SHAPING THE COLLEGE CURRICULUM

More Praise for *Shaping the College Curriculum, Second Edition*

"A solid concept—curriculum planning—is couched in a new purpose: curriculum improvement within interactive contexts and cultures. The authors' vision of coherent curricula leading to student engagement and integrative learning is a must-read."

—Marcia Mentkowski, director, Educational
Research and Evaluation, Alverno College

"Anyone serious about engaging in curriculum development or reform should read this book. The concepts presented clarify the complex interactions between curricula and the many internal and external influences that must be accounted for in successful curricular projects."

—Thomas J. Siller, associate dean for academic
and student affairs, College of Engineering,
Colorado State University

"This new edition of an important book is a must-read for college and university leaders trying to foster curricular reform and instructional practices that emphasize student learning, and it is a comprehensive guide for individual faculty who seek a systematic academic plan for designing an effective course or program."

—Constance Ewing Cook, associate vice provost
and executive director, Center for Research on
Learning and Teaching, University of Michigan

SHAPING THE COLLEGE CURRICULUM

Academic Plans in Context

Second Edition

Lisa R. Lattuca and Joan S. Stark

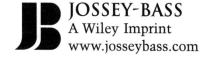

JOSSEY-BASS
A Wiley Imprint
www.josseybass.com

Published by Jossey-Bass
A Wiley Imprint
989 Market Street, San Francisco, CA 94103-1741—www.josseybass.com

Jossey-Bass books and products are available through most bookstores. To contact Jossey-Bass directly
call our Customer Care Department within the U.S. at 800-956-7739, outside the U.S. at 317-572-3986,
or fax 317-572-4002.

Jossey-Bass also publishes its books in a variety of electronic formats. Some content that appears in print
may not be available in electronic books.

Library of Congress Cataloging-in-Publication Data
Lattuca, Lisa R.
    Shaping the college curriculum : academic plans in context / Lisa R. Lattuca and Joan S. Stark.
        p.   cm.
    Includes bibliographical references and index.
    ISBN 978-0-7879-8555-4 (cloth)
    1. Education, Higher—Curricula—United States.   2. Curriculum planning—United States.
    3. Curriculum change—United States.   I. Stark, Joan S.   II. Title.
    LB2361.5.L38   2009
    378.1'990973—dc22
                                                                                    2009012618

Printed in the United States of America
SECOND EDITION

HB Printing   10 9 8 7 6 5 4 3 2 1

CONTENTS

PREFACE

By viewing a college curriculum as a plan, *Shaping the College Curriculum: Academic Plans in Context* encourages instructors and administrators to think about curriculum as a decision-making process with important implications for teaching and learning. The academic plan model we advocate reveals the complexity of curricular decision making, but also clarifies the process, thus enabling instructors and administrators to ask important questions about how curricula might optimize student learning. Updated and substantially revised since its original publication in 1997, this new volume serves as a resource for individuals and groups whose work includes planning, designing, delivering, evaluating, and studying curricula in higher education. Having used *Shaping the College Curriculum* as a text in our graduate courses and in professional development workshops for a number of years, we have learned first-hand how the academic plan concept enables faculty, administrators, and graduate students not only to grasp the complexity of postsecondary curricula, but to see the academic plan as a heuristic for designing curricula and guiding research on curricula. College and university administrators and faculty members, policy makers, researchers, graduate students, and others who share an interest in the improvement of teaching and learning in higher education will find valuable information to guide their practice. Today, concerns about what colleges and universities are teaching and how well, assessment and accountability demands from government agencies and funders, the rise of for-profit higher education, and advances in communications technology have brought curricula and teaching under increased public scrutiny. The potential for change in postsecondary education is enormous. Our efforts aim to promote curriculum change that is guided, not misguided.

In this volume, we focus on the everyday realities of curriculum planning in colleges and universities. Like its predecessor, the revised *Shaping the College Curriculum* stresses research-based educational practices and addresses the concerns of instructors, administrators, and researchers who ask questions such as:

- How can instructors design courses that balance a focus on subject matter with attention to students' needs?
- How can instructors and programs accommodate students' diverse educational, social, and cultural backgrounds?
- What does research tell us about how to create educational experiences that effectively support students' learning?
- What impact do institutional and program contexts—missions, resources, cultures, and histories—have on curriculum planning?
- How can the results of courses and programs, as well as the achievements of students, be evaluated and improved?
- How can programs and institutions achieve needed curricular change in complex environments?
- How can administrators promote continuing attention to curricula and support a culture of improvement?

The academic plan concept, introduced and elaborated in the original *Shaping the College Curriculum*, provides the framework for this volume. However, because our thinking about academic plans is always evolving, this volume reflects refinements and extensions of our understanding of postsecondary curricula. For example, we have expanded our discussion of the sociocultural contexts in which students learn and curricula are created. This is reflected in the change in the subtitle of the volume—from "Academic Plans in Action" to "Academic Plans in Context." An expanded review of theory and research on learning enhances our discussion of how the needs of learners can be addressed in the design of academic plans. A new chapter on curricular change builds on research on organizational change and provides practical guidance to assist faculty members and administrators who are considering and implementing substantial improvements in programs. Each chapter includes updated research findings relevant to curriculum planning, accreditation, teaching, and learning. Finally, information on curriculum planning in for-profit institutions and online education programs supplements our primary focus on planning in not-for-profit institutions.

To purposefully and effectively improve teaching and learning, educators must consider how educational research may be applied. Whether instructors and administrators are engaged in the ongoing task of curriculum revision for courses or programs, in revising general education requirements, incorporating new instructional technologies, or refining student evaluation, assessment, or program review processes, their work is enhanced when they are knowledgeable about research findings as well as about current practices. Those who study higher education—researchers and graduate students—also require resources that synthesize relevant theory, research, and practice so that investigations are well-grounded and well-informed. Accordingly, we have expanded our emphasis on the practical use of the academic plan concept in this revised volume while simultaneously building on past and current research to expand our framework, deepen our understandings of curriculum development and reform, and support our recommendations.

An Overview of the Contents

In 1997, we wrote, in the preface to *Shaping the College Curriculum*, "Faculty, administrators, and scholars need new ways of thinking about curriculum if they are to respond to current challenges and future demands for excellence in higher education." The need for new thinking remains. To produce this revision, we asked ourselves what we had learned about postsecondary curricula, teaching, and learning since *Shaping the College Curriculum* was first published. We questioned our prior understandings and considered how new information from research, theory, and practice might add to—or alter—those ideas. We added two new chapters and rearranged content from existing chapters to facilitate use of the book by researchers, faculty, administrators, and graduate students. We also pruned carefully but purposefully, eliminating a few chapters entirely and substantially reworking others to promote understanding of essential issues.

In the first edition of *Shaping the College Curriculum*, the elements of the academic plan served as the organizational scheme for individual chapters. In this revision, the model still provides the backbone of the book, but it guides its overall conceptualization more fully than the organization of each chapter. The overview that follows briefly summarizes each chapter.

Chapter 1 sets the stage for an extended discussion of the development and revision of college and university curricula by explaining the academic plan model. We define academic plans, discussing each of the eight elements that comprise a plan—purpose, content, sequence, learners, instructional processes, instructional materials, evaluation, and adjustment. We also introduce the concept of educational contexts, particularly noting the many influences—social, cultural, historical, and institutional—that shape postsecondary curricula.

Having defined the concept of the academic plan in Chapter 1, we explore in Chapters 2, 3, and 4 the variety of influences that affect curriculum planning in colleges and universities. Each chapter treats a different, but critical, set of influences. Chapter 2 provides an historical overview of social, cultural, economic, and political forces and debates that have shaped higher education curricula in the United States. Chapter 2 also presents current information on the nation's higher education institutions and student populations. Existing educational structures both constrain and facilitate curriculum planning and reform. By tracing the evolution of several elements of the academic plan (for example, educational missions and goals, content, instructional processes, learners, and evaluation), this chapter reveals the sources of contemporary thinking about postsecondary programs, teaching, and learning as it provides an historical perspective on the current state of higher education in the United States.

Different histories lead to different institutional structures and cultures that can significantly affect educational decision making and processes. In Chapter 3, therefore, we examine the varying organizational structures and cultures of colleges and universities (for example, research universities, community colleges, liberal arts colleges, for-profit institutions), consolidating information about institutional characteristics and influences that was embedded in several chapters in the original *Shaping the College Curriculum*. This chapter will be particularly useful for those with limited familiarity with different higher education sectors and how variations in institutional characteristics generally affect curricular and teaching practices; in short, it offers a primer on faculty and administrative roles and responsibilities in U.S. colleges and universities.

Although college and university missions, structures, and cultures are important influences on faculty members as they plan curricula, the influence of academic fields on course planning, program planning, and educational beliefs is pervasive. In Chapter 4 we rely on research about course planning to help readers understand how instructors in different fields of study approach the task at the course and program levels. Since views about course planning and teaching vary by discipline, this chapter is essential to understanding why instructors from different fields have different views of what and how they should teach. Tapping the knowledge base about the influence of academic fields on faculty work, we describe how socialization in an academic field shapes an instructor's course planning decisions and complicates program and college-wide planning. Importantly, Chapter 4 recommends strategies for sensitizing instructors to the assumptions they bring to the table when they engage in curriculum planning and the sources of their disagreements, thus suggesting how educators might bridge differences to enable curricular improvements.

With Chapter 5 we begin a multi-chapter discussion of curriculum planning that describes current strategies for course and program planning, considers research and theory about learners and learning, and discusses the implications of this information for the development of instructional processes, as well as for the effective evaluation and improvement of academic plans. Chapter 5 focuses on current curricular planning processes at the course, program, and institutional levels. Our review of research on course planning allows us to contrast what college and university instructors typically do when planning courses with what they might do more effectively in a purposeful and ongoing curriculum planning process.

We turn our attention to learners in Chapter 6. To provide the groundwork for improved attention to learners and learning, we present an interdisciplinary treatment of how students learn drawn from the fields of education, cognitive psychology, educational psychology, anthropology, and sociology. This introduction to the complex phenomenon of human learning emphasizes intellectual development and thinking, but also considers how personal characteristics such as academic preparation, interests, and cultural background influence can influence what is learned as students interact with course content, peers, and instructors.

College and university instructors are typically unfamiliar with research on learning, but should be aware of its many implications for the purposeful design and delivery of courses and programs. In Chapter 7, we offer many empirically or theoretically grounded recommendations for improving instructional processes at the course, program, and college levels. Each section of this chapter builds on the research findings on learning discussed in Chapter 6.

In Chapter 8 we turn to evaluation and adjustment, the final two elements of the academic plan model. We describe current practices in course and program evaluation, but also suggest procedures and systems to encourage periodic, rather than episodic, review of curricula at the course, program, and institutional levels. The chapter covers classroom assessment techniques, program review approaches, accreditation, and college-wide assessment programs—all of which are increasingly prominent in the minds of educators in an era of heightened demands for accountability and quality assurance.

The final chapters of *Shaping the College Curriculum* treat the issues of improvement and innovation in academic planning. In Chapter 9 we discuss administrative responsibility for, and leadership of, curriculum development and improvement processes. In doing so, we return once more to the academic plan model elaborated in the early chapters of the book, highlighting the local educational environment in which curriculum plans are constructed. Although faculty members, as experts in their academic fields, are responsible for academic planning in not-for-profit colleges and universities, administrators have a critical role to play in creating a supportive environment in which experimentation and innovation can be pursued. Administrators are also responsible for helping instructors recognize and respond successfully to external challenges that might influence curricula in colleges and universities. This chapter includes many practical checklists that can help instructors and administrators assess and promote the efficacy of their curriculum planning efforts.

Curriculum change in higher education is often portrayed as a slow, tedious, and contentious process—but does it have to be so? Chapter 10 is devoted to the issue of curricular change, assuming that, while innovation is a regular feature of academic life in institutions committed to improvement, any change presents a challenge. This chapter synthesizes recent research on organizational and curricular change to identify principles and conditions that facilitate improvement. From this review, we have drawn many practical recommendations for productive renewal and innovation processes. Ideally, curriculum change is a continuous and collaborative learning process in which faculty members and administrators work together to learn what works and why.

Acknowledgements

Many individuals contributed to the completion of this volume. India McHale and Jennifer Domagal-Goldman, doctoral students and graduate research assistants in the Higher Education program at Penn State, devoted many hours to research for the book and more hours than they will wish to recall to fact-checking, table and figure construction, formatting, and the reference list. India and Jen supplied sharp minds, good humor, and moral support at crucial times, and their work is greatly appreciated. In addition, a number of other graduate students at Penn State researched specific issues for this volume. Most have since completed their degrees and taken faculty or administrative positions in higher education. We are grateful to Christian Anderson, Sam Museus, Joan Pecht, and Stephen Quaye for their valuable contributions. Publishing technologies have changed since *Shaping the College Curriculum* was first published in 1997, and Beverly Ladrido, administrative assistant in the Center for the Study of Higher Education, effectively bridged the gap for us, updating computer files from the first edition so that we had a reasonable facsimile of each chapter to work on for this revised volume.

Colleagueship is the lifeblood of academia and many friends in the field have encouraged us over the years to produce this revised volume. We thank them for that encouragement, as well as for their insights, from which we benefitted as we wrote the new *Shaping the College Curriculum*. Finally, we are exceptionally indebted to Josephine Lattuca and Malcolm Lowther, who patiently and lovingly waited for us to be done.

THE AUTHORS

Lisa R. Lattuca is an associate professor of higher education and a senior research associate in the Center for the Study of Higher Education at The Pennsylvania State University.

Dr. Lattuca's research and teaching interests focus on the intersections of curriculum, teaching, learning, and faculty work in higher education. Three key questions guide her work: (a) how do faculty members' attitudes, values, and behaviors influence curricula and instruction, and in turn, student learning; (b) why do faculty adopt specific forms of knowledge production (such as interdisciplinary research) and how do their choices shape their research and teaching; and (c) how do disciplinary and interdisciplinary contexts and perspectives affect faculty work and student learning in colleges and universities? She has addressed these overarching concerns in several studies of undergraduate engineering education, an evaluation of the impact of outcomes-based accreditation on undergraduate engineering programs and student learning, explorations of interdisciplinary research and teaching among college and university faculty, and investigations of the influence of academic disciplines on research and teaching.

In addition to journal articles and chapters on these and other topics, Dr. Lattuca is the author of *Creating Interdisciplinarity: Interdisciplinary Research Among College and University Faculty* (2001) and co-author (with Joan Stark) of *Shaping the College Curriculum: Academic Plans in Action* (1997). She is also co-editor of *Advancing Faculty Learning Through Interdisciplinary Collaboration* (2005), *College and*

University Curriculum: Developing and Cultivating Programs of Study That Enhance Student Learning (2001) and *Qualitative Research in Higher Education: Expanding Perspectives* (2001). Dr. Lattuca has served on the editorial boards of *The Journal of Higher Education, The American Journal of Education, Higher Education,* and *Research in Higher Education.* She and her colleagues at the Center for the Study of Higher Education have received several grants from the National Science Foundation to support their research on engineering education.

Before joining the faculty of Penn State's Center for the Study of Higher Education and Higher Education program, Dr. Lattuca served on the faculty at Loyola University Chicago, as an associate program officer at the Spencer Foundation (Chicago), and in a variety of college administrative positions. She earned a Ph.D. from the University of Michigan, a master's degree from Cornell University, and a bachelor's degree from Saint Peter's College.

Joan S. Stark is professor emerita in the Center for the Study of Higher and Postsecondary Education and dean emerita, School of Education, The University of Michigan. From 1978 to 1983, she was dean of the School of Education at the University of Michigan. From 1986 to 1991, she was director of the National Center for Research to Improve Postsecondary Teaching and Learning (NCRIPTAL), a national research center funded annually at $1 million by the U.S. Department of Education. From 1991 to 1996 she was also editor of *The Review of Higher Education.* She has received the Howen Bowen Career Achievement Award, the Research Achievement Award, and the Service Award from the Association for the Study of Higher Education. She has also received the Sidney Suslow Career Award and the Distinguished Membership Award from the Association for Institutional Research and the Exemplary Research Award from Division J of the American Educational Research Association. She retired in 2001.

Before moving to Michigan, Professor Stark was associate professor and chairperson of the Department of Higher/Postsecondary Education at Syracuse University (1974–1978) and associate dean of Goucher College in Maryland (1970–1974). She has also been a community college and high school science teacher, and an editorial writer for major textbook publishers.

A 1957 magna cum laude graduate in chemistry of Syracuse University, Professor Stark received a master's degree from Teachers' College, Columbia University, and a doctorate in administration of higher education from the State University of New York at Albany.

Professor Stark's research and teaching interests include curriculum development, evaluation and assessment, and undergraduate professional education in colleges and universities. She is the author or editor of numerous other books and monographs, including: *Shaping the College Curriculum: Academic Plans in Action*

(1997); *Responsive Professional Education: Balancing Outcomes and Opportunities* (1986); *Strengthening the Ties That Bind: Integrating Undergraduate Liberal and Professional Study* (1988); *Reflections on Course Planning* (1988); *Improving Teaching and Learning Through Research* (1988); *Student Goals for College and Courses* (1989); *Planning Introductory College Courses* (1990); and *Assessment and Program Evaluation* (an Association for the Study of Higher Education Reader, 1994). She has also published many articles on curriculum, assessment, accreditation, and professional education in such journals as *The Journal of Higher Education, Research in Higher Education,* and *The Review of Higher Education.*

Professor Stark has directed several projects for the Fund for the Improvement of Postsecondary Education. She has been president of the Association for the Study of Higher Education, and a consulting editor for numerous journals in the United States, the United Kingdom, the Netherlands, and South Africa. Professor Stark also has been a member of the U.S. Education Commissioner's Advisory Committee on Accreditation and Institutional Eligibility; the publications board of the Association for Institutional Research; the board of directors of the Land Grant Deans of Education; the College Board Long-Range Planning Committee; the Harry S Truman Fellowship Regional Review Panel; a trustee of Kalamazoo College; and a member of the Accounting Education Change Commission.

CHAPTER ONE

CURRICULUM: AN ACADEMIC PLAN

Ask any college student or graduate "What is the college curriculum?" and you will get a ready answer. Most think of the curriculum as a set of courses or experiences needed to complete a college degree. Some will refer to the total set of courses a college offers, others will mean the set of courses students take, and a few will include informal experiences that are not listed in the catalog of courses. Some may include teaching methods as part of their definitions, while others will not. At a superficial level the public assumes it knows what a college curriculum is, but complex understandings are rare. Even those closely involved with college curricula lack a consistent definition. A few may point out that we cannot define curriculum without reference to a specific institution because college and university missions, programs, and students vary widely in the United States.

Over the years, we have solicited definitions of curricula from faculty, administrators, graduate students, and observers of higher education. Most people include at least one and usually more of the following elements in their definitions:

- A college's or program's mission, purpose, or collective expression of what is important for students to learn
- A set of experiences that some authorities believe all students should have
- The set of courses offered to students
- The set of courses students actually elect from those available

- The content of a specific discipline
- The time and credit frame in which the college provides education. (Stark & Lowther, 1986)

In addition to the elements that provide the primary basis for an educator's definition of curriculum, individuals often mention other elements, sometimes including their views of learners and learning or their personal philosophy of education. Faculty members with broad curriculum development responsibilities typically mention several elements in their definitions and may be more confident about which of those elements should be included or excluded.

These instructors seldom link the elements they mention into an integrated definition of the curriculum. They tend to think of separate educational tasks or processes, such as establishing the credit value of courses, selecting the specific disciplines to be taught or studied, teaching their subjects, specifying objectives for student achievement, and evaluating what students know. Probably the most common linkage faculty members address is the structural connection between the set of courses offered and the related time and credit framework. Colleges and universities in the United States have emphasized the credit hour since the early 20th century, having modified the Carnegie "unit" first introduced into secondary schools in 1908 (Hutcheson, 1997; Levine, 1978). Curriculum change efforts in the United States often focus on structure because numbers of credit hours and other structural dimensions of curricula are common to all fields. In fact, some observers believe that the most common form of curricular change is "tinkering" with the structure (Bergquist, Gould, & Greenberg, 1981; Toombs & Tierney, 1991), for example, changing course listings, college calendars, or the number of credits required for graduation. Although discussions of curricular reform seem to focus on these structural dimensions rather than on the overall experience envisioned for students, when legislators, policy makers, and the general public talk about "improving curriculum," they have something more in mind than structural adjustments. To them, curricular changes should result in substantive improvements in student learning, and colleges and universities should be able to demonstrate such improvement. Today, demands for accountability and increased scrutiny of higher education call for greater consensus on what we mean when we say "curriculum."

The Need for a Definitional Framework

Since the mid-1980s the extensive literature urging educational reform has focused on the ambiguous term "curriculum." This word has been frequently modified by several equally ambiguous adjectives such as "coherent" and "rigorous" or linked with processes such as integration. Is it the set of courses offered that lacks coherence or integration? The choice of courses made by the students? The actual experiences students take away from the courses? The teaching styles and strategies chosen by the professors? Or all of these? To discuss curriculum reform meaningfully, we need a working definition of curriculum to guide discussion and help us determine what needs to be changed.

The lack of a definition does not prevent faculty members, curriculum committees, deans, academic vice presidents, instructional development specialists, institutional researchers, and teaching assistants from regularly making decisions about curricula. These individuals talk about "curriculum" with the untested assumption that they are speaking a shared language (Conrad & Pratt, 1986). This illusion of consensus becomes a problem when groups with different views come together to work for curricular improvement. In such circumstances, participants often argue from varied definitions and assumptions without spelling them out, particularly in working groups that include many disciplines. Such discussions can be frustrating and even grow contentious. For these and other reasons, curriculum development or revision is typically not a popular task among college faculty.

Many faculty and administrators will resonate with the definition of an undergraduate curriculum as the formal academic experience of a student pursuing a baccalaureate degree or less, particularly because this definition is broad enough to include learning experiences such as workshops, seminars, colloquia, internships, laboratories, and other learning experiences beyond what we typically call a "course" (Ratcliff, 1997). This definition may remind them that a curriculum, from the student perspective, is a very particular set of learning experiences. Yet, to provide a framework for productive discussions and wise decisions, faculty and administrators need a more precise understanding that can help them identify the specific aspects of curricula that must be addressed. Should we adjust the content of a curriculum or use different teaching methods to build student competencies? Should we consider new methods of delivery, such as distance or online learning, to reach different student populations? Should new assessment procedures be adopted to better measure student learning and thus inform curricular revisions?

Most definitions are too general to be very helpful to faculty and administrators faced with the task of curriculum development or revision because they do not identify the many decision points that, together, produce a specific curriculum. Overly general definitions hinder the ability to communicate the intentions of a curriculum to students, to evaluate it effectively, and to make the case for particular changes. Definitions, of course, are not prescriptions. Defining the term curriculum does not mean that everyone must agree on the content to be studied, how it should be studied, or who should study it. It does not mean that everyone must agree on the specific skills or outcomes students must achieve. Our higher education system is characterized—indeed distinguished—by diversity of programs and institutions that serve different students and different needs. A definition of curriculum that can be applied across these differences is required.

Defining Curriculum as an Academic Plan

To remedy the lack of a comprehensive definition of curriculum, we propose the concept of the "academic plan." Plans, of course, can be variously successful once they leave the drawing board. Our goal in conceptualizing curriculum as an academic plan is to identify the critical decision points that, if effectively addressed, will enhance the academic experience of students.

A plan for any endeavor incorporates a total blueprint for action, including purposes, activities, and ways of measuring success. A plan implies both intentional and informed choices among alternatives to achieve its intentions; in this sense, it strives for the ideal. The intention of any academic plan is to foster students' academic development, and a plan, therefore, should be designed with a given group of students and learning objectives in mind. This focus compels course and program planners to put students' educational needs, rather than subject matter, first. The term "plan" communicates in familiar terms the kind of informal development process recognized by a broad range of faculty members across academic fields.

The academic plan definition implies a deliberate planning process that focuses attention on important educational considerations, which will vary by field of study, instructors, students, institutional goals, and so on. Despite such variations, the notion of a plan provides a heuristic that encourages a careful process of decision making. Every curriculum addresses each element of the plan described below—whether conscious attention has been given to it or not, whether a deliberate decision has been made, or whether some default has been accepted. Thinking of curriculum as a plan encourages consideration of *all* of the major elements, rather than attention to singular aspects such as specific content or particular instructional strategies.

In our view, an academic plan should involve decisions about (at least) the following elements:

1. PURPOSES: knowledge, skills, and attitudes to be learned
2. CONTENT: subject matter selected to convey specific knowledge, skills, and attitudes
3. SEQUENCE: an arrangement of the subject matter and experiences intended to lead to specific outcomes for learners

4. LEARNERS: how the plan will address a specific group of learners
5. INSTRUCTIONAL PROCESSES: the instructional activities by which learning may be achieved
6. INSTRUCTIONAL RESOURCES: the materials and settings to be used in the learning process
7. EVALUATION: the strategies used to determine whether decisions about the elements of the academic plan are optimal
8. ADJUSTMENT: enhancements to the plan based on experience and evaluation

This set of elements provides a definition that is applicable to all levels of curriculum. An academic plan can be constructed for a single lesson, for a single course, for aggregations of courses (for example, a program or major), for broader organizational groupings of majors (such as schools or colleges), and for a college or university as whole. Moreover, defining a curriculum as a plan allows plans at these several organizational levels to be examined for integrity and consistency.

The model of the academic plan, however, includes more than the eight elements that define the plan itself. As we show in Figure 1.1, our complete model makes explicit the many factors that influence the development of academic plans

FIGURE 1.1. ACADEMIC PLANS IN SOCIOCULTURAL CONTEXT

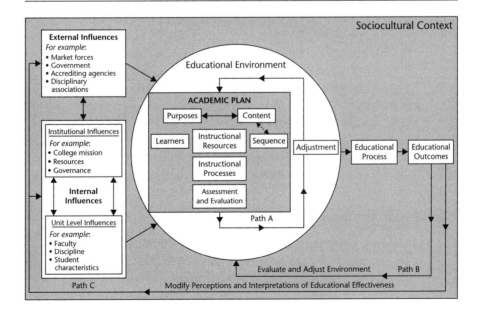

in colleges and universities. In the first edition of this book (Stark & Lattuca, 1997), we divided these influences into three sets, building on work published by the Carnegie Foundation for the Advancement of Teaching (1977) and that of Joan Stark, Malcolm Lowther, Bonnie Hagerty, and Cynthia Orcyzk (1986). In this revised edition, we clarify the nature of these influences by further elaborating the role of social, cultural, and historical factors on curricula, faculty, and learners.

Our slightly revised model of "academic plans in context" emphasizes the influence of sociocultural and historical factors by embedding the academic plan in this temporal context. Within the sociocultural context, we include two subsets of influences, divided into (a) influences external to the institution (such as employers and accreditation agencies) and (b) influences internal to the college, university, or educational provider. We further divide internal influences into institutional-level influences (for example, mission, resources, leadership, and governance) and unit-level influences (such as program goals, faculty beliefs, relationships with other programs, or student characteristics). These distinctions acknowledge the many levels (college, department, program, or course) at which academic plans are created and implemented.

Internal and external influences vary in salience and strength depending on the course, program, or institution under study. In Figure 1.1 we portray these specific influences as interacting to create an educational environment. We place educational processes and outcomes outside the educational environment for planning but within the larger sociocultural context. We recognize a multitude of influences that are beyond the control of planners, such as the attitudes and preparation of students who enroll in a course or program and the social and cultural phenomena that affect perceptions in a given time and place.

Figure 1.1 also shows the evaluation and adjustment processes both for a plan (Path A) and for the educational environment (Path B), which may itself be affected by the outcomes of academic plans. Finally, in Path C, we suggest that external and internal audiences can form perceptions and interpretations of the educational outcomes that may cause them to modify the kinds of influences they exert.

In the following sections, we elaborate on each of the main components of our model, discussing first the elements of the academic plan and next exploring the different influences on the plans, planners, and planning processes.

Elements of Academic Plans

Figure 1.2 isolates the elements of an academic plan. From interviews with faculty members we know that purposes and content are nearly always closely related elements of academic plans in the minds of instructors (Stark, Lowther, Bentley, Ryan, Martens, Genthon, & others, 1990). We illustrate

FIGURE 1.2. ELEMENTS OF ACADEMIC PLANS

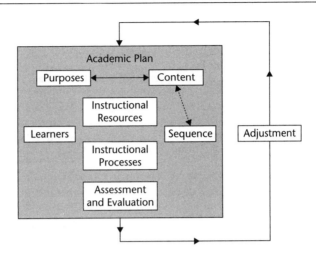

this relationship with a double arrow in Figure 1.2. Frequently, instructors also link content with a particular sequence (or arrangement of content) as they plan. We show the relationship between content and sequence with a dotted double arrow to indicate that, while these elements are often linked by instructors, they are not consistently connected. We have arranged the other elements in their approximate order of consideration by college and university faculty members based on reports of how they plan (Stark & others, 1990). For example, faculty members tend to consider learners, resources, and sequence simultaneously, but after purposes and content.

We have not inserted additional arrows into the academic plan model because we do not wish to imply that all curriculum planners do or should carry out their planning activities in a particular sequence. In fact, instructors reasonably make decisions in different orders and do so iteratively rather than in a linear fashion. This is especially true as they revise courses or programs based on their experiences in the classroom. In the following sections, we briefly describe each of the eight elements of an academic plan.

Purposes: Knowledge, Skills, and Attitudes to Be Learned

Discussions about college curricula typically grow out of strong convictions. Thus, we have placed the intended outcomes, which we call purposes, as the first element in the academic plan. The selection of knowledge, skills, and attitudes to be acquired reflects the planners' views—implicit or explicit—about the goals of

TABLE 1.1. STATEMENTS OF EDUCATIONAL PURPOSE COMMON AMONG COLLEGE FACULTY

A.	In general, the purpose of education is to make the world a better place for all of us. Students must be taught to understand that they play a key role in attaining this goal. To do this, I organize my course to relate its content to contemporary social issues. By studying content that reflects real-life situations, students learn to adapt to a changing society and to intervene where necessary.
B.	The main purpose of education is to teach students how to think effectively. As they interact with course content, students must learn general intellectual skills, such as observing, classifying, analyzing, and synthesizing. Such skills, once acquired, can transfer to other situations. In this way, students gain intellectual autonomy.
C.	Education should provide students with knowledge and skills that enable them to earn a living and contribute to society's production. I believe a fundamental role for me as an instructor is to help students achieve their vocational goals.
D.	Education should involve students in a series of personally enriching experiences. To meet this broad objective, I select content that allows students to discover themselves as unique individuals and thus acquire personal autonomy and improved self-concept. I discuss appropriate activities and content with students in an effort to individualize the course.
E.	In my judgment, education should emphasize the great products and discoveries of the human mind. Thus, I select content from my field to cover the major ideas and concepts that important thinkers in the discipline have illuminated. I consider my teaching successful if students are able to demonstrate both breadth and depth of knowledge in my field.
F.	Whatever the curriculum, it should help students clarify their beliefs and values and thus achieve commitment and dedication to guide their lives. For me, the development of values is an educational outcome as important as acquisition of subject knowledge in the field I teach.
G.	Education should cultivate the latent creative talents of students. To help achieve this, I give my students maximum freedom to explore their own ideas as well as constructive opportunities to interpret the works of creative individuals.

From: Stark and others, 1990. Reprinted by permission of the University of Michigan.

postsecondary education. Research demonstrates that college faculty members in different fields hold varying beliefs about educational purposes (Braxton & Hargens, 1996; Smart, Feldman, & Ethington, 2000; Stark & others, 1988). Table 1.1 includes several broad statements describing some of these views. The second purpose listed in this table, "learning to think effectively," is a commonly espoused purpose, but in any faculty group there are likely to be strong proponents of other statements as well. Some purposes will be strongly endorsed at one type of institution and minimized at another type. Considering a curriculum as an academic plan can direct attention to these differences in basic purposes and aid in the identification of underlying assumptions that can interfere with shared understandings of curricular goals.

Content: Subject Matter for Learning

Educational purposes can be achieved in many ways. For example, it is difficult to argue that any field has a monopoly on encouraging intellectual development or effective thinking. Similarly, values and ethics can be taught using different subject matter. The academic plan model acknowledges that some instructors typically select subject matter to facilitate learning, but the separation of the first and second elements of the plan emphasizes that purposes (or desired learning outcomes) and subject matter are not synonymous.

Although not identical, subject-matter goals and educational goals are interdependent. Moreover, faculty members teaching in specific fields are more likely to endorse certain educational beliefs than others and to view their disciplines in ways related to these beliefs (Braxton & Hargens, 1996; Cross, 2005; Smart, Feldman, & Ethington, 2000; Stark & others, 1990). For example, professors in social science fields are more likely than those in physical sciences to endorse Purpose A in Table 1.1, "making the world a better place for all of us" (Stark & others, 1990). Furthermore, faculty from different fields define desirable educational outcomes such as "thinking effectively" in different ways (Donald, 2002). These disciplinary differences, in both intent and meaning, complicate discussions of the curriculum. Placing purposes and content in the academic plan as two different but interacting elements allows us to emphasize the distinction and aids discussion.

Sequence: A Curricular Arrangement

By curricular "sequence" we mean the ways in which subject matter is arranged to facilitate learning in an academic plan. We emphasize here not the mechanical and bureaucratic devices by which colleges organize their relationships with students (such as credit hours) but rather the assumptions of instructors about how knowledge is conveyed and learned. For example: Is historical material presented chronologically or thematically? What basic mathematical concepts and principles are students expected to learn before moving on to more complex topics in engineering? Does a practice component accompany theoretical presentations in a teacher education program? Are students introduced to a broad picture, such as how inquiry is conducted in biology, before delving into advanced topics? In any discussion about sequence, educational benefits and instructional rationales should drive discussions about subject matter arrangement, rather than the reverse.

Learners: Student Characteristics and Needs

Discussions about purposes, content, and sequence, like discussions about other elements of an academic plan, must be informed by knowledge of the abilities, previous preparation, and goals of learners. Although there is little danger that faculty members will forget the sequencing typical of their discipline, some may overlook the specific students for whom the curriculum is intended. Yet whether a curriculum "works" may depend on whether the plan adequately accounts for students' goals and needs and addresses students' preparation and ability. Stated another way, educators and students have their own goals and intentions. The interaction between the goals and intentions of instructors and those of students requires attention if an academic plan is to succeed. Student motivations to learn are influenced by their interest in the topic and their judgments of its relevance, as well as the instructor's ability to stimulate interest and demonstrate relevance (Pintrich & Schunk, 2002).

Instructional Processes: Learning Activities

Instructional processes are often discussed separately from curricula, but we include them in the academic plan because the method of instruction influences student learning. In colleges and universities, instructors are often unfamiliar with or uncomfortable with teaching strategies (other than lecturing) that are effective in both large and small classes. We believe that faculty members will expand their repertoire of teaching strategies if such choices are consciously recognized as part of curriculum development and based on knowledge about learning.

Instructional Resources: Materials and Settings

Curriculum discussions do not always include considerations of learning materials, such as textbooks and media, or settings, such as classrooms, laboratories, course management platforms, and practicum sites. Yet educational programs are frequently structured by these resources. Sometimes they are the primary consideration in an academic plan. Faculty members may, for example, sequence a course according to the organization of the selected textbook or allow class size and the configuration of the classroom to determine their use of discussions or small groups. As importantly, resources such as textbooks, supplemental reading materials, and visual aids (for example, slides of artwork) are cultural artifacts laden with meanings that may or may not be fully recognized. Consider, for example, how different students may react to a textbook that only uses the pronoun "he" or an anthology that only includes authors from the West. Because these artifacts, tools, and resources shape learning—whether we recognize this or not—they must be purposefully considered as part of any academic plan.

Evaluation: Assessing Plans and Outcomes

In the past twenty-five years, evaluation of the curriculum, through both program review and assessment of student outcomes in specific courses, has become increasingly important in higher education. Effective assessment is viewed as critical because educators must understand how well students have made sense of what they encounter in courses or programs. We consider assessment of student learning in the context of a course to be most directly connected to instructional process. Evaluation, in contrast, is a broader term that encompasses activities such as self-study and program review as well as assessment (Stark & Thomas, 1994). The term evaluation also implies that judgments will be made regarding the overall effectiveness of a course or program. In the academic plan terminology, evaluation involves considerations of the suitability of all of the plan elements.

Typically, academic program review is viewed as a separate process from curriculum planning, but the best time to devise an evaluation is when the goals and objectives of the program are being clarified and the program designed. We suggest also that the list of elements we have defined in the academic plan helps to draw attention to the students' perspective in the evaluation process. Evaluation plans often emphasize educators' goals as measured by student achievement rather than acknowledging and assessing the extent to which plans address relevant student goals as well.

Adjustment: Improving Plans

Curriculum development and change efforts that include appropriate evaluation plans can be used to improve both the plan and the planning process. The academic plan model calls attention to this component of the curriculum development process and of the revision process. Careful specification of the elements of an academic plan can help to identify which aspects need improvement when the plan is revised.

Contextual Influences on Academic Plans

Understanding a curriculum requires more than an examination of its different elements. To grasp why, and often how, a particular curriculum is organized, we need to consider the contexts in which it was created and implemented. In a larger sense, a complete picture of college and university curricula in the United States (or any other country) requires a sense of how and why these institutions evolved over time.

Contemporary colleges and universities in the United States derive their structure and purposes from several western European models of higher education whose impact can still be seen today. The English and Scottish residential colleges emphasized character development inside and outside the classroom, and their influence is still felt in the emphasis on general education requirements and the co-curriculum of some institutions. Later, the German university model promoted disciplinary specialization for both faculty and students and transformed the educational experience by creating curricula based on the pursuit of inquiry and new knowledge. This influence resulted in the organization of major fields. To this mix, the French *grandes écoles* contributed the ideals of meritocracy and professorial autonomy, encouraging a form of higher education that stressed rigorous intellectual training for the professions (Lattuca, 2006a).

External Influences

As a growing nation, the United States borrowed heavily from other countries' higher education systems, but it also created its own structures, norms, and values. The emphasis on both liberal and professional education in undergraduate education in the United States, for example, is unusual compared to the programs offered by most African, Asian, and European universities, which focus on professional education. The emphasis on broad access to higher education was unique to the United States until the latter part of the 20th century but now has been widely adopted in Western Europe as well as throughout North America (Wittrock, 1993). The critical point is that institutions and curricula serve social needs and change as national, cultural, and other needs evolve. In the 1970s, for example, U.S. colleges and universities responded to the influence of the civil and women's rights movements. These movements began outside the academy, but as students and faculty members joined these causes, both groups promoted changes in curricula. Today, academic programs in women's studies and ethnic studies are found on many college and university campuses: courses in disciplinary majors often incorporate the perspectives of African Americans, Latina/os, women, and others who had been historically excluded from higher education.

We could name countless other sociocultural influences on higher education—language, family structures, television, the Internet, computer technologies, to name a very few. Our goal, however, is not to create an exhaustive list but rather to note that, depending on the academic plan under consideration, different sociocultural influences come into play.

External influences is our encompassing term for factors such as market forces, societal trends, government policies and actions, and disciplinary associations that exist outside colleges and universities. Curriculum planning is subject to the influence of disciplinary associations (for example, the National Communication Association, the American Chemical Society), media (for example, The *U.S. News & World Report* annual college rankings issue), funding agencies that support curricular and instructional reform (for example, The National Science Foundation), and regional and specialized accrediting agencies that have increasingly focused on the specification and assessment of student learning outcomes.

When designing their courses and programs, some instructors believe they need not be overly concerned about external influences, but may be more attentive than they realize. Enrollments, the state of the job market, and social needs may seem muted because their influence often is filtered through such groups as accreditors and professional associations. External groups such as employers, however, exert strong and direct influences on academic programs in community colleges, for-profit institutions, and some professional fields (for example, accounting). Liberal education is also subject to the influences of groups advocating dramatically different themes, including internationalization, civic engagement, and interdisciplinarity. The question of what knowledge is most worth having takes on new meaning in a pluralistic and global society with diverse educational institutions.

Defining curriculum development as a planning process helps us identify the elements of a plan that are particularly sensitive to external forces. For example, decisions about purposes, content, learners, and instructional resources are more often subject to pressure from external constituencies. Choices of instructional processes and evaluation approaches are more likely to be influenced by forces internal to the institution.

Internal Influences

As noted earlier, we divide internal influences into institutional-level influences and unit-level influences because academic plans are developed at several levels. Although we discuss them separately, we stress that institutional-level and unit-level influences are interrelated (to varying degrees depending on the curriculum in question), if not always consistent or complementary.

Institutional-Level Influences Most academic programs we will discuss exist within institutions and are thus supported by organizational infrastructures. Aspects of these infrastructures, particularly college mission, financial resources, and governance arrangements, can have a strong influence on curricula. Although infrastructures support the planning and implementation of academic plans, this support varies depending on the centrality of the specific course or program to the college or university mission, as well as on resource availability, advising systems, opportunity for faculty development and renewal, and so on. For example, some courses are linked to a wide variety of departments and programs because they are "service" courses needed by students in a number of degree programs. Service courses are influenced strongly by this interdependence. Courses without such linkages can be planned more independently.

Unit-Level Influences We distinguish between institutional-level influences and unit-level influences, which are characteristic of the organizational unit where the academic plan is created. Unit-level influences may most directly affect the selection and sequencing of content and the choice of instructional processes. Instructors' backgrounds, educational beliefs, and disciplinary training are particularly strong unit-level influences. Student characteristics, when recognized, are also influential. Unit-level influences vary in salience and intensity at various levels of curriculum development and in different kinds of institutions. When an instructor works alone in planning a course, some influences, like personal beliefs about how students learn, may be more potent than when a group of colleagues plans an entire program.

   In thinking about the curricular planning process, we need to consider many types of influences simultaneously, since they do not operate independently. The influences we describe as "external" and "internal" all occur within the sociocultural context. For simplicity's sake, we say that the interaction of these many influences produces a dynamic environment in which curriculum plans are developed—as the following examples illustrate:

- Faculty members consider their educational beliefs and values, their views of how humans learn, and labor market needs to produce a set of educational objectives for a program.
- Cultural beliefs about the purposes of higher education and institutional missions influence choices of general education subject matter.
- Knowledge of instructional techniques, technology, and available materials, as well as publications of a disciplinary association, influence faculty choices of instructional processes.
- Leadership by deans, associate deans, and chairpersons influences the use of results of evaluations of academic plans for improvement, as does the allocation of organizational resources for data collection, accreditation criteria, and public policies, such as state mandates for accountability.

These examples illustrate that an academic plan is not the product of totally rational and context-free deliberations but rather results from a complicated process embedded in a larger, complex, and somewhat unpredictable set of contexts.

Constructing Plans: Curriculum Development

To make the most of the opportunity supplied by our definition of curriculum as an academic plan, we distinguish an academic plan itself (a curriculum) from the iterative process of planning (curriculum development). Defining a curriculum as a plan calls attention to the need for a planning process, helps to identify parts of the plan that are subject to specific influences, and reveals intervention points for productive curricular change. Each of the eight elements of the plan implies an associated decision:

1. PURPOSES: choosing educational goals and objectives
2. CONTENT: selecting subject matter
3. SEQUENCE: organizing content appropriately
4. LEARNERS: accommodating characteristics, goals, and abilities of learners
5. INSTRUCTIONAL RESOURCES: selecting learning materials and technologies
6. INSTRUCTIONAL PROCESSES: developing learning and teaching activities
7. EVALUATION: assessing student outcomes as well as learner and teacher satisfaction with the plan
8. ADJUSTMENT: improving both the plan and the planning process

Breaking down the planning process in this way enables us to ask questions about the process itself and begin to develop agreement about who bears responsibility for it. For example, we might ask such questions as:

- Who constructs the plan? (Who are the curriculum decision-makers operating at each curriculum level?)
- How is the plan constructed? What knowledge of curriculum planning do faculty members bring to the task? What knowledge do they need?
- What premises or purposes undergird the plan? Are these purposes representative of individuals, faculty views in general, or of specific disciplines?

- Whose interests are considered in the plan? Are students included? To what degree are specifications of accreditors, employers, and other external agents attended and accommodated?
- How is the plan described or represented both formally and informally? How is it articulated to students?
- What educational outcomes are achieved by different types of students? How will we know how various types of students experience the plan?
- Who decides when changes in the plan are needed?
- What provisions are made that changes in the plan can be made promptly?
- What expertise must leaders have to guide the planning process?

Answering these questions invariably includes discussion of the many influences on curricula discussed earlier. For example, the planning process may be hindered by lack of available information on learner goals or characteristics, or by lack of contact with local employers who could provide important information for planning a vocational or professional program. As instructional processes are considered, it may become apparent that faculty members need more knowledge about research supporting particular instructional strategies. Decisions about assessment of student outcomes, for instance, may be influenced by the availability of assistance from teaching and learning centers, professional development funds, or an institutional research office that collects and analyzes data concerning students, alumni, and institutional operations.

Evolution of the Academic Plan Concept

Perhaps because higher education in the United States is so complex and diverse, few scholars have attempted to develop comprehensive frameworks about what is taught, why, and how. However, several researchers and theorists in both higher education (especially Clifton Conrad, Paul Dressel, David Halliburton, and William Toombs) and K–12 education (especially Geneva Gay, George Posner, Joseph Schwab, and Hilda Taba) have struggled with how to think about curriculum issues and we have built on their work. These scholars have influenced our thinking about college and university curricula.

Broad Curriculum Frameworks

One of the most prolific analysts of college curricula was Paul Dressel (1971, 1976, 1980; Dressel & DeLisle, 1970; Dressel & Marcus, 1982). Over a career of sixty-five years, he moved steadily toward a conceptualization of curriculum as a comprehensive academic plan. Dressel frequently tested his ideas and conceptual frameworks, and often re-formulated and clarified the ideas of others (for example, Phenix, 1986). Yet, there is little evidence that his work informed empirical studies of the curriculum, perhaps because his normative views did not provide an open framework to guide thinking.

Dressel directly addressed the element of the academic plan that we call purposes, arguing that, while affective development is an important correlate, the primary purpose of college instruction is to promote students' cognitive growth. Further, the primary objective of emphasis on cognitive growth is to make learners self-sufficient thinkers and lifelong learners. Dressel further asserted that attention to the structure of the disciplines is essential if students are to achieve the appropriate higher education outcome. In his view, the disciplines are artifacts of human intellectual development that serve as organizers of human history and experience. Consequently, they represent useful and essential classifications for organizing teaching and learning; the educated person must know about the objectives, methods, concepts, and structures of disciplines and their interrelationships. This view of the proper content of higher education led Dressel to express the hope that students would read classical works for the satisfaction they received. But he also realized that individuals are unlikely to acquire knowledge, skills, or values unless they attach some importance to what they are learning. He did not, however, provide guidance for those wondering how to motivate students who find little satisfaction in learning or do not see its benefits.

Although he wrote before developments in cognitive psychology that many now consider foundational, Dressel presaged the need for the learner to associate new and prior experiences. He believed that colleges and universities should provide a structure and arrangement for learning—that is, to develop instructional processes—that help learners integrate what they learn in a course and to relate that to other courses and experiences. Dressel also devoted much attention to the evaluation of students, of teachers, and of programs. In *Improving Degree Programs,* he observed:

> An ongoing program evaluation that transcends courses should attempt to find out what students have gained from a course or program, what elements of the program have been successful or unsuccessful in promoting this development, and what aspects of the course, content, resource materials, and experiences need to be revised to maintain vigor and enthusiasm. This form of evaluation produces information that tends to modify instructional materials and processes and also the manner in which they are conjoined into courses. In an integrated, cumulative curricular experience, evaluation must be a major structural component, but it cannot be the sole instrument for developing or maintaining such a program. (Dressel, 1980, p. 57)

Ultimately, he argued, evaluation should become a review of the actual outcomes of a course or program and a reflection upon the processes, content, and instructional patterns used. His flow model of steps in course and program development and evaluation (1980) included attention to internal, organizational, and external influences on college curricula. Finally, he noted that information about unintended outcomes of curricula, as well as evaluation of their intended objectives, should be considered in any adjustment processes.

Our debt to Dressel is great. Whereas a number of scholars have connected two or three elements of what we call an academic plan, Dressel discussed in detail nearly all of the eight elements we identify and also acknowledged some of the important influences on curriculum development that we include in the academic plan concept. In this sense, we continue the work Dressel began, applying it to the process of curriculum development—that is, the development of academic plans.

Just before we began to outline the academic plan concept, Clifton Conrad and Anne Pratt (1986) published a non-prescriptive curriculum model. Like us, they viewed the development of a curriculum as a series of decisions or "options." They called some of these options "curricular design variables" and, following William Toombs, divided them into content and form. Internal and external influences on curricular in this model are "input variables" that are considered by those involved in the curriculum development process (such as faculty, students, and administrators). These decision-makers produce two types of outcome variables: curriculum design outcomes and educational outcomes. In our terms, curriculum design outcomes are the decisions that shape the academic plan.

Conrad and Pratt recognized that planning is not a linear process and acknowledged the importance of academic fields, external stakeholders (like the professions and employers), and interest groups in curricular decision making. Their model is comprehensive and highly specific, identifying six different interest groups and the particular perspectives they bring to the curriculum development process. Among these interest groups, Conrad and Pratt include faculty members, whom they view as bringing disciplinary and expertise orientations to the task of curriculum planning, and students, who bring concerns about curricular relevance and transferability. Administrative groups, the model suggests, have responsibility for supporting curriculum planning, as well as monitoring budgets and costs. We agree that such perspectives come into play in curriculum planning processes, but we streamlined the academic plan concept in the belief that a more parsimonious model may have greater utility for guiding practice. The academic plan model allows us to acknowledge the variety of perspectives that exist among, as well as within, interest groups and additionally to suggest ways in which these perspectives can be accommodated and utilized.

Curriculum Design Frameworks

By definition, both "academic plan" and "curriculum design" imply deliberate decisions about desired relationships among settings, students, purposes, and processes. Consequently, the process of creating the plan involves more than getting a few people with different views to compromise; it involves consideration of many influences and circumstances. A few frameworks serve as lenses through which to examine attempts at systematic curriculum design. The concept of "design," for example, can be employed to discuss both curriculum planning and curriculum analysis (Toombs, 1977–1978; Toombs & Tierney, 1993). Design is a process that involves deliberate decisions about curriculum and can be understood by faculty members in diverse fields ranging from art to engineering. By curriculum "analysis," William Toombs means design in reverse, that is, the process of analyzing the curriculum plan to determine whether it contains the assumptions, structures, and activities necessary to meet the objectives (1977–1978). Toombs and Tierney also laid out three essential parts of the curriculum design process to be acknowledged and considered: the context in which the design is developed; the content that is to be taught; and the form or decisions that are made about the design. This work served as the basis for the contextual filters model of course planning (Stark, Lowther, Ryan, Bomotti, Genthon, Martens, & others, 1988) that was used to interpret national data on course planning activities of faculty members. Other useful course design frameworks have been proposed by Robert Diamond (2008), George Posner and Alan Rudnitsky (2006), and Grant Wiggins and Jay McTighe (2005). Although these models come close to implementing a view of a curriculum as an academic plan, they focus on the activities of the planners rather than providing a comprehensive understanding of academic plans themselves.

Other curriculum frameworks focus on the processes and politics of curriculum change. David Halliburton (1977a, 1977b), for example, developed a reasonably complete and useful framework for viewing curriculum planning in higher education. In his view, curricula become obsolete because (a) the role of education changes with respect to broad historical and social needs, (b) new trends occur within the higher education system itself, and (c) the disciplines undergo paradigmatic shifts or changes in accepted assumptions. Halliburton categorized curricular change as typically occurring according to one or more of three processes of curriculum planning: (a) mechanism or statics (a process of tinkering or curriculum maintenance rather than overhaul); (b) dualism (curriculum change that swings from one popular trend or focus to another), and (c) knowledge-ism (a focus on changes in disciplinary content).

Halliburton stressed his belief that academic fields, which reflect the assumptions, values, and habits of their practitioners, play a large part in determining which change process is used. Others have shown, however, that local contexts act as filters, modifying the influence of academic fields at both the course level and the program level (Stark & others, 1988). At the program level, resource allocations, structures, and leadership may be equally crucial frames or filters (Seymour, 1988). At the institutional level, competing societal and political interests may also serve to filter the influence of academic fields. Instructors' orientations to their academic fields are likely to be potent influences at all levels of curriculum planning, but may be manifested in somewhat different ways at various levels of the academic plan.

Drawing on the work of others, Halliburton (1977a) argued that systematic curriculum planning needs a built-in process for curricular change, should be articulated across levels, and should include evaluation. Current processes are bound to assumptions about teaching and learning and thus limit the ability to create effective academic plans. Escaping these assumptions "will depend upon our learning to see the curriculum as a process that is subject to change, and our discovery of how to bring about change" (Halliburton, 1977a, p. 45).

At every turn, observers have noted the important associations among educational purposes, instructional processes, and change processes; the strong impact of the disciplines on each of these; and the influences of forces both external and internal to the university. The academic plan concept is an attempt to tie together meaningfully ideas that are repeated throughout the literature on curriculum. Curriculum planning, however haphazard, occurs. The academic plan concept encourages faculty members and leaders to carry out curriculum planning as an intentional and informed design process.

Advantages of the Academic Plan Model

Historically and currently, debates about the purposes and content of college education have produced much rhetoric but little real understanding or consensus. Multiple definitions of curriculum are both cause and effect of this rhetorical excess. Our definition of the academic plan includes the major elements and influences that regularly surface in discussions of the planning, implementation, evaluation, or improvement of teaching and learning. Without prescribing specific curricula, the academic-plan-in-context framework provides a conceptual umbrella that can accommodate the plans constructed for diverse fields, including liberal arts disciplines and professional fields as well as vocational programs taught in community colleges and by for-profit providers. The academic plan concept, however, has additional advantages.

- *Promotes clarity about influences on the curriculum.* As an academic plan is developed, educators are subjected to influences from many quarters. Both planning and implementation occur in a specific context composed of influences from inside and outside the institution. Once these contextual influences are recognized, faculty and administrators can assess how the context will or does affect academic plans. Awareness of this educational environment is important if meaningful plans are to be constructed and enhanced over time. Any comprehensive model of academic planning must identify the influences within the sociocultural and historical context to be recognized and accommodated.

- *Helps separate facilitators and constraints from educational assumptions.* When curriculum is viewed as a plan, faculty and administrators can recognize both facilitators and constraints for what they are, rather than confusing them with basic assumptions. This recognition is particularly useful in separating instructional process decisions based on constraints due to materials, settings, and structure from the decisions about desired educational outcomes.

- *Focuses attention on decisions to be made.* In distinguishing the plan from the process of planning, we focus attention on the decisions being made rather than the content of those decisions.

- *Guides planning at the lesson, course, program, and college levels.* The definition of curriculum as an academic plan is applicable at all levels. A plan can be constructed for a single lesson or module, for a single course, for groups of courses (usually called programs or majors), and for a college or university as a whole. Defining curriculum as a plan urges faculty and administrators to consider the consistency and integrity of plans within and among these various levels.

- *Encourages explicit attention to student learning.* The definition of curriculum as an academic plan is consistent with current understandings of student learning. Attention to the elements of the academic plan can help faculty members understand the importance of student needs, clarify expectations for students, encourage student engagement, and aid assessment of student achievement by clearly specifying educational purposes, content, and processes.

- *Offers a dynamic view of curriculum development.* The academic plan concept assumes that all plans are subject to evaluation and adjustment; iterative improvements are an expected part of practice. Evaluation is more likely to be useful—and seems less daunting—when it is viewed as a normal and periodic process that produces results relevant to solving particular problems. Unlike the static definition of curriculum as a set of courses, an academic plan implies strategic decision making as conditions—student goals, social needs, accreditation standards, resources, and so on—change.

There is no one way to construct an academic plan. In keeping with the diversity of postsecondary institutions and learners in U.S. higher education, there are many possible processes. Some variations in processes are associated with disciplines, others with institutional or program missions, and still others with leadership styles. This diversity exists, in part, because as the plan is developed, planners are subject to influences from internal and external influences. Thus, both planning and implementation of plans occur in specific contexts. As we shall show in the next chapter, awareness of this educational environment is important if meaningful plans are to be constructed and enhanced.

CHAPTER TWO

EXTERNAL INFLUENCES: SOCIOCULTURAL CONTEXT

American higher education has experienced a long-term trend toward diversification of institutions, educational missions, students, and academic programs, accompanied by recurring debates about key curricular issues. These debates, spurred by influences both internal and external to colleges and universities, have resulted in significant changes in the educational environment during the relatively short history of higher education in America.

Changes in the nation's economy, in the policies of state governing boards, and in the standards for regional and professional accreditation are a few examples of external influences that have altered higher education curricula. Changes in program resources or alterations in academic missions are among the organizational influences that may require faculty members to revise their academic plans. Additional internal influences stem from changes in faculty expertise or the nature of emerging topics. The academic plan concept acknowledges the complex set of influences that act upon higher education and cause adjustments in the educational environment (see Figure 2.1).

The two types of influences on postsecondary curricula that we have noted—external and internal—are not, of course, independent of each other. For example, we classify accrediting agencies as an influence external to academic programs, while we view instructors' impacts as internal influences. Yet colleges and universities voluntarily (if not enthusiastically) undergo regional and specialized accreditation, and most external examiners are faculty members; the

FIGURE 2.1. ACADEMIC PLANS IN SOCIOCULTURAL CONTEXT: EXTERNAL INFLUENCES ON EDUCATIONAL ENVIRONMENTS

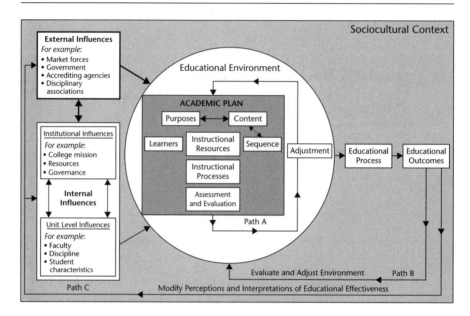

accrediting process is thus strongly influenced by faculty expertise. Accreditation also provides a good illustration of the interaction of external and internal influences and the reciprocal nature of the influences we discuss. We focus this discussion on a single direction of influence—from society (external) to higher education (internal), rather than the reverse—but recognize that colleges shape society, just as society shapes academic plans.

Categorizing the many influences operating on academic plans simplifies discussion and maintains awareness of the varied influences. It also highlights the complexity of the sociocultural environment, reminding us that developing or analyzing academic plans, particularly in the U.S. educational environment, is not a simple task.

A general trend toward diversification of institutional missions, students, academic programs, financial support, and accountability is reflected in changes in curricular purposes, content, and sequence, as well as in instructional process and assessment. A number of key curricular issues surface periodically, but their impact on various elements of the academic plan varies over time. Some have likened this pattern of recurring debate—which has occurred at all levels of American education—to a swinging pendulum (Cuban, 1990; Hansen & Stampen, 1993; Southern Regional Education Board, 1979). Our discussion highlights these patterns as well as variations in these themes.

To place current influences on higher education curricula into historical perspective, we have identified recurring debates about persistent issues, paying particular attention to how these debates have affected the various elements of an academic plan. We emphasize those forces that seem to have influenced the intensity of each debate, providing timelines illustrating periods of significant debate for each issue. Historical perspective helps us to recognize the relationship of current reform efforts to continuing tensions. (A timeline of U.S. curriculum history is available; see Stark & Lattuca, 1997.)

Patterns of Curriculum Debate

In his classic work, *Curriculum: A History of the American Undergraduate Course of Study Since 1636*, Frederick Rudolph (1977) observed that curricular history is American history, "revealing the central purposes and driving directions of American society" (p. 24). In this chapter, we demonstrate the truth of Rudolph's claim about the impact of societal influences on higher education, focusing on five recurring debates about educational purposes, content, learners, instructional processes, and evaluation. For each of these debates, we review the prevailing influences on colleges and universities, thereby providing a thematic, rather than chronological, curricular history.

Our discussion of educational *purpose* centers on debates about whether undergraduate education should be general or vocationally oriented and whether it should transmit a common view of culture or reflect the variety of cultural backgrounds and interests of students. These debates coincide with a more general trend toward increasing diversity in educational missions and types of institutions.

Our second discussion focuses on external influences that have fostered increasing diversity of *learners*. Although difficult to document, we have identified alternating periods of relatively stronger and weaker emphasis on elitism and access and, perhaps, periodic neglect of the expanding pool of students. Debates about access must be viewed in the context of a long-term trend toward greater access and greater diversity in student enrollments.

Third, we discuss *content*, recalling how different educators have taken up the question of whether the curriculum should be prescribed, either fully or partially, for students. The proliferation of knowledge and changes in the personal characteristics and backgrounds of students have engendered considerable debate between the necessity and desirability of a common foundation of knowledge and the need to respond to social needs. This debate also involves questions of institutional mission and raises the question of the balance between general and specialized education.

Fourth, we examine changes in *instructional process*, describing a relatively few periods of modest experimentation with teaching methods and curricular arrangements at the course, program, and college level. After only modest change thus far, the pace of change in instructional process appears to be escalating as a number of forces—calls for accountability, improvements in educational technologies, funding from government agencies, and further diversification in educational providers (for example, for-profit companies)—result in educational innovations.

Finally, we discuss the relationship of these four debates to periods of emphasis on *evaluation*. Calls for greater accountability have been raised many times in the past, often with the intention of changing the direction or pace of change. Nonetheless, evaluation and adjustment efforts in higher education remain unsystematic.

External influences such as economic trends (for example, recessions and depressions), technological developments (the industrial and information revolutions), globalization, and international or domestic conflicts have produced the most significant undulations in the intensity of these five debates. Relatively speaking, internal influences have spurred less dramatic changes. Meanwhile, the tendency toward greater diversity in curricula continues.

Evolving Educational Purposes

U.S. college and university curricula gradually changed from educational programs designed with a common purpose in the colonial period—to prepare a select group of young men for the ministry or gentlemanly status—to programs that must prepare students of different ages, genders, social classes, races, and ethnicities for work and life. Changing social needs initially inspired debates about educational purpose and often produced changes in college curricula. Over time these recurring debates also reflected the growing influence of students' diverse backgrounds, interests, and pre-college preparation, as well as differences in educators' judgments about the preservation, transmission, creation, and/or construction of knowledge.

Debates over educational purpose resulted in the evolution of distinctly different types of postsecondary institutions and in the development of institutions with multiple missions. Discussions focusing on the merits of general and specialized education can best be begun by considering three distinct prototypical college missions that had emerged by the end of the 19th century.

Utilitarian Mission

The utilitarian mission was based on the belief that colleges should train citizens to participate in the nation's economic and commercial life. The Morrill

Land-Grant Act of 1862 provided the framework for large numbers of state institutions that espoused this mission and stressed the study of agriculture and engineering. By the 1920s, teacher education and other occupational fields such as social work and nursing grew in popularity, and private colleges as well as public ones offered career-oriented programs in business and science. Many state colleges and universities emphasized a mission of practical education and social improvement through economic growth and upward mobility, as they attempted to meet the practical educational needs of their regional constituencies. Despite the early introduction of Harvard Law School in 1817, most colleges and universities did not house professional schools (as we know them today) until early in the 20th century when the prestigious professions of medicine, dentistry, and law joined research universities.

Research Mission

The research university espoused another type of mission, primarily dedicated to the production of new knowledge. Adapted from German universities, this model developed in the mid- to late-1800s as Americans educated abroad returned to the United States to found new institutions. In its purest form, the research mission focused on graduate education, but financial concerns and faculty sentiment convinced universities in the United States to include both graduate and undergraduate programs rather than devote themselves exclusively to research. Research universities tended to attract large numbers of undergraduates due to institutional prestige and substantial resources.

Liberal Arts Mission

The liberal arts mission evolved from earlier forms of classical education that stressed the study of classical languages and literatures. The liberal arts mission, which became prominent just before the turn of the 20th century, emphasized the great artistic, literary, and scientific works of humankind. This mission, and the resulting curriculum, stressed the preservation of knowledge and the improvement of students' abilities to appreciate knowledge and think effectively. These abilities, in turn, were believed to transfer to other tasks and settings, allowing graduates to serve society as productive citizens.

Increasing Diversity of Missions

With the expansion of knowledge, faculty members became increasingly interested in advancing new specializations and less concerned with defending the classical course of study. In the early 1800s, the first academic departments emerged to organize curricula, followed by disciplinary associations that motivated their members to stay on the forefront of knowledge. By the late 1800s, undergraduates, too, could specialize in most colleges, complementing their broad education with a concentration in a single liberal arts field. The last half of the 19th century saw an increase in the number of subjects taught and the emergence of new fields like science and psychology. As social and economic needs multiplied and deepened, majors in these new subjects began to focus students' academic programs more closely on future careers. The major field, created in the late 1800s partly to stem the rising tide of student choice, is now an important component of education in all but a handful of four-year institutions.

Although the emergence of majors allowed students to specialize, after 1900 the pendulum swung back from its emphasis on professional and specialized study as faculty groups reacted to the threat of over-specialization. A period of resurgent interest in general education marked the first thirty years of the 1900s (Bell, 1966). The rise of communism and the entrance of the United States into World War I increased awareness of political ferment abroad, and discussions of ideology once again joined technical discussions in college classrooms. During the Great Depression of 1929–1932, students faced with a dismal job market majored in more general fields to enhance their career flexibility.

Mixed Missions

By the mid-1900s most colleges and universities pursued a mixture of the three prototypical missions and continue to do so today. State colleges and universities still emphasize a mission of practical education and social improvement but include elements of liberal education in their academic programs. Independent and denominational colleges (also called private college), which once focused on the classics, also responded to local influences that encouraged specialized occupational programs serving home communities and local employers. The difference between state colleges and independent colleges is often one of emphasis: whereas state colleges use liberal arts education to buttress career programs, many independent institutions add professional and pre-professional majors to supplement liberal arts programs. With less than half of their student enrollment in undergraduate programs, research universities often struggle to balance general and specialized study as different groups within the organization focus on the discovery of new knowledge in their fields of study.

The two-year junior college further diversified institutional missions when it emerged in the early 1900s. Originally designed to provide the academic foundation for students planning to transfer to four-year institutions, public and private two-year colleges soon also provided continuing education, developmental education, skill training in technical education, and community service. After 1950, private junior colleges (never a large number) began to close or merge with four-year institutions, while the number of public two-year colleges grew significantly through the 1960s. Like state colleges and universities, these "community" colleges define service to their communities as part of their mission. They often contract with local businesses to offer professional development courses tailored to their employees' specific needs and provide adult education for populations beyond the age of eligibility for secondary school services. The missions of two-year and four-year colleges overlap somewhat, and thus they compete in many areas, particularly for students who wish to specialize in occupational programs.

The postsecondary landscape also includes various types of for-profit institutions that focus heavily on career preparation. Although structurally and operationally different from traditional two- or four-year colleges, these commercial educational institutions offer associate's, bachelor's, and graduate degrees (as well as non-degree programs) that are tailored to the needs of particular segments of the education market (for example, part-time adult students).

For-profit institutions made their presence known in U.S. higher education in the 1960s, when "proprietary schools" with a purely occupational focus began to seek accreditation so that they might capitalize on federal financial aid programs. At that time, this sector of the higher education enterprise was composed of institutions such as schools of business or cosmetology. The for-profit universe expanded rapidly after the 1990s (Kinser, 2007). Today, for-profit institutions constitute a sizeable proportion of postsecondary institutions in the United States, but only about 40 percent are eligible for federal financial aid through Title IV of the Higher Education Act, which provides direct funding to students via an array of grants, loans, and work-study opportunities (Tierney & Hentschke, 2007).

The Education Commission of the States identifies three types of for-profit colleges and universities (FPCUs). Enterprise colleges are local, privately owned institutions with small, primarily undergraduate, enrollments. Supersystems are multi-campus organizations with large enrollments that are owned by publicly traded corporations. Finally, Internet institutions are virtual universities that provide online education exclusively. William Tierney and Guilbert Hentschke further distinguish among FPCUs by determining whether they offer certificates and short-term programs or degrees, but note the difficuly of developing fixed categories. Counting for-profit institutions is also complicated by the existence of corporate and virtual universities and the dynamic nature of the market, which spawns hybrid institutions (Kinser, 2007) and which promises to remain volatile for the near future (Tierney & Hentschke, 2007). Kinser (2007) recommends a multidimensional classification scheme that combines geographic scope, ownership, and the highest degree offered by an institution.

Despite variations in markets, funding sources, and structure, the three institutional missions we have discussed—research, liberal arts, and utilitarian preparation—are still broadly applicable and exist in varying proportions in different colleges. For-profit institutions that award bachelor's degrees, for example, may require that students take general education courses in communications and mathematics, even as they emphasize vocational training.

These three missions have spawned a wide variety of subjects that almost defies classification. The scope of subjects taught in two-year and four-year institutions can be grasped by reviewing the U.S. Office of Education coding system that colleges use to report their majors, courses taught, and degrees granted. This comprehensive system, the Integrated Postsecondary Education Data System (IPEDS), classifies and describes courses and programs currently offered in postsecondary schools of all types. Another method of classification, developed in the mid-1970s by the Carnegie Foundation and revised several times, originally classified the institutions themselves by degree level, selectivity, and mission. The most recent revision in 2005 additionally uses degree programs, size, and location to classify nearly 4,000 U.S. colleges (Carnegie Foundation for the Advancement of Teaching, 2006).

Short-term certificate programs are also increasingly common in all kinds of institutions, although they tend to be most prominent in the for-profit sector. Tierney and Hentschke (2007) identify two kinds of certificate programs. The first type, which consists of courses added to existing diploma programs to allow students to meet the requirements set by an organization or agency, can be found in a variety of fields and types of institutions (for example, a certificate in cardiopulmonary resuscitation). Stand-alone certificate programs, which are more specialized, prepare individuals to compete for a specific job. They are increasingly common in the information technology field, where computer technicians must complete certificate programs to qualify for examinations that assess specific competencies and thus provide a gateway to employment. Such programs are not included in the IPEDS system because providers that offer information technology certifications do not participate in federal student aid and reporting systems (Adelman, 2000).

Debating General Education and Specialization

In most four-year colleges, undergraduate students include both general and specialized studies in their degree programs. Debate continues over the balance between these program components and has been intense periodically during the last two hundred years. The varying periods of emphasis on either general education or specialization are illustrated in Figure 2.2.

FIGURE 2.2. PERIODS OF EMPHASIS ON GENERAL AND SPECIALIZED EDUCATION

Classical/Liberal/General Education	Direction of Influence ← Year →	Practical/Specialized/Vocational Education
	1650	
	1675	
European model: classical education	1700	
	1725	
		Parallel course in science offered
	1750	
	1775	State colleges established Normal colleges established
Growth of denominational colleges begins	1800	U.S. military academy founded Department system emerges
Yale Report supports classical education	1825	
	1850	Morrill Act fosters study in agricultural and mechanical arts
Liberal education evolves from classical education	1875	Growth of state colleges Research universities emerge
	1900	Disciplinary associations arise Research specialization continues
General education movement Rise in nationalism	1925	Professional fields strengthen
Liberal education re-emphasized	1950	G.I. Bill veterans arrive on campuses Community colleges grow Technological development – reaction to Sputnik
Multiculturalism movement Reports call for reform	1975	Interdisciplinarity encouraged
Core/coherence urged	2000	

General Education

The sheer number of higher education institutions in the United States and the lack of a central agency that coordinates their efforts make it difficult to generalize about postsecondary curricula. The typical four-year college degree consists of 120 credits, and roughly one-third of the credits for a bachelor of arts or bachelor of science is often taken in general education courses, with the remaining two-thirds divided between a major (or specialization) and electives. The two-year college curriculum may also include a general education segment, a major specialization, and some electives, totaling about 60 credits. Thus, many students begin their studies with general education courses intended to provide any or all of the following: (a) a broad base of knowledge and skills thought to be useful to all students in and beyond college, (b) a foundation of skills and knowledge needed for further study, and/or (c) an introduction to different fields of study. But the amounts of general education required for graduation have varied over time and still vary among colleges.

Sometimes the general education a college requires is referred to as the "core curriculum" and is based on the belief that all students should have a common experience or obtain a common foundation of knowledge during college. Few colleges in the United States have an entirely prescribed general education core, but modified core curricula gain ground during the periods when institutions seek to increase the coherence of their general education programs. Various models may include a set of courses (perhaps six to eight) that are required of all students; a single course, perhaps interdisciplinary in nature, required of all; or a set of two or three courses in different disciplines or domains of knowledge that are substantively linked to one another. Most commonly, however, the general education requirements are expressed as "distribution" requirements. In a distributed core, students must fulfill requirements in specified areas but may choose among a range of courses to satisfy those requirements.

Because of the persistent debate about the balance of general and specialized study, considerable efforts have been undertaken to document actual student course patterns resulting from distribution requirements (Adelman, 1990, 1992, 1999, 2004; Ratcliff, 1992; Zemsky, 1989) and the status of curricular components such as general education (Adelman, 2004; Blackburn, Armstrong, Conrad, Didham, & McKune, 1976; Dressel & DeLisle, 1970; Locke, 1989; Ratcliff, Johnson, La Nasa, & Gaff, 2001; Toombs, Amey, & Fairweather, 1989). To summarize this research briefly: in 1967, 43 percent of the courses taken by the average college student were in general education; by 1976, general education requirements had decreased to about 33 percent of a student's program; but by 1988, general education rebounded a bit, accounting for 38 percent of the average student's program. The number of required courses in mathematics has also been documented. In 1967, one-third of all colleges required mathematics as part of general education. By 1974, only 20 percent of colleges required students to study math. The trend reversed itself significantly by 1988, when 65 percent of colleges and universities required the study of mathematics. A recent study in more than five hundred colleges suggested that mathematical requirements have increased again; 88 percent of all responding colleges indicated that they required mathematics or a quantitative reasoning course (Ratcliff, Johnson, La Nasa, & Graff, 2001). The same study indicated that more than 85 percent of institutions required general education courses in the natural and social sciences. Slightly fewer required courses in the humanities (78 percent), fine arts (71 percent), or literature, history, and philosophy (61 percent each). Fewer than half of the five hundred responding institutions reported requirements in foreign language. Despite fluctuations in general education requirements over time, English composition has remained a constant; since 1972 English composition has been the most common course taken by bachelor's degree recipients (U.S. Department of Education, 2004).

Specialization

In four-year college programs, academic specializations are typically of four types: (a) an academic major (intended either to prepare students for graduate school or employment in the same or a related field), (b) a preprofessional major, (c) an interdisciplinary major, or (d) a general education or liberal studies major.

The important concepts of a major field and the methods of inquiry to be taught are determined by the community of scholars in that field. In fields in which there is considerable consensus on key information and methods of inquiry, the undergraduate curriculum tends to be tightly structured; scholars generally agree on concepts, theories, skills, and methods of inquiry and how these should be sequenced. In those fields for which inquiry is more wide-ranging, a more loosely structured undergraduate curriculum results; individual instructors choose what they want to emphasize from a broad range of topics, ideas, and skills. Especially in colleges and universities in which instructors maintain close ties to the disciplinary associations in their fields, the major may reflect key debates among the members of the discipline.

Typically, the undergraduate major follows a sequence in which the student gains progressively more depth of knowledge in a field of study. The major typically includes an introductory course (which may double as a general education requirement), a set of intermediate courses, and some advanced courses. It may require a thesis, a senior paper, or some other culminating experience such as a seminar or comprehensive examination that requires demonstration of the ability to synthesize knowledge. Some students who major in an academic discipline plan to continue study in the field at the graduate level, but most seek work after graduation.

Students who begin pursuing professional majors at the undergraduate level (for example, architecture, business, education, engineering, nursing, social work) often practice their future occupations in fieldwork settings as undergraduates. In these fields, some of which require more than four years to complete, the major conveys a knowledge base of skills, attitudes, and behaviors needed for entry into a specific occupation upon receipt of the bachelor's degree. Students' curricular choices are influenced by many factors, but the job market figures prominently. For example, enrollments in education programs declined drastically as the number of teaching jobs decreased in the 1970s and as opportunities simultaneously arose for women in formerly male-dominated fields like business, medicine, and law.

By the late 1990s, nearly 60 percent of all bachelor's degrees in the United States were granted in professional and occupational fields (Brint, 2002). The most common career majors in recent years have been business and management (22 percent of all bachelor's degrees awarded in 2004–2005), education (7 percent), and the visual and performing arts (6 percent) (U.S. Department of Education, 2007). Career majors are even more popular in two-year institutions: in 2004–2005, 18 percent of all associate's degrees were awarded in health professions and clinical sciences; 16 percent in business; 8 percent in engineering and engineering technology; and 5 percent in computer and information sciences. Thirty-five percent of associate's degree recipients majored in the liberal arts and science, general studies, or the humanities (reflecting, in part, the extent to which associate's degree holders plan to transfer to four-year bachelor's programs) (U.S. Department of Education, 2007).

Students may combine two areas of study through a "double major," which typically requires them to complete all the requirements for two separate academic programs. Interdisciplinary majors also permit the study of two or more fields of study, but do not require students to complete separate academic programs. Rather, students either create an "individualized" major, combining courses from two or more fields of their choosing, or pursue a formal interdisciplinary major that draws on the courses and/or faculty from several academic departments. Common interdisciplinary majors include environmental science, international studies, women's studies, American studies, neuroscience, and a variety of ethnic studies programs (for example, Chicano studies and African American studies). Like the disciplinary major, these programs often require students to engage in a culminating experience like a capstone seminar or senior thesis.

Some colleges offer general education or liberal studies majors, which offer greater flexibility and a wider choice of courses than do majors in specific disciplines. A liberal studies major is intended for students who wish to learn about many fields of study and who resist specialization. In some colleges, it is viewed as a catch-all category for students who are undecided about which specific field to pursue in depth, or as an "escape hatch" for unmotivated students. Such negative reaction to the liberal studies major in some colleges provides evidence of how far higher education has moved from a core curriculum to more specialized programs of study.

Some colleges and universities offer preprofessional majors—a set of recommended courses for students intending to pursue graduate-level professional education in fields such as medicine, law, dentistry, and veterinary medicine. Frequently, a special advisor helps students select the appropriate courses and complete their graduate school applications. Students may also prepare for graduate study in such professions by taking relevant courses outside the preprofessional major.

What is called a major specialization in a transfer curriculum in a two-year college may be the approximate equivalent of introductory and intermediate courses in the four-year baccalaureate program in the same field. (Community and for-profit colleges may also offer occupational majors that have no equivalent at the baccalaureate level but that are instead gateways to employment.) Institutions that seek to facilitate the transfer of students from two- to four-year programs develop "articulation" agreements that specify courses that are equivalent at the two- and four-year levels and thus can be transferred for credit. Articulation agreements not only involve administrators who coordinate the process, but instructors who are responsible for aligning course content and syllabi to ensure substantially equivalent educational experiences. In some states, articulation agreements are written into state educational codes (Cohen & Brawer, 2003).

Over more than 350 years, U.S. higher education programs have become both more diversified and more specialized, fragmenting into subfields such as biomedical engineering, supply chain economics, public relations, and advertising, to name a few. Faculty members cite expanding knowledge bases and increasing demand from disciplinary accrediting agencies as unrelenting pressures toward specialized study. Specialization and diversification of academic programs are closely related and both are opposed by advocates of educational breadth who periodically call for greater attention to a broad set of liberal education goals and outcomes (see Figure 2.2).

The three missions—utilitarian, research, and liberal arts—still form the primary basis for the diversity among colleges, but the debate over general and specialized study sometimes occurs within a single institution. For example, the concept of liberal arts as a foundation for life or further study for all college students may pervade the undergraduate programs in many large universities. Here the colleges of arts and sciences provide a general education curriculum intended to complement students' specialized studies in the major. Faculty members in disciplines and fields with tightly prescribed curricula (such as engineering or music) may seek to reduce the proportion of the undergraduate program dedicated to general education requirements to achieve greater specialization. In all kinds of institutions, competition for resources also impinges on the general education program. As programs and colleges are pitted against one another in the budget process, debate about the relative merits of general and specialized study is often viewed in very pragmatic terms.

Learners: An Emphasis on Access

With very few exceptions, the American colonial colleges educated only a small proportion of the white male populace. In 1850 it is estimated that only 1 percent of the population actually finished college. The rapid rise in bachelor's degrees after records were begun in 1870 is illustrated in Figure 2.3. Since then, an ever-increasing portion of the U.S. population has attended college. By 2000, some eight years after most had graduated from high school, 29 percent of the 1988 eighth-grade cohort had earned a bachelor's, master's, or higher (Ph.D. or professional) degree (Ingels, Curtin, Kaufman, Alt, & Chen, 2002). Almost half of the cohort (46 percent) had accumulated some postsecondary credits or earned an associate's degree or certificate. In tracking female City University of New York students twenty and thirty years after they initially entered college, researchers found that 70 percent had earned a postsecondary degree and more than three-fourths of those had earned a bachelor's degree (Attewell & Lavin, 2007). In a similar analysis of data from the National Longitudinal Survey of Youth, which tracked students for twenty years, the same researchers found that 61 percent of students entering college graduated (Attewell & Lavin, 2007).

Opportunity Increases

The Industrial Revolution and the spread of settlement across the continent inspired a number of changes in higher education. The country needed expertise in areas such as surveying and agriculture. An education encompassing these practical subjects appealed to a broader spectrum of the population, and public pressure led to passage of the 1862 Morrill Act, which provided funds for the creation of land-grant universities that would provide the opportunity for every American

FIGURE 2.3. BACHELOR'S DEGREES CONFERRED BY U.S. INSTITUTIONS OF HIGHER EDUCATION: 1869–1870 TO 1996–1997

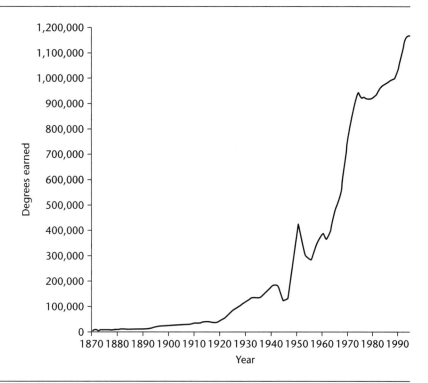

From: Gerald and Hussar (1999); U.S. Bureau of the Census (1975)

citizen to receive some form of higher education (Brubacher & Rudy, 1976). In addition, a growing number of families were willing and able to finance a son's education to prepare him for entry into a world of greater opportunity. Figure 2.4 illustrates the periods of emphasis on access.

For the first half of the 19th century, women desiring a college education were largely confined to "seminaries," institutions that aimed to prepare women for their future roles as wives and mothers (Lucas, 2006). In the U.S., this changed mid-century with the opening of teachers colleges, women's colleges, and founding of co-educational institutions. Later in the 1800s, some of the leading U.S. women's colleges, many of which evolved from earlier seminaries (for example, Mount Holyoke), were founded (Horowitz, 1993). During the Civil War, significant decreases in male enrollments caused many formerly all-male institutions to encourage women to enroll. After the Civil War, reformist ideals supported the continuation of this trend. By 1860, approximately forty-five colleges and

FIGURE 2.4. PERIODS OF EMPHASIS ON ACCESS

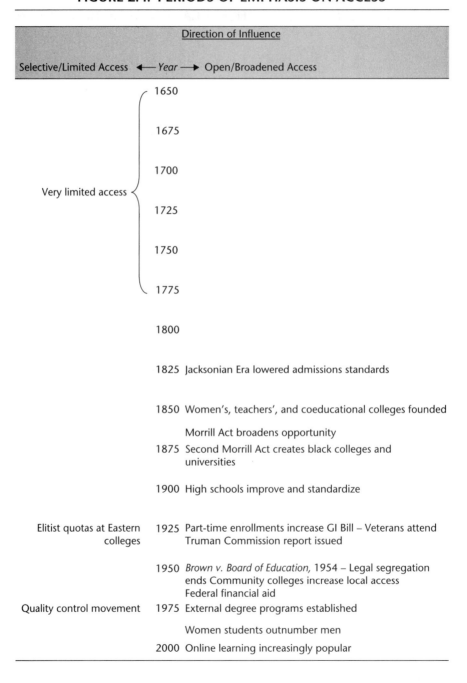

	Direction of Influence	
Selective/Limited Access ◄— *Year* —► Open/Broadened Access		

Very limited access

1650

1675

1700

1725

1750

1775

1800

1825 Jacksonian Era lowered admissions standards

1850 Women's, teachers', and coeducational colleges founded

Morrill Act broadens opportunity
1875 Second Morrill Act creates black colleges and universities

1900 High schools improve and standardize

Elitist quotas at Eastern colleges 1925 Part-time enrollments increase GI Bill – Veterans attend Truman Commission report issued

1950 *Brown v. Board of Education,* 1954 – Legal segregation ends Community colleges increase local access Federal financial aid
Quality control movement 1975 External degree programs established

Women students outnumber men
2000 Online learning increasingly popular

universities, some of which enrolled only female students, offered women the opportunity to earn a degree (Geiger, 2000; Thelin, 2004).

Reforms of the post-Civil War period, and the passage of a second Morrill Act in 1890, which funded the creation of what we now call "historically black colleges and universities" (HBCUs), increased access to higher education for African Americans, although this was accomplished primarily through the creation of segregated institutions. By 1900, all of the southern and border states had state-funded black institutions (Lucas, 2006). However, even as access increased throughout the 19th century, negative assumptions about the suitability of women and blacks, as well as students of lower socioeconomic status, for higher education remained (Lucas, 2006). Although more white men of various social classes sought the education provided by land grants and black institutions, black Americans did not have full access to the types of education provided to white students until well after World War II. A 1917 survey of black higher education suggested that only one of the sixteen black land-grant institutions in the South offered college-level curricula; similarly only thirty-three of nearly one hundred private black colleges provided collegiate-level study (Lucas, 2006).

In 1870 less than 2 percent of the 18- to 24-year-old population in the United States was enrolled in college (Snyder, 1993). In the same year, most of the nation's existing colleges offered preparatory programs for the many students who were not ready for college-level study (Rudolph, 1977). The next period of increased access accompanied the expansion of high school attendance and was fueled by improvements in public high school education. The efforts of the University of Michigan, which developed the first articulation agreements with secondary schools during the 1870s, encouraged standardization of high school curricula. The creation of "standard units" also promoted conformity in the high school course of study, by specifying the amount of time a student had studied a subject. One hundred and twenty hours in one subject area was equivalent to one standard unit of high school credit. Fourteen units were considered to be the minimum academic preparation for college admission (Carnegie Foundation for the Advancement of Teaching, n.d.). As a result, college preparation no longer required private schooling or tutoring.

Improved Preparation Fuels Rapid Growth

Enrollments at colleges and universities in the Eastern United States also swelled with the influx of Jewish immigrants from Europe at the turn of the 20th century (Wechsler, 1977). In the period immediately following World War I, however, many Eastern colleges began to limit the sizes of their entering student cohorts. Newly developed standardized admissions tests intended to ensure adequate preparation allowed institutions to select students based on their test scores. Raising admission standards was a positive step for many institutions, signaling improved educational standards, but at some institutions the standardized tests and other admissions requirements such as assessment of "character" served to limit access (Soares, 2007). For example, "college boards" were first offered by the College Entrance Examination Board, which, according to Nicholas Lemann (2000), was a "clubby association" between a few dozen private schools and colleges with the aim of perfecting the close fit between New England boarding schools and Ivy League colleges (pp. 28–29).

The "Typical" Student Disappears

Most liberal arts colleges enrolled primarily full-time residential students until well after World War II. By mid-century, however, many urban institutions in areas heavily populated by immigrants served commuter and part-time students, establishing large evening divisions to permit the enrollment of working adults. World War II was, however, the most significant catalyst in diversifying college student attendance nationwide. Stimulated by worries about mass unemployment when large numbers of service personnel were demobilized, Congress passed The Servicemen's Readjustment Act of 1944, popularly known as the G.I. Bill. Although the government assumed that only a small number would take advantage of this offer to finance their education, about 2.2 million veterans returned to college with the help of the G.I. Bill. Their enrollment challenged existing visions of the typical student, required massive expansion of higher education, and paved the way for further enrollment growth and student diversity in the following decades. The influx of returning veterans left fewer admission slots for women, however, and women's enrollments declined in the 1950s (Schwartz, 2002). These women were likely to study fields traditionally relegated to them, such as nursing, home economics, and teaching (Goldin, 1992).

Access to higher education became an expectation in the latter half of the 20th century. In a 1947 report entitled *Higher Education for Democracy*, The President's Commission on Higher Education (the Truman Commission) asserted that citizens were "entitled" to higher education regardless of their ability to personally afford it. Reaffirming the usefulness of a college education, the report declared that the nation would benefit when postsecondary education was available to all with the requisite ability (which it estimated at 50 percent of the population). The Commission's report laid the foundation for the Higher Education Act of 1965, which created grant and loan programs that provided financial aid to deserving students with demonstrated financial need. These financial aid programs bolstered college attendance once more and increased students' ability to choose among colleges. The creation of federal financial aid programs also paved the way for federal influence on higher education.

In 1947, the year of the President's Commission report, African American students represented only about 6 percent of all college enrollments in the United States (Lucas, 2006). Access to higher education for African Americans increased following the U.S. Supreme Court's 1954 *Brown v. Topeka Board of Education* decision declaring racial segregation illegal. Desegregation of white institutions in the South accelerated in the years following the decision, sometimes voluntarily and sometimes only following legal action (Wallenstein, 2008). Still, enrollments of black students grew slowly. Between 1960 and 1980, however, after passage of the Higher Education Act, enrollments of African American students in both historically black colleges and universities and predominantly white institutions doubled (Lucas, 2006). Social movements such as the civil rights and women's movements of the 1960s also contributed to the growth and diversification of postsecondary enrollments, encouraging many more women and African American students to enter college. It is only in recent years that African American postsecondary participation rates have been proportional to their representation in the U.S. population. Between 1984 and 2004, minority students had greater growth rates in postsecondary participation than their white counterparts. By 2004, African Americans were the largest minority student population, comprising 13 percent of the total undergraduate student enrollment (Li, 2007).

The number of women undergraduates has increased substantially since the 1960s, and women now constitute more than half of all undergraduate college enrollments. Women also receive almost 60 percent of the associate's degrees awarded and just over half of the more than one million bachelor's degrees awarded annually in the United States. International students also contribute to the diversity of the undergraduate population. In 2006, there were more than 580,000 international students enrolled in U.S. colleges (Institute of International Education, 2007).

New Institutions Appear

By the mid-1900s, the public two-year sector began to expand. Today, most states join with local governmental units to sponsor community colleges that collectively account for more than half of all undergraduate enrollments (Snyder, Tan, & Hoffman, 2006). These colleges (and a few four-year colleges that also grant two-year degrees) now award more than 700,000 associate's degrees annually (*Chronicle of Higher Education Almanac*, 2008). Community colleges account for nearly 40 percent of all enrollments and half of all public college enrollments (Snyder, Tan, & Hoffman, 2006). About 20 percent of students who begin college in a two-year school later enroll in a four-year institution. These students seek to "transfer," or apply the credits they earned in the two-year college to their baccalaureate programs.

Other institutions designed to increase access to college, namely "external degree" colleges or "universities without walls," emerged in the late 1960s to serve adult learners unable to attend formal classes on campuses. This small but distinctive group of colleges, which often award some degree credit for life experiences outside of formal education, typically station faculty in locations convenient to clusters of students. Although these external degree colleges preceded the introduction of computers, by the end of the 20th century substantial numbers of students were enrolled in online education courses and programs using the Internet. For-profit institutions such as the University of Phoenix captured a significant proportion of the adult population seeking credentials and access to employment opportunities. Largely in response to the competition for the growing adult population, public and independent colleges and universities fielded their own distance or online learning programs to serve part-time students. Some created distance learning programs that enroll part-time students as well as residential students seeking flexibility in their course schedules. A few institutions have special units that are dedicated to providing instructional development assistance to instructors developing online courses. In return for supporting these electronic platforms, these units, such as Penn State's World Campus, share the revenues generated through online and hybrid courses with academic programs.

Maintaining Access in the 21st Century

With entitlement and anti-discrimination laws firmly in place in the United States, the years since 1960 can be characterized as a period of particularly strong emphasis on access. Whereas only 5 percent of the population had completed college in 1940; as of 2005, more than 25 percent of individuals in the 25- to 29-year-old age had earned a bachelor's degree (Snyder, Tan, & Hoffman, 2006).

As of fall 2003, about seventeen million students were enrolled in American collegiate education (Snyder, Tan, & Hoffman, 2006) and nearly thirteen million of these attended public colleges. More than ten million were enrolled in four-year institutions (Snyder, Tan, & Hoffman, 2006), but two-year and community colleges are the largest single segment of higher education. Four in ten undergraduates, that is, about 7.6 million students, attend community colleges (Horn & Nevill, 2006). Although the for-profit sector is also growing, one scenario suggests it will account for one out of ten students by 2015 (Blumenstyk, 2005).

Approximately 40 percent of all students in the United States are over 24 years old (Snyder, Tan, & Hoffman, 2006), and many attend on a part-time basis.

Part-time students account for about 60 percent of the undergraduate population in two- and four-year colleges combined (Snyder, Tan, & Hoffman, 2006).

Today, more than two-thirds of all students enrolled in degree-granting institutions in the United States are white. Black students represent just less than 12 percent of graduate and undergraduate enrollments. Hispanic students account for about 10 percent, Asians and Pacific Islanders, 6.5 percent, and American Indians about 1.0 percent of all postsecondary enrollments (U.S. Department of Education, 2005). At four-year institutions (including independent and public institutions and those that award doctoral and master's degrees), about one-quarter of students are minorities, although public two-year institutions enroll more minority students (36 percent) than four-year institutions do. Black and Hispanic students are more likely than other students of color to attend an institution with a high concentration of their own racial/ethnic group. About one-fifth of each of these groups of students attend an institution where they are the majority (U.S. Department of Education, 2005).

Arthur Cohen and Florence Brawer (2003) note that the most rapid change in the two-year college curriculum has been the growth in English as a second language (or ESL) courses. The growth in ESL enrollments reflects the growing diversity of college-going adults in the United States and the growing number of immigrants enrolling in postsecondary education. In 1983, ESL accounted for 30 percent of foreign language enrollments. By 1991, it was over 50 percent and, together with Spanish, accounted for three-quarters of all foreign language credit sections. In 1998, more than half of all two-year colleges offered ESL courses, but students may or may not earn academic credit for them. In some states, state funding and student financial aid policies classify ESL as less-than-college-level work (Cohen & Brawer, 2003, p. 327).

Despite the increasing diversity of U.S. higher education, there are gaps in college achievement. Although the number of historically underrepresented students enrolled has reached record highs, degree attainment levels are considerably higher for white adults than for African Americans and Hispanics. Two-thirds of white Americans in the 25- to 29-year-old age group have attended some college, and about one-third hold a bachelor's degree. In the same age group, only 50 percent of blacks and 30 percent of Hispanics have attended some college, and less than 20 percent of blacks and 10 percent of Hispanic citizens have earned bachelor's degrees. Less than 4 percent of each of these groups has advanced degrees, compared to more than just over 7 percent of whites (U.S. Census Bureau, 2008). (See Figure 2.5.)

Older and part-time students who live off-campus and are financially independent more commonly attend public two-year colleges, and these students often are ineligible for financial aid. Historically underrepresented students are also

FIGURE 2.5. DEGREE ATTAINMENT BY RACE/ETHNICITY (%), AGES 25 TO 29

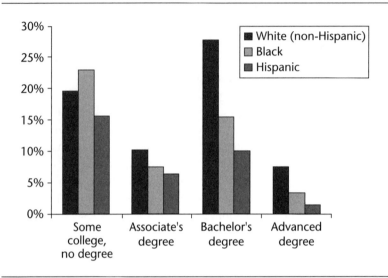

From: U.S. Census Bureau, 2008

disproportionately enrolled in two-year institutions. A student's choice of colleges may be limited by his or her previous academic preparation and success. Because most community colleges have "open door" admissions policies, they are more likely than four-year colleges and universities to offer remedial programs for students who need to develop basic skills in mathematics, writing, reading, or English before or while they enroll in college-level coursework. All public two-year colleges offer at least one remedial course (Kirst, 1998), and about 40 percent of all community college students have taken a remedial course (compared to 28 percent of undergraduates in four-year institutions) (U.S. Department of Education, 2004). In most colleges, enrollment in remedial courses is voluntary, but a few institutions, such as Miami Dade Community College, require students to acquire basic skills before taking courses that require their use.

The sheer number of students in U.S. colleges and universities has caused many to characterize the nation's higher education enterprise as one of "universal" access. This term is somewhat exaggerated since many Americans still do not attend college. External influences, including wars, immigration, desegregation, the shift from an agrarian to a post-industrial society, and various social movements have promoted the diversification of the student population, and the nation has moved steadily from a view of education as a privilege for a few toward an entitlement for citizens of all ages, genders, races, and interests.

Content Debates: Prescription vs. Choice

Curricular choice debates date from the earliest decades of U.S. higher education. Each recurrence yields a temporary victory for one side or the other. New college missions and broader access for diverse students have contributed to the growing variety of courses and programs that colleges and universities offer. This abundance periodically spurs discussions about the extent to which postsecondary institutions should prescribe curricular requirements for their students. Despite this debate's obvious periodicity, it is difficult to separate these discussions from others concerned with the relative virtues of general and specialized education.

Colleges Choose; Students Follow

Today's college students face a daunting array of options compared to the first American students, who lacked the option to choose majors, areas of concentration, or even individual courses. For over fifty years, the colonial colleges offered one program of study, usually incorporating Greek, Latin, Hebrew, rhetoric, logic, moral philosophy (ethics), and natural philosophy (the precursor to what we know as physics).

Colleges gradually responded to a rapidly expanding knowledge base. For example, in 1714 a donation of several hundred new books to Yale University required improvements in mathematics preparation (Rudolph, 1977). Even so, the first mathematics professorship at Yale was not established until 1770. The first real "elective" may have been offered in 1755, when Harvard continued to provide instruction in Hebrew, but no longer required it for graduation.

As new colleges entered the scene, curricular choices expanded somewhat. When it opened in 1754, King's College (now Columbia University), for example, offered courses in commerce and husbandry. By 1776, six of the eight colonial colleges had created professorships in mathematics, a course of study previously neglected, and the study of Newtonian physics was beginning to emerge from natural philsophy. The College of Philadelphia (today the University of Pennsylvania) provided instruction in political science, agriculture, history, and chemistry (Rudolph, 1977). Options of this type, however, did not challenge the assumption that the college, not the student, determined what was to be learned.

New subjects and new institutions were the primary sources of increased choices for students in colonial American colleges. Social and economic changes, however, precipitated more curricular change as the population of a growing nation increasingly questioned the idea that the nation was best served by men significantly familiar with ancient languages and literature but with little knowledge of practical subjects. Colleges gradually introduced subjects such as astronomy, mathematics, engineering, and natural sciences into their curricula. Just before 1800, English supplanted Latin as the language of instruction.

Pressure for Choice Increases

By the early 1800s, prospective and enrolled students, as well as some faculty, were growing dissatisfied with the classical college curriculum, which they perceived to be dated, inflexible, and dull. Colleges first attempted to address student complaints by adjusting the structure of their programs rather than their purpose and content. For example, Harvard offered tutorials and a few electives and began to group students according to ability. The first significant curricular changes came as colleges reluctantly allowed "partial" or "parallel" courses of study in the sciences. Traditionalists viewed these degrees as less prestigious alternatives to the more established requirements of the classical program, but students enrolled nonetheless. In many institutions, students created their own avenues for intellectual pursuits, forming literary and debating societies that enjoyed great popularity.

The "college" system at the University of Virginia, where students chose an organizational unit in which to pursue their studies, represented another early and significant move toward student choice. Once a student at the university enrolled in a particular "college," he had few choices, but the structural subdivision of the university into departments planted the "seeds of the elective system" (Brubacher & Rudy, 1976, p. 99). As other institutions copied this scheme, courses and specializations mushroomed, rendering choice and elective courses possible—and even necessary.

The Yale Report of 1828, which asserted that the classical curriculum provided the only suitable college education, was an extraordinary (although temporary) victory for the conservative faculty forces and a setback for those advocating greater curricular choice. Within a few decades, however, elective reform again emerged as an important topic, even at campuses that had fully subscribed to assertions of the Yale Report. The development of new universities with new missions, such as the land-grant universities, colleges for freed slaves, and coeducational and women's colleges, contributed to the proliferation of new options and fields of study. The Morrill Act encouraged institutions to permit students to choose elective courses, while colleges and universities admitting women added fields such as domestic science, social work, and fine arts, thought to be better suited to women's "gentler" minds and bodies. (See Figure 2.6.)

Debate and Change Intensify

Even as electives became more numerous and evolved into entire new programs, faculty members opposed to choice tried to thwart them—for example,

FIGURE 2.6. DEBATES ABOUT CONTENT:
CHOICE AND PRESCRIPTION

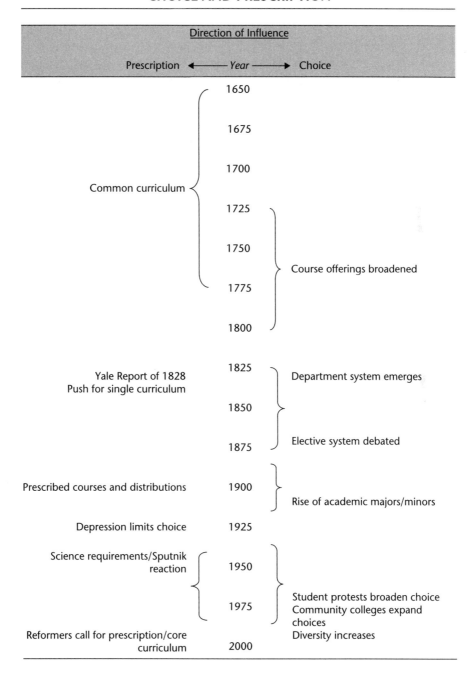

by requiring a higher passing grade for elective courses than for required ones (Brubacher & Rudy, 1976). Each time institutions instituted electives over faculty objections, faculty members resisted.

The forty-year campaign for the elective system waged between 1869 and 1909 by Charles William Eliot, president of Harvard University, is legendary. Through Eliot's efforts, Harvard abolished all course requirements except English composition by 1897. Yet detractors claimed that the new elective system failed to guide students toward clear and coherent educational programs. An 1898 study at Harvard showed that 55 percent of students elected only elementary courses and nearly three-quarters followed a course of study without any clear focus (Rudolph, 1977). With insufficient guidance, many students avoided pursuing any subject in depth.

Between 1885 and 1905, educators responded to the proliferation of elective courses by shaping the system of general education and academic concentrations that is still common in U.S. colleges and universities. The major system, first introduced in 1885 at Indiana University and put into place at Harvard by 1910, coincided with the rise of specializations. Retreating from the ideology of total choice, the major system sought to remedy the lack of structure and coherence that resulted when colleges eliminated all or most curricular requirements (Rudolph, 1977).

By 1920, the system of the major and general education distribution requirements was widely established. Colleges allowed students to choose an area of specialization but required them to also enroll in a general education program, often structured as a set of "distribution requirements" to be fulfilled by courses in subjects the faculty believed supplied a foundation of common knowledge. Departments specified foundation courses and other requirements for their majors, and then allowed students latitude in filling other credit-hour requirements. In some fields of study, the major was nearly as structured as the prescribed curricula that preceded it.

As the 20th century progressed, so did interest in majors such as business and education, which prepared students for specific careers, and in new majors, such as sociology and psychology, which grew out of existing disciplines like philosophy. As options increased, more educators became concerned that students share a common knowledge of Western culture and values. Spurred by nationalistic sentiments during and following World War I, colleges reintroduced core curricula in the humanities and social science and renewed their emphasis on general education requirements.

In 1957, when the Russian launch of the satellite Sputnik challenged notions of U.S. competitiveness and scientific preparedness, educators responded by establishing rigorous scientific requirements for students in high school and college.

Postsecondary institutions strengthened and expanded their general education distribution requirements, including those in laboratory sciences. Colleges and universities frequently used this tactic to prevent students from avoiding laboratory courses.

Students Demand Greater Choice

In the 1960s and 1970s, students became the strongest advocates of greater curricular choice, protesting curricular restrictions by arguing that they faced the draft for the Vietnam War but were denied adult choices on campuses. An increasingly diverse group of students labeled requirements as "establishment"—detrimental to individual development and freedom. Students rejected certification mechanisms such as theses and comprehensive exams as well as curricular prescription. Clifton Conrad and Jean Wyer (1980) described this period as a "virtual free-for-all of the distribution approach" (p. 17). Colleges and universities responded to students who wanted relevant educational programs by experimenting with pass-fail grading options, independent study courses, greater elective choice, and student-designed majors. Buoyed by the civil and women's rights movements, underrepresented women faculty members and their students created programs in women's and black studies.

Despite many concessions to student demands during this turbulent period, the dominant structural features of the curriculum did not change. Most colleges managed to retain, if not fully enforce, programs in general education (required or distributed in groups of courses), a major field of study or combined related studies, and limited electives. As the job market tightened in the 1970s and 1980s, students themselves selected more structured programs in the hope of improving their marketability. As students have become more and more career focused, they have pursued "double majors" and multiple minors to enhance their "credentials."

Whatever curricular constraints students might feel today, the growth in number and variety of programs, majors, and degrees over time has been formidable. As Frederick Rudolph (1977) noted: "It is one thing to describe the curriculum under which Harvard for decade after decade awarded nothing but the B.A.; it is almost an affront to the imagination to be expected to make sense of the almost two hundred different degrees offered by the University of Illinois in 1960" (p. 10). Had Rudolph included the "feeder" community colleges from which students transfer to and from the University of Illinois as well as the university itself, his statement might have been even stronger. The IPEDS includes nearly one hundred categories of subjects, each divided into many subcategories. Traditional programs of study like American history and newly developed specialties like biochemistry exist beside vocational offerings such as refrigeration technology, restaurant management, and horticulture. In some colleges, academic credit is given for life experience, for remedial study, and for career exploration.

Calls for Curricular Coherence

Historically, debates about curricular prescription and choice occupied higher education faculty, administrators, and leaders like President Eliot of Harvard, who supported elective choice, and President John Maynard Hutchins at the University of Chicago, who argued that all students should have a common foundation of knowledge and skills. In the latter quarter of the 1900s, the array of voices grew as additional stakeholders vociferously entered the conversation about curricular content. Originally an internal concern, questions about postsecondary curricula have become more visible as more and more students in the United States attend college and as stakeholders external to higher education institutions, such as employers, legislators, and government officials, have sought to influence college and university curricula.

The 1980s and 1990s saw a wave of reports from blue ribbon committees appointed by state and federal agencies, as well as recommendations from higher education advocacy organizations. These reports (see Table 2.1) assessed the condition of higher education and called for various reforms. The reports that focused primarily on curriculum (for example, Association of American Colleges, 1985; Bennett, 1984; Boyer, 1987; Cheney, 1989; National Institute of Education, 1984; Wingspread Group on Higher Education, 1993) typically decried curricular fragmentation and overspecialization resulting from the lack of coherent general education programs. Although focused on many of the same problems, the authors of these reports arrived at a variety of solutions. William Bennett, chair of the National Endowment for the Humanities, and his successor Lynne Cheney, both published reports that called for greater attention to Western civilization and culture, while the Association of American Colleges called for greater focus on transferable learning skills such as critical thinking and communication.

These reports, particularly Bennett's (1984) "To Reclaim a Legacy," which placed the blame for students' flight from the humanities at the feet of research-oriented and/or ideological faculty, inspired a backlash from critics of the traditional, Eurocentric liberal arts core. Proponents as diverse as educational theorist Henry Giroux (1992) and philosopher and classicist Martha Nussbaum (1997) argued for an education that would prepare students for life in an increasingly diverse nation and world. Although united in their call for greater attention to national and global diversity, these commentators espoused a variety of goals. Some, like Giroux, advocated curricula that would enable students to critique

TABLE 2.1. A CHRONOLOGY OF CRITICAL REPORTS AND PROPOSALS FOR REFORM, 1984–1994

1984	*To Reclaim a Legacy: A Report on the Humanities in Higher Education.* William Bennett, National Endowment for the Humanities.
1984	*Involvement in Learning: Realizing the Potential of American Higher Education.* Study Group on the Condition of Excellence in American Higher Education, National Institute of Education.
1985	*Integrity in the College Curriculum: A Report to the Academic Community.* Task Force of the Association of American Colleges.
1985	*Higher Education and the American Resurgence.* Frank Newman. The Carnegie Foundation for the Advancement of Teaching.
1986	*To Secure the Blessings of Liberty. Report of the National Commission on the Role and Future of State Colleges and Universities.* American Association of State Colleges and Universities.
1986	*Time for Results: The Governors' 1991 Report on Education.* National Governors' Association, Center for Policy Research and Analysis.
1986	*Transforming the State Role in Higher Education.* Education Commission of the States.
1987	*College: The Undergraduate Experience in America.* Ernest L. Boyer. The Carnegie Foundation for the Advancement of Teaching.
1988	*A New Vitality in General Education.* Task Group on General Education. Association of American Colleges.
1988	*Unfinished Design: The Humanities and Social Sciences in Undergraduate Engineering Education.* Joseph S. Johnston, Jr., Susan Shaman, and Robert Zemsky.
1988	*Humanities in America: A Report to the President, the Congress, and the American People.* Lynne V. Cheney. National Endowment for the Humanities.
1988	*Strengthening the Ties That Bind: Integrating Undergraduate Liberal and Professional Study.* Joan S. Stark and Malcolm A. Lowther. Professional Preparation Network, University of Michigan.
1989	*50 Hours: A Core Curriculum for College Students.* Lynne V. Cheney. National Endowment for the Humanities.
1990	*Scholarship Reconsidered: Priorities of the Professoriate.* Ernest L. Boyer. The Carnegie Foundation for the Advancement of Teaching.
1991	*The Challenge of Connecting Learning.* Project on Liberal Learning, Study-in-Depth, and the Arts and Sciences Major. Association of American Colleges.
1991	*Reports from the Fields.* Project on Liberal Learning, Study-in-Depth, and the Arts and Sciences Major. Association of American Colleges.
1992	*Program Review and Educational Quality in the Major.* Project on Liberal Learning, Study-in-Depth, and the Arts and Sciences Major. Association of American Colleges.
1993	*An American Imperative: Higher Expectations for Higher Education.* Wingspread Group on Higher Education. The Johnson Foundation and others.
1994	*Sustaining Vitality in General Education:* Project on Strong Foundations for General Education. Association of American Colleges.

and address social inequities and encourage social transformation. Others, such as feminists like Elizabeth Minnich (1990), sought to redress the distorted view of U.S. history and society resulting from a curriculum that excluded discussion of the experiences of historically underrepresented students and women. Others who focused on economic competitiveness rather than social justice made the case that students must be well prepared for the contemporary, global workplace (Bollinger, 2007).

Another call for curricular reform focuses on the value of interdisciplinary study at the undergraduate and graduate levels. Such calls, although more persistent of late, are not new. During the general education movement after World War I, a number of reformers emphasized interdisciplinary study as a means of connecting the knowledge of the diverse disciplines that comprise general education programs. During the 1960s, the women's studies movement took up the cause, arguing that the traditional academic disciplines provided only partial and limited perspectives from which to view social problems. Viewing interdisciplinarity as the antidote to incomplete understandings of the lives and issues faced by marginalized populations, faculty in these programs encouraged students (and instructors) to critique and expand traditional disciplines. In the late 1980s, a new group of advocates, this time from the sciences and professional fields, grew in force. These proponents of interdisciplinarity asserted that the disciplines in their traditional form were no longer adequate to solving social and scientific problems. They argued that students needed to develop the ability to work in interdisciplinary teams and attack problems from multiple disciplinary viewpoints to spur scientific breakthroughs and innovation. Unlike their predecessors in women's studies, however, science faculty who advocate interdisciplinarity are more likely to believe that students need a strong foundation in the scientific disciplines—rather than simply the ability to critique those disciplines—to advance knowledge (Lattuca, 2001).

Instructional Process: Occasional Innovations

Temporary victories in the debate about content choice and prescription occasionally inspired instructional innovations. In colonial higher education, faculty members typically subscribed to a view of learning as the exercise and discipline of the mind. Students learned through memorization and recitation, as well as through processes of logical disputation. Instructional processes changed somewhat in the middle 1800s as land-grant colleges, with a mission to serve the state and community, focused instruction on improving agricultural and business production. Learning by demonstration and by laboratory practice became common in these fields.

The history of higher education in the United States, however, boasts a few distinct periods of educational experimentation, notably in the 1920s, 1930s, 1960s, and 1990s. Early scientific studies in the psychology of learning, begun by Columbia University professor Edward Thorndike in the early 1900s, stimulated instructional innovation by calling into question the credibility of the mental discipline theory of learning (Bigge & Shermis, 1992). From the field of philosophy, John Dewey and his followers in the field of education argued for the primacy of experience in education, promoting course instruction based on projects, field work, and inquiry, all relevant to the student, rather than memorization and recitation. Rapid enrollment increases following World War II, however, checked the spread of discussion-based courses. The need to teach large numbers of students simultaneously, combined with a faculty reward system that emphasized the importance of research, seemed to cement the lecture as an instructional method. (See Figure 2.7.)

Students Seek Relevance and Freedom

During the experimental years of the 1960s, faculty introduced some alternatives to large lecture classes. Many small colleges experimented with competency-based learning programs like self-paced instruction, which encouraged instructors to specify behavioral objectives (Keller, 1968). During this same period, the demands for "relevance" prompted some colleges to create study arrangements that allowed students to focus on one subject at a time (such as the one-month intensive term, typically during the mid-year break between terms, of the 4-1-4 calendar system). Others combined living and learning experiences in residence halls to foster closer interaction with faculty and a sense of community intended to offset the impersonal nature of large universities. Students also demanded and won new grading systems, such as pass/fail options, and a few experimenting colleges eliminated grades entirely to encourage students to explore new topics without threat of failure. While exciting to faculty and students, many of these experiments were short-lived because they consumed large amounts of faculty time and often limited students' options for transfer or graduate study.

The 1960s also witnessed the founding of several innovative colleges, such as Evergreen State University and Hampshire College. These institutional experiments spawned a considerable literature documenting the efforts and their effects (for example, Smith & McCann, 2001). Arthur Levine (1978) traced some of the sources and results of curricular reforms, concluding that there has been ongoing change in the predominant view of educational purpose and related instructional processes. Since the elements of the academic plan do not operate independently, it is easy to understand why Levine did not distinguish among purposes, content,

FIGURE 2.7. PERIODS OF CHANGE IN INSTRUCTIONAL PROCESSES

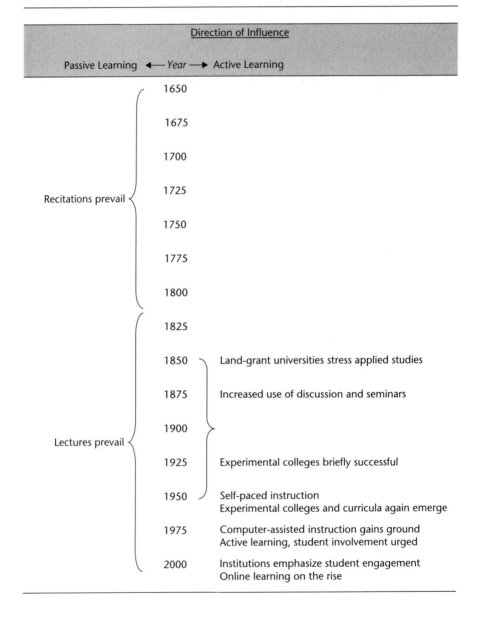

sequence, and instructional process. We have added to his summary for the 1960s and 1970s our own assessment of the 1980s through 2000s.

- 1960s—Dominant educational philosophies are education for life (relevance) and education for personal development. Characteristic experiments include new interdisciplinary studies (ethnic studies, environmental studies), reductions in curricular requirements, and customized courses and programs (for example, independent study, student-created majors, pass/fail grading, and experimental colleges).
- 1970s—U.S. colleges and universities become committed to social justice and universal access. Nontraditional students are admitted and, to accommodate them, variable scheduling, alternatives to courses, off-campus study, credit for experience, and compensatory education are introduced. A strong concern for education and work emerges.
- 1980s—A number of 1940s-era reforms are revived. Curricula move away from electives and toward greater structure in attempts to achieve curricular "coherence." More prescribed distribution requirements emerge, except in two-year colleges, where requirements continue to be reduced. Employers complain that graduates lack basic skills; observers express concerns about educational quality and its measurement and about general education. Decentralization of higher education leads to greater state responsibility and funding for higher education. Experimental colleges and free universities almost disappear.
- 1990s—The catch phrase "student-centered teaching" buoys discussions about instruction. Advocates of active learning and student engagement seek ways to convince faculty of the need for instructional reforms. The emphasis on the quality of teaching gains momentum as a number of accreditation agencies stress the importance of assessment of student learning to demonstrate the quality of a college or university. Online learning begins a rapid ascent as traditional institutions and for-profit educational providers vie for enrollments.
- 2000s—Student-centered teaching becomes "learning centered" as instructional reforms refocus faculty attention on designing curricula and instructional approaches to maximize student learning. Active learning gets a boost with increasing institutional participation in the National Survey of Student Engagement, which collects information about students' involvement in their academic programs. Debates about quality assurance, particularly through general and professional accreditation, take the national stage. Concerns about economic competitiveness and globalization influence calls for educational reforms in the professions. Interdisciplinarity and integration are new watchwords for coherence.

Some innovations from the latter half of the 20th century, notably pass/fail grading, independent study, interdisciplinary area studies, and student-created majors, have endured. Most of the surviving changes, however, are structural rather than philosophical or systemic.

Technological and Instructional Change

Among the educational debates we consider, discussions about instructional processes have been muted, a lifted eyebrow compared to the raised voices generated by purpose, access, and choice. Moreover, most of these discussions about instructional process, as we have noted, occurred internally. Only recently has pressure for reform come from external sources. Today, technological advances appear to have great potential for influencing instruction, as online learning and instructional interfaces like Blackboard™ change the nature of course delivery and student-instructor interactions. These new instructional technologies have the potential to increase significantly both access and student choice.

In fall 2006, online course enrollments reached nearly 3.5 million students, or nearly 20 percent of all enrollments in degree-granting postsecondary institutions in the United States (Allen & Seaman, 2007). More than two-thirds of all higher education institutions offered at least some online offerings in 2006. (Allen, Seaman, & Garrett, 2007). Public institutions were the most likely to offer online education; almost 90 percent of public institutions reported offering at least one online course. Two-year institutions have more online enrollments than all other types of institutions combined (Allen & Seaman, 2007). In fall 2004, half of all institutions offered at least one "blended" course that combined face-to-face and online instruction. Roughly four out of five public institutions offered at least one blended course at the undergraduate level, compared to about a third of independent non-profit institutions, although that gap is beginning to close (Allen & Seaman, 2007). Private, for-profit institutions are more than twice as likely to offer online rather than blended courses.

Institutional size and mission are strongly correlated with decisions about what kinds of courses to offer. Nearly three-quarters of doctoral/research institutions offered both online and blended courses in 2004, compared to about 30 percent of baccalaureate institutions. The baccalaureate category, often composed of residential colleges, has the least number of schools offering blended or online courses (Allen, Seaman, & Garrett, 2007) and accounts for less than 5 percent of U.S. online enrollments (Allen & Seaman, 2007).

Lecturing and demonstration may remain the predominant instructional method among college and university teachers in face-to-face instruction (Lindholm, Szelényi, Hurtado, & Korn, 2005), but advances in instructional and communications technologies are rapidly changing the nature of student and faculty interaction. Data from the National Survey of Postsecondary Faculty (NSOPF) reveals that from 1994 to 2000, instructors' use of email and Internet resources increased "from a curiosity in one of ten courses in 1994 to a dominant instrument in the majority of courses by 2000" (Schuster & Finkelstein, 2006, p. 110). According to Kenneth C. Green (2002), about one-fourth of all college courses use course management software (for example, to post information, provide links to resources, and/or conduct synchronous or asynchronous discussions).

Evaluation Debates: Emphasis on Quality Control

At different points in the history of U.S. higher education, expressions of concern about educational quality and institutional accountability have emanated from society, from educators, and from students. (See Figure 2.8.) Most frequently, however, they come from those who fund higher education—philanthropic foundations, business and industry, and state and federal governments. Although calls for accountability have a financial dimension, they typically emphasize the need for assessment and evaluation to demonstrate educational effectiveness.

Calls for evaluation are often linked with other debates. For example, when educators and government officials believe higher education has overemphasized specialized study, they initiate discussions about the neglect of general education. Conversely, when educational purpose seems divorced from the country's civic and commercial needs, stakeholders argue that college graduates need to improve their mathematical, scientific, and technical knowledge and skills to enable the United States to compete in a global economy. Increased access is linked by some critics to declines in academic rigor and curricular standards. The creation of the land-grant universities with practical programs of study, open-access community colleges, and financial assistance programs all produced some level of backlash. Similarly, the recurring debates about curricular choice are couched as concerns for educational quality and control. Cycles of relaxed curricular requirements to provide more choice for students give way to cycles of tightened requirements to increase "rigor."

Government Funding Begins; Accountability Increases

Throughout U.S. history, sources of funding for higher education have become more heterogeneous and more numerous. Federal support for higher education originally was very small and, despite a few proposals, no "national" university

FIGURE 2.8. EMPHASIS ON EVALUATION AND QUALITY CONTROL

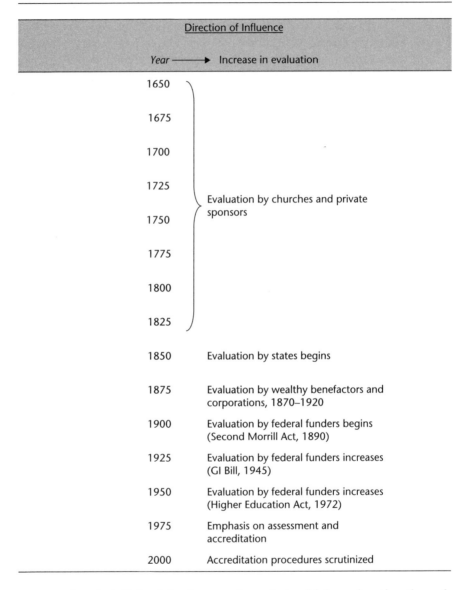

Direction of Influence	
Year ⟶ Increase in evaluation	
1650	⎫
1675	
1700	
1725	
	Evaluation by churches and private sponsors
1750	
1775	
1800	
1825	⎭
1850	Evaluation by states begins
1875	Evaluation by wealthy benefactors and corporations, 1870–1920
1900	Evaluation by federal funders begins (Second Morrill Act, 1890)
1925	Evaluation by federal funders increases (GI Bill, 1945)
1950	Evaluation by federal funders increases (Higher Education Act, 1972)
1975	Emphasis on assessment and accreditation
2000	Accreditation procedures scrutinized

was ever founded. Federal funds were channeled to higher education through special purpose legislation such as the Morrill Land-Grant Act (1862), the Hatch Act (1887), and the Second Morrill Act (1890). With each new federal initiative, record-keeping and evaluation processes developed to ensure that funds were properly spent. These factors created the first period of emphasis on quality control in the final decade of the 19th century.

World War II helped forge strong ties between universities and the federal government. Because the nation needed defense research and because it was efficient to use talent and resources already in place, the federal government directly funded research at major universities, an arrangement that continues today through research grants from agencies such as the Department of Defense, the National Institutes for Health, the National Science Foundation, and others. These agencies created systems to ensure effective and legitimate use of funds. The Servicemen's Readjustment Act of 1944 (G.I. Bill) enlisted already existing accrediting agencies to ensure the quality of institutions enrolling veterans whose tuition would be paid with federal entitlements. While the accreditors did not exactly welcome this responsibility, they accepted it because it strengthened their role by placing quality control in the hands of educators (Stark & Associates, 1977).

The National Defense Education Act (1958), and the Higher Education Act (1965) and its subsequent amendments (1968, 1972, and later) continued to spur the development of accountability requirements. Especially after 1972, when new types of students became eligible for financial aid, the federal government took on increased responsibility to monitor many aspects of college activity and responsiveness. Institutions that accept students who have federal financial aid grants and loans are regularly subject to quality-control initiatives.

In the United States, responsibility for operating public systems of higher education rests with the states. States founded the normal schools that later became teachers' colleges, as well as comprehensive colleges with broader missions. Universities initially supported by the Morrill Acts now receive regular appropriations of state and federal funds, although the proportion of such funds is typically a very small percentage of a university's operating budget (National Association of State Universities and Land Grant Colleges, 1995). With state funding came varying degrees of state coordination and supervision. Many states use state-wide commissions and governing boards to coordinate college missions and programs for efficiency; thus some academic programs are subject to numerous quality control procedures and central reviews. Community colleges are subject as well to local control (usually from their home county or school district). In many states, formal articulation agreements between the community colleges and the four-year state colleges create uniformity in the curriculum by developing guidelines for transferring credits from the sending to the receiving institution.

State-level accountability efforts in the 1980s focused on assessment of student learning, but in the 1990s, a number of states shifted their emphasis to funding, reviewing their funding formulas for public higher education and seeking to link funding to institutional ability to achieve important goals and objectives.

Rather than providing institutions with state funds based on other formulae, some states developed "funding for results" programs that awarded funds to public institutions that met performance goals on particular indicators. Others linked funding to achievement indirectly through *performance budgeting*, which considered reports of achievements of public colleges and universities in budget determinations (Burke & Serban, 1997). In the 1990s some states had adopted, some were considering adopting, and some had dropped or suspended performance funding, suggesting a dynamic legislative environment; changes in state governments led to frequent changes in policies.

In 2000, the National Center for Public Policy and Higher Education, an independent, nonprofit, and nonpartisan organization, issued its first state-by-state "report card," giving each state an "incomplete" grade for assessment of student learning in postsecondary institutions. The absence of acceptable and comparable data for higher education, the publicity surrounding the state report cards, and the growing popularity of performance-based management elevated performance reporting as the preferred accountability mechanism in public higher education (Burke, 2002; Burke & Minassians, 2002). Performance reports offer a "middle ground" between performance funding and outcomes assessment, allowing states to evaluate higher education on critical issues such as access, quality, affordability, and workforce development, while also permitting many colleges and universities to maintain autonomy over their budgets and expenditures (Burke, 2002).

State funding for independent colleges and universities takes a different form. Some states offer tuition grants to state residents who choose to attend in-state colleges, whether public or independent. Some states provide per-capita funding to independent colleges based on their student enrollments. The result of this heterogeneous funding of all types of colleges and universities is that institutions that had been independent are now quasi-public, and some public institutions are now quasi-independent, garnering much of their revenue from alumni donations, foundations, and corporations that underwrite research (and the faculty and students who conduct it). Governmental control has strengthened with increases in student support and subsidies for academic research. Today, institutions face demands for evaluation and quality control from many sources, although accountability to the federal and state governments may be the most keen.

Concerns About Student Preparation

Academic aptitude and achievement test data show that the academic preparation of students attending college is highly variable. Average scores on college admissions tests such as the SAT and ACT began to decline in the late 1960s and continued to decline through the 1970s. Verbal scores stabilized in the 1980s, but math scores declined even further. In the 1990s, verbal scores were at record lows, but math scores rebounded. Since the mid-1990s, average scores of verbal ability have remained fairly stable, while scores of mathematical ability have continued to rise slowly, even as more and more students take admissions tests (College Board, 2007). High school grades are also on the rise, as are the numbers of students who take a college preparatory curriculum in high school (four years of English and three years of mathematics, science, and social studies). Yet, a 2007 report by ACT, a nonprofit testing organization, found that only one in four of the more than 647,000 ACT-tested students who took a college prep curriculum met all four of ACT's College Readiness Benchmarks (Redden, 2007). (A student who meets or exceeds an ACT College Readiness Benchmark can be expected to earn a "C" or better in courses like algebra, composition, and biology taken at a four-year college.)

As a result of the variability in high school preparation and basic skills readiness, many four-year institutions require students to take remedial (also known as developmental) education courses in mathematics, writing, or reading before they are admitted or during their first year of college. In some ways, the situation is similar to that facing colleges in the mid-1800s, before the widespread development and standardization of secondary schools. To remedy that problem, many early colleges and universities established their own preparatory divisions for students lacking needed skills.

Today, more than a quarter of all entering first-year students enroll in one or more remedial reading, writing, or mathematics courses. About 20 percent take a remedial math course, compared to 14 percent for writing and 11 percent for reading (Parsad & Lewis, 2003). A government survey of remedial education in degree-granting institutions indicated that more than three-quarters of all two- and four-year institutions offered at least one remedial math, writing, or reading course in fall 2000. Public two-year institutions are more likely than any other type of institution to provide remedial education, enroll more of their entering students in these courses than other kinds of institutions, and report longer than average time periods of student enrollment. More than two-fifths of all public two-year college students took at least one remedial course (Parsad & Lewis, 2003).

Adelman (1999) reported that the type of remedial courses a student takes influences college degree completion. Analyses of longitudinal data from a nationally representative sample indicate that students who take remedial reading are the least likely to complete their bachelor's degrees (39 percent earn their degrees) (Adelman, 1999). In contrast, students who take one or two remedial courses, and do *not* take remedial reading, are much more likely to persist to graduation. Nearly 60 percent of this group of students successfully completed college, compared with 69 percent of students who took no remedial courses (Adelman, 1999).

In a study designed to determine whether the lower levels of academic achievement of students in remedial courses were due to the effects of remediation or of pre-existing differences among students, Eric Bettinger and Bridget Terry Long (2004) found that remediation had positive effects on persistence to degree. They estimated that, over five years, math and English remediation reduce a student's chances of stopping out nearly 10 percent and increase the likelihood of completing a baccalaureate degree by 9 percent. Compared to students with similar backgrounds and academic preparation, students in remedial courses obtain better educational outcomes. An analysis of community college students (Bettinger & Long, 2005) similarly revealed some positive outcomes of remediation.

Of the colleges and universities that have compensatory courses, the majority use placement tests, given to all entering first-year students, to identify students in need of remedial education. More than three-quarters of the institutions that have such courses require students to enroll in these courses if their scores on math, writing, or reading placement tests fall below a specified criterion (Parsad & Lewis, 2003). About three-quarters of institutions offering remedial courses award institutional credit for them. However, less than 5 percent give degree credit for these courses, and about 10 percent do not award any credit at all for remedial coursework (Parsad & Lewis, 2003).

State legislation requiring assessment has raised questions about the validity of placement tests (Berger, 1997) and the definition of college-level work (Merisotis & Phipps, 2000). Critics argue that most four-year postsecondary institutions should not offer remedial courses. Underprepared students, they insist, are best served at community colleges whose mission is to provide access to higher education (Ignash, 1997). Cost is also a concern. Opponents argue that remediation education utilizes human and financial resources that might be applied to other institutional priorities, or that public funds should not be used to pay, a second time, to develop academic skills that students should have mastered in high school (Parsad & Lewis, 2003). The number of states that are discouraging four-year institutions from offering remediation education is growing (Jenkins & Boswell, 2002). In 2002, the Board of Regents of City University of New York approved a plan to eliminate most remedial education courses from the system's upper division colleges and to locate these in community colleges or in alternative programs (Hebel, 2003a). Other states have limited the amount of time that a student can be enrolled in remedial courses (Hebel, 2003b).

Pressure for Assessment Mounts

Although educators and the general public tend to believe that students from disadvantaged backgrounds should have equal access to a college education, concerns about the levels of remediation underprepared students need at the postsecondary levels fuel public discussion about the higher education quality. Concerns increased throughout the 1980s, and discussions of quality have continued largely unabated. Increasingly, legislators and government officials are engaged in efforts to scrutinize and improve the performance of colleges and universities.

During the 1980s, most colleges and universities considered various assessment techniques and strategies in an effort to respond to public and policy makers' concerns about quality. In 1989, 70 percent of administrators surveyed reported that their institutions were engaged in some kind of assessment activity—but 40 percent indicated that this was in response to mandates. Only about half of those responding believed that assessment had the potential to improve undergraduate education. Moreover, 70 percent feared that assessment data would be misused by public authorities and agencies (El-Khawas, 1989). By 1992, two-thirds of public institutions reported state-mandated assessment procedures and nearly 60 percent of colleges surveyed had made program or curricular changes as a result of assessment (El-Khawas, 1992).

Institutional responses to public and legislative questions about higher education quality have not, however, quelled concerns. During Congressional hearings on each reauthorization of the Higher Education Act, the emphasis on assessment of student learning and quality assurance mechanisms shifted to high gear. In 2006, U.S. Department of Education Secretary Margaret Spellings convened a blue-ribbon panel that produced a report critical of higher education (U.S. Department of Education, 2006). The Spellings report questioned the value of accreditation as a quality assurance mechanism, arguing that it did not provide useful information on the quality of student learning to the public. As a result, the report concluded, prospective students and their parents have limited ability to choose wisely from among the vast number of the nation's colleges and universities.

Prior to the appointment of the Spellings Commission, accreditors had acknowledged the growing consensus that student learning outcomes should be the ultimate test of the quality of academic programs (Council for Higher Education Accreditation, 2003). The Council for Higher Education Accreditation (CHEA), which recognizes individual accreditation agencies, endorsed assessment of student learning outcomes as one dimension of accreditation, and many regional and professional accreditation agencies had already refocused their criteria, reducing the emphasis on quantitative measures of inputs and resources and requiring judgments of educational effectiveness from measurable outcomes (Volkwein, Lattuca, Caffrey, & Reindl, 2003). A study of the impact of a new set of outcomes-based accreditation criteria in undergraduate engineering programs revealed changes in curriculum and instruction, students' classroom experiences, and student learning before and after the implementation of the new criteria (Lattuca, Terenzini, & Volkwein, 2006). While supporting the use of assessment of student learning as a condition of accreditation, many in the higher education community (including representatives from accrediting agencies, institutions, and higher education advocacy organizations) worried that the reforms sought by the Department of Education threatened to create a new level of federal control on colleges and universities (Basken, 2007). In fact, members of Congress themselves demanded that Secretary Spellings desist from establishing new rules for accreditors until they finished the reauthorization discussions and then prohibited her from doing so in the legislation. Clearly, the accountability debate remains in full swing.

Influences and Potential Reforms

Historian Frederick Rudolph characterized the curriculum as a battleground for society, a locus and transmitter of values, a social artifact, a reproduction of the national ideology, a reflection of faculty research interests and student desires, a mixture of the cultural and the utilitarian, and sometimes a creature of convenience. The main thesis of Rudolph's (1977) history, and ours, is that curricular history is American history; college and university curricula both reflect societal needs and shape them. This interaction is often pragmatic, as Rudolph suggested, and on occasion the pace of cultural, economic, and technological changes temporarily outstrips the capacity of colleges and universities to respond.

Overall, societal influences have encouraged colleges and universities to expand access and to balance attention to general and specialized education. The mix of internal and external forces operating on curricula, and the relative strengths of those influences, may be changing as a result of new calls for quality control through assessment and external evaluation. The model of the academic plan introduced in Chapter 1 alerts us to the variety of influences active in the sociocultural environment for education at any given time and enhances our understanding of how these affect curriculum planning. In future chapters, we note variations in the impact of different influences on academic plans, demonstrating how some components of these plans are open to direct societal influences, while others are buffered from external forces, but subject to internal influences such as faculty views about education.

Our historical overview of recurring curricular debates situates the current set of influences we discuss throughout this book. As societal influences have increased student access and student choice, academic decisions have become more visible and more likely to kindle public debate. Educators are increasingly aware that matters once left to college and university presidents and faculties are being observed by other interested factions. Higher education institutions are responsive to social needs and, consequently, more vulnerable to demands for accountability and quality control.

CHAPTER THREE

INTERNAL INFLUENCES: COLLEGE AND UNIVERSITY CONTEXTS

Curricula are subject to varied influences, including cultural and social trends, economic conditions, and national and state policies that shape higher education institutions and the academic programs they provide. Yet, each college and university may respond differently to these external forces. For example, while many universities responded to student demand for online education in the 1990s and 2000s, most small liberal arts colleges did not (Allen, Seaman, & Garrett, 2007). Such variations in institutional responses to external influences can be explained, at least in part, by examining how the organizational features of colleges and universities affect their interpretations of external influences and their ability and willingness to address them.

For example, the differing missions of public universities and independent liberal arts colleges might affect their responses to increased demand for online courses and programs. The mission of comprehensive public universities is to serve the population of their states or regions through undergraduate and graduate education. To help them achieve that mission, online courses can provide access to residents who might not be able to attend campus-based programs. Many small liberal arts colleges, in contrast, are committed to providing residential undergraduate education and personal attention to a small number of students. Online educational programs that forego face-to-face instruction typically will not be viewed as achieving that mission.

Institutional resources also play a role in decisions regarding online curricula. Large universities often have financial resources to support online programs until they are self-sustaining or profitable and the human resources needed to staff online courses or programs. Moreover, because they serve a sizeable student market, they may achieve economies of scale that contribute to the profitability of online programs. In comparison, the financial and human resources of many smaller colleges are more limited. Committing instructors who already teach several courses a year to online programs may strain human and financial resources.

Consider, too, how the mission, culture, and staffing of a particular academic unit, such as a department or program, might influence curricular decisions about online education. In considering whether to add an online program, administrators and faculty might first ask whether the subject matter is adaptable to online methods. Will students learn as much if they do not have access to laboratory equipment? Are there instructors in the program who are interested in, and willing to teach, online courses? Do these individuals have the necessary technological skills? Or will they need professional development to mount and teach these courses? Will staffing online courses affect the program's ability to provide face-to-face instruction to students who live on campus or commute from home? The organizational features of a given department or program, our example reveals, also affect its response to external forces.

The academic plan concept recognizes that various external and internal factors influence a college or university's curricular choices (see Figure 3.1). The impetus for online education is external to colleges but highlights two major categories of internal influences: those that operate at the institutional level and those that are specific to a particular unit (such as a college of arts and sciences, a department of organizational behavior, or a program in exercise physiology). Institutional-level features include (but are not limited to) the mission and goals of the institution and its governance structure, leadership, and resources. At the college, department, and program levels, differences in program goals, faculty beliefs about teaching, student characteristics, available resources, and curricular relationships with other programs are some salient unit-level influences. Discussing institutional and unit-level influences separately is, admittedly, somewhat artificial. It is the interaction among different influences that creates a particular educational environment in which curriculum decisions are made. This interaction is depicted in the academic plan figure through the use of bi-directional arrows between the boxes defining institutional and unit-level influences. In this chapter, we define and clarify these two categories of internal influence individually. Temporarily separating these influences allows us to show that institutional and unit-level influences are not necessarily in harmony: differences in perspectives

FIGURE 3.1. ACADEMIC PLANS IN SOCIOCULTURAL CONTEXT: INTERNAL INFLUENCES ON EDUCATIONAL ENVIRONMENTS

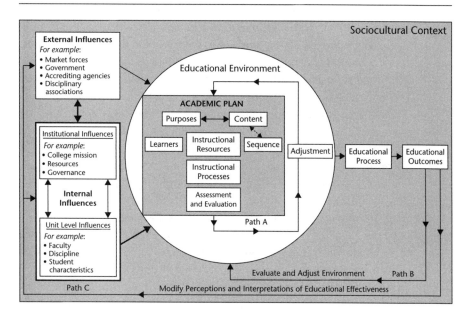

and perceived needs at the institutional and unit levels often complicate the task of curriculum development and revision.

Our discussion of internal influences follows the logic of the academic plan concept. We address institutional-level influences first, and then describe typical influences found at the unit level. Finally, we consider how these levels are inter-related in the task of curriculum planning and discuss some current trends that are emerging as significant influences at both levels. Thus we re-integrate the two levels we temporarily separated for the sake of clarity and emphasis.

Institutional Influences

Unlike business organizations and for-profit institutions, which tend to have a sin-gular purpose, most higher education institutions embrace several goals (Gross & Grambsch, 1974). For example, most four-year institutions in the United States emphasize goals of research, teaching, and service. Although these goals may be interrelated and mutually reinforcing, they typically rely on different organiza-tional structures for support and different types of faculty roles for success. For example, academic departments organize faculty members' teaching activities;

research centers or institutes often support research activities; and outreach (or "extension") units engage in community service (Birnbaum, 1988). Traditionally, faculty members have been expected to fulfill each of these goals, although few formally affiliate with all three organizational units (Birnbaum, 1988).

In addition to missions and goals, the history and culture of institutions shape their responses to external forces and new ideas. Institutional culture is related to, but not identical with, structural features of the institution, such as its governance system and administrative arrangements. Finally, financial and human resources play a large role in curricular decisions. A department faculty may propose a new academic program that is entirely consistent with the mission and culture of a given institution, but access to human and financial capital will ultimately determine the fate of the proposal. Even in colleges and universities with large financial endowments, economic considerations strongly influence curricular decision making.

Although other institutional characteristics clearly can affect curricular decision making (for example, consider the role of geographic location in determining the viability of graduate programs in music or drama), we focus on three features (mission, culture, and resources) that typically have the greatest influence on substantive decisions made about curricula and/or the procedures by which they are created and revised.

Institutional Mission, Type, and Control

In Chapter 2 we noted the diverse types of colleges and universities in the United States, as well the convergence of three prototypical missions that have shaped American higher education over time: the utilitarian, research, and liberal education missions. Since most contemporary colleges and universities pursue a mixture of these missions, they are often best distinguished by their relative emphasis on teaching, research, and service. Research universities, as their name implies, are particularly dedicated to the creation of new knowledge. Community colleges and smaller baccalaureate colleges, in contrast, are more teaching-oriented, expecting faculty to spend more of their time on interactions with students. Institutional control, that is, whether an institution is public or independently controlled, can also influence its curricular choices. On the whole, however, there are many more curricular similarities between public and independent institutions in the United States than there are differences.

Institutional Mission Although they are occasionally used synonymously, *institutional type* and *mission* are not the same thing. The confusion arises because we often use the term mission loosely (as in "the research mission of the university").

While a mission communicates information about what an institution values, different types of institutions can and do share common objectives or missions. Despite significant structural and cultural differences, liberal arts colleges, community colleges, and research universities all strive to prepare students to live and work in a diverse world.

A mission is a statement about an institution's identity or vision of itself, articulated to provide its members with a sense of institutional goals and shared purpose. Mission statements also communicate purpose and values to external audiences (Hartley, 2002; Morphew & Hartley, 2006). Whereas some argue that mission statements are typically too vague to be useful guides for action (Chait, 1979; Delucchi, 1997), others see them as essential to the strategic planning process (Keller, 1983) and to determining which educational programs are appropriate for a given institution (Carnegie Foundation for the Advancement of Teaching, 1977). In many institutions, missions are an important influence on curriculum.

Institutional Type In the United States, the taxonomy called the Carnegie Classification was developed in 1970 to differentiate types of institutions and has been revised a number of times, most recently in 2005. Originally intended to serve researchers' needs, the Carnegie Classification has become a "general purpose" tool that is used in higher education research and policy formulation (McCormick & Zhao, 2005). For purposes of curricular discussion, the "basic classification" (1973) remains the most meaningful. It identifies six kinds of institutions (for more information, see http://www.carnegiefoundation.org/classifications/):

- *Associate's colleges* primarily offer associate degree and certificate programs; the few that offer baccalaureate degrees account for less than 10 percent of all bachelor's degrees awarded.
- *Baccalaureate colleges* are primarily undergraduate colleges that emphasize baccalaureate degree programs, but in the revised classification, may also award associate's degrees and certificates.
- *Master's colleges and universities* offer a wide range of baccalaureate programs and are committed to graduate education through the master's degree at least in selected fields. In previous classifications, these institutions were referred to as comprehensive institutions, and that name is still in use today.
- *Doctorate-granting institutions* offer a wide range of baccalaureate programs and are committed to graduate education through the doctorate. Those with greater emphasis on research are often referred to as research universities.
- *Special focus institutions* (also known as specialized institutions) vary in the level of degrees offered (from bachelor's to doctorates) but award at least half of their degrees in a single field of study. Medical schools, schools of engineering

and technology, Bible colleges, theological seminaries, schools of art and music, and the U.S. military and naval academies are examples of specialized institutions that stand alone. (Specialized schools that are part of larger universities are not considered specialized institutions.)

• *Tribal colleges* are typically tribally controlled, located on reservations, and are members of the American Indian Higher Education Consortium.

To some extent, these Carnegie "types," partially based on stated mission and degree offerings, predict specific educational characteristics of a college such as teaching responsibilities and research emphasis. Since the mid-20th century, the number of hours faculty members devote to their instructional activities has been relatively stable. The typical faculty member in a not-for-profit college or university spends the majority of his or her time on instructional duties (Schuster & Finkelstein, 2006). On average, faculty members spend just over 60 percent of their time in teaching activities, devote another 18 percent to research, and allot about 20 percent of their working time to service. Such averages, however, mask differences among types of institutions. At two-year colleges, research efforts account for only about 5 percent of faculty time, whereas teaching occupies more than 70 percent. In contrast, in doctorate-granting institutions, the average faculty member spends only about 50 percent of her time teaching and nearly 30 percent on research. Faculty in doctorate-granting universities also teach substantially less than those in master's level (comprehensive) institutions and tend to be less involved in undergraduate teaching than those at other types of four-year institutions (Middaugh, 1998).

Institutional type seems to have little relationship to teaching style. Faculty in all types of institutions report using lectures, classroom discussions, small groups, and activities such as service-learning in roughly the same proportions (Lindholm, Szelényi, Hurtado, & Korn, 2005), although faculty in the same academic field tend to use similar teaching approaches (Einarson, 2001).

Knowledge of the influence of institutional type on teaching and learning is often based on surveys of students reporting the extent of their engagement in academic processes. Scholars have expected institutional characteristics to influence levels of student engagement on a campus (Astin, 1993; Kuh, Kinzie, Schuh, Whitt, & Associates, 2005; Pace, 1980), but have found that the influential characteristics, for the most part, stem from an institution's culture rather than its structure. Jillian Kinzie, John Schuh, and George Kuh (2004), for example, cite the role of institutional policies that emphasize the importance of undergraduate education as key, while Gary Pike (1999; Pike, Schroeder, & Berry, 1997) emphasizes the role of specific educational practices such as learning communities in levels of engagement. The key influence appears not to be institutional type *per se*, but rather how an institution intentionally shapes its academic and co-curricular programs to encourage student involvement in the educational process. This line of research supplies evidence that the same influence—such as mission—may produce different policies at different institutions.

Institutional type, nonetheless, is often used as a rough proxy for institutional policies and practices. For example, one study of a nationally representative group of institutions found that attending a doctoral-research university is negatively related to student engagement, even after student characteristics such as socio-economic status and ability and the size of the institution are taken into account (Pike, Smart, Kuh, & Hayek, 2006). Although the overall data pattern suggested that high levels of student engagement did not characterize doctoral-research institutions, some doctoral-research universities demonstrated relatively high levels of student engagement. These institutions are those that have, probably intentionally, made curricular and other decisions that enhance student engagement in the learning process.

Institutional Control Like institutional type, institutional "control"—that is, whether an institution is public or independent—is an organizational feature that may affect development of academic plans. In the United States, public institutions are funded partly through state appropriations and are accountable to state government in various ways. To confuse the picture, independent colleges in the United States also receive government funding through student aid, research sponsorship, and per capita grants. Still, colleges that see themselves as "independently controlled" usually have more autonomy in constructing academic programs than do public institutions.

Both public and independent institutions, however, may provide similar academic programs, may be large or small in size, and may be resource-rich or resource-poor. While many independent institutions are non-sectarian, others are affiliated (weakly or strongly) with particular religious denominations. Institutions with strong ties to faith traditions (such as Bible colleges or institutions closely connected with particular denominations) provide one of the best examples of how institutional control affects curriculum. Most institutions with denominational ties offer academic majors similar to those of public institutions (for example, business, education, and psychology). But they also require students to take courses in religion or theology. In such colleges, there may be an emphasis on religious interpretations of phenomena and texts in both religion and non-religion courses. In contrast, some public institutions are restricted from offering majors in religion. Like institutional type, institutional control can be, but is not always, an important influence.

Governance: Faculty Roles

The academic governance systems of not-for-profit colleges and universities typically distribute curricular responsibility among many members of the institution;

decision making is said to be "shared" among trustees, presidents, administrators, and faculty. This relationship evolved over time as the small colleges of the colonial and post-colonial era in the United States grew in size and complexity. Originally, a college's board of trustees and president exercised authority over all of the institution's functions, including its curricula and teaching. Gradually, as faculty professionalized and specialized during the early 20th century, institutions delegated much of the responsibility for the academic programs and related academic decisions (such as faculty hiring, promotion, and tenure) to their faculties. Boards of trustees (or in the case of some multi-campus systems, coordinating boards) establish institutional missions and have legal obligations and responsibility for an institution's academic programs, but leave most day-to-day decisions regarding the academic program to faculty and administrators (Birnbaum, 1988). The details of governance systems vary by institution, so the broad picture we paint here presents curricular decision making (and its variations) in the typical not-for-profit college or university. Management systems and curricular decision making are quite different in for-profit institutions, however, so we discuss these as well.

In the unique organizational structure of not-for-profit higher education, an administrative hierarchy exists in parallel with faculty decision-making structures. Corson (1960) noted that this dual system of authority and control varies somewhat among colleges and universities, depending on particular needs and situations. Typically, the administrative structure of a college or university relies on a hierarchy of officers with budgetary and legal authority to control and coordinate its activities. Faculty members, in contrast, accept academic authority based on individual knowledge and expertise. Whereas the assumption of administrative authority serves to resolve conflicts in business organizations, it may *cause* conflict in a college or university, particularly in matters where the professional knowledge base of faculty is relevant (see Birnbaum, 1988; Etzioni, 1964). With respect to curricular matters, this tension is usually resolved in one of three ways: (a) faculty control through a committee system and academic senate, (b) by negotiating responsibilities through collective bargaining, or (c) by a combination of a senate and collective bargaining. Institutional cultures on campuses with these three systems may differ greatly.

To describe an optimum system of academic governance, the American Association of University Professors (AAUP), the American Council on Education (ACE), and the Association of Governing Boards of Universities and Colleges (AGB) published, in 1966, the "Joint Statement on Government of Colleges and Universities" (AAUP, 1990), which they still espouse. That statement identified "an inescapable interdependence among governing boards, administration, faculty, students and others" that requires not only communication among them, but "joint planning and effort" (p. 120). Once the educational policy of an institution is determined, the Joint Statement asserted, the faculty are primarily responsible for the curriculum, methods of instruction, and student instructional progress, as well as the authority to set degree requirements and determine when requirements have been met. In addition, the faculty of an institution are primarily responsible for research, faculty status (for example, promotion in academic rank), and student life as it pertains to the educational process. The governing board or president should have power of review or final decision in these areas only in "exceptional circumstances" (p. 123), and when boards or presidents fail to concur with faculty judgment, they should do so "for compelling reasons which should be stated in detail" (p. 123).

The faculty senate is a common governance structure that enables faculty participation in the decision-making processes of a college or university. A small college may have a single faculty governing board (such as an academic senate) in which all faculty participate, while a large and/or multi-campus institution may rely on committees in departments and schools as well as (or in place of) a larger, elected senate for the institution as a whole. Representatives on these bodies are selected by the faculty according to a set of procedures they have devised. They may act on policies directly related to the educational programs and sometimes on budgets, as well as on peripherally related matters like faculty parking and evaluation of administrators.

In the most complex systems, curriculum proposals that originate in an academic department may undergo review at several levels, first by college- and university-level curriculum committees, and, in some cases, also by the university faculty senate and the institution's governing board, which is legally responsible for oversight of the institution's overall educational program and its quality. In contrast, some large universities (for example, the University of Michigan) do not require curriculum approval beyond the school, college, or department directly involved. It is obvious that curriculum change becomes slower when more levels of approval are needed, especially when competition for financial resources is keen. With fewer approval levels, time and conflict are reduced, but costly duplication of some academic courses and programs as well as academic isolation of departments may occur. Systems of shared governance are not as frequently found in for-profit colleges and universities. Although some individuals with faculty titles participate in making curricular decisions, hiring and evaluating instructors, and performing other similar duties, these individuals operate more like department-level administrators (Tierney & Hentschke, 2007). As is true in the not-for-profit sector, there is considerable variation in faculty contracts and responsibilities among the for-profit colleges.

In some public colleges and universities, collective bargaining is an additional or alternate route to faculty participation in academic decision making. A traditional governance structure, such as a faculty senate, represents faculty interests broadly, while faculty unions usually negotiate agreements regarding the terms and conditions of faculty employment. Although the scope of collective bargaining varies by state, in a typical unionized college or university, decisions regarding matters such as faculty appointments, tenure, promotions, sabbaticals, and research support are often subject to joint senate and union review. Although joint review may appear to limit the impact of collective bargaining on an institution's educational program, the secondary impact may be substantial. Agreements about working conditions can affect, for example, the number of courses offered in a given term, the provision of monetary incentives for curriculum development or reform efforts, the number of students advised, and other activities that are "academic" in nature but that are also considered part of the terms of employment of an instructor.

About 61 percent of public institutions in the United States have faculty unions (Rhoades, 1993) and about 94 percent of unionized faculty work at public institutions (National Center for the Study of Collective Bargaining in Higher Education and the Professions, 2006). Most faculty in independent institutions are not eligible to bargain collectively as a result of the 1980 *NLRB v. Yeshiva University* Supreme Court ruling, which determined that because faculty participate in decisions regarding academic affairs and personnel, they are really managers, not employees.

Governance: Administrative and Board Roles

Historically, presidents and boards of trustees exerted significant influence on their institutions' curricula. In colonial colleges, the president was closely involved and often taught a senior-level "capstone" course that helped students synthesize what they had learned during their studies and consider its implications for their lives. Through the 19th and into the 20th centuries, presidents like Jeremiah Day at Yale, Charles Eliot at Harvard, Eliphalet Nott at Union College, James Burrill Angell at the University of Michigan, Robert Maynard Hutchins at the University of Chicago, and Alexander Meiklejohn at the University of Wisconsin brought their particular visions of the purposes of the college curriculum to fruition in the institutions they led. In a few cases, presidential influences were also strongly felt beyond the walls of their home institutions. President Eliot of Harvard championed the general education distribution system (an alternative to the core curriculum then common in colleges and universities) that greatly altered the university curriculum in the late 1800s.

Boards of trustees have also been influential, particularly when they have sought to represent the interests of particular groups of stakeholders (Hawthorne, 1996). At The Pennsylvania State University during the 1860s, for example, trustees, with the aim of protecting the original agricultural focus of the institution, were able to temporarily block the addition of engineering programs at the university (Bezilla, 1981). At the University of Michigan in the 1980s, lobbyists and legislators approached the Board of Regents when, with the concurrence of university administrators, the School of Education closed some popular programs it believed to be understaffed and of poor quality. Typically, however, boards exercise oversight but entrust the conduct of educational programs to the faculty and academic administrators.

Although the extent to which he or she is directly involved in curriculum decisions is limited, the president of a not-for-profit college or university is often required to articulate and defend his or her institution's educational programs to external stakeholders such as legislators, accreditors, and potential donors. Especially in large institutions, presidential duties focus more on external relations and fundraising than on academic decision making. Whether an institution is large or small, however, the president is likely to be involved when substantial changes in academic directions are considered. The addition of new academic units and decisions to discontinue existing programs are typically made by an institution's academic leadership in consultation with its president and governing board. For example, when the president of The Pennsylvania State University proposed the addition of a law school, he and his cabinet necessarily sought the advice and approval of the University's Board of Trustees. Similarly, the trustees were apprised of a proposal to make substantive change in the general education requirements for undergraduates. In the first case, the decision to open a law school required significant commitment of financial and human resources; in the second, the role of the trustees and president in ensuring educational quality, rather than the need for capital expenditures, created the rationale for their involvement. In some cases, involvement may be largely symbolic, signaling that presidents and boards are fulfilling their obligation for oversight of the academic program. For public institutions in some states, new programs or even changes in existing programs may be subject to statewide review to avoid costly duplication of state resources.

Even in small baccalaureate colleges, the primary responsibility for oversight of academic programs is now delegated from the trustees and presidents to vice presidents, deans, and associate deans at the college level. These individuals can exert extremely strong influences on academic planning. They carry out several important leadership roles, including emphasizing curriculum and teaching, facilitating innovation, providing budgetary resources, and structuring reward systems. Failure to perform these roles is as great an influence as performing them.

Jerry Gaff (2007) argues that the bifurcated governance system in colleges presents two problems. It gives faculty responsibility for academic decisions related to educational programs, but does not give them control over resources or responsibility for the fiscal repercussions of their decisions. Conversely, while administrators and trustees have bureaucratic and fiscal authority for an institution's academic programs, they have little accepted authority to intervene to control program quality. The degree to which the dual culture of responsibility is a positive influence on academic planning depends heavily on the provosts and deans who share the responsibility for accomplishing change so that institutional environments support and enhance the contributions that faculty members can make to their institutions (Gappa, Austin, & Trice, 2007).

Institutional Resources and Costs

Institutional resources significantly influence curricular decisions at all levels—program, department, unit, and college-wide. This is true of traditional not-for-profit institutions as well as the for-profit institutions that recently have entered the U.S. higher education market. Resources affect the numbers and types of courses and programs that can be offered, the number of instructors who can be hired, the number of students who can be admitted, and the adequacy of teaching facilities. Less directly, perceptions of priority of resource use (whether or not accurate) influence instructors' attitudes and behaviors and thus the institutional culture.

Most colleges and universities in the United States rely on varied revenue streams, including student tuition and fees, grants and contracts, individual donations, corporate and foundation sponsorship, and student financial aid to sustain their operations. Public institutions rely more heavily than independents on state appropriations, but both public and independent institutions are affected when the federal and state governments face budget shortfalls. As a sector, higher education typically suffers more stringent cuts than mandated services such as K-12 schools, welfare, and Medicaid (Callan, 2002), and few expect state support for higher education to improve in the future (Gappa, Austin, & Trice, 2007). The common phenomenon of mid-year budget cuts, or the expectation of them, can affect faculty members' willingness to engage in curriculum planning.

Institutions differ in the autonomy they have over resources and expenditures. Independent colleges and a few large public and independent universities have extensive authority to allocate their own budgets. Many public colleges have far less discretion because tuition goes directly to state coffers and line allocations are given by coordinating boards and legislatures. In any case, personnel costs account for a very large share of college budgets, leaving limited maneuverability for experimentation and enhancement of academic programs. In this constrained fiscal environment, colleges and universities must make decisions about how to allocate limited funds to institutional priorities, including but not limited to their educational programs. Fiscal constraint has been a strong internal influence on college programs throughout American history.

Unit-Level Influences

In the academic plan model (portrayed in Figure 3.1), we classified the influence of faculty views and disciplines as unit-level influences and separated them from broader institutional influences. Typically, faculty perspectives differentiate one academic unit or program from another. College and university instructors are trained in a particular field of study, and that field, as well as their personal beliefs and experiences, strongly influences the decisions they make about courses and programs. In fact, while institutional types and missions broadly define the scope of faculty work, establishing, for example, expectations regarding the relative emphasis on teaching and research, an instructor's academic training and program affiliation have a greater direct effect on academic planning. In fact, in all types of institutions, instructors in the same field tend to choose the same kinds of educational goals (Stark & others, 1990) and instructional methods (Antony & Boatsman, 1994; Einarson, 2001; Fairweather, 1997).

Here we focus on the general roles and responsibilities of faculty in curricular decision making and explore other unit-level influences, such as program mission and student characteristics. Because academic field is such a strong influence, we explore it in detail in Chapter 4.

Faculty Roles

Many facets of faculty work contribute to the development and maintenance of academic programs in not-for-profit colleges and universities. Typically, faculty members are expected to plan, prepare, and deliver the courses they offer. Many also evaluate their own courses, if only informally, to determine whether to change texts or reading, in-class exercises, assignments, and assessments. In addition to responsibilities for teaching courses, faculty members may also advise students who are majoring in their fields. They work together with their colleagues to devise programs, that is, sequences of courses that constitute major fields. As we discuss the instructor's role in teaching and learning, we will contrast the roles of faculty in different type of institutions.

Not-for-Profit Colleges and Universities Faculty members typically revise courses and programs to incorporate intellectual advances in the field or to better meet the needs of employers—two key external influences. Revisions to courses can be accomplished by individual instructors—and often appear to be driven by them (Lattuca, Terenzini, & Vokwein, 2006). More extensive changes for an academic program, however, require collective action by the faculty responsible for the program. For instance, a decision to revise the introductory sequence of courses in an undergraduate program has implications for the intermediate and advanced courses that follow—and build upon—the knowledge base that is developed in the first-level courses. In these cases, a committee of involved instructors may collaborate on the design of the affected courses to ensure students are well prepared for subsequent work in the field.

Unit-level influences vary in salience and intensity at various levels of curriculum development. When planning a course, an instructor is likely to be working alone; her own experiences and beliefs thus largely shape the academic plan she designs. If the same individual is part of a departmental subcommittee examining the introductory sequence of courses in the major, her educational beliefs may be tempered as program resources and staffing concerns or competing educational views are addressed.

The relative emphasis institutions, colleges, and departments place on the different elements of faculty work—teaching, research, and service—influences faculty engagement in academic planning at the unit level. Both strong and weak expectations for research can have direct effects on an academic program. In institutions with high research expectations, hiring a new tenure-track faculty member with a particular research expertise, for example, may result in the addition of new specialized courses in an academic program. On the other hand, some faculty members may be released from teaching duties so they can devote more time to new or ongoing research projects or teach an advanced seminar. In contrast, in colleges where research is not expected, such as community colleges, there may be clearer expectations for involvement in curriculum development at the program level. High or low expectations for research productivity can also affect levels of participation in departmental and college-level curriculum committees, advising, academic program reviews, assessment activities, and off-campus and online academic programs. The effect of institutional missions and values is thus felt at the unit level.

External influences can also influence unit-level faculty activities. For example, the regional accreditation agencies that accredit colleges and universities (for example, the Middle States Commission on Higher Education), as well as many of the specialized agencies that accredit individual academic programs (for example, Association to Advance Collegiate Schools of Business; Accreditation Board for Engineering and Technology), require institutions or programs to establish specific student learning outcomes. Some further require evidence of assessment of student performance for these desired outcomes and use the findings from their assessment programs to improve their programs. Such efforts require communication among faculty in a program or department and, in all likelihood, promote collaboration on curricular matters.

In not-for-profit colleges and universities, a faculty member's career status affects curriculum development. The stakes for promotion and tenure are high because once a faculty member earns tenure (typically after an extended probationary period), he or she is considered a permanent employee of the institution. However, to manage enrollments more readily, colleges and universities often hire part-time (adjunct) non-tenured instructors to cover extra sections of courses or to teach lower-division courses. To avoid long-range tenure commitments, they also may hire full-time "contingent" faculty who have renewable contracts but are not eligible for tenure. These solutions are expedient and cost-effective. The question of whether hiring contingent faculty affects academic planning positively or negatively, however, remains unanswered, partly because the institutional contexts vary substantially. Community colleges tend to hire many part-time instructors, as do practice fields like business, education, and fine arts, where almost half of instructional appointments are part-time. Contingent faculty members are particularly prominent in health sciences fields, where half of the instructors are on non-tenure-track appointments, and in education, where 40 percent of faculty are not tenured or tenure-eligible (Cataldi, Bradburn, & Fahimi, 2005).

Paul Umbach (2007) found that full-time tenure-ineligible instructors are similar to full-time tenured and tenure-track faculty in terms of course-related interactions with students. These full-time instructors, even if they are on term appointments, are likely to view themselves as teaching professionals and devote their time and energy to their teaching duties (Baldwin & Chronister, 2001). In contrast, instructors who are part-time or on limited term contracts may hold other jobs that prevent them from interacting with students and colleagues outside of class. Some research indicates that they may also spend somewhat less time preparing for class, be less likely to use active and collaborative instruction, and be less likely to challenge students academically (Umbach, 2007). Yet, others argue that contingent faculty are, in some institutions, more student-centered than tenured or tenure-track faculty who value research more than teaching duties. Roger Baldwin and Jay Chronister (2001) suggest that contingent faculty are more practitioner-oriented and can help students bridge the theory-practice divide.

Full-timers (both tenure and pre-tenure) may participate more actively in curriculum planning at the program and college-wide levels. Once the curriculum is planned and approved by the faculty, the norm of professional autonomy that characterizes not-for-profit colleges and universities frequently takes over. In teaching the revised courses, a single faculty member, regardless of status (who may not have been involved in the revision), typically will have a great deal of freedom to choose her own texts, readings, assignments, methods of instruction, and assessment strategies. In fields in which curricula tend to be hierarchical, with courses tightly linked to one another, instructors may have less latitude in the selection of topics to be covered, but nonetheless will have much autonomy regarding instructional and assessment methods. The extent of autonomy depends on the unit culture.

For-Profit Higher Education In response to the demand for practical career-oriented training, for-profit colleges and universities stress the importance of student satisfaction. Instructors who work in for-profit institutions are therefore encouraged to think of the student as a customer or consumer. Very few for-profit institutions offer instructors long-term contracts; the protections of tenure or collective bargaining are virtually non-existent (Tierney & Hentschke, 2007). Instructors who do not receive good student ratings are dropped from the corporation's payroll. The employer-employee relationship in these ventures is a business relationship that can be readily terminated to improve productivity or efficiency.

The typical instructor in the for-profit sector is a part-time employee whose responsibilities are largely limited to delivering lessons and grading students. The larger national providers in this sector, such as the University of Phoenix, assign the task of curriculum development and revision to a small group of core faculty specialists who serve as content experts and work closely with instructional specialists to ensure that the content is carefully packaged (Farrell, 2003; Lechuga, 2006). The goal of the process is standardization: courses must be fully developed and carefully scripted so that students—no matter where they are located, who their instructor is, or in what term they are enrolled—have essentially the same experience in a given course (Berg, 2005). Although some institutions involve instructors in course development, in most for-profit institutions, they receive course manuals that describe the use of predetermined content, texts, assignments, and assessments (Lechuga, 2006; Tierney & Hentschke, 2007). The learning objectives for each course are predetermined, and each course is evaluated to ensure student satisfaction. At many for-profit institutions, instructors must also undergo training that prepares them to teach and acquaints them with policies and procedures. This "unbundling" of curricular responsibilities allows these institutions to maximize efficiency and minimize instructional costs. Clearly, however, the influences on academic planning at the unit level are much different in for-profit colleges than in traditional not-for-profit colleges.

Program Mission, Culture, and Leadership

Even within the same college or university, academic programs can have distinctive values and cultures. Differences arise not only from different missions but from the mix of instructors and students within a unit, the leadership styles of department chairpersons, and, in larger institutions, the leadership styles and priorities of deans, associate deans, and program coordinators.

The mix of faculty in an academic program determines the breadth of courses that can be offered, the educational experiences that students have in the classroom, and even the role of co-curricular activities, such as presentations by guest speakers, clubs and organizations, and internships. In not-for-profit colleges and universities, faculty members' specialization areas, values, and beliefs about education create a culture for teaching and learning in a program that influences how academic plans are created and implemented. Activities that support teaching and learning, such as curriculum planning, tend to reflect this culture and therefore vary by unit. For example, an economics program in which equal numbers of faculty espouse conflicting schools of economic thought will develop academic plans different from a program in which thinking is uniform. Research by Charlotte Briggs, Joan Stark, and Jean Roland-Poplawski (2003) and by Betty Harper (2008) reveals differences in levels of faculty engagement in curriculum planning processes among and within fields of study. Although faculty attitudes and behaviors contribute to a program's culture for teaching and learning, strong leadership can also shape a unit's attention to curriculum, teaching, and learning.

The president, chief academic officer, or dean may or may not be the most visible influence on academic planning and may or may not provide curricular leadership. Nevertheless, academic leaders in not-for-profit institutions influence academic plans through their communications to faculty, especially through the faculty reward system that provides strong messages about what academic leaders believe is important. Even in baccalaureate colleges at which teaching traditionally has been highly valued and rewarded, nearly two-thirds of faculty members agree that it is hard to earn tenure without a record of scholarly activity and publication. In universities, nearly all faculty members (94 percent) agree with that assessment (Schuster & Finkelstein, 2006). The same acclamation, however, is not uniformly given to effort devoted to teaching and academic planning. Some believe that the more faculty perceive rewards for research, the less incentive they have to devote time and energy to teaching, advising, mentoring, curriculum development and revision, and other learning-related activities. Others believe that faculty members simply expand their work time to allow for sufficient time for all rewarded activities.

Rewards come in many shapes and sizes. They can include summer salary supplements or incentive funds to support faculty who are creating new courses or program sequences, merit raises for exceptional teachers, release time from teaching, and teaching and advising awards to recognize excellence in instruction.

Colleges and programs also send messages about the value they place on teaching by the evaluation systems they use to assess the quality of teaching, courses, and student learning and how deans and chairpersons use the results of these evaluations. The willingness (or lack of willingness) of the dean to compensate faculty for unit- or program-wide contributions or to fund professional development to enhance faculty members' knowledge and skills signals a particular type of culture with respect to these kinds of contributions to the educational program. Such organizational arrangements strongly influence the way academic plans are constructed.

Student Characteristics   Changes in the characteristics of college-going students in the United States are significant impacts on postsecondary curricula. As we have noted in Chapter 2, the increasing diversity of students over time, declines in the academic preparation of the college-going population, the growing need for remedial programs at the postsecondary level, and the increase in student interest in career-oriented majors such as business have shaped academic programs. Forces such as these operate on academic plans, even if faculty do not acknowledge or address them.

Just as the mix of faculty in a program or college affects its culture, so does the mix of students it enrolls. In their model of the college experience, Patrick Terenzini and Robert Reason (2005) posit a "peer environment" that is influenced by the characteristics of the students who attend a college or university. This peer environment, in turn, both affects and is affected by the curricular, classroom, and co-curricular experiences of the students in the institution. Although Terenzini and Reason developed their conceptual model to describe institutional environments, the concept can as easily be applied at the program and course levels. When considered at these different levels, the model suggests that peer environments may vary considerably across academic units, depending on the kinds of students they attract, choose, and retain.

Student characteristics may include demographic characteristics, academic preparation, student goals, attitudes, and personal traits. Not only do the students vary in different units, but academic programs and institutions vary in the ways that they gather and use data about student characteristics in course and program planning. For example, through end-of-course evaluations, students can formally express their opinions about their instruction and may influence the conduct of a particular course or instructor. Many programs conduct exit interviews or surveys with students who leave an academic program (at graduation or before) or conduct town hall meetings to collect information on perceptions of the educational experience and satisfaction with that experience. Other academic units do none of these things to acknowledge student influence.

Unit Relationships Institutional leadership may generally support the careful planning and implementation of academic plans, but the actual level of this support and faculty perceptions of it depend on how central a course or program is to the institution and unit missions. A program may be central to an institution because it has achieved national prestige, because it is considered important to the college's mission, because it produces strong enrollments and accompanying revenues, or simply because the program leaders are successful advocates for it.

Within a unit, centrality can be affected by these and other factors. Typically, courses directly relevant to students who are majoring in the academic field are more central than those less relevant. Courses provided to other majors may be perceived as less important. Because plans for these "service" courses must be negotiated between two departments, their development and maintenance depend heavily on relationships between the units. The relationship among academic units that offer and utilize service courses can therefore be critical, encouraging or discouraging cooperation in course planning.

Effective leadership and personal relationships may facilitate conversations and efforts to customize service courses for particular groups of students. Yet pragmatic concerns can affect the willingness of academic units to respond to the needs of those in other fields. For example, the chemical engineering department in a large independent institution needed the cooperation of the chemistry department in the college of arts and sciences to revise its chemical engineering major. The chemistry department, however, had little interest in redesigning introductory chemistry courses to meet the needs of chemical engineers because a larger "client"—the institution's well-respected medical school—commanded its attention by providing a steady stream of student enrollments in chemistry courses. The much smaller engineering school, and the even smaller chemical engineering department, had little influence in the shadow of this more prominent academic unit (Lattuca, 2006b).

Emerging Internal Influences

The nature and salience of influences on the educational environment in which academic plans are made change over time. Recent changes in postsecondary education have produced new or stronger influences that are worth noting. These internal influences are sometimes related to the societal debates we described in Chapter 2.

Changing Faculty Roles and Composition

The roles of college and university faculty members and the conditions under which they are hired are changing. The difficulty of balancing attention to all three college goals (teaching, research, and service) is one factor leading to change in instructors' roles and in the mix of full- and part-time teaching staff. Some institutions are hiring tenured and tenure-eligible faculty members to conduct research and teach graduate courses while part-time instructors teach undergraduate courses. Along with the increased use of part-time instructors, colleges and universities are also experimenting with contract faculty, that is, full-time fixed-term faculty who are not eligible for tenure. One factor propelling this change is cost containment. Tenure creates a financial obligation on the institution that limits flexibility to respond to enrollment shifts overall and within a given academic specialization.

Both for-profit colleges and not-for-profit colleges and universities hire instructors whose responsibilities are limited to teaching. Although colleges and universities have long relied on part-time (or adjunct) instructors to supplement the full-time faculty, the recent steep increase in part-timers is striking, particularly in the two-year college sector where part-time instructors now represent two-thirds of faculty. Some believe that non-tenure faculty may soon be the norm (Schuster & Finkelstein, 2006).

Yet, under current circumstances, contingent faculty may not yet fill the gap in curriculum development. Umbach (2007) writes:

> As social exchange theory suggests, contingent faculty are likely to reciprocate the support they receive from colleges and universities. Faculty in contingent appointments earn low wages, receive little support for professional development, and work in environments that often marginalize them . . . Given these work conditions, it should surprise few that contingent faculty display a lack of commitment and perform less effectively than their tenured and tenure-track peers. (p. 110)

Critics claim that hiring contingent instructors creates a two-tier system on a campus: those faculty members who have tenure and have the power to shape academic programs, institutional practices, and policies (but are not always involved in teaching), and those who are not eligible for tenure and have little power and little voice. This situation may affect the quality of academic programs and student experiences. Because contingent faculty appointments are rapidly increasingly, colleges and programs need to find ways to engage those who are teaching off the tenure track in the academic life of their programs.

Another related role change is the practice some have called "academic capitalism" to describe the reliance of faculty members on supplementary income from research grants and contracts. In some fields it may be linked to faculty opportunities to patent and sell the results of their research to commercial entities. Academic capitalism, it is argued, leads to the privatization of faculty work and research and increases faculty autonomy (Fairweather, 1996; Slaughter & Rhoads, 2004).

Although this trend is most noticeable in research universities, it is becoming more evident in all types of institutions and across fields of study. The result is that new tenure-track faculty members are socialized to believe that involvement in activities external to the institution is more important than engagement in campus based activities like teaching (Kezar, Lester, Carducci, Gallant, & McGavin, 2007).

Technology and the competition from for-profit higher education for online education may also cause substantial changes in instructional practices and faculty roles. Gappa, Austin, and Trice (2007) describe how the processes of producing, delivering, and assessing curricula and students are being separated:

> Curriculum designers may prepare a course; technology specialists may develop the appropriate software to facilitate teaching the course online or in another technology-mediated environment; public relations specialists may market the course; a teacher may work with the students; and an evaluator may determine the effectiveness of the course, of the related technology, and of the instructor. (p. 17)

The "unbundling" of these formerly linked responsibilities for teaching and learning, these authors argue, diminishes faculty control and ownership of the curriculum. Although this differentiation of work roles is most common in for-profit institutions, it also reflects the approach taken by colleges and universities that have aggressively moved into the online education market. Changes such as these lead Tierney and Hentschke (2007) to conclude that over time the distinctions between traditional and for-profit institutions will blur and for-profit institutions will be viewed less as departures from the norm and more as variations within the larger higher education environment.

In addition to their academic training, instructors' personal experiences and characteristics also influence their curricular and instructional decisions. Gender, age, and ethnicity appear to be related to instructional approaches. Women, for example, report greater use of active learning methods such as cooperative learning, class discussion, and student self-evaluations of their work (Lindholm, Szelényi, Hurado, & Korn, 2005). The percentage of women professors has been growing in most types of colleges, and the proportion of women who are top administrators has also increased dramatically. Therefore, it seems logical to expect changes in institutional and unit-level cultures as the gender and ethnic composition of faculty and administrator groups changes.

Budget Constraints and Financial Accountability

College and university budgets are increasingly constrained: the operating costs of most institutions have increased due to rising energy and personnel costs, and some state budgets have been in deficit. Such situations lead to increased pressure for cost containment and cost effectiveness. Even so, many institutions feel pressured to improve their educational and technology infrastructure and physical plant and to offer additional student services to meet the needs of increasingly diverse student populations (Gappa, Austin, and Trice, 2007).

Reductions and cost-containment strategies are one approach to rising costs. Another approach is to reward faculty for developing revenue-producing academic programs, such as continuing education, online, and certificate programs that open new markets. Commercial viability is increasingly considered in decisions to maintain, consolidate, or terminate academic programs. These efforts, combined with greater emphasis on technology development and transfer, can change institutional and unit-level cultures as new measures of success, efficiency, and productivity emerge. Whether these efforts are sources of positive or negative change may depend on the nature of the effort and its congruence with traditional institutional norms and values.

The relation of cost containment to academic quality is difficult to measure. There is a small body of research on the effects of institutional resources (as reflected in institutional expenditures) on student learning in higher education. Although there are many intervening variables, some studies have revealed statistically significant relationships between the level of expenditures and college students' learning outcomes (Astin, 1993; Gansemer-Topf & Schuh, 2003/2004; Hayek, 2001; Ryan, 2004; Smart, Ethington, Riggs, & Thompson 2002; Toutkoushian & Smart, 2001) or between expenditures and student engagement in the learning process (Pike, Smart, Kuh, & Hayek, 2006). Pike and his colleagues suggested that an institutional culture that values student achievement and individual differences may influence how an institution invests its human and financial resources.

The pressure for greater accountability on the part of colleges and universities has prompted a search for more efficient and effective instructional programs. Two of these efforts, the instructional costs benchmarking effort known as the Delaware Study (Middaugh, 2001) and the course redesign program of the National Center for Academic Transformation (2005), highlight increased interest in instructional costs and suggest some concrete approaches to understanding and controlling them. These efforts bear watching to determine their impact on the educational environment. We discuss them further in Chapter 8.

Pressure for Assessment and Evaluation

Federal and state governments, as well as accreditors, are more actively demanding quality assurance from colleges and universities, especially with respect to student achievement. In part, demands for testing of student outcomes follow the pattern set by the No Child Left Behind program for elementary and secondary schools established by the Bush administration in the early 2000s. Not all public school teachers and relatively few college teachers are convinced that testing programs are the primary key to improving educational quality. The end result of this ideological struggle about the best means and ends for education is unknown. It is clear, however, that uniform testing, if broadly adopted, would substantially change the way college faculty members design and implement academic programs.

Some emerging influences stem from the new ethos in for-profit colleges and universities. For-profit colleges elevate instructor attention to student needs, and some provide professional development to help instructors understand and learn how to respond to and teach students with different needs and academic preparedness. Some faculty members in for-profit colleges argue that the student-as-customer approach goes too far, forcing instructors to acquiesce to students, whether they are right or wrong, in order to receive good course evaluations and remain employed (Lechuga, 2006). However, in not-for-profit colleges also, new research on student learning and learning environments and new ways of measuring how students experience the curriculum (student engagement) seem to be gaining credence and usefulness. Ernest Pascarella and Patrick Terenzini (2005, p. 602) write that because individual student effort is the "critical determinant of the impact of college," educators must focus on "the ways in which an institution can shape its academic, interpersonal, and extracurricular offerings to encourage student engagement"—and, ultimately, the quality of student learning. The shape of a college or university's academic and co-curricular offerings, of course, depends on how it chooses to work with what it has—and to change what does not work.

Converging Influences

Writing about curriculum at the postsecondary level, William Toombs and William Tierney (1991) defined a curriculum as "an intentional design for learning negotiated by faculty in light of their specialized knowledge and in the context of social expectations and students' needs" (p. 183). This definition identifies at least three different sources of influence on faculty: those of the society in which a curriculum is taught, those of practitioners in a given academic field, and those of students in a given course or program. Thus far in our discussions, we have classified the first of these, societal expectations, as an external influence; and the others—faculty and students' characteristics and expectation—as internal influences. To the discussion we have added institutional-level influences that result from passage of social expectations through the filter of institutional culture and the network of interprogram relationships. In the academic plan model, we connect institutional- and unit-level influences with bi-directional arrows to signify their interaction.

In this chapter we have considered how the organizational features of colleges and universities at both the institutional and unit levels influence curricular decision making. The story is not a straightforward one. Missions, governance structures, leadership styles, institutional resources, department cultures, and student characteristics can all affect how academic plans develop. The same influence affects two colleges or programs in quite different ways. One important influence that we have not yet discussed is typically more consistent in its influence on how faculty members plan courses and programs. That influence stems from academic fields or disciplines. We turn our attention in Chapter 4 to the strong influence of academic fields on instructors' decision making as they develop academic plans.

CHAPTER FOUR

INTERNAL INFLUENCES: ACADEMIC FIELDS

We have focused on the institutional contexts that influence college and university faculty as they plan and deliver courses and programs, discussing in general terms how institutional and program missions shape the environments in which academic plans are constructed. Substantial empirical evidence indicates that the academic fields in which instructors teach exert a very strong influence on their decisions about curricula. In this chapter, we consider this influence in detail, examining how and why academic fields affect instructors' thinking about the nature of knowledge, the purposes of education, course and program goals, content sequencing, and instruction (see Figure 4.1).

Some use the words discipline and field interchangeably—but they are not, in our view, synonymous. The typical college or university is home to an extensive variety of fields. These include (a) subjects traditionally viewed as academic disciplines (for example, chemistry, philosophy, sociology), (b) those that aim to prepare students for professional and occupational careers (for example, computer engineering, nursing, hotel management), and (c) those that are interdisciplinary (for example, women's studies, neuroscience, international relations). We believe that "field" is the more inclusive term, encompassing disciplines, undergraduate professional study, and occupational study. We reserve the term "discipline" for academic subjects traditionally taught in arts and science colleges. We use the terms "applied," "career-based," and "professional" for other programs, such as those in business, engineering, library science, nursing, and education, and we

FIGURE 4.1. ACADEMIC PLANS IN SOCIOCULTURAL CONTEXT: FOCUS ON PURPOSES, CONTENT, AND SEQUENCE

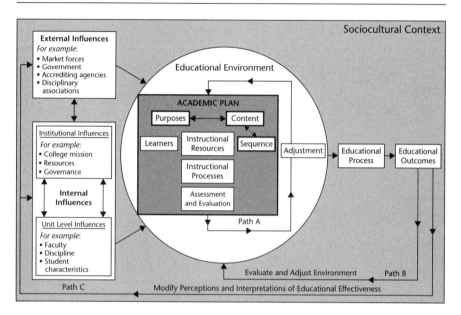

reserve the adjective "occupational" for career-directed programs taught in two-year colleges or for-profit institutions.

The organizational separation of academic fields into programs, departments, and colleges is often criticized for fragmenting the higher education curricula. Yet, most educators would agree that some structure is needed to facilitate students' learning. Academic fields, many have argued, offer such a structure.

Jerome Bruner argued that the structure of the disciplines provides an appropriate organizing framework for students as early as elementary school (Phillips & Soltis, 2004). The Association of American Colleges (1985) asserted that college students should understand the organization of their major fields of study and, by the end of their undergraduate education, be able to think like practitioners in their fields. In 1982, Paul Dressel and Dora Marcus noted:

> For effective learning, a student needs a framework made up of an appropriate set of clear stable concepts, principles or ideas at various levels of generality or inclusiveness. Such a structure provides the optimal possibility for correlating, anchoring, bridging or grouping new ideas in relation to those already known by inserting them in the existing framework. (Dressel & Marcus, 1982, pp. 164–165)

Today, most instructors will agree that academic success depends, in part, on how well students decipher the ways of thinking and inquiring used in the various disciplines they encounter. Not all instructors would agree, however, that disciplinary frameworks are superior to interdisciplinary frameworks for promoting student learning. Just as educators recognize the need to help students understand the nature and knowledge of different fields of study, they also focus on helping students integrate the knowledge they gain from the varied fields they study during their undergraduate programs (Huber & Hutchings, 2005; Schneider, 1997). Debates about the appropriate organizing and integrating schemes for undergraduate education will likely continue, but most college-level courses and programs remain, as they have developed historically, organized around academic fields.

Characterizing Academic Fields

Academic fields are often roughly grouped as the humanities, social sciences, sciences, and professional fields (see, for example, Table 4.1), and observers see at least some similarities among the fields within each of these groups. For instance, some have described the sciences as hierarchical and tightly knit knowledge structures; the social sciences as more loosely connected structures of concepts, principles, and relationships; and the humanities as relatively free-form disciplines with little apparent structure (Bell, 1966; Harvard Committee, 1945; Toulmin, 1962). Others have focused on specific characteristics of academic fields (such as inquiry methods) as a source of distinguishing features. We review these efforts because they help us understand the various orientations that college and

TABLE 4.1. TYPICAL GROUPINGS OF ACADEMIC FIELDS

Humanities	Social Sciences	Sciences	Professional Fields
• Classics	• Anthropology	• Anatomy	• Architecture
• Literature	• Economics	• Biology	• Business
• History	• Geography	• Chemistry	• Communication
• Modern languages	• Political science	• Computer science	• Education
• Music	• Psychology	• Geology	• Engineering
• Philosophy	• Sociology	• Math	• Nursing
• Visual arts appreciation		• Physics	• Social work
			• Visual and performing arts

*These groupings are representative of typical undergraduate fields of study and, therefore, do not include professional fields such as medicine, dentistry, and law, which are studied at the graduate level.

university instructors bring to the task of curriculum development and because they have served as grounding for empirical investigations of the attitudes and behaviors of faculty in different academic fields.

Phillip Phenix (1986), who argued that academic disciplines represented a natural ordering of knowledge and thus served as appropriate organizing schemes for curricula, sought to understand their common elements—or realms of meaning. Dressel and Marcus (1982) built on Phenix's work, positing five components—or structures—of academic disciplines:

- *Substantive structures*: the assumptions, variables, concepts, principles, and relationships of interest that control the questions asked and inquiries undertaken by individuals in the field.
- *Symbolic structures*: the symbolic language that allows elements to be identified and relationships defined and explored.
- *Syntactical structures*: the system for collecting and organizing data, posing and testing hypotheses or assertions, and relating justified assertions to the broader generalizations and exploratory schemes of the discipline.
- *Value structures*: a set of embedded values, orientations, or ways of viewing the world that determine what is worth studying and how it should be studied.
- *Organizational structures*: the relationship of a discipline to other disciplines.

Variations in these different components give a field its distinctive character. For example, the substantive structure of mathematics, its symbolic language, its inquiry practices and values, and its organizational structure differentiate it from fields such as history and sociology that study different phenomena in different ways.

Phenix concentrated on the academic disciplines and seemed to ignore professional fields. Although a number of scholars have since developed classification schemes for professional fields (as they have for the pure disciplines), these are not comprehensive or fully developed as those Phenix proposed for the disciplines. William McGlothlin (1964), for example, distinguished "helping" and "facilitating" fields based on the relative amount of time devoted to social understanding or technical competence. Others contrast "enterprising" fields like business and engineering with "helping" fields (Anderson, 1974; Nyre & Reilly, 1979). William McGaghie (1993) proposed four categories of professions: helping, entrepreneurial, technical, and performing.

Based on a survey of faculty members at one research university, Tony Biglan (1973a, 1973b) developed a three-dimensional framework of eight cells to classify many academic fields in a single scheme: hard/soft; applied/pure; life/non-life. Scholars have found support for Biglan's classification and have used four of the categories (pure, hard fields; pure, soft fields; hard, applied fields; and soft, applied fields) extensively in research. Biglan argued that pure fields, like physics and chemistry, are more interested in advancing basic knowledge than in applying knowledge to actual problems. Applied fields like education and engineering, however, find the application of knowledge more compelling. Hard fields (for example, physics and engineering) are marked by a greater consensus on content and methods of inquiry than soft fields (for example, English literature and sociology), which allow more latitude in choices of research and teaching topics and modes of inquiry. In a comprehensive review of the literature, Braxton and Hargens (1996) presented empirical evidence that academic fields can be distinguished from one another, as Biglan suggested, based on their degree of consensus on content and methods of inquiry.

The classification systems typically used to study academic disciplines do not take into account the specialized characteristics of professional fields, which attempt to integrate content, theory, and practice, initiate students into a professional practitioner community outside academe, and pursue pragmatic problems that require interdisciplinary inquiry. Joan Stark (1998) developed a classification scheme based on that proposed by Phenix and elaborated by Dressel and Marcus. Table 4.2 summarizes this work, comparing the components of professional fields to those proposed for the disciplines.

Whereas disciplines have substantive structures that determine the kinds of questions and inquiries they pursue, the kinds of problems pursued in a professional field are determined by the service or technical role. Rather than organizational structures that link the discipline to others, professional fields have a wider set of linkages: they are connected to their foundational (or parent) disciplines, to a practice community, and to other related professional fields. Although disciplines and professional fields each have value systems, the value system of a professional field references its service role and client base, whereas the value structure of a discipline focuses primarily on the questions of what should be studied and why. Both professional fields and disciplines have preferred methods of inquiry, but those of the professional fields tend to be more eclectic because they are adapted from foundational disciplines. Finally, both professional fields and disciplines depend on specialized languages, but professional fields may have both technical and non-technical symbol systems that allow them to communicate internally, with other members of the field, and externally, with clients. In the next section, we explore some of these similarities and differences in greater detail.

Differences in Course Planning

Empirical research reveals that the patterns of variation observed in academic planning among academic fields reflect the kinds of substantive differences

TABLE 4.2. COMPONENTS OF PROFESSIONAL FIELDS AND DISCIPLINES

Professional Fields	Disciplines
Service or technical role: The problems with which the field deals and, specifically, its type of "service" to society. What are the technical and conceptual competencies professionals must acquire to perform their role in society?	*Substantive structure*: Assumptions about the particular concepts of interest that control the questions asked and the inquiries undertaken. What are the types of problems with which the discipline deals?
Connections and linkages: The linkages with foundational disciplines, with the practice community, and with other professional fields. How are conceptual and technical competencies integrated for practice?	*Organizational structure:* The set of principles relating a discipline to other disciplines.
Values: The attitudes the field has about its service role, its clients, and the improvement of the professional field itself. What services are worth providing and what orientation must the professional bring to the role?	*Value structure*: A set of embedded values, orientations, or ways of viewing the world. What is worth studying and how should it be studied?
Methods of inquiry: The methods used to answer questions or solve problems. What are the ways in which the field creates its own unique methods and draws upon the inquiry methods of its foundational fields in developing its knowledge base?	*Syntactical structure:* A system for collecting and organizing data, posing and testing hypotheses or assertions, and relating justified assertions to the broader generalizations and exploratory schemes of the discipline. What are the ways in which evidence is collected, organized, evaluated, and interpreted?
Symbolic and discourse communities: Technical and non-technical symbol system. What symbol systems does the field use in communicating internally and with clients and the public about its role in society?	*Symbolic structure:* A symbolic communication system (frequently linguistic or mathematical but sometimes non-discursive). What is the symbol system that allows the expression of and communication about the unique aspects and relationships?

From: Stark, 1998. Copyright by The Ohio State University Press. Reproduced with permission.

suggested in all of these theoretical classification schemes. Variations in faculty members' course planning, instruction, and perceptions of students can be attributed to these differences (Donald, 2002). Examining the fields through the lenses suggested by Dressel and Marcus and by Stark promotes understanding not only the nature of academic fields, but the curricular implications of differences among them. Janet Donald's research helps to relate the theoretical descriptions to tasks of academic planning.

Substantive Structures and Service Roles

The component that Dressel and Marcus called a discipline's substantive structure includes its conceptual structure and problem base. Research by Janet Donald (2002) provides one indicator of difference in structure: the type and number of concepts in a typical course. This research shows that the courses in the sciences tend to include more specific, explicit, and concrete concepts. In comparison, about 90 percent of concepts that students are expected to learn in social science courses are abstract in nature. Moreover, Donald demonstrates that instructors teaching science courses typically expect students to learn *more* concepts than those teaching social sciences and humanities courses expect. Such differences, she asserts, reflect the nature of the fields, but should not be construed as measures of the intellectual rigor of a course.

Donald (2002) also found that the average number of relationships in science courses significantly exceeds the average in courses in the social sciences and humanities. Moreover, what she calls the logical structure of fields—that is, the patterns of relationships among concepts in a given field—differ. Consistent with theoretical propositions of other scholars, she found that relationships in science courses tend to be hierarchical, with concepts and ideas building one upon the other; students need to understand these foundational concepts and ideas foundation before they can move on to intermediate and advanced ideas and courses. In the social sciences, concepts cluster or tend to pivot on a key concept that provides an entry into a topic. Instructors, of course, may choose different key concepts for this pivot role because social science concepts are related but not necessarily linearly related. Concepts in humanities courses tend to be even more loosely linked than those in social science courses, if they are linked at all.

In professional fields, the analog to the disciplines' substantive structure is the service role, which refers to the problems with which the field deals and the type of service it provides to society (Stark, 1998). The service role determines the knowledge bases and technical skills that professionals in the field must master. Compared to those of the disciplines, the conceptual foundations and skills of a professional field are more varied because they are typically derived from multiple fields of study. Stark suggests at least four different service roles: human client (for example, nursing, social work), information (for example, library science, journalism), enterprise/production (for example, business, engineering), and artistic (for example, music, art, theater). Each of these groups has a slightly different philosophical and ethical orientation toward its role in society.

Syntactical Structures and Methods of Inquiry

Academic fields, scholars have noted, have different ways of seeking and validating knowledge. Donald (2002) provides evidence of how these variations influence the design of college and university courses. In Table 4.3, we present a sample of Donald's findings, comparing thinking and knowledge validation processes for four fields of study: physics, English literature, engineering, and education.

The thinking skills associated with English literature and education, both "soft" fields, are more subjective. English literature faculty stress analysis, criticism, and interpretation of texts. Education faculty members ask students to evaluate and reflect on pedagogical approaches and, as a result, to develop expert processes. In both fields, thinking skills reflect a reliance on professional judgment to validate knowledge.

In general, professional fields tend to be eclectic in their choice of methods of inquiry, borrowing and adapting methods from several relevant fields of study. The range of methods depends on the range of questions that the field seeks to

TABLE 4.3. THINKING AND KNOWLEDGE VALIDATION STRATEGIES IN FOUR FIELDS

	Terms for Thinking	Examples of Thinking	Validation Processes
Physics	• Problem solving and analysis • Visualization • Deductive logic	• Experimentation • Scientific explanation	• Match evidence to theory • Plausible answers that fit expectations
English Literature	• Hermeneutics • Interpretation • Literary analysis • Criticism • Imagination • Rhetoric	• Close reading • Bridging gaps and integrating textual elements • Analyzing the organizing principle	• Critique of others' claims • Peer review • Credibility and plausibility • Testing parts against whole
Engineering	• Problem solving and analysis • Design • Mathematical modeling	• Solve problems given incomplete information • Use procedural knowledge	• Does it work within specific constraints?
Education	• Pedagogical reasoning • Expert processes • Evaluation • Reflection	• Represent ideas in form of new analogies and metaphors • Problem solving in classroom	• Practical judgment • Triangulate evidence • Ecological validity • Utility

Adapted from: Donald, 2002. Reprinted with permission of John Wiley & Sons, Inc.

address and to the diversity of practice settings for which students are prepared. For example, in nursing, the methods of study to address problems of patient relations (psychology, sociology) differ from those to address administration or policy relationships with government (political science, management). In general, there is less consensus on inquiry methods when the professional field is based in parent disciplines that also demonstrate less agreement about methods of studying and solving problems (Stark, 1998). Professional fields rooted in disciplines with strong inquiry paradigms tend to also agree on their own methods of inquiry.

Organizational Structure and Connections

All academic fields have, to varying degrees, connections to other fields of study. Physics, for example, requires a thorough grounding in advanced mathematics; social psychology links the study of individuals (psychology) with that of social organizations (sociology). Professional fields of study, such as education and engineering, are also linked to academic fields that provide conceptual and knowledge bases. The number of such linkages may be modest or extensive. In chemical engineering, for example, students must master advanced mathematics and physics and, in some cases, additional scientific fields to become competent practitioners. Education relies primarily on its parent disciplines in the social sciences (for example, psychology, sociology, anthropology, and political science) for useful concepts, theories, and methods. These differences in lineage are clearly reflected in the terms used for thinking and the thinking skills emphasized in these two fields (see Table 4.3). Engineering faculty and practitioners stress the need to develop students' problem-solving and mathematical reasoning skills; educators attend to development of critical thinking skills (for example, comparison, evaluation) and the use of expert professional judgments or, in Donald's terms, practical judgments.

The differences in thinking skills associated with professional fields such as education and engineering not only result from their connections to foundational disciplines, but they reflect the needs and expectations of the practice communities served by these fields. In general, faculty in professional fields that are strongly regulated by society have close connections with the practice community and supervise their students as they develop "integrative competence"—the ability to meld concepts and skills in practice (Stark, 1998). This connection with the practice field is very tight for the human client fields, involving careful supervision and socialization. In nursing, counseling, education, and social work, for example, students often undergo formally structured field experiences in clinical or supervised settings in preparation for entry to the profession. Supervision is viewed as less critical in the enterprise/production fields like business, where students are

encouraged, but typically not required, to gain work experience before graduation. Students in artistic service fields are more likely to have less formal and more
individualized connections with the practice community (Stark, 1998).

Discourse and Symbolic Structures

Academic fields vary in the degree to which their vocabularies and symbol systems
are accessible to those without specialized training. Although most fields have a
specialized vocabulary for describing the phenomena studied, some fields rely more
heavily on technical language and highly specific symbol systems. The language
and symbol structure of statistics, for example, are not accessible to those without
training in the field. In professional fields, dual symbol structures may exist. For
instance, human services fields employ both a closed symbol system (for example,
technical language used by nurses and pharmacists) and an open symbolic system
to communicate with clients. As a result, the professional fields are somewhat
distinctive in their emphasis on the development of interpersonal skills. Technical
fields, like engineering, that have traditionally relied on closed symbol systems,
recently are emphasizing the importance of developing communication skills that
permit effective interaction with those in related fields and with customers.

Values and Value Structures

Many observers have commented on the deeply held values and orientations that
create, in different fields, particular ways of viewing the world. These values and
orientations help members of the field define what is worth studying and how it
should be studied. Whereas the value structures of the disciplines tend to focus
on the boundaries of the field and its inquiry practices, the professional fields are
distinctive in their emphasis on the development of a set of professional attitudes,
including those related to professional identity, professional ethics, and motivation
for continued learning in the field. In traditional liberal arts and science fields,
professional identity typically is viewed as the province of graduate study and
the career path to the professoriate. In comparison, professional fields like nursing strongly emphasize the development of professional identity and ethics in
their undergraduate curricula. This emphasis, of course, varies by field. Business
and engineering curricula traditionally have stressed the technical aspects of the
field more than professional identity. A related issue is the emphasis placed by
the professional field on a student's understanding of the social, economic, and
political context in which the profession is practiced. In general, the stronger the
value orientation, the stronger the emphasis placed on providing students with
a contextual orientation to practice in society, and the stronger the emphasis on

technical competence to provide the service. Many of the academic disciplines, of course, are themselves studies of the context of human life and society, and some may emphasize the use of such knowledge in societal change.

Illustrative Course Planning Profiles

In this section, we offer profiles of course planning in representative fields, based on reports from college and university faculty collected by researchers at the National Center for Research to Improve Teaching and Learning (NCRIPTAL) (Stark & others, 1990). These profiles provide concrete examples of how differences in structures, roles, methods of inquiry, language, and values influence how instructors in different fields approach curriculum planning.

Profile 1: Literature The literature instructors' profile also illustrates course planning in other humanities fields (such as history and fine arts appreciation). The NCRIPTAL course planning studies found that instructors teaching introductory literature courses attributed strong influence on course planning to their scholarly training but very little influence to pedagogical training. Typically these faculty members have had little formal training to teach. Often, but not always, their goal is to help students clarify their values. Literature instructors tend to select content to maximize students' personal development, enjoyment, search for meaning in life, ability to solve problems, and ability to investigate independently. They stand out, however, from other instructors in the high degree of emphasis they place on values clarification and on students' intellectual and personal development as key educational purposes.

Establishing course objectives seems less important for literature instructors than for those in many other fields; possibly the specific literature chosen for study and the activities based on this literature constitute both the medium and the message. That is, the materials chosen incorporate the objectives of the course within them; choosing and arranging materials is not easily separated from choosing learning activities.

Profile 2: Biology An orientation toward concept learning is exemplified by biology instructors but also fits those in sociology and psychology. Biology instructors attribute strong influence to their scholarly training, tending to view their field as an organized body of knowledge that includes sets of principles, operations, and a mode of inquiry. While hoping to foster effective thinking, biology instructors are committed to concept learning as their primary educational purpose. Some biologists, however, are interested in other educational purposes as well; for example, some are interested in social causes such as environmental concerns, while others may be interested in the relation of biology and values clarification. While they do not attach extremely high importance to vocational purposes, biology instructors are more sympathetic toward them than instructors in literature. This may stem from their responsibility to teach many introductory biology students contemplating careers in the health sciences. Biology instructors, who view their field as consisting of a set of concepts to be learned, are accordingly more concerned with selecting and arranging content than are faculty in some other fields.

Profile 3: English Composition   The fields that teach language skills are represented in our profile of English composition instructors. To varying degrees, this profile also fits introductory mathematics and foreign languages, which are similarly concerned with symbol systems. Some aspects of this profile may also generalize to courses in other fields that are also focused on teaching skills rather than concepts.

Whereas literature instructors tend to view their field as an organized body of knowledge and themselves as members of a community of scholars with like interests, English composition instructors stand out because they view their work as teaching students a body of skills to be learned and applied. To some extent, they may also be interested in selecting content to ensure the development of effective thinking and basic skills useful in problem solving, work, and career choice. English composition instructors also tend to espouse a variety of educational purposes for their students and try to help students achieve these through different types of writing assignments.

English composition instructors report that pedagogical training and teaching experiences are a relatively strong influence on their course planning, perhaps because they have more often been trained to teach and have worked as teachers before or during their graduate studies. In addition, the national associations for composition instructors emphasize teaching in their meetings and publications. Perhaps because of their backgrounds and professional associations, composition instructors see research on teaching and learning as a modestly important influence on their course planning; no other faculty group reported that this kind of scholarship was an important influence on their course planning.

English composition instructors tend to see a number of contextual influences as important. Because most view writing as an active educational process, student characteristics and goals are key. Because they provide general education (or service) courses to students, college and program mission are noted as additional contextual influences. When asked about steps in course planning, they emphasize selection of learning activities and report that they first establish goals for the course or select subject matter. This may be because the skills to be learned in composition are already well defined.

Profile 4: Business Of the profiles illustrated here, business instructors least often consider their scholarly or pedagogical training as a strong influence on course planning. They draw instead on work experience and employer needs outside academe. They tend to characterize their field as both an organized body of knowledge and a set of skills to be learned. Not surprisingly, a strong interest in the vocational development of students (including the search for an appropriate career) differentiates business instructors from others we have profiled. For business instructors, students' goals are more important than students' characteristics, another point of contrast with other fields.

Seeking Academic Community

Academic fields build and maintain consensus through ongoing social interaction, and the differences among them result, in part, from choices and decisions made by the members of these academic communities. Richard Whitley (1976) recognized the centrality of social interactions and the communal nature of academic work, defining disciplines as organized social groupings. Arthur King and John Brownell (1966) viewed them as expressions of human imagination and traditions built on the discourse of forebears and highlighted the role of communications networks and instructional communities in their development. Scholars such as Tony Becher (1989) and Michel Foucault (1980) described how the social relationships within disciplinary groups serve to regulate the conduct of their members and produce roles and norms that are tightly tied to systems of power. Foucault highlighted the ways in which communities "discipline" knowledge, and Becher (1989) explored the self-sustaining functions of academic communities, portraying them as continually engaged in political and territorial disputes and keenly aware of status structures and pecking orders. Becher's "tribes of academe" define their own identities and social practices, including particular traditions, customs, and practices; knowledge, beliefs, morals, and rules of conduct; and linguistic and symbolic forms of communication as well as the meanings they share (1989, p. 24). In the professional fields, of course, the linkage with the field of practice may either enhance or attenuate these identities and social practices.

Although knowledge of differences among academic fields is critical to understanding the variety of curricular and instructional practices in higher education, discussions of these differences tend to fragment our view of the academic landscape. Faculty members in the sciences, social sciences, humanities, and professional fields, it may seem, have little in common and go their separate ways. Higher education, however, often requires that faculty from different fields collaborate on designing educational experiences for students. Faculty members must identify common ground if they are to develop effective general education curricula, construct interdisciplinary majors, and ensure that service courses address the needs of students from different majors. Attending exclusively to characteristics that distinguish one field of study or one undergraduate program from another may have the unintended effect of paralyzing educators interested in curricular collaboration, coherence, and integration. After all, if the disciplines are so distinct from one another, how can educators hope to identify shared learning goals?

Finding Common Ground

John Holland argued that although individuals within a field of study display distinctive professional attitudes and behaviors, there are also fundamental similarities among the fields. Based on his theory of careers, he reclassified the academic fields into six broad categories on the basis of shared characteristics that do not align neatly with the a priori groupings of social sciences, humanities, sciences, and professional fields.

Holland (1966, 1973, 1985, 1997) refined his theory of careers over several decades to explain how personal and interpersonal factors interact to influence the choice of an occupation. According to his theory, most people can be classified into one of six theoretical or ideal personality types (Realistic, Investigative, Artistic, Social, Enterprising, or Conventional) that influence their choice of an occupation. The theory presumes that individuals choose fields consistent with their motivations, knowledge, personality, and abilities, and, once in the field (even as students), those individuals are supported and rewarded for those attitudes and behaviors. Holland thus proposed six environments, created by the people who dominate in that environment, that correspond to his six personality types (see Figure 4.2 for a summary of the personality types). The way individuals respond in a situation is thus partly a function of the situation and partly a function of their behavioral repertoires—the distinctive pattern of interests, competencies, and preferred activities associated with their personality types. Readers may argue with Holland's claim that these types are the result of personality characteristics rather than the effects of socialization. Our concern here is a practical one: identifying common ground upon which college and university instructors can productively work together.

Academic fields as well as occupations have been classified into one of the six personality/environment categories. John Smart, Kenneth Feldman, and Corinna Ethington (2000) pointed out that academic programs in colleges and universities are occupational "homes" to faculty members and students. They bring together groups of individuals with similar interests and characteristics to engage in distinctive sets of activities. The academic program is thus a socialization setting

FIGURE 4.2. HOLLAND PERSONALITY TYPES

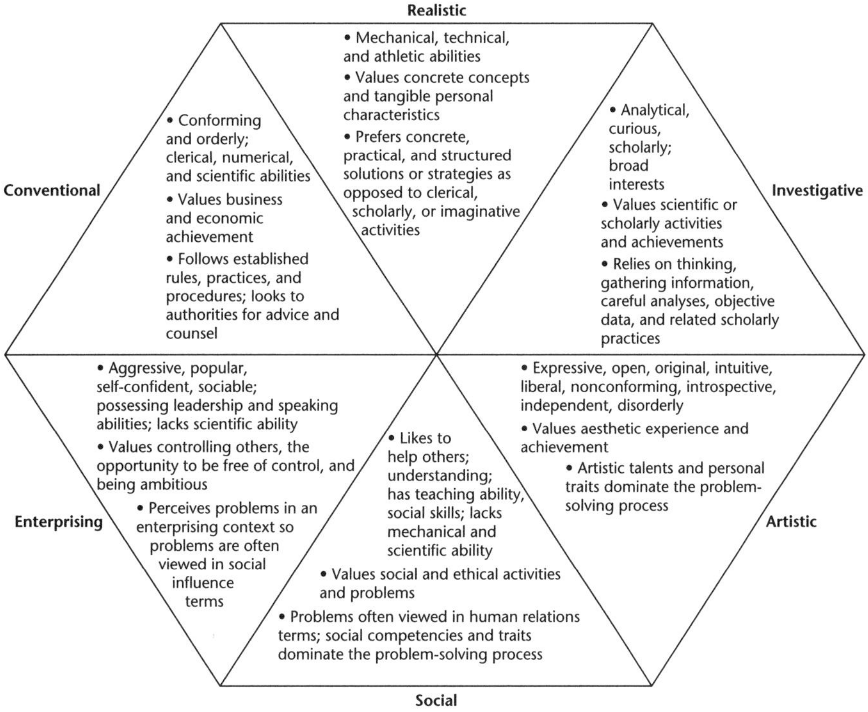
Realistic
• Mechanical, technical, and athletic abilities
• Values concrete concepts and tangible personal characteristics
• Prefers concrete, practical, and structured solutions or strategies as opposed to clerical, scholarly, or imaginative activities
Investigative
• Analytical, curious, scholarly; broad interests
• Values scientific or scholarly activities and achievements
• Relies on thinking, gathering information, careful analyses, objective data, and related scholarly practices
Artistic
• Expressive, open, original, intuitive, liberal, nonconforming, introspective, independent, disorderly
• Values aesthetic experience and achievement
• Artistic talents and personal traits dominate the problem-solving process
Social
• Likes to help others; understanding; has teaching ability, social skills; lacks mechanical and scientific ability
• Values social and ethical activities and problems
• Problems often viewed in human relations terms; social competencies and traits dominate the problem-solving process
Enterprising
• Aggressive, popular, self-confident, sociable; possessing leadership and speaking abilities; lacks scientific ability
• Values controlling others, the opportunity to be free of control, and being ambitious
• Perceives problems in an enterprising context so problems are often viewed in social influence terms
Conventional
• Conforming and orderly; clerical, numerical, and scientific abilities
• Values business and economic achievement
• Follows established rules, practices, and procedures; looks to authorities for advice and counsel

Adapted and reproduced by special permission of the Publisher, Psychological Assessment Resources, Inc., from *Making Vocational Choices*, Third Edition, copyright 1973, 1985, 1992, 1997 by Psychological Assessment Resources, Inc. All rights reserved.

that encourages new members to adhere to prevailing ways of thinking, behaving, and feeling. Smart and his colleagues further noted that "abundant evidence exists that faculty in academic departments, classified according to the six academic environments proposed by Holland, differ in ways theoretically consistent with the postulates of Holland's theory" (p. 83). Their analyses of national data also produced strong support for the assumption that academic environments are socializing mechanisms, reinforcing and rewarding different patterns of abilities, interests, and values while simultaneously discouraging others.

Holland's theory is often used in career counseling offices on college and university campuses to help students select a major and a career. It might also be useful to academic planners who seek to understand the actions of faculty; the classification system suggests new opportunities for helping faculty recognize their common attitudes and values. A focus on shared educational beliefs, rather than surface-level differences in course content or foci, could become the basis for collegial and productive exchange. Research on Holland's typology provides some starting points for these discussions.

For example, Holland (1997) noted that Realistic and Investigative environments are highly consistent. Both share a focus on students' career goals, prefer formal and structured instructional processes, and emphasize grades and examinations more than other Holland environments. These points of common ground among faculty in realistic fields and investigative fields might facilitate cross-disciplinary conversation about general education and elective courses. Beginning with the assumption that students' career-related goals are important, faculty from these fields might fruitfully discuss the specific learning outcomes that should be addressed in service courses. Agreement on student learning outcomes could then facilitate discussions of content and learning experiences to address those learning outcomes.

Holland's typology also suggested that faculty in artistic and social fields are likely to encourage students to set personal goals and pursue personal interests. Faculty in these fields tend to prefer informal teaching approaches, stress student independence in the learning process, and favor collegial interactions with students more than their faculty counterparts in investigative and realistic fields. Faculty in fields such as languages and architecture (artistic fields), many of the humanities fields (history, philosophy, and arts appreciation), and those in several social science fields (for example, anthropology, political science, psychology) share some common views, and curricular discussions might be facilitated by acknowledging these shared perspectives and preferences.

The course planning profiles we discussed earlier represent different categories in Biglan's scheme and they also represent at least three of Holland's environments. English literature was classified by Holland as a social environment. Other fields that Holland classified as social environments include area/ethnic studies, library science, physical and health education, psychology, anthropology, political science, education, and social work. Social environments, Holland asserted, emphasize activities that involve mentoring, treating, healing, or teaching others and thus lead to human relations competencies such as interpersonal and education skills. Biology is representative of investigative fields in Holland's typology. As noted earlier, investigative people prefer activities that involve the study of physical, biological, and cultural phenomena, and investigative environments therefore tend to emphasize analytical and intellectual skills.

Holland classified business as an enterprising field because it emphasizes activities that result in organizational or economic gains and stress the acquisition of leadership, interpersonal, and persuasive skills. These activities focus little attention on scientific forms of inquiry. Enterprising fields include communications and journalism, as well as law and public affairs. The profile for business instructors resembles that of other professional fields classified by Holland as enterprising environments (such as nursing) in its emphasis on vocational purpose and the importance of student goals. In other respects, it diverges. This probably reflects the differences in service sectors associated with professional fields and the differences in Holland career types as well. Future studies are needed to identify clusters related to the four service roles suggested by Stark (enterprising/production, human client, information, enterprise/production, and artistic) and to explore their possible congruence with the Holland categories.

Promoting Linkages Donald (2002) asks us to imagine "the predicament" of an entering university student registered in courses in physics, psychology, and English literature. Each discipline, she reminds us, asks students to think in particular ways and to apply different strategies in reading and problem solving. How do we help students both understand and manage these competing intellectual demands?

As the range of academic specializations has expanded over the past century, so has the array of college and university courses and programs inspired by these advances in knowledge. One challenge at the undergraduate level is to create a coherent and integrated learning experience that spans general education and the major. Although a few colleges and universities offer integrated curricula that help students understand how the disciplines they encounter are connected (for example, the long-standing interdisciplinary programs at Evergreen State and Hampshire Colleges), the great majority do not.

Most institutions employ a distribution approach for general education, allowing students to choose from a large number of potential courses to satisfy these curricular requirements. Although these individual courses may offer excellent learning experiences, the distribution approach leaves the task of integrating the knowledge gained from general education courses entirely up to the student. Major programs may be similarly constructed. Students in business, engineering, and the sciences, for example, may see little connection between the foundational mathematics and writing courses they must take as lower-division students and their subsequent studies in the major. The same might be said of students studying fields in the humanities and social sciences. The Association of American Colleges and Universities (AAC&U, formerly the Association of American Colleges, or AAC) has long urged faculty members to take collective responsibility for creating a coherent and integrated curricular experience. *Integrity in the College Curriculum* (AAC, 1985) called for greater attention to how students experienced the different academic fields they encountered in college while *High-Impact Educational Practices* (AAC&U, 2008) stressed the need for greater integration of general education and major programs. Ernest Boyer (1987) proposed that education should become a "seamless web" with integration between school and college levels, integration of liberal and professional studies, clearly articulated goals, and assessment that supports academic advising and curriculum development at all levels. He saw the ideal college as a learning community in which discussion of varied points of view about all subjects, including the educational process itself, would take place. Instructors teaching in interdisciplinary majors and minors often have such a community in mind, although these programs achieve varying degrees of coherence and integration (Association of American Colleges, 1991b; Klein, 1990).

The primary issue is not the academic fields but "rather that teachers, having become so immersed in the disciplines, no longer view(ed) themselves in relationship to the basic problems and concerns of mankind" (Dressel & Marcus, 1982, p. xii). Relying on academic fields as organizing frameworks for academic program structure can provide students with opportunities to integrate their learning or it can result in a narrow curriculum or overspecialization. The difference depends on whether and how educators choose to help students connect the knowledge learned in separate courses.

Suggestions for integrating curricula that require dramatic changes in college and university organizational structure and relationships are unlikely to be accepted and, experience suggests, often fail (Grant & Riesman, 1978; Klein, 1990). Effective course and program planning does not require overhauling academic departments or units; instead, it acknowledges the essential role of academic fields in curriculum planning and seeks to balance the impact of academic fields with the educational needs of students.

One benefit of the typologies we examined in this chapter is their ability to focus attention on aspects of their fields that instructors tend to neglect in their planning. For example, faculty are often accused of focusing so intently on the content of their fields that they neglect to consider how students perceive the field. The typologies suggest that instructors can help students understand a field of study by explicitly discussing its conceptual or logical frameworks, methods of inquiry, and values. Does a course or a program introduce students to the methods of inquiry in a field and give them practice in the thinking and analytical skills associated with those methods? Does it provide students with adequate and effective opportunities not only to learn the language and symbol system but to use it? How does it make clear the connections between the major and other fields, and does it ask students to explore these connections deliberately? What kinds of content and instructional approaches help students identify and describe the value system that directs the attention of scholars and practitioners in a field to some problems and not others—and how does the academic program as a whole help students understand how the perspectives taken in the field differ from the perspectives of others?

To respond to such questions, instructors must balance their attention in planning to include the various characteristics of the fields. Instructors might also examine the extent to which their academic plans balance learning the knowledge base of a field with opportunities to apply it. As we have noted (and will explore further in the next chapter), instructors tend to link content and purpose when they develop academic plans. Achieving balance, however, means continually checking to see that the desire to cover content does not overshadow the broader purposes of a course or program. Instructional processes may be chosen specifically to refocus attention from the *content* of a field to the *use* of content knowledge to address meaningful problems and issues and thus integrate their knowledge. Similarly, general education programs can place important social problems at the center of attention, encouraging students to draw from various fields of study to imagine solutions to important issues.

Connections among fields can also be made explicit. Instructors in professional fields tend to look to outside practice settings more than to internal sources of influence as they plan courses and programs; the reverse is true for those in the liberal arts disciplines. Consequently, the professional faculty need continually to remind themselves of important internal linkages, especially with fields that provide foundations and contextual study for their students, while the liberal arts faculty need to be aware of the ways in which the external context might modify their plans and make content, sequence, and instructional process more relevant.

The task of curricular collaboration may not be as daunting as our discussion thus far may suggest. We know that faculty can agree on important learning outcomes for students. One vivid example was the Professional Preparation Network, a volunteer national task force of faculty from varied liberal arts and professional fields. Its report, *Strengthening the Ties That Bind: Integrating Liberal and Professional Study* (Stark & Lowther, 1988b), documents the results of extensive discussions among a diverse group of faculty from liberal arts and professional fields. Convened with the sponsorship of the Fund to Improve Postsecondary Education (FIPSE), the report identified ten outcomes, ranging from communication to ethics, that are important in both liberal and professional education. Table 4.4 lists and defines these ten outcomes educators considered important and why they are important to both groups.

Pressing too hard for connections among faculty members from different academic fields, however, may lead to escalated conflict and renewed isolation. Extended discussions may avoid this situation because they offer faculty from different fields opportunities to learn together. In *Contesting the Boundaries of Liberal and Professional Education*, Marsh (1988) documents the positive experiences of a group of Syracuse University faculty engaged in planning an honors curriculum. The group, from different fields of study, chose and read books and viewed works of

TABLE 4.4. OUTCOMES IMPORTANT TO EDUCATORS IN BOTH LIBERAL ARTS AND UNDERGRADUATE PROFESSIONAL PROGRAMS

Communication Competence	The graduate can read, write, speak, and listen and use these processes effectively to acquire, develop, and convey ideas and information. *Comment:* Reading, writing, speaking, and listening are skills essential to professional practice and to continued professional growth as well as to informed citizenry and continued personal growth.
Critical Thinking	The graduate examines issues rationally, logically, and coherently. *Comment:* Although critical thinking is a universally desired educational outcome, professionals particularly need a repertoire of thinking strategies that will enable them to acquire, evaluate, and synthesize information and knowledge. Since much professional practice is problematical, students need to develop analytical skills to make decisions in both familiar and unfamiliar circumstances.
Contextual Competence	The graduate has an understanding of the societal context (environment) in which the profession is practiced. *Comment:* The capability to adopt multiple perspectives allows the graduate to comprehend the complex interdependence between the profession and society. An enlarged understanding of the world and the ability to make judgments in light of historical, social, economic, scientific, and political realities is demanded of the professional as well as the citizen.
Aesthetic Sensibility	The graduate will have an enhanced aesthetic awareness of arts and human behavior for both personal enrichment and application in enhancement of the profession. *Comment:* Sensitivity to relationships among the arts, the natural environment, and human concerns epitomizes aesthetic awareness. Through learning to approach life as an aesthetic experience and by viewing work as an act of aesthetic judgment, professionals can more effectively assess and understand their world and their roles within it.
Professional Identity	The graduate acknowledges and is concerned about improving the knowledge, skills, and values of the profession. *Comment:* Professional identity both parallels and supplements the liberal education goal of developing a sense of personal identity. The sense of personal worth and self-confidence that develops from experiencing success in professional practice, often including a contributing or altruistic relationship with clients, is an effective vehicle for gaining a sense of one's place in the world as an individual and citizen.
Professional Ethics	The graduate understands and accepts the ethics of the profession as standards that guide professional behavior. *Comment:* Liberally educated individuals are expected to have developed value systems and ethical standards that guide their behavior. Since in every field professionals face choice and responsibility in the process of making decisions with full understanding of their consequences, the study of ethics provides a context for development of professional ethics.

TABLE 4.4. *(continued)*

Adaptive Competence	The graduate anticipates, adapts to, and promotes changes important to the profession's societal purpose and the professional's role. *Comment:* A liberally educated person has an enhanced capacity to adapt to and anticipate changes in society. Since professional practice is not static, adaptability can be fostered by promoting the need to detect and respond to changes and make innovations in professional practice.
Leadership Capacity	The graduate exhibits the capacity to contribute as a productive member of the profession and to assume leadership roles as appropriate in the profession and society. *Comment:* All education carries with it the responsibility of developing leadership capacity. This is particularly true for professional education where the problem-decision-action cycle may have broad environmental, social, and individual ramifications. Not only does leadership imply both functional and status obligations, it requires the intelligent humane application of knowledge and skills.
Scholarly Concern for Improvement	The graduate recognizes the need to increase knowledge and advance the profession through systematic, cumulative research on problems of theory and practice. *Comment:* The heart of the intellectual process is attention to a spirit of inquiry, critical analysis, and logical thinking. Although many critical analysis skills are developed as theory and practice are integrated, the professional curriculum can be specifically designed to foster among graduates an obligation to participate in inquiry, research, and improvement of the profession.
Motivation for Continued Learning	The graduate continues to explore and expand personal, civic, and professional knowledge and skills throughout a lifetime. *Comment:* A truly educated person will wish to continue learning throughout life. In professional education, substantial emphasis can be placed on fostering individual responsibility for continued professional growth.

From: Stark and Lowther, 1988b. Reprinted by permission of the University of Michigan.

art deliberately intended to provoke discussion reflecting the differences among their individual disciplines and professional fields.

In a similar way, the Professional Preparation Network used the Collaboration/ Integration Matrix (see Figure 4.3), which is designed to answer the question, "What are the most appropriate types of cross-discipline integration to help students achieve specific important outcomes?" The matrix was originally designed to be used by professional field faculty and their colleagues in foundational disciplines, but its use as a template for discussion can lead to concrete and well-defined relations among many fields.

The key to using the matrix is to base discussion on common goals shared by the various fields. Initially, objectives and processes must be shared without criticism to establish an open climate for exchange. Usually, a brief discussion will

FIGURE 4.3. THE COLLABORATION/INTEGRATION MATRIX: A CONCEPTUAL FRAMEWORK FOR INTEGRATING LIBERAL AND PROFESSIONAL EDUCATION

Program Structure \ Teaching/Learning Emphasis	Specialization	Contextual	Investigation
Internal	I-S	I-C	I-I
External	E-S	E-C	E-I
Collaborative	C-S	C-C	C-I

The rows in the matrix describe structures for coursework or activities established between fields as follows:

Internal: Coursework or activities that occur within the professional program.

External: Coursework or activities that occur in the fields of study outside of the professional program, taught by faculty in other fields.

Collaborative: Coursework or activities (a) taken in other fields but taught by professional program faculty; (b) taken within the professional program but taught by faculty from other fields; or (c) taken within a merged or transformed program structure where two or more fields have united around common goals, themes, or concepts.

The columns in the matrix describe teaching and learning emphases within a field of study as follows:

Specialization: Emphasis on the specialized conceptual, technical, and integrative practice components of study in a particular field.

Contextual: Emphasis on knowledge of broad social, political, historical, and economic issues; values; contexts; and the arts.

Investigation: Emphasis on inquiry, analysis, and the search for innovative and creative solutions based on the active use of knowledge of broad social, political, historical, and economic issues; values; contexts; and the arts.

From: Stark and others, 1988. Reprinted by permission of the University of Michigan.

---

reveal that the groups of faculty are separately developing academic plans and selecting instructional processes intended to achieve these common goals. Once a common set of desired outcomes is identified, discussion focuses on one objective at a time. Defining the objective more fully and exploring the program linkages that might be used to achieve the goal most effectively are critical. Possible types of program linkages are arranged in the nine-cell matrix in Figure 4.3.

The nine cells are defined by the intersection of three possible types of program structures and three possible types of teaching/learning emphases. The three program structures are (a) internal (courses planned and taught internally to a single department), (b) external (courses delegated to another department to be planned and taught), and (c) collaborative (courses planned and taught by the two departments jointly). The three types of teaching/learning emphases include (a) specialization (courses that are highly specialized or technical), (b) contextual (courses that may be specialized but which also consider the context in which the specialization takes place), and (c) investigation (courses that explore questions of mutual interest to one or more programs). The appropriate cell to foster desirable student outcomes depends on the desired outcome; a different degree of collaboration might be appropriate to teach communication skills than to teach professional ethics.

One extreme position, but one which may be typical in many academic plans, is for programs to be both specialized and insular, for instance, teaching students professional and technical skills without reference to other studies (Cell I-S in Figure 4.3). In contrast, the typical general education program, offering primarily contextual knowledge in the first two years of undergraduate study, is represented by Cell E-C. In Cell E-C, contextual knowledge, which may be extremely relevant for professional practice, citizenship, and life, is taught with little or no reference to its connection with the students' planned professions or future lives. More intentional integration of liberal and professional outcomes would occur in any of the three cells in the row labeled "Collaborative." Whether collaborative specialization (Cell C-S), collaborative contextual (Cell C-C), or collaborative investigation (Cell C-I) would be the most desirable strategy would depend on the specific educational objective being pursued.

Building on the Strengths of Academic Fields

A decade-long national effort to identify liberal learning outcomes for all college graduates offers additional evidence that educators can forge consensus on educational priorities. Through studies of high school and college students, faculty, employers, civic leaders, and accrediting bodies, the Association of American Colleges and Universities (AAC&U) determined, and roused support for, a set of liberal learning outcomes for all college students (see Table 4.5). Reported in *Taking Responsibility for the Quality of the Baccalaureate Degree* (AAC&U, 2004), these outcomes include many of the competencies originally identified in the Professional Preparation Network project. Both reports identify thinking and communication skills, lifelong learning, ethics, and contextual competencies as critical priorities. The two efforts, roughly fifteen years apart, also reveal how curricular conversations change as societal values evolve. In 1989, educators focused on students' ability to develop leadership skills; in 2004, the broader concept of teamwork

TABLE 4.5. LIBERAL EDUCATION OUTCOMES

Knowledge of Human Culture and the Natural World
- Science
- Social sciences
- Mathematics
- Humanities
- Arts

Intellectual and Practical Skills
- Written and oral communication
- Inquiry, critical and creative thinking
- Quantitative literacy
- Information literacy
- Teamwork
- Integration of learning

Individual and Social Responsibility
- Civic responsibility and engagement
- Ethical reasoning
- Intercultural knowledge and actions
- Propensity for lifelong learning

Reprinted with permission from *Liberal Education Outcomes: A Preliminary Report on Student Achievement in College,* Copyright 2005 by the Association of American Colleges and Universities

took its place. Now collaborative skills, as well as individual effort, are deemed important. The specification of intercultural competence, which is clearly related to contextual competence, reflects widespread agreement among today's educators regarding the importance of diversity in higher education. Critical thinking, the term used in 1989, is now subsumed in the more broadly construed phrase, "inquiry, critical, and creative thinking," which includes thinking skills associated with a broader array of academic fields. The success of these two efforts, and the similarities in the outcomes they identified, demonstrate that curricular consensus can be achieved with concerted efforts.

The structure of U.S. higher education—which usually includes studies in general education and a specialized major field—reflects its broad educational purposes: preparing students for lives as professionals as well as members of local, national, and global communities. To focus on these purposes, college and university instructors need to be secure in their academic fields but capable of moving beyond their confines. This is a challenge to many faculty members because it requires conversations that span symbolic systems, value systems, and modes of inquiry.

Such conversations are unlikely to start spontaneously and they require regular infusions of energy to maintain. Persistence, strong leadership, and a supportive environment are critical to success.

From our discussions with faculty, we know that educational programs can be modified so that students achieve a more complete and satisfying education. When faculty members take seriously the principle with which we began this chapter—that academic plans should help the learner achieve understanding of various fields of study—they can improve curricula and extend their notions of the place of academic fields in the curriculum. Conscious and vigilant attention to balance among academic fields is necessary to create effective academic plans. Deliberate designs that maximize linkages within and among the fields will lead to greater coherence and integration in course and program plans.

CHAPTER FIVE

CREATING ACADEMIC PLANS

In this chapter we provide an overview of curriculum planning, that is, the creation of academic plans, and discuss how the academic plan concept compares to other frameworks that might be used to guide, and potentially improve, curriculum planning. These frameworks tend to be more systematic, research suggests, than the methods college faculty and administrators actually use. We thus refer to existing activities as *planning*, reserving the term *design* for a more deliberate scheme of choices and decision strategies, such as those suggested by the frameworks we examine. This will help us to distinguish between curriculum planning as it is typically conducted and more deliberative processes of curriculum design.

As we have noted, academic plans may be created at several levels: course, program, and college. The actors and processes, as well as the strength of internal and external influences, differ at each level. To describe how academic planning takes place, we begin with courses as the structural building blocks of curricula and then broaden our discussion to include the creation of academic programs and college-wide curricula.

Course and program planning in higher education is essentially a faculty role. Yet most who aspire to teach in colleges and universities receive little, if any, training in how to construct academic plans. Moreover, much of what we know about curriculum planning is the result of only a few studies. In this chapter, we rely heavily on studies of a nationally representative group of faculty planning a wide variety of introductory and advanced college courses (Stark & others, 1988;

Stark & others, 1990) to explain and explore planning at the course level. These related studies, "Reflections on Course Planning" and "Planning Introductory College Courses," were conducted under the auspices of the National Center for Research in Postsecondary Teaching and Learning (NCRIPTAL) at the University of Michigan. The Curriculum Leadership for Undergraduate Education (CLUE) study of planning in academic departments across the country, sponsored by the Spencer Foundation (Briggs, Stark, & Rowland-Poplawski, 2003), provides a picture of effective planning practices at the program level. We also cite a study of a nationally representative sample of engineering faculty and program heads (Lattuca, Terenzini, & Volkwein, 2006), entitled "Engineering Change: A Study of the Impact of EC2000," sponsored by the Accreditation Board for Engineering and Technology. This study, which focused in part on curricular, instructional, and planning decisions and activities, allows us to confirm and extend some of the findings of the course- and program-planning studies. Because few additional studies exist, we also draw on our own experiences as faculty members in not-for-profit institutions to describe, in general terms, how college and university instructors think about creating academic plans. Course and program planning in for-profit institutions may look very different, and we occasionally comment on this variation. In the final sections of this chapter, we examine systematic design models intended to improve course and program planning.

Course Planning

College instructors spend relatively little time in systematic planning activities prior to teaching an existing course. An early study showed that instructors preparing to teach an existing course spent only about two hours prior to the beginning of the course considering content, intended outcomes, and/or the conceptual structure of the content to be taught (Powell & Shanker, 1982). Rather than planning in advance, instructors tend to plan courses almost continuously by fine-tuning or making adjustments to existing courses when needed. In classifying various patterns of course planning, Joan Stark and Malcolm Lowther (1988a) characterize this dominant pattern for existing courses as "routine course planning." Planning new courses or conducting more extensive routine "reviews" or "major overhauls" of courses are less frequent. But overhauls do occur when, for example, the instructor perceives the course to be unsatisfactory in some respect (Stark & others, 1988, p. 68).

Course planning can "be characterized as decision making about the selection, organization, and sequencing of routines," and then the adjustment of contents of those routines (Yinger, 1979, p. 165). When there appears to be no necessity for major change, routines tend to take over. College instructors in the course planning studies perceived that their students tended to be similar from semester to semester in age, ability, and interests, and thus made few changes in their plans. Structural factors such as types of classrooms and laboratory schedules tend to reinforce routines and inhibit new course plans. Under these circumstances, professors undertake radical changes in courses more to relieve their own boredom than to facilitate specific instructional decisions (Stark & others, 1988).

Although our understanding of planning processes used by college instructors is far from complete, we know that a step-by-step or rational planning model does not seem to describe their actual planning behavior. Instructors, who are usually well-versed in and enthusiastic about the principles and concepts embodied in their fields, tend to start planning by considering content, rather than by stating explicit course objectives for students as design theorists might hope. Also, since they often take for granted the content they will teach, instructors focus on selection of teaching activities quite early in the planning process. Although models of course planning often separate planning from choosing instructional activities, research indicates that the two processes occur interactively. Plans for course structure and course implementation are closely related, as the academic plan concept suggests.

The fact that course content and instructional process are not separate planning issues for instructors is illustrated by research on instructional methods as well. For instance, when Thielens (1987) asked eighty-one faculty members why they lectured, as opposed to using some other instructional technique, their answers revealed a strong need to cover content rather than an explicit choice of instructional process. Faculty members said, for example, that they: (a) must select the correct material; (b) must organize complicated materials for students, even if the text has already done so; (c) must digest material for the student, performing a translation function; and (d) must correct student misconceptions, including those that can be obtained through reading the text.

Influences on Course Planning

Previously, we discussed an array of influences on academic programs, illustrating how their interaction creates a context for curriculum planning and shapes academic plans. We mentioned Toombs' (1977–1978) ideas about course design (Toombs & Tierney, 1991, 1993) and a model of curriculum planning they inspired. Stark and her colleagues later developed these ideas into the contextual filters model of course planning that illustrates the interrelationships among the influences. The studies of course planning (a) confirmed Toomb's hypothesis that *content* and *context* interact to shape faculty members' decisions course design (*form*);

FIGURE 5.1. CONTEXTUAL FILTERS MODEL

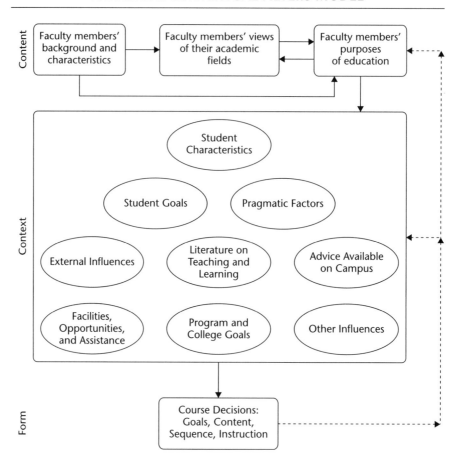

(b) more completely specified the components of content, context, and form; and (c) provided preliminary evidence of how these interact in curriculum planning (Stark & others, 1988; Stark, 2002). To aid and organize our discussion of course planning, we now describe the contextual filters model developed by Stark, Lowther, and their NCRIPTAL colleagues in greater detail (see Figure 5.1).

Although depicted as individual components in Figure 5.1, the influences of faculty members' background and characteristics (for example, their scholarly and pedagogical training), their views of their academic fields, and their beliefs about the purposes of education are hard to separate. Following Toombs' logic, the three together constitute a set of *content* influences that instructors bring with them to course planning. A second content frame includes instructors' views of their academic fields. As shown by the direction of the arrows in Figure 5.1, personal characteristics and academic backgrounds influence instructors' views of the teaching field more than the reverse.

Content influences also include instructors' purposes of education (whether implicit or explicit). In Figure 5.1, the two-way arrow between instructors' views of academic field and educational purposes (beliefs) connotes the dynamic and reciprocal nature of these influences, as described by faculty in the course planning studies. The arrow between instructor background and purposes of education suggests that instructors' characteristics and experiences may have a direct influence on their educational beliefs; views of the field do not necessarily intervene. The course planning studies revealed that most (but not all) instructors selected content as their first step in course planning—further evidence of the strength of the academic field as an influence on course planning. The studies also demonstrated a strong relationship between the subject-matter arrangements that instructors said they use in their courses, their beliefs about educational purposes, and their views of their academic fields. Rather than being mediated by other contextual influences, the arrangement of content may, to a certain extent, be strongly influenced by the field.

Eight specific contextual influences, empirically derived from interview and survey data, are portrayed in the model. These represent instructors' perceptions of what influences them as they plan a course. It is possible, however, that some influences go unnoticed. For example, while faculty members tend to recognize how the academic preparation of the students enrolled in their course affects the kinds of assignments they plan, they may be much less conscious of how pragmatic factors such as the size of the institution shape their course decisions. In the model, each item depicted in the context frame serves as a filter, mediating or modifying instructors' views about their fields and their educational purposes.

Toombs suggested that college faculty members translate considerations about *content*, modified by *context* influences, into *form*. In the contextual filters model, form is denoted as course decisions (see bottom frame in Figure 5.1), including choices of course content (subject matter), identification of course goals and objectives, selection of instructional activities and materials, and sequencing of subject matter.

Although choices about course content tend to drive the course planning process, the role of the contextual filters may be most evident once an instructor has taught a course. For example, if dissatisfied with student learning in a course, the instructor might seek out information about his students' goals in an attempt to understand their motivations for taking the course. Having learned more about why students take the course, he may make adjustments in course topics and classroom activities to help students better understand the relationship between the course content and their career goals. In some instances, feedback might even affect his beliefs about educational purposes. For instance, a new instructor may initially believe that her course should introduce students to the methods of inquiry in the field. The experience of teaching first-year students may, however, convince her that inquiry methods are more appropriately taught at advanced levels and that introductory courses should focus on fundamental concepts and principles.

The broad categories of *content, context,* and *form* provide an organizing scheme to present in greater detail the findings from the course planning studies.

Content Overwhelmingly, faculty members in the course planning studies reported that their own background, scholarly preparation, teaching experience, and beliefs about educational purpose influenced their course planning. These self-reported influences are perceptions, of course, and real influences may differ, but when interviewed, faculty participants in the course planning studies gave concrete illustrations of the sources of influence they reported.

Instructors' beliefs about the purpose of education (a content influence) are closely related to their views of their field. Instructors reported that they typically selected and interpreted content for students based on their own beliefs, assumptions, experiences, and reasoning (valid or invalid). When asked to choose their own beliefs among several statements of educational beliefs, respondents teaching introductory courses had little difficulty doing so, and most chose beliefs about the overall purposes of education that were similar to those chosen by others in their field. Table 5.1 reports the percentage of faculty (in six selected fields) in the introductory course planning studies who chose each of six broad educational purpose statements.

Patterns are also evident in the goal statements that instructors provided when asked about the goals they tried to communicate to students in their specific introductory course. Nearly half of the objectives contributed for introductory courses focus on learning concepts, principles, or facts in the field (see Table 5.2). Thus, although faculty members resonate with broad goals for education such as "effective thinking," the goal of transmitting concept knowledge about a specific academic field tends to provide the initial framework for specifying learning outcomes in course planning. To illustrate, a faculty member might say she believes the primary purpose of education is to develop students' ability to think critically. Yet when asked about goals for her course, she might stress the need for students to first learn specific principles, concepts, or theories. As one faculty member phrased it: "In my field, you have to have concepts and principles to think about before you can learn to think effectively." The primary consideration given to content is also clearly reflected in faculty reports of their "first steps" in course planning, shown in Table 5.3 (Stark & others, 1990).

TABLE 5.1. PURPOSES OF EDUCATION REPORTED BY FACULTY MEMBERS TEACHING INTRODUCTORY COURSES

Educational Purpose Statement Summary	Percent of Faculty Endorsing Educational Purpose Statement*							
	All Faculty	English Composition	History	Biology	Math	Psychology	Business
Personal enrichment: Students discover themselves, develop personal autonomy	36	51	26	17	11	44	34
Social change: To make the world a better place for all	54	54	61	46	23	74	69
Effective thinking: Acquire general intellectual skills to use in many situations	90	94	94	91	93	84	85
Vocational: Prepare to earn a living, contribute to society's production	30	31	31	23	48	23	70
Values: Help students clarify values and beliefs, develop dedication, commitment to guiding principles	60	65	65	51	35	57	58
Great ideas: Emphasize great products and discoveries of the human mind, great thinkers, concepts in the field	50	34	34	50	40	56	43

*Percent reporting that "this statement is much like my belief."

From: Stark and others, 1990. Reprinted by permission of the University of Michigan.

TABLE 5.2. INTRODUCTORY COURSE GOALS CONTRIBUTED BY FACULTY MEMBERS

Percent of Faculty Reporting Course Goals*

Type of Goal	All Faculty	English Composition	History	Biology	Math	Psychology	Business
Personal development or social development	13	10**	10	17	7	20	14
Intellectual development	15	20	22	12	20	10	6
Concepts or knowledge in the field	45	23	53	55	37	57	54
Skill development	15	38	7	2	13	4	6
Value development	2	2	2	2	2	2	1
Great ideas	<1	0	<1	0	0	0	0
Preparation for the future	5	3	<1	6	15	3	12
Aesthetics	3	1	3	3	1	1	2
Unclear	3	2	3	2	5	4	5

*Each faculty member was asked to contribute two goals; a few contributed only one.

**Columns do not sum to 100% because faculty could contribute more than one goal and because some goal categories were omitted for presentation purposes.

From: Stark and others, 1990. Reprinted by permission of the University of Michigan.

TABLE 5.3. FIRST STEPS FACULTY REPORT WHEN PLANNING COURSES

First Step in Planning	Percent of Faculty
Select course content	46
Draw on own background, experience	16
Think about student needs, characteristics	15
Choose activities to promote learning	9
Select textbooks, other resources	6
Set objectives, based on external standards	6
Examine student evaluations from previous courses	<1
Examine examinations from previous courses	<1

From: Stark and others, 1990. Reprinted by permission of the University of Michigan.

TABLE 5.4. REASONS FACULTY SELECT CONTENT IN INTRODUCTORY COURSES

Reason for Content Choice	Percent of Faculty
Conveys fundamental concept	87
Is important concept or principle	88
Contributes to students' development	75
Relates field to other fields	74
Illustrates mode of inquiry of field	74
Helps acquire essential skills	71
Helps integrate ideas	70
Interrelates fundamental principles	68
Encourages investigation	67
Is important example of inquiry in field	65
Is useful in solving problems on job	53
Stimulates search for meaning	49
Links concepts to social problems	48
Examines diverse views	45
Assists in career search	28

From: Stark and others, 1990. Reprinted by permission of the University of Michigan.

Generally, faculty in the course planning studies did not include knowledge of learning theory or pedagogical training among the types of scholarly preparation that strongly influenced their course planning. Only about 30 percent of the college instructors interviewed had any exposure to educational theories through formal courses or workshops. Nonetheless, when asked to choose among reasons for their choices of course content in introductory courses, faculty often chose responses consistent with good educational practice (see Table 5.4).

Context   Although there are numerous potential contextual influences on course planning, internal unit-level influences (within the program) and institutional influences originating outside the program but within the college or university affect course planning most. For example, about two-thirds of faculty in the course-planning studies reported that characteristics of learners in their courses and programs (particularly students' ability and preparation) were strong internal influences in their course planning.

The strength of many contextual influences varies by academic field. For example, availability of facilities influences science instructors more strongly than sociology instructors, while library resources are more important to literature instructors than to mathematics faculty. These differences illustrate why we view the contextual influences as modifiers or "filters" of basic faculty assumptions. The closer the level of institutional influence to the course, the more influential it tends to be. For example, college goals generally tend to be weaker influences than disciplinary or program goals; only one-third of the faculty in the course planning studies said college goals were influential in their course planning. When the program served wider college requirements (for instance, by providing English composition courses to all students), college-wide goals were assigned greater importance. Program goals are important but usually are more salient for courses in the major than for general education courses.

External influences may be most important in course planning for professional and occupational fields where scholarly or professional associations, employers, and accreditors set standards. For example, less than 20 percent of general education faculty members reported being influenced by entry tests for the next level of education, college-wide achievement tests, or external examinations of other types, but more than four-fifths of nursing faculty members reported that external examinations greatly affected their course planning (Stark & others, 1990). External factors may also be strong in community colleges where articulation agreements mandate course content or level for transfer to four-year colleges and in occupational programs where changes in industry practices must be quickly incorporated into degree programs to prepare individuals for career entry or advancement.

Even in professional fields, external influences may be more apparent at the program level than at the course level. Less than one-third of faculty respondents in a nationally representative sample drawn from seven engineering fields reported that a new set of engineering program accreditation criteria had a moderate or great deal of influence on changes in content they made in courses they regularly teach (Lattuca & others, 2006). This is surprising not only because the engineering accreditation criteria specify eleven different learning outcomes that must be assessed, but because more than 95 percent of all engineering programs in the United States are accredited. The findings are consistent, however, with those of the course planning studies. Rather than cite accreditation or industry as influences on their courses, more than four-fifths of the engineering faculty members reported that the changes they made in their courses were the result of their own initiative (Lattuca & others, 2006).

Form *Form* incorporates the various decisions made in planning a course. It translates the interaction of content and context into actual events. Although there are many dimensions of form, four dimensions are key: arranging content, selecting instructional processes, describing the plan, and evaluating the plan. In this section we describe briefly what is known about how instructors arrange course content because that decision is closely related to academic fields and instructors' educational beliefs. As we have seen in Table 5.3, the strong influence of academic field on college course planning means that most instructors select the content first. Many then move quickly to arrange course material in ways that they believe achieve specific objectives.

In the course planning study, faculty members responded to a question about how they arranged content in their introductory courses. The different response options (see Table 5.5) are based on the "sequencing" categories developed by George Posner and Kenneth Strike (1976) but expanded and revised based on the course planning interviews discussed earlier. As shown by the six examples in the table, one or two sequencing patterns tend to predominate in each discipline, suggesting that while there is commonality within a discipline, there is also some variation. These variations are linked with other discipline-related patterns.

Other decisions about the form of a course, such as selecting instructional activities, describing course plans, and evaluating them will be discussed in detail in Chapters 7 and 8.

Faculty Involvement in Course Planning

At the course level, curriculum planning is usually the task of a single individual. In the course planning studies, about two-thirds of faculty reported being highly autonomous and informal in their planning. Most instructors feel that developing a course is a creative act and are more satisfied with their course development role when they have flexibility to be creative. However, we encountered cases, too, where instructors believed that interaction with colleagues enhanced creativity. Colleagueship appears to be important in course planning, even when faculty members teach alone. Congenial colleagues can stimulate new thoughts and provide support and reassurance. For example, Stark found that faculty members who plan in groups (for example, to teach a course with multiple sections) give more

TABLE 5.5. WAYS FACULTY ARRANGE CONTENT IN INTRODUCTORY COURSES

Ways of Organizing Course Content	Percent of Faculty Reporting Organizing Scheme*						
	All Faculty	English Composition	History	Biology	Math	Psychology	Business
Way major concepts and relationships are organized	41	29	26	59	56	59	31
Way I know students learn	20	41	3	10	24	8	9
Way relationships occur in real world	15	5	47	21	4	8	5
Way knowledge has been created in my field	6	5	10	4	4	8	4
Way students will use knowledge in social, personal, or career setting	8	10	2	1	4	10	26
To help students clarify values and commitments	7	6	12	3	0	8	7
So that students prepare directly for careers	4	3	>1	1	8	0	19

*Percent responding "This is the statement most like how I arrange content in my course."

NOTE: Primarily general education courses, not professional or occupational courses. As a result, career development may be understated.

From: Stark and others, 1990. Reprinted by permission of the University of Michigan.

attention to student needs and varied instructional strategies than those who plan alone. Similarly, faculty members responsible for coordinating and supervising the work of laboratory or teaching assistants tend to be more systematic course planners. Some faculty members report that working with others, once they are accustomed to collaboration, is inspiring and reinforcing. Enforced colleagueship, on the other hand, may be detrimental. Linking and integrating courses may require increased interaction among instructors, and it can be challenging to achieve substantive course connections without decreasing individual faculty members' autonomy and flexibility.

Faculty autonomy in course development varies by type of institution, and sometimes within the same institution. In most not-for-profit colleges and universities, courses are developed by faculty on site. For-profit institutions like the University of Phoenix, however, may centralize course development and control course quality by relying on a small group of faculty experts and instructional designers to plan courses and develop the necessary instructional materials (Farrell, 2003). These pre-packaged courses are taught by part-time instructors who may or may not be experts in the field but who must closely follow the course plan and script (Farrell, 2003; Lechuga, 2006). In contrast, in not-for-profit institutions, instructors who have little or no input into the course plans they use (that is, who teach courses devised by others) tend to be discontent with the courses they teach and dissatisfied with the teaching role.

The experience of planning a course in a not-for-profit institution may also vary based on the mode of course delivery. In many colleges and universities, faculty planning online courses serve as content experts, while instructional developers contribute their knowledge of effective online instruction. Unlike those in the for-profit sector, however, faculty who teach online courses in traditional colleges and institutions retain autonomy in their teaching.

Program Planning

We define an academic program as a planned group of courses and experiences designated for a specific group of students. Our definition is broad enough to include academic majors, general education or college studies programs, formal interdisciplinary programs, and individualized programs of study that students construct with instructors' advice. Thus, course sequences, such as study abroad or cooperative education that are parts of a more general program, could also fit the definition of a program. In addition to planning the educational experiences, instructors may also admit the students to the program, provide academic advising, and evaluate students' progress. An academic program is not necessarily congruent with a department or division. One department may be home to more than one program, and some programs cross organizational lines.

Compared to the routine adjustments that regularly take place in course plans, academic program plans are created and revised only sporadically and usually as the result of strong organizational or external influences. External catalysts may include shifts of thinking within the field or changes in job market opportunities or accreditation standards. For example, more than three-quarters of the chairs of engineering programs saw accreditation and industry as influences on curricular changes made in their programs. Still, the vast majority (nearly 90 percent) also credited collective faculty decision making as an influence on changes in their program curricula. Clearly, faculty involvement in curricular decision making remains critical, even when there are strong external pressures for change.

Organizationally, the impetus for program change may be the arrival of a new faculty member with special interests and expertise or a new high-level administrator who implements an assessment program, strengthens the process for academic program review, or needs to cut the budget. Occasionally, major overhauls are due to decisions initiated by program faculty. A primary difference between program planning and course development is that the individual instructor no longer has great discretion in decision making. Consequently, program planning often involves compromises between faculty members in the same field who have slightly different points of view or, in the case of interdisciplinary programs, among faculty members from different fields who may have very different points of view. The more varied the backgrounds and disciplines of the planners, the more complex the process becomes and the more likely it is to be aborted before a satisfactory conclusion is reached. The compromises primarily concern content and sequencing. Although curricular compromises are often political (because power relationships are involved), these decisions are also based on deeply held beliefs about what students should learn. Many colleges and universities offer instructional assistance through teaching and learning centers, but instructors typically do not consult with them during program-level decisions about curricula. Thus, program planning is dominated by scholars, rather than curriculum specialists or other potential contributors.

Instructors generally have less personal interest and investment in program planning than they do in course planning. When asked to describe the process of program planning, most faculty members in the course-planning studies instead described their own course or how their own efforts fit into the program plan. Faculty members often seem reluctant to take responsibility for program planning, but accept the responsibility more readily and pursue it more systematically when strong leadership at the program or college level establishes a climate conducive for planning including a sense of the importance of the academic plans and their effects on students.

Colleges and universities vary in the degree to which they strive to create a supportive climate for planning. In one study that involved a large random national sample of academic vice presidents, presidents, and department chairpersons in both state and community colleges, university vice presidents (58 percent) and program chairs (53 percent) reported that curriculum development or revision was always or mostly systematic and planned. Less than half of community college academic affairs officers reported using a systematic, organized plan for program development all or most of the time (Johnson, Eubanks, Fink, Lewis, & Whitcomb, 1987). When Stark, Briggs, and Rowland-Poplawski (2002) asked vice presidents of academic affairs throughout the United States to nominate departments that were exemplary in systematically planning academic programs, many vice presidents did not offer a single program that fit that description.

Influences on Program Planning

In discussing influences on program planning, we follow our previous pattern, reporting influences on content, context, and, briefly, on form.

Content As is true for course planning, the primary internal influences on program planning are instructors' beliefs about teaching and content expertise. Broad shifts in the content and methods of teaching college fields occasionally are fostered and disseminated through disciplinary associations and accrediting agencies. Examples include the introduction of qualitative research in social science fields, advances in genetic engineering, an emphasis in accounting education on training accountants as users (rather than producers) of information, and the prominence of professional skills in revised engineering education accreditation criteria. In such cases, faculty work together to translate the views of external groups so that what looks like an internal process is really an adaptation of the field to the demands of outside stakeholders.

Context Among the many contextual influences on program planning, program mission may be strongest. Two-thirds of faculty in the course planning studies rated program goals as important considerations as they planned courses—fully twice the percentage who rated college goals as important. In professional fields, the importance of program goals was highest; about 80 percent of faculty in some of these fields rated program goals as a strong influence. Mandates from specialized accreditors to identify and enact program goals reinforce this influence.

Leadership is likely the second-most-important internal influence in program planning. In program planning, major curricular revisions require someone to supply the initiative. Some faculty respondents in the course planning studies reported that their programs had remained unchanged for years for lack of leadership. Others specifically identified the important stimulus provided by a leader. Sometimes this stimulus was as simple as creating a feeling that program excellence was important. In contrast, it was clear that heavy faculty workload was a strong inhibitor to involvement in program planning. One faculty member characterized the ideal situation in which program planning takes place as: "bottom up with support from the top."

In general, faculty members judged a number of external influences to be weak influences on their planning. These include textbooks, alumni, turf battles, enrollment concerns, assessment initiatives, and accreditors (except in specific fields). Although they purported to be strongly influenced by student characteristics and goals, program faculty reported access to little systematic data about learners. Groups of faculty working together as program planners tend to rely on anecdotal information about students rather than carefully collected data. This situation is changing in some fields where program accreditation standards now require the collection of assessment data (Briggs, 2003). The accreditation agency for undergraduate engineering and engineering technology programs, for example, requires programs not only to collect data on student learning outcomes, but also to demonstrate how the program uses this information in a process of continuous improvement.

Form At the program level, sequencing of courses is analogous to sequencing topics in a course. Ideally, an academic program is not just a set of isolated courses but rather an intentional plan to help students integrate knowledge, develop skills, and build a "coherent" view of the field or fields of study. Just as various conceptual links between topics hold courses together, so various types of "binding forces" hold courses together into a total plan or curriculum. These forces differ among academic fields. For example, programs in the social sciences tend to link courses in a relational way, compared with those in the humanities, which exhibit more intricate, web-like relationships. Programs may also be focused on the development of specific skills such as design or problem solving, career preparation (for professional fields), or themes (such as urban development).

Controversies about sequence in program planning are often a function of the structure of the academic field. Some fields require systematic progression through increasingly difficult courses that build upon each other. To illustrate, chemistry programs typically establish a sequence of required foundational courses (prerequisites) that prepare students for advanced study in the field. In other fields, the idea of standard sequences is eschewed altogether. Sociology programs, for example, typically offer a curriculum that gives students broad latitude in course selection. Even in the sciences, however, instructors debate course sequencing. In the course planning interviews, some biologists were convinced that the best course sequence began by focusing on the cell as a microcosm of life and moving outward toward the broader study of ecology. Others believed it was more effective to start at the macro-level ecological perspective and to progress into the cell.

In professional fields, a sequence of courses may be partly dictated by the responsibilities students will undertake in scheduled field experiences. A nursing instructor in a community college described her frustration about attempting to teach a large number of important topics, including not only content material but personal hygiene, ethics, interpersonal skills, and professional demeanor, in the first six weeks of a program before students entered a hospital setting.

Capstone courses are a popular approach in many fields. Typically scheduled in the last year of study in the major, the capstone experience is intended to help students integrate what they learned from the several courses they have taken in their major field of study. In professional fields, an internship or other supervised field experience may, at least in part, serve this function.

Another important debate about sequencing program content is inherent in the development of focused general education programs. Many colleges view general education requirements as foundational to upper-division specialized work in the major, but do not judge any particular sequence within the general studies program as necessarily superior to any other. In contrast, the premier advocacy organization for liberal education in the United States, the Association of American Colleges and Universities (AAC&U), encourages the integration of general education and study in the major so that they form coherent "pathways for learning" for students (AAC&U, 2002). Sequencing learning goals, not simply courses, enables colleges and universities to determine when particular courses or course modules should be required. The curriculum at King's College (Pennsylvania), for example, integrates general education and major courses so that students can repeatedly work to develop skills like writing while learning the subject matter of their field (AAC&U, 2002).

Faculty Involvement in Program Planning

Faculty tend to engage sporadically in program planning—despite the opportunities it can provide for colleagueship and professional collaboration. Academic values such as professional autonomy, some conjecture, tend to focus faculty members' attention on their own instructional responsibilities rather than on program-level curricular planning. In the Curriculum Leadership for Undergraduate Education (CLUE) study, Briggs, Stark, and Rowland-Poplawski interviewed 127 department heads and faculty in forty-four academic departments nominated by their chief academic officers for their success in curriculum planning at the program level. The interviews were designed to elicit "indigenous" descriptions of continuous curriculum planning, as well as to gather information about department roles, processes, and attitudes. The inductive analysis of the interview data produced twenty indicators, which were classified into four broad categories of continuous curriculum planning practices. These four broad criteria focus on (a) the frequency and continuous nature of curriculum planning, (b) program awareness and responsiveness to influences on curricula, (c) faculty participation and teamwork in curriculum planning, and (d) the use of evaluation data for developmental and adaptive change. A comparison of programs that scored in the top and bottom quartiles on continuous curriculum planning revealed that, even among these programs already identified as noteworthy for their planning successes, academic programs in the top quartile were more likely to

- Consider a wide array of curricular issues in their planning process;
- Make an ongoing effort to increase departmental expertise in curricular matters;
- Behave as a curriculum discourse community within the department;
- Participate in curriculum related discourse communities beyond the department. (Briggs & others, 2002, p. 379; reprinted with permission of the authors.)

College-Wide Planning

The diversity of higher education institutions in the United States makes it difficult to generalize about how academic plans are constructed at the "college" level. For example, a college can be a small independent institution that provides either very general (for example, liberal arts) or very specialized (for example, technical or religious) education. It can be a specialized unit, such as a professional school, within a larger complex university. It can be a for-profit enterprise that serves primarily adult and part-time students. The meaning of "college" in each context will determine the types of institution-wide academic plans that are likely to be considered and implemented. To simplify our discussion as we consider academic plans created by and for colleges, we differentiate between two very different settings: a small liberal arts college and a school (such as a school of business or architecture) within a university.

In both examples, a diverse group of faculty members, other experts, administrators, and students tend to be involved in college-wide curriculum planning. In a small liberal arts college, the entire faculty and administration often debate changes in college-wide plans or mission in a committee of the whole. In contrast, in a large unit within a university, plans may be formulated by a committee of respected faculty and presented to a representative governing body that acts on behalf of the faculty. In large institutions where general faculty meetings are sparsely attended, the relevant points of view may be distilled in meeting minutes or bulletins from a committee, through the campus newspaper, and even in student debates. Some lament a loss of faculty community and collective faculty responsibility for the entire curriculum in large institutions and attribute the downward delegation of substantial curricular decision making to faculty members' "overspecialization." In contrast, some universities take pride in placing academic decision making at the grassroots level, seeking to ensure that faculty members retain their interest in and responsibility for the college-wide curriculum. Whatever the cause, delegation is surely why many decisions are located at the program level.

College-wide planning has four purposes: (a) adjusting academic programs to be more congruent with mission, (b) establishing (or adjusting) mission, (c) modifying academic programs to be more responsive to the changing external environment, and (d) joining the bandwagon of innovation. In each case except the first, the impetus for change is predominantly external. Of course, more than one of these purposes can act concurrently.

The impetus to bring an academic program into better alignment with the institutional mission is often internal to the college but outside a specific program. For instance, the faculty or administration may conclude that the liberal arts college curriculum includes too many options or that programs introduced by the business college to serve new clientele are too expensive to maintain. A review of college-wide mission, however, can also be an effort to call faculty attention to the institution's mission or to reaffirm it. These kinds of adjustments are equally possible in small institutions and larger ones. In a small or specialized college, the process is likely to include a broader range of campus stakeholders.

When a college undertakes a total revision of its program, makes a major change in its mission, or tries to achieve a more distinctive environment, the process tends to attract public and professional attention and, temporarily at least, outside funds. Prominent examples include the efforts of Alverno College (Wisconsin) to create and maintain an abilities-based curriculum with a strong emphasis on student assessment; the development of interdisciplinary learning communities of faculty and students at Evergreen State College (Washington); and the creation of a project-based, design-focused engineering curriculum at the College of Engineering (MA), funded by the W.F. Olin Foundation. When innovative academic plans are developed without meaningful faculty involvement in curriculum development, they may be short-lived; yet, in a few cases, institutional survival requires substantial changes. The significant refocusing of the mission and curriculum at Olivet College, which was troubled by a racial incident in 1992, provides a case study of a comprehensive curricular response to an institutional crisis (Walters, 2001/2002).

In large universities, sweeping curricular changes may be discouraged by organizational complexity, faculty size, entrenched bureaucracy, and many required levels of curriculum approval within the institution. Such change efforts can be time-consuming and divisive: the multi-year efforts to revise the general education curricula at Harvard and Stanford Universities are prime examples. Yet, external influences, such as public critiques or data showing that students are not well prepared for careers, can also spur change, especially in colleges that comprise fairly autonomous large units within the university. In the field of engineering, employers' concerns about the lack of professional skills such as teamwork and communication in new graduates stimulated a radical overhaul of accreditation standards that had significant curricular implications (Prados, Peterson, & Lattuca, 2005). Similarly, in the field of accounting, concerns of employer firms stimulated broad curriculum change. Through the national Accounting Education Change Commission, the profession established standards and provided seed grants for programs willing to innovate in reaching these standards.

Occasionally, internal groups stimulate large-scale curricular change. In the 1980s and 1990s, faculty and students seeking greater attention to diversity pressed colleges and universities nationwide to adopt general education requirements focused on developing students' awareness of gender, race, ethnicity, and other differences. Changes in the college-wide curriculum, however, tend to result from "the bandwagon effect" rather than from a systematic assessment of the need for new academic plans. Colleges and universities tend to adopt curriculum plans that peer institutions or programs have implemented. An example was the rapid expansion of the interim term or "January term" developed among liberal arts colleges to allow students to explore topics not in the regular programs. The bandwagon effect, then, is not necessarily bad. Concepts such as active learning, classroom research, and the use of technology in instruction gained national attention because of the efforts of a few innovation leaders.

Small size, a strong sense of community, and a governance system that encourages involvement will foster participation in curricular change typical of small colleges. In contrast, in universities where faculty are more oriented to research than teaching, have little sense of the larger community, and a decentralized system of governance, curriculum planning is often laissez faire. Many large universities are slower to consider broad changes in general education requirements and to initiate assessment procedures than are small colleges (Ory & Parker, 1989). Structural revisions, credit hour adjustments, and calendar revamping tend to dominate the planning process at the college level (Bergquist, Gould, & Greenberg, 1981).

Systematic Design Models

Some believe that college and university professors defend the privacy of the classroom vigorously, plan and teach their courses as they were taught, and oppose new ideas about curriculum or instruction. Based on this false stereotype, curriculum planning in higher education is seen as unequivocally "scholar-dominated" and irrevocably stagnant. During our varied curricular change and research projects, we have found this picture to be inaccurate. Many instructors believe curriculum decisions are important and are reflective about the academic plans they create; those interviewed in the course and program planning studies welcomed the opportunity to discuss these topics. Merely asking about goals and strategies for course and program planning provided an opportunity for faculty members to crystallize their thoughts and consider new alternatives.

Just as our interviews stimulated thought among instructors, collaboration has strong potential to encourage improvement by introducing new ideas and expertise through collegial exchange. One study of curriculum planning efforts revealed that collaborative planning efforts have greater potential for success when faculty approach their task as an opportunity to learn from one another, to gather information and data, and to consult with colleagues with different expertise and experience (Evensen & Lattuca, 2005). Collaborative discussions about course and program design may also be an effective route for instructional development; faculty may be less likely to feel that their personal style is at issue when they discuss curricular decisions rather than teaching behavior.

College faculty members do not typically read much about the educational process (Lattuca, Terenzini, & Volkwein, 2006; Stark & others, 1990), but they are selective in adopting new practices. For example, instructors in different fields have used Bloom's taxonomy of educational objectives (1956), William Perry's work on students' intellectual development (1970), Wilbert McKeachie's "teaching tips" (2006), and Cross and Angelo's classroom assessment techniques (Cross & Angelo,1998; Angelo & Cross, 2002). New educational ideas and methods slowly find their way into curricula through the work of accepted translators such as these authors. For example, the work in the mid-1980s by Stark, Lowther, and others on integrating liberal arts and professional study has been regularly used by faculty members since its publication, but a new interest in it has developed only recently. Increased emphasis on improving undergraduate education may accelerate the dissemination and acceptance of educational ideas and theories, but a wider variety of mechanisms is needed to translate new ideas, to circulate them among faculty members, and to encourage their use.

Exposure to new ideas expands instructors' capacities to think in new ways about curricular design and increase their options (Schubert, 1986, p. 299), but relatively few works addressing course and program design are specifically intended for college faculty. Writings by Robert Diamond (2008) and L. Dee Fink (2003) are two exceptions, written expressly for postsecondary audiences. Materials prepared for elementary and secondary educators (Posner & Rudnitsky, 2006) can also be useful to college instructors if they are adapted to personal course planning styles. In the following sections, we explore models that are well known, tested, and relatively enduring—four models at the course level (Diamond; Fink; Posner & Rudnitsky; Wiggins & McTighe) and one at the program level (Diamond).

Course Design

Most course design models rest on a few common assumptions and share some common elements. For example, they stress the importance of course goals in the design process. George Posner and Alan Rudnitsky's central message is to "teach with a purpose" (2006, p. 183), and their model includes two key components, a "rationale" and a set of "intended learning outcomes" (ILOs), which guide the planning process. The rationale states the general goal that the course is intended to address, while the intended learning outcomes state more specifically what students are to learn. ILOs convert disciplinary concepts to be taught into measurable course objectives. For example, in a history course, the instructor may create an ILO that includes knowing the causes of a particular event. Grant Wiggins and Jay McTighe's (2005) popular concept of "backwards design" shares the same premise: instructors cannot design a curriculum without first establishing what it is that students should know and be able to do at the end of a course or program. Focusing first on the desired results, Wiggins and McTighe argue, helps course planners avoid the "twin sins of design"—activity-focused teaching and coverage-focused teaching—both of which focus on teaching instead of learning. Whether applied at the course or program level, Diamond's model is similarly goal-driven, requiring faculty to state general course and instructional goals. According to Diamond, college and university faculty either resent writing learning objectives or write far too many of them, including trivial ones. In his process, instructors instead answer the question: "If I'm your student, what do I have to do to convince you that I'm where you want me to be at the end of this lesson, unit, or course?" (1998, pp. 134–135). In this way, the design of evaluation procedures occurs at the beginning of the planning process, rather than at the end.

The models provided by Posner and Rudnitsky (2006) and Diamond (2008) have a good deal in common with the academic plan concept itself, specifying the decisions instructors must make in constructing such a plan (see Table 5.6).

TABLE 5.6. COURSE PLANNING STEPS, ACCORDING TO POSNER AND RUDNITSKY

1. Jot down ideas.
2. Give the course a title.
3. Make a tentative outline of what you want to include.
4. Make a list of Intended Learning Outcomes (ILOs).
5. Categorize ILOs as either skills or understandings.
6. Develop central questions addressed by the ILOs.
7. Expand the ILOs based on consideration of student entry skills, prior knowledge, and background.
8. Identify needed new vocabulary.
9. Construct conceptual trees for the concepts embedded in the ILOs.
10. Construct flowcharts for the skills to be developed.
11. State and clarify the rationale for the course.
12. Cluster the ILOs into units of appropriate size (consider pragmatic factors).
13. Prioritize the ILOs.
14. Choose sequencing principles.
15. Choose teaching strategies.
16. Plan course evaluation.

From Posner, George J., & Alan N. Rudnitsky. *Course Design: A Guide to Curriculum Development for Teachers (7th ed.)* Published by Allyn & Bacon/Merrill Education, Boston, MA. Copyright ©2000 by Pearson Education. Adapted by permission of the publisher.

In both approaches, content (what is to be learned) generally derives from an accepted body of knowledge. Both additionally assume that the course planner has sufficient knowledge of the projected course content.

Posner and Rudnitsky suggest that planners begin by listing ideas about content that should be covered in a course, but they encourage instructors to state intended learning outcomes as the ideas develop for three crucial reasons: (a) to guide instructional planning, (b) to communicate the learning goals to important others (for example, students, the public), and (c) to provide a basis for developing indicators of success. The learning outcomes desired in college may be cognitive (knowledge of principles, facts, concepts), affective (attitudes or emotions), or psychomotor skills (physical abilities, such as manipulating a tool).

Posner and Rudnitsky divide planning into three decision areas: (a) deciding *what* is to be learned, (b) developing *why* it is to be learned, and (c) deciding *how to facilitate* the learning. College and university instructors may tend to skip the second step, assuming that learning the field is justifiable on its own grounds, but pressing instructors to be explicit about their rationale for learning and their governing beliefs about educational purpose may create greater awareness of implicit assumptions that guide course and program planning. Research suggests that beginning with learning outcomes may be difficult for college and university instructors, who tend to focus first on the concepts and principles of their field when planning a course. The authors of the curriculum design models we discuss here all acknowledge that course planning takes place most naturally in an iterative rather than a linear fashion. To accommodate this, Posner and Rudnitsky's model specifically recommends that planners reconsider and revise their intended learning outcomes as they rethink their rationales later in their planning.

Posner and Rudnitsky also recommend that instructors develop explicit conceptual maps that relate discipline ideas to one another and create flowcharts that demonstrate the hierarchical or nonhierarchical relationships of skills and concepts necessary to learning. Although the Posner and Rudnitsky work was originally designed for K-12 teachers, Stark has successfully used concept maps in workshops for medical school faculty members at the University of Michigan.

Fink's "integrated model" recommends similar strategies for course design: defining learning outcomes, considering situational factors that influence the course design process, and connecting outcomes, teaching activities, and assessment. What distinguishes Fink's model is his specification of "significant" learning goals that guide faculty to consider more than the cognitive domain as they plan courses. In his judgment, contemporary collegiate learning goals, such as leadership, ethics, interpersonal skills, and lifelong learning, cannot be adequately addressed by most learning taxonomies. His alternative taxonomy (shown in Figure 5.2) includes the following six goals: foundational knowledge, application, integration, the human dimension, caring, and learning how to learn. A course that promotes all six kinds of learning will, he argues, result in a significant learning experience because it will take students beyond content mastery and help them integrate their learning. Integration can occur, Fink argues, because each kind of learning in his taxonomy is related to the others: achieving any one will increase the possibility of achieving the other kinds. This synergy, he further suggests, enhances the achievement of significant learning by students.

Our model of academic planning differs in some respects from the models we have been discussing. Posner and Rudnitsky view curriculum development and instructional planning as separate processes. In their terms, a curriculum is a set of intentions; curriculum development results in a design that specifies a set of intended learning outcomes. Instructional activities seek to produce, stimulate, or facilitate learning, and instructional development is a process resulting in a plan outlining the intended process of instruction, that is, what is to be done or what is supposed to happen during the learning process. In contrast, we consider curriculum design an integral part of a deliberate process to promote learning and thus subsume instructional choices within curriculum development.

We also differ in our ideas about evaluation. For Posner and Rudnitsky (and also for Wiggins and McTighe), evaluation of a course design focuses on measurement of achievement of the *actual* learning outcomes that correspond to the

FIGURE 5.2. FINK'S TAXONOMY OF SIGNIFICANT LEARNING

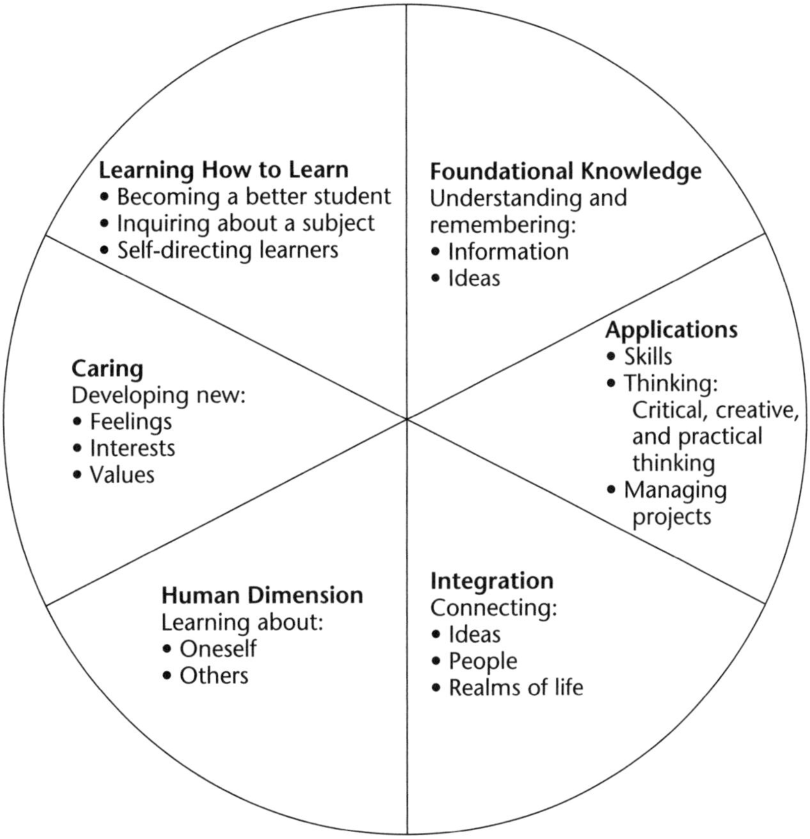

Learning How to Learn
• Becoming a better student
• Inquiring about a subject
• Self-directing learners

Foundational Knowledge
Understanding and remembering:
• Information
• Ideas

Applications
• Skills
• Thinking:
  Critical, creative, and practical thinking
• Managing projects

Caring
Developing new:
• Feelings
• Interests
• Values

Human Dimension
Learning about:
• Oneself
• Others

Integration
Connecting:
• Ideas
• People
• Realms of life

Reprinted with permission from *Peer Review, 9*(1). Copyright 2007 by the Association of American Colleges and Universities.

previously specified *intended* learning outcomes. We view evaluation more broadly, including both assessment of student learning and course/program evaluation that leads to the improvement of an academic plan. We agree, however, that course designers should think early about student assessment. Wiggins and McTighe suggest it as the second step in their course design process. Then they ask instructors to determine what will count as "acceptable evidence" of student understanding and proficiency. Course planners, they suggest, must learn to think "like an assessor" (2005, p. 18). Only after desired results and appropriate evidence of learning are specified can planners think effectively about instructional experiences and approaches.

In the end, we believe the specific framework used to guide course design activities is less important than the process of engaging in reflection and analysis. Reflection on the design of academic plans has two great benefits. First, it challenges instructors to identify appropriate content and effective instructional methods, given explicit purposes, a set of intended outcomes, and a view of how achievement will be recognized. In addition, it promotes attention to the relationships between faculty planning decisions and the learning styles and strategies of students. These kinds of general design processes have the advantage of preserving faculty autonomy and creativity by leaving the determination of a rationale and content base up to the individual professor. Moreover, they reveal that the steps in planning also are varied. The goal is not conformity, but rather to establish a comfortable but systematic approach to course design.

Program Design

Diamond's model is designed for use at either the course or program level. It is valuable because it outlines how instructional experts and other "facilitators" can help instructors focus on important questions and "ideal designs," then adjust for their local environment. In this guide to program design, planners identify general instructional goals (such as the competencies students are expected to achieve in the major), as well as more specific course goals and unit-by-unit objectives. They next gather information, including data on the characteristics of their students (backgrounds, abilities, and priorities), the educational priorities of the institution or program, and the requirements of the field (for example, the academic requirements set by accrediting agencies). Diamond's extended curriculum design process asks faculty members to take into account the kinds of institutional, unit-level, and external influences we identified in the academic plan model.

Diamond's approach is team-based. Professors are the content experts, representing the major academic areas of concern in a program. A team will ideally include experts in instructional design, technology, and assessment, as well as the facilitator who attends to the design process. This process facilitator can be an instructor from another field (to maximize his or her ability to check assumptions and suggest alternatives) or a staff member from an academic-support unit that assists instructors in their teaching. Diamond recommends that the facilitator, whether faculty or staff, have experience in the design process and an understanding of teaching, learning, technology, and assessment. The facilitator helps instructors to focus on content and structure as they work to ensure that assumptions are questioned and alternative approaches are examined. The facilitator, as well as information gathered in the planning process about students, resources, institutional and program priorities, can reveal that perceived limitations to an "ideal design" may be more imagined than real.

The instructional developer's role is to help the instructor think in new ways about program structure, the process of setting objectives, and the simultaneous choice of evaluation strategies to determine success. In this approach, the design process ends with the choice of instructional activities and the production of instructional materials to facilitate learning. Instructors who have successfully completed this process have carefully diagnosed student needs and attitudes, have consciously assessed availability of needed resources and facilities, and have determined how much administrative support for new activities they will receive. They have considered future directions in their discipline, included diagnosis and remediation for students with inadequate preparations, and stated clear evaluation criteria. Many will have developed a working knowledge of the research on teaching, learning, and assessment to inform course design decisions.

As instructors conceptualize academic designs, one idea that needs special emphasis at the program level is coherence. Just as conceptual maps can show students how to integrate ideas within courses, conceptual maps of program content can reveal a program faculty's view of the connections among courses. Just as the sequencing of ideas in a course should attune students to the relationships among those ideas, the sequencing of courses in a program serves to help students conceptualize their fields of study. Diamond's model intends to produce a cohesive curriculum, beginning with an institutional statement of goals and ending with the assessment of student skills both prior to and after graduation.

Although each has excellent qualities, the models we have discussed are fairly elaborate and can require considerable time and resources. Perhaps the simplest framework for systematic program design is a set of questions that instructors can ask as they create an academic plan at the program level. We propose four questions that instructors find hard to answer when working in groups, and thus tend to omit:

- What are our specific purpose(s) and learning objectives?
- What is best sequence for teaching the content and/or skills identified?
- What is the relationship among the concepts to be taught, and how are those concepts related to student understanding and experience?
- What is the best way to evaluate the success of the plan?

College-Wide Design

These methods for increasing curricular coherence may be extended to the academic plan for an entire college. For example, an institution's educational purposes and desired learning outcomes for students suggest ways to select and arrange its general education program. We also find Posner's (1974) classification of curricular content along two dimensions—commonality and temporality—helpful in designing cross-disciplinary programs such as general education.

Commonality refers to the similarity of curriculum units. Some pairs of topics are largely unrelated in purpose or content, such as studying Spanish grammar and studying geometric proofs. In contrast, some curriculum units involve a single purpose or content repeatedly, such as learning Spanish vocabulary or practicing a musical instrument. Between these two extremes are pairs of elements that are neither identical nor entirely unrelated; rather they are related in some identifiable way, such as studying English history and studying English literature from the same period; or studying taxonomic classifications of plants and similar classifications for animals. The closer the relationship, the higher the commonality.

Temporality refers to the relationship of curricular units in time. For example, one may consecutively study U.S. history 1800 to 1865, and then U.S. history 1865 to 1900. These subjects also may be studied concurrently, or their sequence may be interrupted by other activities. The closer the time periods in which they are studied, the higher the temporality.

Posner asserts that a curriculum in which units, courses, or programs are organized with both high commonality and high temporality is a curriculum with high structure. In contrast, in a low-structure curriculum, elements would be both unrelated in time and have little commonality. Colleges with fragmented general education programs allow students to take a series of unrelated courses according to their own time frames; no attempt is made to link these elements. Colleges with limited distribution requirements may attempt to increase either commonality or temporality, or both, in the patterns of study students elect. Finally, colleges with deliberately designed core curricula may achieve both high commonality and high temporality. Focusing general education discussions on these questions of commonality and temporality can help instructors avoid ideological debates about the nature and timing of the core program.

One mechanism for creating commonality is to link content courses and skills courses in developmental education programs. A developmental writing course may be linked with a general education course so that exercises to improve writing can focus on assignments in, for example, a required history course. Clustered courses provide another example of attention to commonality and temporality. At Babson College (Massachusetts), which seeks to integrate liberal and professional studies, a management major simultaneously takes courses in business law, history, and accounting that deal with overlapping ideas, time periods, or issues. Other models, such as learning communities, often require substantive integration of content between or among courses. Freshman interest groups link courses around pre-major topics, enrolling cohorts of twenty or twenty-five in the same large courses to provide a first-year support system. Federated learning communities connect more advanced students in courses with an overarching theme (Gabelnick, MacGregor, Matthews, & Smith, 1990). The coordinated studies model, which is the basis for the curriculum at Evergreen State College, replaces separate courses with a fully integrated program of courses for a term or an academic year.

Alverno College (Wisconsin) offers an instructive example of a systematic, college-wide curriculum design. Beginning in the 1970s and continuing to the present, Alverno's faculty members have carefully and reflectively approached the task of developing and improving their curriculum, which is focused on comprehensive assessment of key student learning outcomes. Alverno's extensive experience in college-wide curriculum development and renewal demonstrates that the process both depends on—and can help build—a positive institutional climate and sense of academic community (Mentkowski & Associates, 2000).

Just as there are few sources of information describing the creation of college-wide academic plans, few frameworks are available to make college-wide design more systematic. With modifications, some of the suggestions we provided for program planning can be applied to college-wide curricula. The focus on student learning outcomes in all the design models we have examined remains an important element of a college-level curriculum design, and the dimensions of commonality and temporality are useful in thinking about sequence. The development of ideal curricula, as recommended by Diamond, can help institutions or units examine alternatives and develop realistic plans based on existing constraints. We will discuss recommended change processes for achieving such results in Chapter 10.

Sharing Responsibility for Curriculum Design

Whether they work alone or in groups to create academic plans—at the course, program, or college level—instructors tend to think first about their academic fields. As we move from the course level, where faculty members typically work alone, to the program and college levels where faculty must work together, differences in educational beliefs emerge, group dynamics become more important, and pragmatic concerns become more potent. As programs and institutions pursue educational improvements, a balanced participation of experts in course and program planning is likely to prove fruitful. An effective process might include greater participation by different individuals who are knowledgeable about how students learn, instructional design, and assessment. Recognition of the contributions these experts have to offer would open the varied and extensive literature relevant to curriculum planning to curriculum decision-makers. We suggest in Chapter 6 that focusing on learning and the learner as well as the academic field presents possibilities for achieving increased success.

CHAPTER SIX

LEARNERS

The capabilities, preparation, motivation, effort, and goals of the students in their classrooms and programs all may influence instructors as they plan. Few instructors, however, systematically consider learners' needs, abilities, and goals as they develop courses. Yet research on learning suggests this is a critical dimension of effective curriculum design. In this chapter, therefore, we draw on research to describe how instructors consider students in their planning and also examine scholarship on learning that can help instructors design academic plans that promote learning. We will return to this research on learning in the next chapter as we discuss how instructors can use it more purposefully to select instructional processes.

When discussing how academic fields influence curriculum planning, we linked three elements of the academic plan—purpose, content, and sequence—acknowledging empirical evidence that instructors in the same academic field tend to hold similar ideas about educational purposes and to arrange course content in similar ways. Now we point to another linkage between elements of an academic plan—that is, between instructors' purposes and their attention to learners' individual educational goals and abilities. This relationship is highlighted in Figure 6.1. Our discussion of the role of students' purposes in learning explicitly acknowledges the possible differences between the goals of learners and the goals of faculty members. If not recognized and addressed, such differences can diminish the effectiveness of academic plans.

FIGURE 6.1. ACADEMIC PLANS IN SOCIOCULTURAL CONTEXT: FOCUS ON LEARNERS

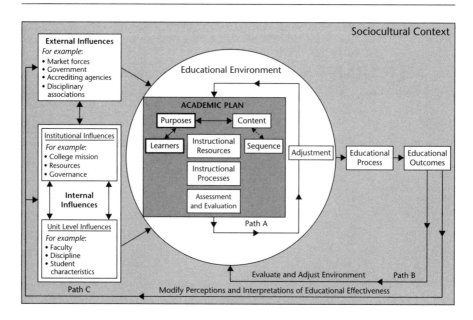

As we show in Figure 6.1, both learners' purposes and instructors' views of them are affected by influences external to the college or university. Variations in students' purposes reflect both the cultural diversity of learners in higher education and variations in other characteristics such as their academic preparation, prior knowledge, educational experiences, and academic and career goals. For the 37 percent of students older than traditional college age (18 to 24 years) (*Chronicle of Higher Education Almanac*, 2007) and the 37 percent who attend part-time (Chen, 2007), external influences may remain very strong through the collegiate experience. For traditional-age students who reside on campuses, influences inside the college—from faculty members, other students, and the educational environments in which they study—may be more salient than external influences during the college years. Our discussion of learners and learning includes both the psychological and sociocultural dimensions of learning and thus provides a comprehensive picture of learning in college.

At the course and program levels, variations in students' interests, preparation, and learning styles present challenges to effective academic planning. Too often, however, learners are not consciously considered at either level of academic planning. Viewing the curriculum as an academic plan makes the learner's presence visible and may encourage educators to focus more systematic attention on learner needs and characteristics.

Learner Influences on Course Planning

Faculty members in most fields report that several influences outweigh that of learners in course planning (Stark & others, 1990). These dominant influences include faculty members' beliefs about educational purpose (the knowledge, skills, and attitudes to be learned), content (the subject matter of learning), and sequence (the arrangement of content to be learned). Not only did most faculty members in the NCRIPTAL course planning studies mention these dominant influences more frequently in interviews, they elaborated on them more fully than they did on the influence of learners (Stark & others, 1988). Although 69 percent of faculty surveyed said that they always considered students at some point when creating plans for introductory courses, only 15 percent said that they thought of students first (Stark & others, 1990).

As instructors described the way they planned courses, they spoke of prototypic groups of learners that they kept in mind. Most based their notions about learners on their past classes; some made assumptions about learner goals and characteristics. Those whose plans were based on untested assumptions often reported rude shocks when their ideals were not met. For example, before relying on current events in courses, instructors will want to check their assumptions that students read a newspaper online or listen to daily newscasts. Those who assume that their students are essentially similar from year to year may also be operating on shaky ground, as student profiles are changing rapidly.

Backgrounds

When discussing the influence of students in course planning, few instructors in the NCRIPTAL studies mentioned considering such demographic characteristics as gender and ethnicity. Instructors seemed wary of appearing to stereotype students based on fixed characteristics. The exceptions were instructors who believed that a neutral attitude toward gender, ethnicity, and culture neglected to address important differences among students. Despite ongoing publicity about the role of students' prior experiences and backgrounds in learning, and the development of "culturally responsive" teaching methods (Gay, 2002; Ladson-Billings, 1995; Murrell, 2002) that show instructors how to accommodate student differences, few instructors report actually adjusting their teaching strategies in response to a more diverse student population (Maruyama & Moreno, 2000). Faculty members in the NCRIPTAL studies did frequently mention age as an influence on their planning, noting that traditional-age college students lacked maturity in dealing with particular topics, while older students were strongly motivated but often lacking in self-confidence and pressured by family and work demands.

Preparation and Ability

Faculty members in the NCRIPTAL studies stressed the influence of student preparation on their course plans, but usually avoided commenting on student "abilities" or "capabilities." In fact, some of those interviewed preferred not to receive information about students' previous academic records because it might influence their thinking about students' capabilities. They feared possible cultural biases in traditional measures of intelligence and aptitude, as well as conclusions hastily drawn and reported by previous instructors.

Research shows that the ways in which instructors think about students' preparation vary with institutional type. National data from the Higher Education Research Institute at the University of California at Los Angeles indicated that 40 percent of faculty in four-year institutions but only 20 percent of those in two-year institutions agreed with the statement that "faculty feel that most students are well prepared" (Lindholm, Szelényi, Hurtado, & Korn, 2005). About one-third of faculty in four-year institutions, compared to more than 60 percent of those in two-year institutions, said that "most of the students I teach lack the basic skills for college level work." Faculty at private four-year institutions were much more positive in their assessments of student preparation: more than 65 percent reported that faculty thought most students were well prepared and only 16 percent thought most students lacked basic skills.

The NCRIPTAL studies identified substantial disciplinary differences in faculty members' impressions of student preparedness. Generally, faculty teaching composition, mathematics, or literature in general education programs viewed their students as reasonably well prepared, even when the preparation was not as strong as they might wish. In contrast, instructors who taught fields typically not stressed in secondary school, such as fine arts, sociology, and business, more frequently judged their students to be underprepared. The faculty members interviewed believed they were sensitive to the limited preparation of students in such basic skills as writing, reading, listening, and numerical literacy. These views of preparation may be based on realities or on the different expectations created by institutional characteristics such as admissions selectivity or national reputation.

Instructors are not always confident about their ability to deal with underpreparation once they recognize it. Few faculty members interviewed or surveyed for the NCRIPTAL studies reported that they knew or had planned their courses based on theoretical or empirical knowledge of how people learn. But they felt that they had developed, over the years, a sense of what worked and did not work for different types of students. They used this practical experience in constructing academic plans aimed at students with average preparation.

Most faculty members created course plans by establishing content goals first. They then considered students' preparation, adjusted content, and made sequencing decisions (Stark & others, 1988). The process, however, varied by discipline. Faculty members in fields that emphasize learning concepts, principles, and other foundational knowledge were most concerned with adequacy of student preparation. Ironically, their tendency to arrange content sequentially may have reduced their ability to adjust to differences among students, for example, by pacing the course differently. In contrast, faculty in fields where content could be arranged in many different ways tended to view students' personal and intellectual development as their primary teaching goal. In interviews, these instructors often remarked on the challenges of working with students at different levels of preparation and frequently noted their satisfaction when students accomplished more than they had anticipated.

Goals

Students today are clearly interested in career preparation. About 70 percent of first-year students nationwide say that two of their motivations for attending college are to get training for a specific job and to make money. Yet, about 70 percent of female first-year students, and about 60 percent of male first-year students, also say that they are attending college to gain a general education and an appreciation of ideas. Roughly 50 percent of male first-year students and 60 percent of female first-year students also report an interest in preparing for graduate study (Pryor, Hurtado, Saenz, Korn, Santos, & Korn, 2006).

Instructors in the NCRIPTAL studies viewed students' intellectual goals as important—in line with national data showing that more than 80 percent of instructors across two- and four-year institutions believe that promoting students' intellectual development is a high priority at their institutions (Lindholm, Szelényi, Hurtado, & Korn, 2005). Fewer reported that they were influenced by students' life or career goals. As usual, differences occurred by type of institution and academic field. Faculty in arts and science fields saw students' career goals as minimally relevant to their course planning, but as might be expected, more than 80 percent of the pre-professional faculty surveyed reported being strongly influenced by students' career goals (Stark & others, 1990). Faculty in the most selective colleges said they were minimally influenced by students' life, career, and educational goals, while faculty in the least selective colleges reported greater influence. The influence of "non-academic" characteristics such as students' goals is relevant to planning a course, yet we note that faculty in the NCRIPTAL studies varied in their willingness to find common ground with students. While some talked about identifying common goals when creating academic plans, others believed that accommodating student goals was "coddling" and inappropriate at the college level.

Effort and Involvement

Most instructors say their academic plans are influenced by anticipated levels of student effort. Typically, faculty reported that students in their general education classes exhibited a "modest amount" of effort. Just over 21 percent of faculty in the course planning survey thought their students expended a "great deal" of effort; nearly 12 percent thought they demonstrated "very little or relatively little" effort (Stark & others, 1990, p. 82). More than 80 percent of the faculty we surveyed said that they tried to find ways to motivate or interest students to help them learn. The form, intensity, and frequency of these attempts varied widely, ranging from holding extra review sessions to requiring students to submit daily homework assignments. Some faculty members who strongly criticized students' lack of effort often indicated they were resigned to it as a "fact of life." Yet the students' quality of effort may be the single most influential variable in accounting for students' progress toward educational outcomes (Astin, 1993; Pace, 1980; Kuh & others, 2005).

Many of the faculty teaching general education courses who were interviewed for the NCRIPTAL studies said they recognized students who were disengaged, even in large lecture classes, and attempted to capture their attention. Some tried to stimulate the inattentive or unprepared by calling on them unexpectedly in class. Some asked students who were not putting forth acceptable effort to visit them during office hours. Others motivated students by using collaborative approaches to learning to create a sense of personal responsibility. The most common strategy that faculty teaching general education courses used to motivate students, however, was grades. Some regularly reminded students that grades would be calculated soon or discussed the weight of a particular exam in the final grade; others devised elaborate systems of bonus points to stimulate students to work hard. Relatively few faculty interviewed believed that students would put forth maximum effort in the absence of extrinsic incentives such as grades (Stark & others, 1988).

In contrast to the need for extrinsic motivating strategies mentioned by general education faculty, professional program faculty felt it easier to capitalize on students' existing motivation by involving them in practical problems related to the career field. In the interviews, faculty in fields like business and nursing, for example, reported that visits with practicing professionals, field trips, observations in work settings, and discussions of current events in the field linked faculty members and students in common purposes (Stark & others, 1988). Scheduling such activities early in the program also helped students know whether they want to continue in a field of study.

Most instructors in the NCRIPTAL interviews said that they formally assessed student satisfaction only at term's end. They also delayed using this feedback to make adjustments until the next course offering. A few faculty members, however, described elaborate evaluation mechanisms employed as their courses proceeded.

These included using frequent "one-minute papers," journals, or student commit-tees (usually in very large courses) to keep them informed of the status of student effort, motivation, and satisfaction.

Learner Influences on Program Planning

In program planning, decisions about educational objectives and choice of specific course sequences should take into account students' needs, abilities, prior preparation and knowledge, and future plans. In a study of colleges and universities that were particularly effective in encouraging active student engagement in academic life, George Kuh and associates (2005) found that instructors used data on their students to inform their decision making and to foster higher levels of student involvement. Yet, program faculty in most colleges seldom collect such data systematically, and most seem to make decisions regarding the content and course sequence for majors based partly on images of ideal students and partly on informal contact with current students. Some programs do, however, collect data regarding student satisfaction, which may include information about the degree of congruence between student and program goals. Many programs monitor student enrollments in courses and program sequences as well, interpreting low enrollments as indications of student dissatisfaction and thus the need to change some element of the academic plan.

Usually, there are at least three groups of students about whom information is needed and from whom opinions might be sought: (a) students majoring in the field to seek a related job after graduation or because of their intrinsic interest in the subject; (b) students majoring in related fields who require a few interme-diate or advanced courses; and (c) students intending to pursue graduate study whom faculty members see as future scholars in their field. In interviews with faculty members about program plans, NCRIPTAL researchers found that plans frequently were designed to assist students aiming for graduate study, even when very few students had pursued such study recently. Programs targeted at the most academically oriented students may be more focused on the scholarly aspects of the field than the majority of student majors believe they need. As a result, sub-stantial efforts may be made to recruit students who will fit an existing plan rather than making adjustments in the program to fit current student characteristics. In two-year colleges, a similar disjunction exists when faculty aim programs at students who plan to transfer to an upper-division program and pay less atten-tion to those with career or shorter-term educational goals. Even in professional fields, differences in faculty and student beliefs about the orientation of programs occur. Faculty members may dwell on theoretical aspects of professional practice, while students are eager to practice skills they anticipate needing on the job.

Such incongruities in educational objectives may produce positive outcomes from an instructor's viewpoint, since research shows that, over time, students come to think more like their instructors and other students in their field of study (Smart, Feldman, & Ethington, 2000). From the student's viewpoint, however, there may be a negative outcome if the discrepancy between the need to prepare for post-college employment and the program plan is too great.

The separation of learners from academic plans at the program level is exacerbated by the physical and philosophical separation between academic and student affairs staff in colleges and universities (Boyer, 1990; Garland & Grace, 1993; Kuh & others, 2005). It is unusual for instructors in academic programs to collaborate with professional student affairs staff to gather information for use in designing academic plans, but such linkages can be quite useful. For example, staff from the career development office might provide data on first job placements for particular majors, as well as career trajectories and patterns that program faculty can use to assess the curriculum's ability to prepare students for particular kinds of work experiences. In a few colleges and universities, student affairs professionals contribute to, or serve as instructors for, first-year seminar programs. This kind of collaboration encourages information sharing and could provide faculty members with a different perspective on college students, their needs, their challenges, and their motivations.

Program faculty members are often unaware that their college institutional research office can also provide information on student characteristics, course-taking patterns, and satisfaction. Although the type of data collected varies, these offices are a potential source of information for program planning. In addition, hundreds of institutions participate in the Cooperative Institutional Research Program (CIRP), which can provide program faculty with information on their students' goals, personal commitments, and activities on campus and off. Since the 1960s, the annual CIRP studies, conducted by the Higher Education Research Institute at the University of California, Los Angeles, have tracked students' reasons for attending college and self-reported preparation and interests, as well as other information. The CIRP survey also gathers information after students have graduated. Since this information can be linked directly to various elements of academic plans, it constitutes important outcome information with considerable promise for educational improvement in an institution.

Learner Influences on College Planning

At the college-wide level, students' influence on the curriculum plan is usually indirect because the institutional mission already states what a college or university believes is important for students to learn. Some colleges, however, are inclined to respond to students' characteristics and needs in college-wide planning. These include community colleges, those that are working hard to adjust to substantial shifts in enrollments, and for-profit institutions that depend on student interest to thrive commercially.

Ironically, systematic data collection about student backgrounds, goals, preparation, and effort may occur more often at the college level than at the program level. It is here that the authority, expertise, and resources needed to collect data, alone or in cooperation with state or private external agencies, are located. Executive officers can authorize voluntary data collection such as participation in the National Survey of Student Engagement (NSSE) or CIRP. Despite the availability of a wide array of information, institutions seem to use such data more frequently for estimating program enrollments and assessing the need for remedial services than to help plan college-wide or program curricula. For example, CIRP data could be used to document gradual and sometimes little-noticed changes in college programs that result from shifting student populations and changing levels of preparation (Dey & Hurtado, 1995).

Multiple Perspectives on Learning

As we noted earlier, many faculty members are willing to address students' intellectual (cognitive) development but uncomfortable with the idea that they are responsible for personal, attitudinal, or career development. Separating intellectual outcomes from others, however, is both artificial and counterproductive because intellectual development is inextricably linked to students' emotions and attitudes, that is, their affective development. To involve students in their learning, instructors need to promote the development and/or maintenance of positive attitudes and motivation as well as create appropriately challenging educational environments. Information about learning and learners can thus be used to make academic plans more effective.

Since college and university instructors typically are trained as disciplinary experts, rather than experts in teaching and learning, our goal in the following sections is to present information that is relevant to constructing academic plans. Our review draws from varied empirical and theoretical literature to describe what postsecondary instructors need to know about students. We hope to simplify and translate existing research so that it is useful to instructors.

Views of learning are evolving and expanding as scholars from many fields—education, cognitive psychology, educational psychology, anthropology, sociology, and neuroscience—study this complex phenomenon. The diversity of perspectives in this scholarly domain is reflected in the literature; there is no single definition or description of learning that is accepted by all. To some extent this definitional diversity reflects the fact that there are different kinds of human learning (Phillips & Soltis, 2004). Consider, for example, the following learning experiences and goals: mastering a yoga pose, solving a calculus problem, and developing empathy for individuals from different cultures. Each requires the individual to learn something specific—psychomotor skills, mathematical knowledge and problem-solving skills, and cultural understandings and self-knowledge. Moreover, some complex learning tasks (for example, the planning and execution of a student video or the conduct of an undergraduate research project) require a combination of knowledge and skill sets. Different theories of learning allow us to explain these different kinds of learning tasks.

Different theories of learning, however, also emphasize different aspects of the phenomenon of learning. There are at least three distinctive traditions of thinking about how people learn—the behaviorist, cognitive, and sociocultural perspectives. Because each tradition defines learning differently, each offers a unique vantage point for understanding the phenomenon (Collins, Greeno, & Resnick, 2001; Greeno, Collins, & Resnick 1996). The research associated with these three perspectives contributes important knowledge of how people learn.

Behavioral Perspectives

Until the late 1800s, discussions of learning were largely philosophical in nature, but became more empirical as researchers sought to understand learning by asking people to reflect on their thought processes. As the field of psychology matured, however, the subjectivity inherent in individuals' reports of their learning became suspect. In the early 1900s, psychologist John Watson argued that psychology should limit itself to the study of observable behaviors. The behavioral psychologists who followed, such as B.F. Skinner, studied only what could be measured, defining learning as a change in behavior. In time, the focus on measurable behavioral change broadened as other psychologists argued that the potential for a change in behavior, as well as an actual change in behavior, should be considered evidence of learning. This view of learning as change still underlies many perspectives on learning.

Behavioral theories view learning as a process that occurs incrementally through reinforcement of behaviors that approximate a target (or desired) behavior. Many concepts that emerged from behavioral studies are still applied in classrooms today. For example, the practice of "drills" in mathematics and languages is derived from the concept of conditioning (the idea that behavior that is reinforced and rewarded is more likely to be repeated) and the law of exercise (which states that practice enhances learning). Other instructional practices, such as the identification of learning objectives, derive from the behavioral assertion that learning is promoted by breaking a desired behavior into a sequence of easy-to-achieve steps. Today, this assumption is reflected in the set of specific learning objectives that many instructors include in their course syllabi (although few instructors limit these to behavioral objectives). The practice of criterion-referenced testing, which sets a standard for performance rather than comparing students against one another to determine a grade, is another outgrowth of behavioral research. Finally, and importantly, behavioral theories stress the importance of immediate feedback and rewards to encourage correct responses and discourage incorrect ones.

Behavioral theories emphasize learners' responses to stimuli in their environment. While still influential in education, they are criticized for portraying the learner as a passive recipient of stimuli (Phillips & Soltis, 2004). Most contemporary theories of learning, in contrast, cast the learner as an active participant in the construction of knowledge. Behavioral theories are also criticized for neglecting the role of emotions in learning (Schunk, 2004). Today's theories attend to the affective (emotional), as well as the cognitive, dimensions of learning.

Cognitive Perspectives

Experience is often the catalyst for changes in the individual (Slavin, 2000). Cognitive psychologists argue that changes in knowledge and understanding, which may or may not be evidenced in observable behaviors, are evidence of learning. Accordingly, they define learning as a process of conceptual growth that involves the formation, strengthening, or weakening of connections that influence the individual's ability to organize information (Greeno, Collins, & Resnick, 1996). Cognitive theories thus emphasize understanding of ideas and concepts, as well as behaviors exhibited in problem solving or reasoning.

The idea of conceptual change challenges the behavioral portrayal of the human mind as passively responding to environmental stimuli. Humans don't simply react to the world, cognitive theorists argue, they actively interpret sensations, manipulate ideas and things, make intellectual connections, and give meaning to phenomena they encounter. Whereas behavioral theories see the environment as shaping behavior, cognitive theorists view the individual as the locus of control in learning. In this perspective, learning is both goal-directed and adaptive as people seek out information to understand and control their environments. It is the product of interactions among personal, behavioral, and environmental influences (Schunk, 2004).

Research in cognitive psychology has cemented the idea that individuals construct understandings of themselves and their world rather than simply receiving information about them. Emphasis on active learning in the classroom is aligned with this constructivist view of learning. Just how knowledge construction occurs, however, is not yet understood. Cognitive psychology also provides information on the role of memory and prior knowledge in learning. While praised for conceptualizing the learner as an active inquirer and explaining how memory functions, cognitive theories can be criticized for downplaying the role of the environment in learning and focusing too narrowly on individual cognition.

Sociocultural Perspectives

Like cognitive theories, sociocultural perspectives view learning as the active construction of knowledge. Sociocultural perspectives, however, focus as well on the role that social contexts and interactions play in the construction of meaning. Learning and meaning-making, they assert, is not only a cognitive process that is influenced by the contexts in which it takes place; it is itself a social process. Soviet psychologist Lev Vygotsky, whose work has helped shape the sociocultural perspective, explained that we cannot understand the individual without understanding the social and historical context in which he or she lives (Wertsch, 1985). Languages, as well as ways of thinking and communicating, emerge from particular cultural contexts (Rogoff, 2003; Rogoff & Chavajay, 1995). Cognitive processes are therefore also cultural processes because they are situated in, and thus created by, relevant interpersonal, social, cultural, institutional, and historical contexts.

The American educational philosopher John Dewey shared this view, writing: "As a matter of fact every individual has grown up, and always must grow up, in a social medium. His responses grow intelligent, or gain meaning, simply because he lives and acts in a medium of accepted meanings and values. Through social intercourse, through sharing in the activities embodying beliefs, he gradually acquires a mind of his own. The conception of mind as a purely isolated possession of the self is at the very antipodes of the truth . . . the self is not a separate mind building up knowledge anew on its own account" (Dewey, 1916, p. 344).

As we have noted, both behavioral and cognitive psychologists are also interested in how environments shape—or mediate—learning. A key difference, however, between these perspectives and the sociocultural perspective is the degree to which they focus on the role of the context and experience in explaining learning. The behavioral and cognitive perspectives both view the environment as a source of experiences (albeit to differing degrees) that produce learning, and each is concerned with understanding the cognitive development of the individual. For those working in a sociocultural perspective, the contexts in which an individual grows and learns powerfully enlarge but also limit his ways of thinking and acting. In this perspective, learning is a social activity, rather than a purely cognitive one, because it requires participation in the social practices of a specific community or communities.

This attention to an extensive array of contextual factors is the basis for one criticism of this perspective: sociocultural descriptions of learning can be very complex as they consider a vast array of mediating factors in learning. In addition, research guided by this perspective is in a relatively early stage. Still, the work of sociocultural theorists and researchers has helped to replace the conceptualization of the learner as a "lone inquirer" (Phillips & Soltis, 2004) with a view of learning as a social and cognitive process in which thinking and learning are "situated in a particular context of intentions, social partners and tools" (Greeno, Collins, & Resnick, 1996, p. 20).

Each of the perspectives we have discussed—behavioral, cognitive, and sociocultural—contributes to our understanding of learning and learners in postsecondary settings. In the sections that follow, we distill critical insights from these perspectives for college and university instructors, presuming that a basic understanding of how students in college courses learn will help instructors construct effective academic plans.

Developing Competence

Psychologists use the term "cognition" to describe learning processes, which include individuals' general strategies for processing information, their prior knowledge about content, and their problem-solving and thinking skills. Cognitive psychologists are particularly interested in the ways new information is processed and organized in memory because this can influence learning (Ausubel, 1963; Ausubel, Novak, & Hanesian, 1978; Shavelson, 1974). For example, the ability to store extensive sets of ideas and experiences in long-term memory, and to efficiently access them for use in problem solving, distinguishes novices in a domain, such as college students who are learning biology, from those who are experts in that domain, such as faculty members in the biology department (Chi, Glaser, & Farr, 1988). Experts can solve problems effectively because, when faced with a problem in a domain, they can quickly select and apply approaches that have worked in the past to solve that problem. The large amount of information experts possess allows them to quickly recognize the characteristics of a situation, and this suggests to them what to do and when to do it. Long-term memory makes it possible for people to engage in simple everyday tasks, like sewing a button on a shirt, as well as much more complex tasks, such as solving mathematical problems or identifying allegorical elements in a science fiction novel.

While expert-novice theories help distinguish experts from those who are new to a field of study, they tell us little about how individuals develop competence or expertise (Alexander, 2003). Other theories are therefore needed to expand our understanding of learning. Some cognitive researchers try to explain how individuals learn by observing people in social settings. Students, for example, can learn how to conduct an experiment by watching a teaching assistant or faculty member demonstrate a set of procedures. While imitation of observed behaviors can produce learning (Miller & Dollard, 1941), this type of learning can also be vicarious; individuals can learn from observing the consequences of others' behaviors without having to imitate what was observed. Learners can also self-regulate their behaviors by visualizing the anticipated consequences of their actions (Bandura, 1976). Much postsecondary teaching seems to be predicated on the fact that students learn, at least in part, through observation and imitation. Mathematics instructors often solve calculus problems on the chalkboard and then ask students to do the same in homework assignments or tests. Nursing instructors model patient interaction for student nurses in order to demonstrate appropriate interpersonal skills and attitudes.

Educators assume that what is learned in courses and programs will be used in work and community settings. Educational anthropologists, however, have demonstrated discontinuities in individuals' abilities to perform mathematical activities in different settings. Studies of adults, for example, show that individuals in a testing situation were correct less than 60 percent of the time when asked to solve simple mathematics problems that would be encountered in shopping. Among the same individuals, however, 90 percent correctly solved the same problem when actually calculating prices and identified the best buy while shopping (Lave, 1977; Reed & Lave, 1979). Such findings raise the question of the extent to which competence is situation-specific rather than invariant. Some psychologists are addressing these concerns. Ecological psychologists, for example, view individuals and environments as interdependent. Their studies demonstrate how environments provide opportunities for action to individuals who have the needed abilities or competences to take advantage of those opportunities. A pool is swimmable, for example, to adults and children who know how to swim (Barab & Plucker, 2002).

The following example suggests how the cognitive and sociocultural perspectives on learning may yet be bridged. At the postsecondary level, students in a major are expected to learn the conceptual and methodological tools and practices of that field of study. Students majoring in political science, for example, must learn the assumptions, concepts, and theories that define the field. They also come to understand the kinds of questions posed by scholars, as well as how inquiry is conducted using the research tools and methods particular to the field. Finally, they learn what kinds of evidence are deemed credible. Some cognitive theories portray this learning over time as the development of expertise and stress the role of knowledge organization and pattern recognition (for example, this problem looks like the one we discussed last term). Other cognitive theories suggest that some of this learning is achieved as students observe and then practice the kinds of thinking and inquiry taught in courses. Sociocultural theories explain learning in terms of the students' increasingly competent participation in the social practices of the discipline; skills develop through social interactions in the program. These different perspectives are not incommensurate. Each assumes that learning is a process of developing competency in thinking and other skills particular to a given field. By framing particular ideas—such as that of competence—differently, they provide different vantage points to view them. Importantly, each implies that educators can create the conditions that facilitate learning.

Learners and Learning Processes

Cognitive psychology has provided educators with much useful information on learners. Earlier we noted two important dimensions of students' learning—cognitive and affective (emotional). In this section, we review theories on ability and intelligence, students' approaches to learning tasks, and the related concepts of motivation, goals, interest, and engagement. When appropriate, we note how sociocultural or behavioral theories of learning challenge or extend these theories.

Intelligence and Ability

After many years of research, scholars still do not agree on the nature of human intelligence. Many psychologists accept a multidimensional, hierarchical model of intelligence that includes the concept of "general intelligence," and more than seventy primary cognitive "abilities" (such as memory span, mechanical knowledge, and reading speed) as well as nine broad groupings of more general factors (for example, processing speed, visual processing, reading and writing, quantitative knowledge). As one moves up the hierarchy, from the primary cognitive abilities to the nine broad groups of general factors, and finally to the concept of general intelligence, the psychological clarity of the concepts in each stratum decreases (Ackerman & Lohman, 2006). Some psychologists do not accept the idea of general intelligence at all and, among those who accept the hierarchical model, there is disagreement on the nature of the influence of general intelligence on the range of human abilities.

Many psychologists subscribe to an information-processing model of learning that stresses the dynamic nature of intelligence. Information-processing approaches emphasize how the learner can learn to perceive and process information and store it in memory for further use. Using an information-processing approach, Robert Sternberg (1985) introduced a three-part model, the "triarchic theory of successful intelligence," which includes analytical (or academic) intelligence, creative intelligence, and practical intelligence. Sternberg asserts that successful learning does not rely on analytical intelligence alone. Learning also requires the ability to be creative, going beyond the routine tasks to synthesize experiences in new and insightful ways. He uses the term "practical intelligence" to describe the ability to adapt to, use, and manipulate the environment to serve one's needs. This ability enables individuals to achieve better fits with their environment; it includes both problem-solving skills and social skills in relating to others in the environment.

Howard Gardner, a contemporary of Sternberg, developed another theory, which he called "multiple intelligences," during the same time period. Like Sternberg, Gardner (1983, 1993, & 2003) also posits that intelligence is multifaceted, arguing that individuals have different intelligence profiles. He has proposed several different kinds of intelligences, including logical-mathematical, linguistic, visual-spatial, musical, kinesthetic, interpersonal, intrapersonal, and naturalist, all of which enable individuals to process information in certain ways. Gardner (1993) does not deny that general intelligence exists, but rather questions its explanatory power, asserting that the construct is largely useful for measuring performance on a relatively narrow range of tasks that involve logical and linguistic intelligences particularly valued in school settings.

Critics of Sternberg's and Gardner's theories argue that some of the kinds of intelligences proposed (for example, linguistic, logical-mathematical, creative) overlap with traditional ability constructs (Gustafsson & Undheim, 1996). They also believe that further testing is needed to validate the theories and their component parts. Still, many believe that Sternberg and Gardner have highlighted important issues in the study of intelligences.

One important conclusion drawn from research on intelligence is that, as behaviors become more contextualized, measures of general intelligence become less useful for predicting and explaining achievement. More specific knowledge and skills become the more useful explanations because, in all domains of knowledge, prior knowledge and skills are the best predictors of future success. This is especially true when future learning is similar to the learning that has occurred to date (Ackerman & Lohman, 2006). For college students, a successful learning experience with particular types of problems and in certain types of settings may be a better predictor of future success than a measure of generalized capability. This may explain why standardized test scores, such as the SAT, are reasonable predictors of first-year college grades, but not of overall achievement.

Most theories of intelligence acknowledge the role of environmental contexts or culture, but focus primarily on the individual and do not describe how social and cultural interactions influence the development of intelligence. Similarly, most concepts of talent and giftedness tend to focus on the qualities of the person rather than on how individual and environmental factors may interact to produce "talent" (Barab & Plucker, 2002). In contrast, sociocultural perspectives suggest that, while intelligence or ability involves individual processes, particular contexts may or may not enable intelligence and talent to manifest themselves. For example, in colleges and universities, educators tend to value particular kinds of knowledge and learning and sometimes fail to recognize other kinds of knowledge and interactions that are valued primarily outside of schools. Because there is a perceived gap between life skills and academic skills, most students will need help in understanding and appreciating the relevance of formal educational activities to their broader lives (Barab & Plucker, 2002). From a sociocultural perspective then, the educator's emphasis is not on identifying talented individuals but on initiating them into academic practices and supporting meaningful interactions. In short, the question is how to develop "smart contexts" for learning, not just identifying "smart individuals" (Barab & Plucker, 2002, p. 175). In the following sections, we begin to see how individual and contextual factors interact to shape learning in academic settings.

Approaches to Learning

Many researchers believe that a key difference in how students pursue their academic work is whether they pursue meaningful learning (in which the learner extracts personal meaning from what is being taught) or rote learning (in which the student simply seeks to remember what is taught (Entwistle, 2008). Researchers have also identified variations on this theme, finding that students use two different approaches when reading textbooks: a "surface" processing style and a "deep" processing style. Surface processors simply plow through text and are satisfied that they have completed the reading task. In contrast, deep processors think about the meaning. Research has confirmed this distinction in many fields of study (Long, 2003; Richardson, 2000).

Learning strategies, however, vary according to the situation. Students may use a surface processing approach in one subject area, for example, as they read for a general education course in which they have little interest, and a deep processing approach in courses in their major which they perceive as enabling them to achieve personal goals. The difference in the approaches is a result of the students' differing motivations to learn in these different situations, which influences their learning outcomes as well as their choice of learning processes. The choice of a learning approach also depends on the existence of prior knowledge that allows the student to make sense of the subject matter under study. The learning approach chosen will affect retention and the integration of the materials learned. In sum, not only do students use different strategies as they approach learning tasks, but the process they select depends in part of the features of the learning environment.

Learning Styles

Some psychologists (for example, Kagan & Kogan, 1970) argue that socialization experiences in the family, at school, and at work influence the development of consistent and distinctive learning styles in individuals. People, they suggest, learn to choose between certain styles—for example, between acting quickly or reflecting on their proposed action, between using concrete experience or abstract analysis in solving problems, between learning alone or with others, between preferring complex material and preferring simple material, and between the tendency to focus on one solution versus considering a wide set of solutions.

Educational psychologists, however, no longer believe that learning styles are immutable personality characteristics. While one's learning style may have some structure, that structure is responsive, at least to some degree, to the immediate demands of the situation (Cassidy, 2004). Although students choose preferred sets of strategies and approaches to learning, instructors can help them develop the ability to make choices.

Learning Strategies

How one processes information (that is, how one learns) can be influenced by the use of learning strategies. Claire Weinstein and Richard Mayer (1986) identified four aspects of information processing that are within the learner's control: selection, acquisition, construction, and integration. In selection, the learner controls the attention given to stimuli or information in the environment; in acquisition, she transfers information from working (short-term) memory to long-term memory (permanent storage); in construction, the learner actively builds connections among ideas in working memory; and in integration, she connects new information with prior knowledge. Each of these steps in information processing is important for effective learning and retention.

Weinstein and Mayer outlined several learning strategies that can be used to control how information is processed and thus help to ensure that effective learning take place. Each of these—rehearsal, elaboration, organization, and monitoring—can be basic or complex, depending on the task. Table 6.1 provides examples of some of these learning strategies.

Rehearsal strategies influence how information is encoded in memory but do not generally help individuals connect new information to prior knowledge. Rather, these strategies help to focus attention on the material to be learned.

TABLE 6.1. COMPLEX LEARNING STRATEGIES

Cognitive Strategies	Complex Tasks
A. Rehearsal strategies	Shadowing; Copying material; Taking verbatim notes; Underlining text
B. Elaboration strategies	Paraphrasing; Summarizing; Creating analogies; Taking generative notes; Answering questions
C. Organizational strategies	Selecting main idea: Outlining; Networking; Diagramming

From: McKeachie, Pintrich, Lin, and Smith, 1986. Reprinted by permission of the University of Michigan.

A basic rehearsal strategy involves reciting names or items from a list; a more complex strategy involves highlighting material in a text or copying it into a notebook. In contrast, elaboration strategies help students transfer information to long-term memory by building connections among concepts, facts, principles, and so on. Basic elaboration strategies include creating mental images and using mnemonic keywords; more complex strategies include paraphrasing, summarizing, creating analogies, and answering questions.

Organizational strategies help the learner select appropriate information and build connections. Clustering words into taxonomic categories is one basic organizational strategy. Students can select the main idea from a text or analyze the structure of the text through outlining or networking (linking ideas).

Monitoring strategies are used to deliberately regulate and control learning and assist in integration. Self-monitoring can take the form of self-testing to check comprehension or regulating the speed of reading to fit within a specific time frame. Such monitoring activities are all forms of metacognition (awareness of one's learning), which we will discuss shortly.

Motivation

Whereas learning styles and strategies explain how students approach learning, motivation theories explain why individuals initiate and persist in a certain activity.

Motivation, however, should not be equated with achievement. Students can achieve at high levels without having high levels of motivation (Anderman & Wolters, 2006) and, of course, students can be highly motivated but not achieve well. Motivation influences learning and achievement—but so do a host of other variables, such as cognitive abilities and prior knowledge.

Behavioral theories assert that motivation is the result of rewards and punishments that affect the individual's response to the learning environment. Rewards such as grades and bonus points can influence motivation levels. Such incentives are external to the individual student, and their effect is mediated by the individual's goals and needs (Greeno, Collins, & Resnick, 1996). Thus motivation can also come from within the individual, arising from personal needs or interests or stimulated by external factors other than rewards supplied by the instructor. Instructors, for example, create "situational interest" (Hidi, 1990; Renninger, 2000) when they provide particularly engaging examples of a new concept that grabs students' attention and engages their imaginations. Students whose personal interests are not stirred by the instructor's presentation, however, may not respond positively to the situation designed to provide incentives.

Many cognitive psychologists believe that motivation depends, at least in part, on an individual's estimates ("expectancies") of what will happen if he or she engages (or does not engage) in a behavior or activity. These expectancies can be powerful motivators. Students with different estimates of their potential for academic achievement in an organic chemistry course will react differently to the activities required for that course. Expectations of success can supply motivation, while expectations of failure can reduce it. Consciously or unconsciously, psychologists contend, learners also assign a "value" to a particular task by assessing its ability to fulfill their intrinsic needs or to achieve desired rewards. From this perspective, students' motivation can be thought of as varying with (a) the value of a task in achieving incentives and (b) the estimated "expectancy" of success or failure. Knowing that motivation is related to task value and expectancy is useful because it suggests that motivation can be influenced by the instructor's abilities to design educational experiences that students perceive as helping them to succeed. It also can be influenced by deliberate strategies to help students see value in particular learning activities; for example, by explicitly discussing how and when practicing engineers use particular physical laws in their work.

In forming expectancies, students rely on perceptions of self-competence (How well can I do this?) and estimates of task difficulty (How hard will it be to succeed?) (McKeachie, Pintrich, Lin, Smith, & Sharma, 1990). In addition to estimating expectancies of success, students attribute their successes and failures to various causes. Some attribute their success to personal factors, such as their own ability and effort; others attribute success to external (situational) causes. This tendency to attribute success or failure, an affective component of expectation, is not separable from motivation. Students, for example, may attribute a failure on a writing assignment to their lack of ability and believe this to be a stable, unchanging, personal trait. As a result, a student may feel ashamed and hopeless. If these feelings occur repeatedly, the student is likely to avoid similar writing experiences whenever possible (Anderman & Wolters, 2006).

In addition to such attributions, psychologists have studied how individual self-assessments influence learning. Albert Bandura (1977) referred to individuals' evaluation of their ability to do something as "self-efficacy." Self-efficacy, unlike one's self-concept or level of self-esteem, is situation-specific. A student may have one level of self-efficacy in a biology course and quite another estimate in English composition. Self-efficacy and expectancy are closely related and both are related to learning effectiveness. Students who tend to attribute success (or lack of success) to their own ability are likely to make this attribution consistently over time and in different contexts. In contrast, students who attribute their successes or failures to situational causes (for example, the difficulty of the test or their level of effort) tend to make less consistent estimates of self-efficacy because they realize difficulty and effort level change with each situation.

Motivation is also affected by educational contexts in which learning occurs. Peers, families, classroom communities and larger communities, as well as teachers, shape motivation (Anderman & Anderman, 2000). Some researchers argue that individual motivation cannot be disentangled from culture: what some students find motivating may diminish the motivation of others (Wlodkowski & Ginsberg, 1995). The emotions of joy, frustration, and determination may differ across cultures because cultural definitions of novelty, opportunity, and gratification, as well as assumptions about the appropriate responses to these reactions, differ across cultures (Kitayama & Markus, 1994). For example, differences in how students in different cultures view success in their studies appear to be culturally based. Japanese students, for instance, tend to believe that academic achievement is the result of hard work; American students are more likely to view achievement as related to innate ability and therefore less variable (Chen & Stevenson, 1995). Understanding assumptions like these about learning and achievement can help instructors address motivational issues in the classroom. For example, a student who experiences difficulty learning calculus, and who believes ability is a fixed trait, may decide that no matter how hard he tries to learn calculus, he won't succeed. Instructors can help students like this improve academic performances by teaching effective learning strategies or can refer them to campus services designed to improve study skills. Adopting improved strategies may improve motivation as students see the fruits of their efforts.

Goals

Faculty interviewed about course planning seldom considered students' personal, social, and career goals as they developed or revised courses, but believed students' intellectual goals were relevant to course design (Stark & others, 1988). College students' intellectual goals, however, are usually related to, rather than distinct from, their personal and career goals (Stark, Shaw, & Lowther, 1989). Intellectual goals include, for example, students' broad goals for attending college as well as their goals for completing specific courses, programs, and academic tasks.

Students' goals influence the value they place on a given endeavor or task and, consequently, drive motivation and effort. Goals have a variety of attributes, including specificity, clarity, difficulty, temporality, importance, ownership, commitment, and stability (Stark, Shaw, & Lowther, 1989). Variations in these attributes influence how students perceive and engage in the course or program in which they are enrolled. Especially relevant to our discussion of learners are two types of goals students may adopt as they engage in an academic task: performance goals and learning goals (Dweck & Elliott, 1983; Nicholls, 1984). Students who adopt a performance goal, such as learning to play a musical scale correctly, focus on their own ability to do a task, rely on firmly established standards, and tend to see errors as failures. Under these circumstances, attribution of success or failure to personal factors can clearly be dysfunctional and decrease self-efficacy. Students who adopt a learning goal, such as the ability to interpret a musical composition in their own style, focus on the process of how to master the task. They view their performance on a flexible personal standard, are involved in the task rather than the outcome, and see errors as useful in learning. Students may adopt a performance goal for one task or academic course and a learning goal in others. The student having trouble in calculus, for example, may decide that earning a grade of "B" is a reasonable performance goal, but may set higher learning goals in his major field of study.

Interest

Some psychologists believe students' estimates of task value and expectations of success are insufficient to explain motivation in intellectual and creative realms. Intrinsic interests, they contend, can motivate individuals to pursue activities or objects that have no apparent use to them (Deci & Ryan, 1991). Although there are different conceptions of interest, researchers typically believe it emerges from an individual's interaction with the environment (Krapp, Hidi, & Renninger, 1992). One example might be a student's interest in studying ancient languages. Typically, such an interest might emerge from travel, from religious experiences or cultural background, or from a particularly stimulating class in high school or college. More commonly, a student might be interested in studying sports training because of local, parental, or peer group influences.

Interest may be individual or situational. Individual interests, as the name suggests, are specific to an individual, relatively stable, and usually stem from or lead to increased knowledge (such as the study of ancient languages). Situational interests, in contrast, are generated by an environmental stimulus and tend to be shared among individuals (such as the interest in sports training). Instructors often try to stimulate students' situational interests in a topic in hopes of producing longer-range individual interests, but situational interests may be short term and have a marginal influence on the individual's long-range thinking. Rather, it is individual interest that motivates students' growth toward competence and expertise in goal-directed ways (Alexander, 1997). Fortunately, situational and individual interests can be complementary—and situational interest can, in some instances, lead to individual interest. An instructor's use of content that is personally involving, for example, may be effective in developing and maintaining the interest of students with little knowledge of a subject area (Mitchell, 1993). An instructor teaching theories of human development, for example, might ask students to test the theories against their own experiences to illustrate the concepts and their limitations.

Engagement

The concept of student engagement, which has been popularized through the National Survey of Student Engagement (NSSE), appears related to concepts like motivation and interest. The construct is based on the ideas of C. Robert Pace and Alexander Astin, who both contributed to its definition and measurement. Pace used the term *quality of effort* to make the assertion that the more a student is meaningfully engaged in an academic task, the more he or she will learn. Astin developed a similar concept, which he called *involvement*, defined as a student's engagement with his or her academic environment.

Pace (1998) argued that quality of effort is not the same as motivation, describing the construct instead as "voluntary effort." Quality of effort reflects initiative, as Pace puts it, the strength and scope of the personal investment a student makes in his or her own education. Pace acknowledged, however, that student effort does not exist in a vacuum. Quality of effort is relative to a specific environmental context "and its strength probably depends on [that] context" (Pace, 1998, p. 31).

Astin also studied the interaction between students and educational environments. He developed his concept of involvement inductively, since survey research revealed that undergraduate student degree attainment was positively affected by a number of seemingly unrelated things—participation in co-curricular activities, having a part-time job on campus, participating in an honors program, and so on. In addition, degree attainment (or persistence) was also negatively associated with certain activities such as commuting and working full-time off campus. According to Astin, "Every positive factor can be seen as a form of engagement, effort, commitment, 'time on task,' or involvement in the college experience. In other words, the student who is most likely to complete college is heavily involved in the college experience, while the most dropout-prone student shows minimal involvement" (Astin, 2003, p. 26). Like Pace, Astin distinguishes involvement from the concept of motivation, noting that motivation is a psychological state while involvement connotes behavior.

The NSSE survey instrument is premised on the belief that individual effort and involvement influence the extent to which students benefit from their educations (Kuh, 2007). It should be noted, however, that a strict causal relationship cannot be documented. Researchers are beginning to study the relationship between engagement and specific learning outcomes such as critical thinking and academic achievement (Carini, Kuh, & Klein, 2006). Many colleges regularly participate in the NSSE data collection, and local studies are possible on these campuses.

Understandings of Learning and Knowledge

College instructors know that students vary in awareness of their own learning approaches. Some students have a good sense of the kinds of learning strategies they use and when these are effective; others have little understanding of how their learning strategies fail to foster progress as they struggle with unfamiliar ideas or problems. Students also vary in their intellectual sophistication. Some want instructors to identify what is important for the test and to arbitrate among conflicting ideas, research findings, and opinions. Others view knowledge as complex and manage this complexity with relative ease. Research on metacognition (also called self-regulation) and conceptions of knowledge and learning help instructors understand these variations and how they might be addressed.

Metacognition

Recent research suggests that students' motivational patterns are related to their ability to consciously reflect on their own learning, a process called metacognition. Those who can reflect on their learning can also manage and monitor it (Greeno, Collins, & Resnick, 1996). Metacognition (or self-regulation) refers to deliberate control of cognitive activities (Flavell, 1985), such as planning how to approach a specific learning task, monitoring one's comprehension during reading, and evaluating progress toward the completion of an academic task. To control these activities, an individual must understand what skills, strategies, and resources are needed to complete a task—and know how and when to apply those skills and strategies. For this reason, metacognition is often described as "thinking about thinking." Flavell (1979, 1987) argued that metacognition consists of (a) acquired knowledge about cognitive processes, which learners can use to manage their own learning, and (b) metacognitive experiences, which involve the use of specific strategies to regulate or control learning activities.

Some scholars have linked metacognition to intelligence. Sternberg (1986), for example, included it in his theory of intelligence. For Sternberg, meta-components help individuals figure out what is required in a task and enable them to determine if the task is done correctly. The ability to allocate cognitive resources appropriately, he argued, is central to intelligence. Metacognition, however, is also linked to development since over time students become more able to understand the demands of particular tasks and their ability to complete them.

Learners' beliefs about themselves influence metacognition. Students who consider themselves, in general, to be effective learners (have high self-efficacy about learning) are likely to do so because they believe they have the skills and strategies they need to learn (Schunk & Zimmerman, 2006). Some research suggests that students' beliefs about learning begin to emerge in middle school as students develop detailed understandings of how learning occurs (Schommer-Aikins, Mau, Brookhart, & Hutter, 2000). These beliefs about learning are related to, or perhaps precursor of beliefs about the nature of knowledge. Both types of beliefs influence learning, affecting, for example, comprehension, cognitive processing, and conceptual change (Hofer, 2001).

Beliefs About Knowledge

Student learning in college can be understood from many perspectives. One stream of research considers students' intellectual development, specifically how they develop their beliefs about knowledge (epistemological beliefs) and how these beliefs influence their learning. A number of frameworks describing epistemological development were inspired by research conducted by William Perry, who studied the intellectual development of male students at Harvard in the 1960s. Based on extensive interviews over many years, Perry (1970) described how students gradually change their views, developing from stereotypic thinking and reliance on moral and intellectual absolutes to a view of knowledge as plural and contextualized. Most college students, he found, begin college in a "dualistic" stage, seeing the world in absolute terms—right/wrong or good/bad—relying heavily on their judgments of what they had learned at home. In the college setting, students in the dualistic stage expect, for example, that courses will exhibit clear structures and that instructors are the authorities. While teachers might not be the source of complete truth, they are seen as the source of the right answers in their field of study.

Following the dualism stage, Perry's male subjects moved into a stage characterized by "multiplicity." They began to see issues from multiple perspectives, coming to understand that a problem might have more than one solution or a dilemma more than one right choice. Students in this phase began to consult with others. They viewed instructors as individuals who, rather than providing truth, provided methods for getting answers. In the multiplicity stage, students were comfortable with less structure in the classroom and enjoyed, or at least tolerated, more participatory course activities.

When students left multiplicity, they entered a stage in which they took responsibility for making choices in the face of multiple alternatives. While still consulting with others, they realized that choices must be their own. During this stage of "relativism," students accepted the complexities of knowledge and observed that, while there may be many alternatives, some answers were better than others. Finally, a very few students moved during the college years to Perry's final stage of "commitment," choosing from among potential stances or answers those they would espouse consistently.

The transition from dualistic to relativistic thinking can be difficult. Perry noted that dualistic students often had difficulty making their own decisions and commitments in a relativistic and complex world. Some students were threatened by new ideas and held tightly to stereotypic beliefs. These threats could lead to psychological or even physical withdrawal from the source of the challenge.

Aware that Perry's research investigated the epistemological beliefs of male students only, Mary Field Belenky and associates (1986) framed a study of women's ways of knowing that included young women from college, and also from local community organizations. They found that young women experienced patterns of intellectual development similar to those discovered by Perry with one significant difference. Belenky and her colleagues added a new category, "constructed knowledge," in which the individual uses both head and heart to see truth in a complex, ambiguous world. These researchers distinguished between "separate knowing" and "connected knowing." Separate knowing (perhaps more typical of males) focuses on formal analysis of the object or topic under study, while connected knowing (more common among females) focuses on a personal understanding of the object or topic. Separate learning emphasizes competition, logical reasoning, and other approaches that separate self from subject. Connected learning emphasizes cooperation, discussion, and clarification, approaches that involve learners with the subject and with one another. Adaptations in learning tasks may be used to accommodate these gender differences.

Marcia Baxter Magolda (1992, 2001) extended the work of Perry and Belenky and her colleagues through a longitudinal study of college students of both sexes. Her model of epistemological reflection is grounded in observations that college-age men and women actively construct perspectives on knowledge by interpreting their experiences, constructing accounts of those experiences, and changing their assumptions based on experiences that are dissonant with their current understandings. These meanings are socially constructed, that is, they are grounded both in the student's own assumptions about knowledge as well as the particular contexts in which meaning-making takes place. In this model, most students begin as "absolute knowers" and progress through a stage of being "transitional knowers" while "contextual knowing" is the ultimate phase of epistemological development. Baxter Magolda's research indicates that only a few students achieve the stage of contextual knowing during the college years. Some, she notes, may never achieve this stage. According to data collected by Baxter Magolda, about 70 percent of college freshmen are absolute knowers; the rest are transitional knowers. Sophomores are about evenly divided between absolute and transitional knowers. Some juniors and seniors show significant growth beyond this point, toward contextual knowing.

Baxter Magolda argues that understandings of oneself are intertwined with understandings of the world. She observed that the participants in her study could only realize gains in epistemological complexity when they developed complex understandings of themselves in relation to others. For example, students had to see themselves as individuals capable of judging claims (regardless of how others saw them) before they could make determinations about what would be evidence and reasonable knowledge claims in a particular context. To encourage students to achieve "self-authorship," Baxter Magolda (2001) recommends that instructors design curricular (and co-curricular) activities to validate students as knowers, to situate learning in students' experiences, and to define learning as the mutual construction of knowledge rather than as the receipt of information from others. These types of academic plans encourage students to take an active role in knowledge construction and self-definition.

King and Kitchner (2004) have studied students' beliefs about knowledge from a different angle, examining how personal epistemologies affect students' ability to think in complex ways about "ill-structured problems" for which all the information is not known and for which there may be more than one acceptable answer. Complex reasoning, King and Kitchner argue, affects an individual's ability to master learning outcomes often associated with college, such as moral reasoning, tolerance for diversity, and intercultural competence.

Like others who have studied students' personal epistemologies, King and Kitchener found that individuals progress from absolute to relative views of knowledge and finally accept the idea that some knowledge is more certain or more true. Individuals in the lowest developmental stage (absolute knowledge) could not distinguish between well-structured problems (those that have answers) and ill-structured problems (those for which no clear answers exist). Instructors who do not realize that their students may have very different views of knowledge may, King and Kitchener suggest, overestimate the intellectual maturity of their students and their ability to contend with ill-structured problems in courses and programs. Such unrealistic expectations can lower students' expectations of success, decreasing their self-efficacy and decreasing engagement.

Some have offered the idea that students' beliefs about knowledge are not the same across different settings and domains of knowledge. Some research suggests that students' "personal epistemologies" are composed of multiple beliefs and each can have a different effect on learning (Schommer, 1990). Research on high school and college students and adults indicates four types of beliefs about knowledge and learning:

- Ability to learn—beliefs range from the idea that ability to learn is fixed at birth to the idea that it is acquired;
- Structure of knowledge—ranging from a belief that knowledge is composed of isolated bits of knowledge to one in which knowledge is organized as complex and interrelated concepts;
- Speed of learning—learning is quick (or doesn't occur at all) to learning is gradual; and
- Stability of knowledge—knowledge is unchanging or evolving. (Schommer, 1990)

Some researchers hold that these beliefs are independent—a student can believe that knowledge is fixed and certain while also viewing it as complex and interrelated. These beliefs may also change over the life span (Schommer-Aikins, Brookhart, & Hutter, 2000). Others observe that in different social settings and academic situations, the same individual will treat knowledge in different ways (Hammer, 2002). One student, for example, may treat knowledge in history as simple and static when it is provided by an instructor, but that same student may understand that texts in a literature course are influenced by the different perspectives of their authors. Individuals may have a coherent set of beliefs, but these may be context-specific. Viewing epistemological beliefs as multidimensional suggests a shift in instructional practices (Hammer, 2002). An instructor who is confronted with a student with a counterproductive epistemology does not assume the student has only one set of resources at his or her disposal, but rather seeks to activate other epistemological resources that the student may have to help him or her apply those resources to the problem at hand.

Because so much of learning in college is focused on mastering particular domains of knowledge such as that in academic fields, the question of whether epistemological beliefs are tied to domain knowledge is worthy of consideration. Research, however, has not yet provided a clear answer to this question. Several questions must be explored before an answer is reached: (a) Do both domain-specific and general epistemological beliefs exist? (b) How broadly applicable are domain-specific beliefs? (Can I extend my view of knowledge in mathematics to the field of physics? To biology? To political science?); and (c) Do general systems of epistemological beliefs, generated in childhood, become domain-specific as individuals acquire knowledge in a domain? (Schommer-Aiken, 2002). While there is still uncertainty surrounding the nature of epistemological beliefs, the impact of such beliefs on learning seems clear. Instructors who understand the influence of students' beliefs about knowledge may be able to determine when students' thinking involves simple misunderstandings and when academic learning challenges more basic beliefs.

Cultural Conceptions of Learning

Students' reactions to academic work and educational settings are also influenced by their culturally generated conceptions of learning. Research evidence from developmental psychology and anthropology suggests the existence of (at least) two contrasting "pathways" of learning (Greenfield, Trumbull, Keller, Rothstein-Fisch, Suzuki, & Quiroz, 2006). One is individualistic; the other is collective. The individualistic pathway emphasizes the development of individual identity, independence, and self-fulfillment; the collective pathway stresses group identity, interdependence, and social responsibility. In the individualistic conception of learning, the student's goal is to stand out and excel; in the collective conception, it is preferable to fit in and contribute. Both idealized pathways have historical and sociocultural roots. The individualistic pathway appears to be an adaptation to life in large, urban, commercial societies; the collective pathway appears to be more typical in small-scale, face-to-face societies relying on subsistence economies and informal systems of education.

These learning pathways represent general patterns that do not describe specific individuals or even all members of a particular societal group. Cultural patterns of learning, however, may persist over generations and in new contexts. Immigration and colonization, for example, bring people from individualistic societies into collective ones (and the reverse), exposing persons who have experienced varied pathways to one another and often to contrasting social expectations and practices. This intersection of contrasting patterns can lead to conflict and misunderstanding among students and educators in colleges and universities as students from other cultures enroll in institutions with contrasting traditions. Some educational theories suggest bridging these differences when they arise in the classroom by making the expectations of each culture explicit and encouraging students to develop competencies associated with both pathways.

Learning in Academic Fields

Understanding how the many different influences on learning that psychologists have studied might interact is not as overwhelming as it might appear. Pintrich (1988a), for example, stresses the dynamic interplay of motivation, cognition, and metacognition in the college classroom, suggesting that instructors encourage students to reflect on their motivations, learning strategies, and attributions to understand their own learning. Ideas of how students learn in specific domains of knowledge are helpful for thinking about how motivation, interest, prior knowledge, and epistemological beliefs affect what is learned and how well it is learned. In this section, we review cognitive and sociocultural theories to highlight key processes and influences on learning within a particular academic field.

Conceptual Change

Research soundly refutes the idea that students come to education as blank slates, revealing instead the critical role of prior experiences and prior knowledge in learning. Moreover, the conceptions a student brings to the college classroom are the result of both previous school experiences and other life experiences. When a student encounters a new field of study, some of these conceptions will be primitive and limited. In fact, they may be incorrect—misconceptions that will interfere with learning in that domain. Science educators have been particularly active in documenting the kinds of persistent misconceptions that not only impede learning in the sciences but that are resistant to change (Murphy & Mason, 2006). Students come to education with naïve understandings of biology, physics, and other subjects that explain phenomena they observe in the world. The folk theories they espouse may be coherent, but they are not necessarily aligned with disciplinary knowledge and therefore require some degree of restructuring as students learn more about a science (Carey, 1985).

There are varied ideas about how misconceptions can be altered. As one example, Posner, Strike, Hewson, and Gertzog's (1982) model of conceptual change views learning as an interaction between new and old conceptions. For students to learn, four conditions must be met: (a) the student must be dissatisfied with her current conceptions, viewing them as inappropriate explanations of events and phenomena; (b) the student must understand the new conception; (c) the student must find the new conception initially plausible (perhaps because it comes from a credible source like an instructor) and it must be consistent with other personally held concepts; and (d) the student must think the new conception is a fruitful one, capable of accounting for many different events and phenomena. Although this change process seems rational, researchers have challenged the lack of attention to the role of emotions—or affect—in investigations of conceptual change. Paul Pintrich, Ronald Marx, and Robert Boyle (1993), for example, argued that researchers must account for the role of motivation and contextual factors in knowledge revision. Appropriate models would examine how knowledge and beliefs work together or separately to influence conceptual change during learning.

One model seemingly meeting this criterion posits that both cognitive processing and emotional investment are necessary for conceptual change to occur. Students must have an interest in the topic at hand and have personal characteristics or needs that motivate information processing. They must also be able to understand the new material and revise their own knowledge (Dole & Sinatra, 1998). Another model incorporating both affective and cognitive factors in knowledge change focuses specifically on how learners' prior knowledge, beliefs about a topic, and interest in the topic interact with the characteristics of texts (such as persuasiveness or comprehensibility) to influence conceptual change (Murphy, 1998). Researchers have found that when students read texts, strong beliefs about a topic inhibit knowledge acquisition and interest, and that too much topic-specific knowledge can impede changes in beliefs about the topic (Murphy, 1998).

In addition to prior knowledge, which plays a significant role in conceptual change and text comprehension, one's knowledge about her knowledge and thought processes is critical to conceptual change in science (Kuhn, Amsel, & O'Loughlin, 1988). Students must be able to think *about* conceptions rather than just thinking *with* them. They must be aware of their own presuppositions about a concept and the need to change these to develop a correct understanding of a concept. The recommendations of researchers who study conceptual change are similar to those who study epistemological development: students must be provided with opportunities to understand that what they believe is not necessarily factual but rather a personal construction that can be verified or refuted (Murphy & Mason, 2006).

Domain Learning

Patricia Alexander's (1997) model of domain learning (MDL) synthesizes information about motivation, cognition, and metacognition to understand how students develop competence in a particular academic subject. The model seeks to explain how cognitive and motivational factors come together in a process of academic development in a particular discipline or field. The MDL is based on theory and research on development, strategic processing, motivation, and expertise. Elements of the model have been tested on college students, and the MDL thus has implications for curriculum development in higher education.

Alexander suggests that students move through three stages of proficiency in an academic domain: acclimation, competence, and proficiency/expertise. Acknowledging that all students do not have the ability or desire to become experts in all the domains they study, Alexander contends that a student's journey toward competence occurs through gradual transformations in three areas that operate in association with one another: domain knowledge, interests, and strategic processing. Alexander argues that proficiency or expertise requires a student to invest him- or herself in the domain over an extended period.

Domain knowledge refers to the depth and breadth of a student's knowledge about a given academic subject area, such as history or physics (Alexander, Schallert, & Hare, 1991). Individual interest energizes and motivates a student's thoughts and actions toward a goal (Ames, 1992; Ames & Archer, 1988; Dweck & Leggett, 1988; Pintrich & Schrauben, 1992). The third component of the model of domain learning, strategic processing knowledge, is a learning strategy that is intentionally invoked when individuals want to maximize their performance or circumvent problems in understanding or learning (Alexander, Schallert, & Hare,1991; Garner & Alexander, 1989). It includes general cognitive and meta-cognitive processes used in performing a task. Strategic knowledge serves as a link between cognitive (subject-matter knowledge) and motivational (that is, interest) forces because learning strategies are purposefully invoked; thus they are tied to students' goals and can reflect a learner's sense of self-efficacy.

Comparing the first two stages of the MDL, acclimation, and competence makes the connections among the three dimensions of domain learning clearer. When students enter the first stage of domain learning, *acclimation*, they focus primarily on orienting themselves to the field, constructing and organizing a base of domain knowledge that will serve as the foundation for further development. Because they lack a deep understanding of the domain, students in this early stage are more dependent on guidance than those who are competent in the domain. These beginning students need assistance in distinguishing domain-related knowledge from other knowledge and separating important from less-important information. Learners in this stage must rely on general strategic knowledge (activities such as note-taking, summarizing, and re-accessing text) to navigate this foreign academic territory.

Situational interest generated by class activities and context is likely to motivate students in the acclimation stage, and they are likely to be more oriented to task completion or pleasing others, like instructors, than mastering the domain. This is logical, Alexander (1997) argues, for students in the acclimation stage have more limited goal orientations due to their limited understanding of the domain. Because they have a fragmented knowledge base and lack a personal commitment to the domain, learners who are acclimating to a domain often use general strategic processes inefficiently (Alexander & Judy, 1988). Some students, of course, come to the study of a new domain as "intelligent novices" (Brown & Campione, 1990) who have a strong repertoire of general strategies on which they draw as they learn. These students should have greater self-efficacy and proceed more quickly toward competence than their less-well-equipped peers. Most newcomers to a domain, however, will require instructional resources to make progress toward competence.

Whereas the problem-solving approaches of acclimated learners are highly contextualized and functional, *competent* learners (at the second stage of development) should rely less on the situational and contextual factors in the learning environment and are better able to function at a more abstract level. The move to competence, Alexander argues, is marked by transformations in a student's knowledge base, level of individual interest, and strategic abilities. Competent learners not only have significantly more information about a domain, but they know more about important concepts in that domain. Gains in knowledge, however, are not enough for the transformation to competence; they must be accompanied by a major shift in the nature of that knowledge base. The knowledge base of the acclimated learner, we noted earlier, is fragmented; students acquire information in a piecemeal fashion. Competent learners, in contrast, begin to form a coherent knowledge base anchored by key concepts or principles. Domain and topic knowledge become more cohesive as this occurs.

As a result of this shift in domain knowledge, students' strategic processes become more automatic. Problems and tasks in the domain are no longer as cognitively demanding and become more routine through practice. While learners in this stage still encounter problems that are novel and complex and therefore require strategic effort, competent learners can make intelligent decisions about the strategies they have at their disposal (Alexander & Judy, 1988; Harris & Graham, 1996). This should lead to greater efficiency and greater effectiveness.

With gains in domain knowledge, students should also become more personally invested in the domain. Research supports this relationship (Alexander, Jetton, & Kulikowich, 1995; Alexander, Kulikowich, & Schulze, 1994; Alexander, Murphy, Woods, Duhon, & Parker, 1997). As undergraduates progressed in their understanding of a field over the course of a semester, they reported a significant increase in interest in domain-specific concepts (Alexander & others, 1997). The combination of a shift in domain knowledge and personal interest not only lessens the need for general strategies, but it can stimulate deeper processing as well.

Interviewees in the NCRIPTAL studies teaching basic courses in their academic fields independently described a process of gradual student transformation much akin to that described in the model of domain learning. Using language common in their fields, they stressed the importance of acquainting students with domain knowledge first (acclimation), then fostering the development of student competence, especially achieving the integration of ideas and principles and understanding the ways of learning new information in the domain. Study participants who taught majors clearly recognized points at which upper-class students began to aim for proficiency in the field. Interviewees often mentioned the importance of creating situational interest by choosing instructional processes. A key item in the MDL, which most faculty members failed to stress as they described planning courses, was the students' learning strategies. Most instructors assumed that students possessed (or lacked) such strategies before college and didn't mention planning to improve them so that students could progress in the field. The exception was English composition instructors, who had more exposure to educational and psychological theories and were especially concerned with motivation and self-efficacy as well as domain knowledge and interest (Stark & others, 1988).

Participation and Identity Development

In a sociocultural perspective, the emphasis is on understanding how knowledge, understandings, and meanings emerge through interactions in specific contexts. People are members of many, often overlapping communities (nation, city, local neighborhood, religious institution, family, and so on). To participate effectively in any community, individuals must learn its social practices and become competent in the use of its characteristic tools. Academic fields and programs in colleges and universities are also communities, and learning in these contexts requires students to become familiar with, and eventually competent in, the use of a field's specialized language, vocabulary, methods of inquiry, and ways of thinking. Participation in these knowledge communities is both the process and the goal of learning in higher education.

As students participate in these knowledge communities, the communities shape their learning by framing their thinking and intellectual activity. Some sociocultural theorists use the term "apprenticeship" as a metaphor to explain learning because it captures the situated nature of learning, the changing nature of participation in social practices, and its transformative possibilities (Lattuca, 2002). Lave (1997) explains that "apprentices learn to think, argue, act, and interact, in increasingly knowledgeable ways, with people who do something well, by doing it with them" (p. 19).

Learning is thus a vehicle of socialization (the process of learning) and at the same time the result (or goal) of socialization. Learners adopt the existing strategies of the field and reproduce its existing cognitive and social order by working with more skilled members of the community (Wertsch, Del Rio, & Alvarez, 1995). (In some cases they may also challenge the existing order and encourage innovation, enabling a field to change and develop.) During the learning process, learners develop an identity associated with that field. The adoption of the belief system and behaviors of social groups has also been described as enculturation (Seely Brown, Collins, & Duguid, 1989) or acculturation (Bruffee, 1999). While not every student who majors in philosophy will become a professor of philosophy, a successful student will develop at least some of the habits of mind associated with the philosophy community and think of himself as someone who can use the knowledge tools of the philosopher. Identity development is, in this sense, the process of learning to see the world through a philosopher's eyes.

Considering Learners in Curriculum Design

Course planning and curricular revision need no longer be simple exercises in upgrading content and tinkering with sequences. Research on learning suggests how curriculum planners may choose and organize course material to facilitate its meaningful acquisition by students. Bransford, Brown, and Cocking (2000) suggest that three research-based conclusions, with strong implications for teaching, can be drawn from studies of learning:

- Students' preconceptions about how the world works must be engaged if students are to fully grasp new concepts and information and retain these ideas after testing and outside the classroom;
- To develop competence in a domain of knowledge, students must (a) have a deep foundation of factual knowledge, (b) understand and organize these facts and ideas in a conceptual framework, and (c) organize knowledge in a way that facilitates retrieval and use; and
- A metacognitive approach to learning in which students define their learning goals and monitor their progress toward those goals can help students take control of their own learning.

These conclusions all imply that academic plans should engage students in active processes of knowledge construction, enabling them to incorporate new information into their existing understandings of the world—or, when necessary, to build new understandings that replace inaccurate ones. Research on

TABLE 6.2. LESSONS FROM THE LEARNING LITERATURE

Assess students' prior knowledge and skills to avoid unfounded assumptions about what they know about the subject matter being studied.
- Identify misconceptions about subject matter that interfere with learning and dispel these through learning activities that make misconceptions explicit *and* rectify them.
- Ascertain whether the college or university institutional research or assessment offices possess or can collect data about students that can inform course and program planning.

Don't assume that students know how to learn.
- Develop students' awareness of different learning strategies and how these enhance or impede learning.
- Orient students to the field by teaching them effective learning strategies for that field.
- Design learning activities that require students to reflect on what they are learning and to assess their own understanding and progress.
- Help students see how their beliefs about their abilities can affect their performance in courses.

Acknowledge that learning, motivation, and engagement are affected by attitudes and emotions.
- Identify and address student attitudes that hinder learning.
- Consider how program and institutional conditions (for example, student-to-student interactions, classroom environments, or program cultures) can affect students' attitudes or ability to learn well.
- Collaborate with student affairs professionals to develop holistic understanding of students' college experiences and to identify local resources for connecting curricular and co-curricular experiences.

Design academic plans that connect students' personal and academic goals to enhance motivation and engagement.
- Gather information on students' goals to support effective course and program planning.
- Design instructional processes that help students see the value and/or personal relevance of learning activities to help them succeed in their fields of study.
- Create situational interest in a new field or topic and explore ways to turn situational interest into intrinsic interest.

Recognize that students with different beliefs about knowledge have different expectations of their instructors and different attitudes toward learning activities.
- Urge students to take responsibility for their learning by asking them to examine their views about knowledge and to consider how these views affect their learning and attitudes toward learning.
- Recognize cultural variations in attitudes about knowledge and learning and consider how these might influence student behavior in courses.

Treat students as apprentices who need assistance in learning the language, ways of thinking, and inquiry methods of academic fields.
- Design learning activities that acknowledge variations in students' experience in, and understanding of, the field.
- Help students who are new to a field to understand how knowledge in the field is organized and encourage advanced students to develop their own understandings of the field.
- Orient students to field by teaching them effective learning strategies.

TABLE 6.2. *(continued)*

Promote development of complex views of knowledge and recognize that students are at different stages of epistemological development.
- Ask students to reflect periodically on their views of knowledge and how these change throughout their college experience.
- Promote reflection on the many views of knowledge, as well as views of how knowledge is created and validated, that students encounter inside and outside academia.
- Encourage students to view themselves as knowledge producers as well as knowledge consumers.
- Challenge students to apply, integrate, evaluate, and construct knowledge by engaging them in collaborative, complex problem-solving activities.

Learn about learning and discuss with colleagues how knowledge about student learning can be put to use in courses and programs.
- Promote—among instructors and students—a multidimensional view of intelligence that recognizes different abilities to be tapped in courses and programs.
- Encourage faculty and students to view individuals' abilities as malleable rather than fixed and unchangeable.

student engagement and motivation also suggests that academic plans should create opportunities for active student involvement in the process of knowledge construction. The challenge for instructors is to focus less on content and more on what students are actually doing and thinking in and out of the classroom. This change is a difficult one for instructors who teach large classes or who believe that there is insufficient time to "cover" the required content. The change may occur when instructors recognize that, although they are "covering" knowledge, many students are not learning.

Most instructors interviewed for the NCRIPTAL course planning studies said they could readily tell if their students were actively involved in their learning by informally observing their behavior in class. What sometimes seemed to baffle them, however, was how to plan courses to promote greater student engagement and encourage more positive attitudes toward learning. In Table 6.2 we summarize the findings from the literature on learning that we have reviewed in this chapter to provide a set of guidelines to enhance student learning in courses and programs. In Chapter 7, we discuss the practical implications of each of the major findings highlighted in this table.

The degree to which students construct knowledge may be significantly altered if instructors take seriously the ideas about learners and learning discussed in this chapter. In addition to being versed in the central concepts of their discipline, college and university faculty must design courses and programs that build on the insights of learning research. These same insights, as we discuss in the next chapter, should inform the selection of a repertoire of instructional strategies.

CHAPTER SEVEN

INSTRUCTIONAL PROCESSES

Many factors influence instructors' choices of instructional processes. Previous experiences and beliefs about education, as well as organizational factors such as college and program goals, administrative structures, and institutional traditions all affect the shape of college courses and academic programs. The academic plan concept depicted in Figure 7.1 gives an overview of the relationships among these influences and three closely linked elements of an academic plan, namely faculty views of learners and learning, availability of resources, and choice of instructional processes.

National surveys of postsecondary faculty consistently show that, despite the emphasis on active learning in discussions of teaching, lecture is the most common instructional process used in college and university classrooms; more than half of all instructors use "extensive lecturing" in their courses (Lindholm, Szelényi, Hurtado, & Korn, 2005; Schuster & Finkelstein, 2006). Early career faculty members, however, are more likely to report using student-centered or active learning instructional methods than their mid- or advanced-career colleagues. For example, 57 percent of early career faculty report using small groups in instruction, compared to 36 percent of advanced-career faculty (Lindholm, Szelényi, Hurtado, & Korn, 2005). The NCRIPTAL studies of course planning (Stark & others, 1988, 1990) are among the few that have provided some insight into the variety of factors that influence the choice of lecture or other teaching strategies. Our review of what affects faculty decisions at the course, program,

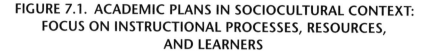

FIGURE 7.1. ACADEMIC PLANS IN SOCIOCULTURAL CONTEXT: FOCUS ON INSTRUCTIONAL PROCESSES, RESOURCES, AND LEARNERS

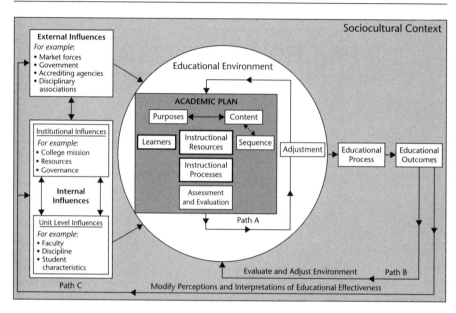

and college levels extends the examination of course planning presented in Chapter 5 by focusing specifically on the choice of instructional processes.

Following this review we discuss instructional processes themselves, exploring implications for teaching of the research and theory on learning that we presented in Chapter 6. While it is challenging to translate empirical studies on learning into instructional practices, these studies often provide powerful lenses for analyzing classroom practices without directly specifying teaching practices (Shuell, 1986). In connecting theory and research to effective instructional processes, our goal is to expand the array of teaching strategies that college and university instructors consider as they design and deliver courses and programs, so that teaching practices are consistent with what we know about how students learn.

Teaching Styles

Research on teaching styles at all levels of education suggests that individuals' beliefs about teaching are deeply held and enduring, even when those beliefs are contradicted by reason, experience, time, and schooling (Floden, 1995;

Pajares, 1992). Studies of teachers in elementary and secondary schools have established the role that personal influences, schooling experiences, and formal knowledge play in shaping beliefs about teaching (Woolfolk Hoy, Davis, & Pape, 2006). In higher education, the contextual filters model of course planning developed by the NCRIPTAL research team posits the influence of a very similar set of factors, suggesting that an instructor's views of her academic field (a type of formal knowledge) interact with her experiences, beliefs, and views of students to produce decisions about a particular course. The results of this interaction may produce quite different decisions for courses of different sizes and levels so it is likely that teaching styles are not context-free.

A few investigators have studied teaching styles at the postsecondary level, often centering on the extent to which an instructor consistently focuses his attention on academic content or student learning (see Kane, Sandretto, & Heath, 2002, for a review). Joseph Axelrod (1973), for example, compared the didactic teacher, who is inclined to tell students what is known, to the evocative teacher, who encourages students to discover it. Subdividing this classification, Paul Dressel (1980) suggested that the evocative teacher may be oriented in one of four ways: toward her discipline, toward herself, toward developing students' minds, or toward developing students as persons. Others have classified teaching styles based on their reliance on teacher-directed activities. Peter Jarvis (1985), for example, identified a teacher-controlled didactic style, a Socratic style in which instructors direct and students react, and a facilitative style in which the instructor focuses on creating learning experiences and holds students responsible for their own learning.

Empirical investigations have partially validated a few of these dimensions of teaching style. David Kember and Lyn Gow's (1994) study of teaching orientations in higher education revealed two contrasting orientations—learning facilitation and knowledge transmission—that were associated with instructors' espoused goals, attitudes, and beliefs about education. Instructors with a learning facilitation orientation, they explain, depend on student participation in their courses, think of themselves as facilitators of learning, care about students, and believe instructors should motivate student learning. Those instructors favoring knowledge transmission have a good understanding of the discipline or of the knowledge students will need for specific jobs and believe their role is to impart information to students. Keith Trigwell and Michael Prosser (2004) identified two conceptions of, and approaches to, teaching similar to those observed by Kember and Gow: an information transmission/teacher-focused approach and a conceptual change/student-focused approach. Instructors who use an information transmission/teacher-focused approach are primarily concerned with teaching content and they focus on how to organize, structure, and present course content in a way that students can understand. Instructors identified as having a conceptual change/student-centered approach see their role as facilitating student learning and knowledge construction or as supporting conceptual change. These instructors focus on what students do and encourage them to develop their own understandings of knowledge.

Teaching styles are often strongly associated with academic fields (Dressel & Marcus, 1982). This assertion is supported by the NCRIPTAL course planning studies, by investigations of faculty preferences for educational goals and emphases (Donald, 2002; Smart & Ethington, 1995; Smart, Feldman, & Ethington, 2000), and by studies of instructors' choices of teaching processes. Instructors in hard disciplines (classified according to Biglan's typology) were more likely to report using teacher-focused approaches, while those teaching in soft fields were more student-focused (Prosser & Trigwell, 1999; Lindblom-Ylanne, Trigwell, Nevgi, & Ashwin, 2006; Lueddeke, 2003; Trigwell, 2002). The differences appear to be related to the characteristics of the fields; hard fields contain many concepts to be learned, whereas soft fields focus more on exploring relationships and ideas.

A common critique of studies that use interview and survey data to study teaching style is that they typically are self-reports and do not include observations of teaching, examinations of course materials, or evidence of actual practices (Kane, Sandretto, & Heath, 2002). However, researchers have examined the relationship between instructors' intentions and their actual teaching practice and observed "a good, but far from perfect, fit" between instructors' beliefs and knowledge about effective practices and what they do in the classroom (Hativa, Barak, & Simhi, 2001, p. 725; Martin, Prosser, Trigwell, Ramsden, & Benjamin, 2000). Data from the National Survey of Student Learning (NSSE) and the Faculty Survey of Student Learning (FSSE) also indicate that, at institutions where instructors say they emphasize particular educational practices, students report engaging in those practices to a greater degree than peers attending other institutions (Kuh, Nelson Laird, & Umbach, 2004).

Teaching style is important because empirical evidence links instructional choices to students' learning strategies (Trigwell, Prosser, & Waterhouse, 1999). For example, use of passive learning methods that focus on knowledge transmission (Kember & Gow, 1994), assessment practices that test superficial knowledge (Entwistle, 2008; Kember & Gow, 1994) and lack of freedom for students in the learning environment (Ramsden & Entwistle, 1981) are all related to the development of undesirable learning behaviors such as the use of surface approaches to learning. Additional studies of teaching style are needed to determine the strength of the association between styles, instructional choices, and student learning. However, if, as Kember and Gow (1994) concluded, a knowledge transmission approach to teaching can depress students' use of deep learning approaches while a learning facilitation approach tends to discourage the use of surface approaches, efforts to improve teaching will need to make these connections explicit and engage instructors in discussions and examinations of their consequences for students.

Considerable evidence indicates that teaching styles can change and evolve, as a result of both experience and conscious effort. Furthermore, although college and university faculty tend to espouse a particular teaching style, they are not restricted to the type of teaching typically associated with that style (Dressel & Marcus, 1982). Instructors may gradually change their teaching styles as they gain teaching experience. Maryellen Weimer (1987) argues that experienced instructors more often view students as partners in learning. It seems likely that a number of personal characteristics and contextual factors need to align to foster this kind of development among instructors. First, the instructor must be reflective about her teaching practice and willing to learn and change. The institution, in turn, must encourage instructional experimentation.

Contextual Influences on Courses and Programs

Research suggests that instructors who teach in different contexts may adopt different approaches to teaching to accommodate those contexts (Lindblom-Ylanne, Trigwell, Nevgi, & Ashwin, 2006). A list of the most common influences reported by more than 550 instructors who attended teaching workshops included the nature of the course (required or elective, for majors or non-majors), student level (first-year students, seniors, graduate students), and departmental norms (Grasha, 1994). The contextual filters model, which we introduced in Chapter 5, describes a course planning process in which contextual influences such as the ones on Grasha's list modify the strong influence of teaching views and discipline (see Table 7.1 for the survey results). The contextual influences change how faculty construct academic plans and limit or expand the variety of plans they construct. Some influences—or filters—may influence course planning positively, as when an instructor takes into account student goals in designing course assignments. In other cases, filters may act as constraints; for example, when there is no suitable textbook for a course or when the length of class periods doesn't facilitate effective teaching.

Contextual influences may also modify teaching style by accentuating or attenuating the influence of the academic field. An instructor teaching a required course for senior majors may use different instructional methods than she would in an introductory course for non-majors. The adequacy of laboratory facilities and equipment strongly influences science instructors as they plan courses;

TABLE 7.1. FACULTY REPORTS OF CONTEXTUAL INFLUENCES ON PLANNING IN GENERAL EDUCATION AND PROFESSIONAL FIELDS

Influence	Percent of Faculty*	
	General Education	Professional Fields**
Goals of my college	35	49
Goals of my program	65	83
Program's contribution to college	65	63
Students' preparation	63	60
Students' effort	53	50
Students' ability	67	61
Students' interests	58	59
Students' life goals	35	54
Students' career goals	35	78
Students' educational goals	51	73
Success of previous students	59	56
Accreditors	29	65
Employers	28	69
Professional associations	28	57
External examinations	14	54
College-wide achievement tests	17	26
Other colleges' requirements	40	40
Available textbooks	54	60
Available facilities	34	46
Available opportunities (clinical, etc.)	22	48
Available teaching assistants	12	17
Available secretarial help	11	19
Available supplies	21	30
Class size	53	54
Class schedule	37	41
Assigned workload	37	43
Promotion or tenure pressure	9	11
Required instructional method	11	20
Advising office	7	13
Instructional development office	4	7
Student services office	4	7
Library services	38	49
Audiovisual services	35	50
Program chairperson	27	39
Colleagues	33	41
Articles/books on teaching/learning	31	55
Articles/books on my field	45	62

*Percentage of faculty who rated the item as a "very strong" or "strong" influence on course planning.

**Professional fields included were nursing, business, and educational psychology.

From: Stark and others, 1990. Reprinted by permission of the University of Michigan.

historians are more concerned with appropriate library resources. The influence of contextual factors also varies with the type of college or university. Choices of instructional processes by vocational faculty in community colleges may be strongly influenced by the needs of local employers and the desire to give students hands-on experience in a career field. Liberal arts college faculty, in contrast, may be more likely to choose instructional approaches that prepare students for admission requirements of graduate and professional schools.

The strong influence of academic field on instructional choices is reflected in the sources of assistance in teaching cited by faculty in the NCRIPTAL studies. The most useful sources of assistance were a departmental colleague at the institution (78 percent), a department or division chair (48 percent), course evaluations from students (48 percent), books or articles on instructional design (41 percent), a colleague from another institution (40 percent) or another department (23 percent), and one's disciplinary association (27 percent). These figures reveal the strong dependence on disciplinary colleagues in course planning. Faculty members who reported being influenced by one of these on- or off-campus sources of assistance were influenced by other sources as well. Instructors who consult others in course planning also tended to seek a wide variety of sources of assistance; those who consulted little appeared to prefer working alone.

Other contextual features also influenced the course planning practices of instructors in the NCRIPTAL studies. More than half of the instructors surveyed reported that the availability of an appropriate textbook was an important influence on their planning. In structured fields such as mathematics and science, respondents often reported following the textbook sequence rather than making individual decisions about when to introduce a topic. Commercially prepared materials, especially electronic ones, that accompany textbooks increasingly influence instructors. The adoption of such resources, of course, can both facilitate and constrain effective curriculum planning.

In all fields, classroom facilities, such as rooms with fixed seating, may constrain the choice of instructional methods. For example, instructors may forego small-group discussions or project work if classroom spaces are not conducive to these arrangements. Resources such as time and teaching assistance can also influence how a course is designed and taught. Instructors may avoid writing assignments because they have a large class and no assistance with grading. Despite such obvious pragmatic constraints on instructional process, faculty in the NCRIPTAL studies seldom viewed their course planning as strongly influenced by them. Exceptions occurred if resources had recently been cut or if new resources, such as instructional technologies, had raised instructors' hopes but were insufficient in supply. It appears that instructors are so accustomed to working with limited help and within constrained environments that they overlook all but the most severe situations. Although unnoticed, insufficient time and material resources, nonetheless, limit instructional innovations.

Although they may also go unnoticed, organizational structures influence choices of instructional strategies. Academic credits and degrees, advising systems, tests, grading practices, and the semester and quarter academic calendars all shape college curricula. Typically, instructors do not question the educational efficacy of these structures; they merely work within them, arranging the material they teach to accommodate student vacation periods, facility schedules, and even the time of the day.

At the program level, instructors often make decisions by adopting instructional policies rather than selecting instructional processes. Policies articulate and codify beliefs about instructional processes that program faculty view as appropriate for their students. Like decisions about course form, these policies and the practices they generate are influenced by organizational conditions and external forces such as the college mission, relations with other units, available resources, and accreditors. At the college level, instructional processes may be viewed as the aggregation of program policies, which can vary considerably within a single institution and within a specific organizational unit such as a department or a college within a university.

Institutional conditions and college-level policies can create a supportive or constraining atmosphere for instructional innovation. A college provides instructional resources to support those aspects of an educational environment (including instructional processes) it deems important to its purposes. Conversely, it may deny resources to programs perceived to be tangential to established educational goals or instructional policies. In many colleges and universities, the traditional division between general education and major fields also shapes the instructional processes chosen for students.

Disciplinary associations, accreditors, employers, and government agencies may also influence program content and instructional practices and policies. For example, the Conference on College Composition and Communication (CCCC) has influenced instruction in many major fields with its advocacy of writing across the curriculum. Similarly, by mandating that all engineering students demonstrate learning outcomes in design and teamwork, the accrediting body for engineering programs encourages the use of active and experiential learning in the field. In many career-oriented fields, the choice of instructional policies and processes is influenced directly when professional associations and accrediting groups set standards for specific numbers of hours of clinical experience and ratios of students to faculty (for example, in speech and hearing science) or prescribe detailed instructional objectives (for example, in architecture). Regional accreditors, in contrast, may indirectly influence instruction by assuring collegial governance structures and providing a resource base, but have little direct impact on instructional planning.

Employers are a strong influence on professional and vocational programs that have statewide certification and licensing examinations or consult advisory boards of local employers to assist them in program planning. Four-year college programs, such as business and engineering, have such boards, which sometimes provide monetary resources for program development and improvement as well as advice.

Instructional policies may also be affected by student transfer to other institutions. Community college programs often adjust instructional policies to prepare students for entry into four-year colleges with which they have articulation agreements. If four-year engineering programs require students to use graphing calculators, these skills may be introduced in the two-year college curriculum. Conversely, four-year colleges adjust in anticipation of receiving transfer students whose initial preparation was provided elsewhere.

At the college level, institutions that adopt a distribution system of general education requirements have, de facto, made policy decisions that affect instructional process at the course level. The decision to use a distribution system virtually assures classes of substantial size and may create the need for multiple sections of a course, sometimes taught by instructors who do not teach from the same syllabus and texts. Some courses that fulfill general education requirements may also serve as the introduction to a major, effectively defaulting instructional decisions to the program specialties or individual instructors. Faculty, who are organized into departments based on their field affiliations, may have little motivation to contribute time or resources to the distribution-based general education program. In contrast, general education programs with specific core requirements often require that a group of faculty members from several disciplines devote considerable time to discussing decisions about instructional policies and processes. Such a group may have leadership, a budget, and the authority to choose instructional processes, for example, designing small seminar classes rather than large lecture courses.

Ideally, a college or university purposefully cultivates an educational environment that encourages faculty members to use varied instructional processes at the course level. Such an institution also establishes instructional policies at the program- and college-wide level that support faculty learning about how instructional processes are consistent with what is known about student learning.

Expanding Choices Among Instructional Processes

Observers of higher education often comment that few college and university instructors have been formally trained in teaching. This situation is slowly changing as more universities develop training programs to prepare doctoral students—the faculty of tomorrow—to understand, appreciate, and fulfill the teaching role. At present, however, most college and university instructors learn to teach by teaching or imitate their own teachers. Some read journals or books about teaching in their field, take advantage of professional development opportunities on or off campus, and hear about instructional alternatives from colleagues, but most have limited exposure to the variety of instructional processes that are possible and limited knowledge of the educational theories and research that support them. The following discussion of instructional processes provides an overview of approaches that align with the research and theories of learning reviewed in Chapter 6 (the bulleted text in each section corresponds to major findings highlighted in Table 6.2). The instructional choices we describe apply primarily to the course level but can also affect program and college planning.

Good teaching is, in large measure, the consequence of an academic plan that includes informed and conscious decisions about instructional processes and how they will enable student learning. To develop a good plan, an instructor must consider how the plan will contribute to students' development as learners in the course. After determining a set of broad course goals and more specific learning objectives, instructors must determine how each instructional strategy they propose will help students achieve those goals and objectives. What will be achieved by the set of readings assigned for a given week, by the assignment of a term paper, through laboratory exercises, from a field observation, small-group discussion, or demonstration? What learning should occur for each strategy? In evaluating a course, the instructor must determine whether the selected texts and readings, in-class activities, course assignments, and assessments actually worked. To what extent did they contribute to students' development and capacity to learn independently?

Knowing Learners

> - Assess students' prior knowledge and skills to avoid unfounded assumptions about what students know about the subject matter being studied.
> - Don't assume students know how to learn.
> - Acknowledge that learning, motivation, and engagement are affected by attitudes and emotions.

Contemporary views frame learning as a process of constructing new knowledge and understandings, building on prior beliefs and knowledge. The implication of this view, supported by considerable research evidence, is that learning is enhanced when instructors pay attention to the beliefs and knowledge learners bring to a task (Bransford, Brown, & Cocking, 2000). In some cases, students have prior knowledge that instructors can build upon to provide more complete understandings of ideas or phenomena. In other cases, incorrect views of phenomena, that is, misconceptions, can get in the way of an accurate understanding of the topic and subject being studied. And, in an educational system in which students from many different cultures interact with peers, instructors, and content, there is the potential for new ideas to conflict with values and practices common in students' homes and communities.

Prior misconceptions can be particularly problematic at the college level. Numerous studies reveal that college students' misunderstandings of scientific phenomena—already studied in elementary and/or high school—persist despite accurate instruction in these concepts. When misconceptions interfere with understanding, active learning is more effective than lecturing because it can make students' thinking visible to the instructor, who can then search for ways to help students replace their faulty understandings (Bransford, Brown, & Cocking, 2000). Effective assessment strategies provide specific feedback about where misconceptions lie so that instructors can explicitly correct these misunderstandings.

Capitalizing on Students' Goals Motivation is required for active learning, but active learning can also increase student motivation. This reciprocal relationship, based in research and theory on learning, highlights the importance of the interaction between the learner and the learning experience in producing learning. To promote this interaction, instructional processes must motivate students by capitalizing on their goals and interests and showing them how what they are learning can be valuable personally, intellectually, socially, or occupationally.

Given the motivational power of student goals, instructors developing academic plans should be deliberate in their explorations of the goals students bring to classes and programs. In addition to acknowledging these personal goals, instructors can, at the very least, discuss with students how a course may be useful to them in their lives and careers. Faculty and professional advisors can do the same when discussing general education goals with students who come for curriculum planning.

The Student Goals Exploration (SGE) inventory (Stark, Lowther, Shaw, & Sossen, 1991) can help instructors understand students' goals in relation to course goals and can also be used to foster a classroom dialogue about the congruence between these often disparate goal sets. Instructors will likely be surprised about the misunderstandings that entering college students have about the purposes of different college courses and fields of study. Some students, for example, assume that studying psychology will help them solve personal problems. Instructors who fail to recognize that some students are naïve about the purposes of different courses and programs may perceive their students as lacking learning-directed goals. Learning-directed goals develop, however, when students understand the relevance of what they are learning to their own career and personal goals. True mismatches between student goals and program goals can be remedied through advising, discussion, and intentional decisions to link coursework to students' interests and goals.

Course goals and demands can be positive influences on students, but they can also decrease motivation and even threaten students, leading to anxiety, ineffective learning behaviors, or lack of incentives. Knowing students' abilities and their perceptions of their abilities allows instructors to interpret student behaviors and feelings about a course. Designing academic tasks that are challenging but not threatening requires some knowledge of students' feelings of self-efficacy in the specific course or program. With such information, instructors can gradually increase the difficulty and types of learning activities to enhance students' expectations of success, improve their academic confidence, and increase their interest in the field. Instructors may be able to motivate students by capitalizing on their intrinsic and extrinsic needs, helping them succeed, and increasing their self-efficacy by attributing success to individual ability and increased effort (Weiner, 1986).

Establishing Classroom and Program Environment Students with differing levels of preparation, aptitude, experience, motivation, and self-confidence frequently are in the same classrooms and academic programs. Many instructors manifest their concern and respect for these student differences and preferences and try to create opportunities for all students to achieve. Some of these required accommodations are fairly simple to implement; others are far more difficult.

Since psychologists tell us that students need a modest level of anxiety and a supportive climate to learn well, students will learn best when the classroom and program offer them academic challenges but treat them with trust and respect. Positive classroom experiences result when students believe they are valued members of a learning group, that instructors respect their contributions in the classroom, and that taking intellectual risks is not only accepted but encouraged. A positive classroom climate reduces student anxiety, promotes linkages with students' goals, and meets students where they are intellectually and as developing learners. Students can find academic work challenging or threatening. Too little or too much stress can diminish learning. The key to reducing harmful stress is to help students understand what to expect, give feedback, and provide them with a sense of control over their own education (Whitman, Spendlove, & Clark, 1984).

Svinicki (ca 1989) observed that, while learning involves risk taking, teaching involves trust building. Students put their self-esteem on the line whenever they actively participate in a course (Gaff, 1991). If their attempts at making contributions are met with empathy and understanding, the results will be increased trust, self-confidence, and self-esteem. In contrast, "learning abuse" occurs when students' comments are ignored, rejected out of hand, or met with derision. Such treatment bruises students' self-esteem and confidence and, if continued over time, turns learning into an anxiety-producing experience. In the face of this kind of treatment, students respond by restraining their curiosity, read only what is assigned, answer questions only when they cannot be avoided, and keep the instructor at a distance. When these coping mechanisms are unsuccessful, a student may withdraw from a course or from an institution.

College-level learning is the joint responsibility of faculty and students, who must create and maintain an atmosphere of mutual respect, a common interest in inquiry, and freedom from anxiety. Instructors should make it clear to students that their ideas will be respected, but also open to scrutiny. Prior to college, many students have learned in schools where the teacher's answer is the correct answer and their ideas are not solicited. Students schooled in this way may be unwilling to risk sharing their ideas, so instructors must clearly establish the importance of hearing what students think. Many of the instructional processes we describe are possible only if a favorable learning climate exists.

Helping Students Learn to Learn Individuals select learning strategies that they believe will help them understand and make meaning of the information they encounter. Sometimes this choice of learning strategies is productive, enabling the individual to develop a clear understanding of what must be learned. In other cases it is less productive because the individual lacks an understanding of which learning strategies will be effective for a given learning task and why. Metacognition describes this reflective process of thinking about thinking and learning to learn. In colleges and universities, metacognition often calls up the idea of "study skills" courses or workshops, but the term is more encompassing.

First-year orientation and other kinds of study skills courses often focus on the development of metacognitive processes such as comprehension, monitoring, reviewing, and test-taking strategies. The topics in such courses can help students improve the ways in which they learn from lectures, reading assignments, discussions, and peers. They may also help students develop strategies to improve their ability to recall information, as well as introduce topics such as self-management, time management, motivation and anxiety, and test-taking strategies. Pintrich and his colleagues found that they could successfully teach students to "learn how to learn" while teaching them about psychological principles underlying metacognitive strategies. They also successfully used these ideas in courses other than psychology where the subject matter is less closely related to the learning tasks (Pintrich, 1988a, 1988b; Pintrich, McKeachie, & Lin, 1987).

Instructors can teach study skills in their own courses, regardless of their familiarity with research on metacognition, by devising a set of questions for each reading assignment that prompt students to practice deep processing. Knowing what study strategies students already possess, and assessing whether they are expanding their available strategies, is a bit more complex and requires initial diagnosis. One useful tool for instructors is the Learning and Study Strategies Inventory (LASSI), which measures strengths and weaknesses related to academic success (Weinstein & Palmer, 2002). The inventory is administered in about thirty minutes and easily scored. It assesses a student's attitude, motivation, time management, anxiety, concentration, information processing, ability to select main ideas, study aids, self-testing, and test strategies. Diagnosis, of course, should and can be combined with skill development.

At the program level, faculty collectively can decide to diagnose study skills, as well as content knowledge, when they conduct placement tests. They can ensure that some basic-level courses include exercises and assignments to develop relevant study skills, and they can examine advising structures to be sure that students are directed to support services when needed. Where learning skills services do not exist, programs can train peer tutors to help with the task. These program-level decisions deliberately address elements of the program's academic plan that are too often neglected.

Engaging and Motivating Students

> • Design academic plans that connect students' personal and academic goals to enhance motivation and engagement.

Courses that treat students as passive spectators usually do not help them learn or prepare them well for other learning experiences in or out of college. To learn well, students must actively engage with course content—questioning, applying, testing, and reflecting on what they are learning. Students who are listening intently to a lecture and taking notes are active learners, as are those who are using deep processing strategies to understand texts and complete assignments. Too often students do not engage in this kind of active learning inside or outside the classroom because they are not asked to do so by instructors.

Instructional development experts observe that they repeatedly hear instructors who cling to the lecture methods of teaching lament: "I have too much content to cover!" (Svinicki, 1991, p. 1). Mere exposure to material does not constitute learning. It is not the lecture that produces learning, but the studying, summarizing, and organizing of lecture notes on which learning depends. Instructors who emphasize content coverage are not acting on empirical evidence that active learning experiences are the closest we have to a gold standard in instruction. Course content is critical, but so are instructional processes that require students to grapple with that content and its application. Such activities demonstrate the value of course content, sustain student attention, and increase motivation. Furthermore, because much learning occurs outside of the classroom as students wrestle with content on their own, instructors should ensure that students engage in active learning between class sessions as well as in class.

Weston and Cranton (1986) differentiated instructional strategies according to the extent to which they engaged students in learning:

- Instructor-centered strategies place the greatest responsibility on the instructor. Lectures are most common, but demonstrations may be incorporated.
- Interactive strategies use communication among students as well as between students and instructors. Discussions are the most common interactive teaching method and are believed to be effective for developing skills of analysis, synthesis, and evaluation.
- Experiential strategies, such as service learning and internships, often take place outside the classroom, but role playing, simulations, laboratories, and games can bring it into the classroom. Although experiential learning is by definition active learning, it varies in the degree to which it is instructor-led.
- Individualized strategies are used to accommodate students who learn at different rates and to provide immediate feedback intended to reinforce student effort. These methods emphasize pacing and may include computer-based instruction and the use of learning modules.
From: Weston & Cranton, 1986. Copyright by The Ohio State University Press. Reproduced with permission.

The following sections describe various instructional processes that exemplify these different categories of instruction.

Modifying Instructor-Centered Lectures

The size of many academic programs and the pressure to provide cost-efficient instruction in colleges and universities suggest that lectures will continue to be common instructional strategies. The lecture method is appropriate when instructors want to provide up-to-date information, summarize widely scattered material, adapt material to student interests and backgrounds, and build connections (Cameron, 1992; McKeachie, 2006). Good lectures are characterized by expressiveness, clarity, and organization. Nonetheless, they hold students' interest for relatively short periods of time and are less effective than more active learning methods for developing students' thinking skills or promoting motivation. Any lecture, however, can be improved by increasing students' engagement with the ideas under study.

In a lecture, the instructor controls how information is presented, sequenced, and paced. A well-organized lecture presents a coherent set of ideas that help students organize the material they are learning. Yet, it may not ensure that students understand or integrate the ideas it delivers. Depending on their prior learning and experiences, students may or may not construct the same meaning of the ideas as their instructor.

The traditional fifty-minute lecture period is too long for the human attention span. So those who modify the lecture to be more effective often seek to break up the length of time the instructor speaks. Even in a large lecture hall, a number of techniques can involve students in the lectures by incorporating activities that ask students to analyze situations, solve problems, or evaluate ideas. Expert instructors give overviews of their lectures at the beginning, perhaps introducing a concept map or outline to help students understand the relationship of ideas to be presented. They include a limited number of ideas in a single lecture; research suggests no more than five major chunks. These expert lecturers involve students by questioning, posing problems, using examples, and checking to see whether students understand key points. Occasionally they may stop and ask students to summarize, synthesize, and reflect on what has been said. They summarize key ideas at the end of class or, alternatively, leave students with a problem to solve for the next meeting. They may also use writing exercises to help students articulate their thoughts and integrate material. In modern lecture rooms, electronic devices at each seat such as "clickers" allow students to submit their answers to instructor questions following these activities, see how their answers stack up against those of their peers, and receive immediate feedback from the instructor on correct and incorrect answers and solutions.

Activities such as one-minute papers and group discussions can be effectively incorporated within lectures to test student understanding and encourage integration. In the one-minute paper, the instructor interrupts the lecture and asks the class to write their ideas or questions or to solve a problem. The questions may concern any element of the course that an instructor wants to stress or examine (Cross & Angelo, 1988, p. 148) and should require students to synthesize information and provide opportunities for students to practice effective thinking skills.

Collaborative learning groups also may be used to divide a lecture, focus attention on a key issue, and serve as a mechanism for active learning. Small groups of students, usually five to eight, briefly discuss a concept or problem suggested by the lecturer. All or a few of the groups then present their ideas to the class. Such groups allow students to digest the information they have received, making sense of it as they discuss it with others and compare understandings. Group reports also provide the instructor with feedback regarding the general level of comprehension of the class and an opportunity to provide corrections, amendments, amplifications, and/or additional examples to ensure students understand the material. In a format that can be used to summarize small-group discussions or to close a lecture, the instructor asks the class to identify the main points in a lecture, recording all the responses, good or bad. He then elaborates on various points, restating them if necessary, adding detail. This method can be used to help students relate their own experiences to the course content and also provides the instructor with immediate feedback about the success of the activity or lecture. These and other techniques for segmenting lectures can be adapted to suit the discipline taught.

Using Interactive Instructional Processes

Class discussions, used as a primary instructional method or interspersed among mini-lectures, seek to engage students actively with the content of a course. Other interactive strategies, however, such as collaborative and cooperative learning, peer teaching, and the use of case studies, simulations, and role plays, provide additional methods for engaging students as active participants in the learning experience.

Discussions Discussions are usually more motivating to students than lectures, maintain their interest more fully, and are an effective means of developing thinking skills. Discussions differ from lectures because the instructor is not the only individual in the room assumed to have the ability to answer the questions asked or solve the problem that is posed. Students are encouraged to give their opinions, test their theories, and even offer guidance to others.

Faculty often lack training in posing the right kinds of discussion questions for students. The questions need to be tailored to both the students' level of understanding of the topic and the learning objective sought. Instructors may pose questions designed to clarify ideas, to develop relationships, to summarize, and to challenge. Each of these is useful in specific situations; instructors can develop a sense for which type is appropriate. Instructional development staff can assist faculty who are new to discussions methods as they master this technique.

Different questions can be used to facilitate different stages of discussion. For example, to initiate a discussion, change the subject, or modify the direction of the discussion, instructors can ask students to think about their reactions to the information at hand, about how other approaches might work, or about how the approach being discussed would work in other situations. To lead a student to a particular statement or to get students to progress through a set of logical steps to a conclusion, instructors can frame questions about the factors that might explain an occurrence or phenomenon, ask students to propose next steps, and have them relate their comments to those of other students. It is also helpful to ask students to clarify or amplify what they have said and to rephrase answers.

Questions that involve memorization, comprehension, and application generate fewer statements from students than questions that demand analysis, synthesis, or evaluation. Those that have a single correct answer nature (for example, those that ask students to respond with a memorized fact) inhibit students from offering expanded responses that better reveal what they know and can do with their knowledge. Investigators have found that student responses to questions tend to reflect the demands placed on them by instructors and that the amount of student participation also appears to be positively influenced (Dunkin & Barnes, 1986). The most useful questions encourage further responses from students without threatening, judging, or turning them off.

Leading discussions that produce positive results is a demanding task. Whole-group discussions are difficult to manage with classes of more than thirty students. They are typically less efficient than lectures in presenting large bodies of information and may be minimally effective (or even threatening) for students who are reluctant to participate. Instructors must therefore deliberately create a classroom environment in which students' questions, as well as their answers to the instructors' queries, are appropriately acknowledged and corrected constructively.

Case Studies, Simulations, and Role Plays   Case teaching is a well-established strategy for interactive learning that originated in professional fields such as legal and medical education to serve as proxies for real situations in which decisions or actions are usually required. The case study is usually short, focusing on a specific idea or dilemma to be addressed. It may require that students critique a decision or make a recommendation. Instructors can use case studies to address a variety of course and program goals, including building students' content knowledge; exercising and strengthening their skills in analysis, synthesis, and collaboration; and enhancing their self-confidence (Boehrer & Linsky, 1990). Well-developed case studies, properly used, can also encourage student responsibility, promote self-directed learning, and develop questioning skills.

Role playing, simulations, and guided design (a type of structured problem solving) also require that students analyze complex problems, often collaboratively. These processes are often enjoyable for students, as well as replicable and convenient. Like cases, computer simulations and role plays can be realistic and may be modified or manipulated in response to student input. Computer technology also permits instructors to expand the boundaries of the classroom or laboratory through simulations that bring learning experiences into residence halls and student homes.

Collaborative and Cooperative Learning Strategies for group learning are based on a solid base of knowledge about student learning and have proven successful in practice. Despite widespread discussion of their educational benefits, adoption has been slow. Some instructors are reluctant to use groups because they fear students and colleagues will view this as reneging on teaching responsibilities. Contrary to such beliefs, well-designed group learning activities require instructors to prepare and orchestrate student learning deliberately.

Positive group learning experiences are more likely to result if students understand why the collaborative learning experience is important and what it will help them achieve (Feichtner & Davis, 1984). In addition to explaining the purposes of group learning, instructors must assist students throughout the process by helping them set realistic expectations and ground rules, creating diverse groups, providing multiple decision-making opportunities, listening in on group discussions and offering advice or assistance as needed, providing immediate feedback, and allowing groups to meet occasionally during regular class time. Undergraduate students report that their best group experiences were those in which the instructor formed the group (Common, 1989), possibly because instructors are able to match student learning styles or join students with complementary talents.

The terms "group learning," "collaborative learning," and "cooperative learning" are often used synonymously, but actually vary in meaning. *Collaborative learning* is the umbrella term for instructional approaches that involve students in joint learning activities with peers and/or instructors (Smith & MacGregor, 1992). Learning activities may take the form of extended projects, mentoring, or peer teaching, but all are based on the assumption that learners must construct their knowledge. To develop students' awareness of learning as a process of discovery, they share responsibility for both shaping the learning experience (or course) and teaching. Collaborative learning strives to create an atmosphere of community in which students solve problems, but also develop interpersonal, teamwork, communication, and leadership skills. In some forms of collaborative learning, the status differential between teacher and student is purposefully reduced to encourage students to view themselves as essential participants in the learning process.

Cooperative learning generally describes a more structured type of collaborative learning. Five basic elements are characteristic of this teaching approach: (a) positive interdependence, (b) face-to-face interaction, (c) individual accountability, (d) social skills, and (e) group processing (Johnson, Johnson, & Smith, 1991). The first, *positive interdependence*, is multidimensional, involving decisions and behaviors related to goals, roles, resources, and rewards. Goal interdependence is achieved by requiring all group members to agree on the answer and strategies for solving each problem; the existence of a mutually shared goal is the most important element in cooperative learning. Role interdependence requires that each group member be assigned a role—for example, the role of reader, facilitator, checker, etc. The instructor creates positive resource interdependence by giving each group only one copy of the problem or assignment; all members work on the same problem sheet and share their insights with one another. Interdependence is rewarded through assignments of points or credit based on each team member's performance.

Face-to-face interaction is the second element required in cooperative learning. Students encourage, assist, and support one another in the process of learning together. The third element, *individual accountability*, exists when the instructor assesses each individual's performance and gives the results to the group. One strategy for structuring individual accountability is to test each student and then select one grade at random to be assigned to all group members. This strategy not only promotes individual responsibility, but it encourages group members to work together to ensure that all fully understand the material under study. Advocates note that the *social skills* needed for successful cooperative group learning must be taught "as purposely and precisely as academic skills" (Johnson, Johnson, & Smith, 1991, p. 7).

Finally, instructors who use cooperative learning must assist in *group processing* of information that helps them assess how well they are achieving their goals and maintaining working relationships. In addition to addressing progress toward the goal and group dynamics, the instructor also facilitates the learning of social skills by giving all members feedback on the quality of their participation in the group.

Cooperative learning can be used to achieve a variety of purposes: teaching content, ensuring active information processing during a lecture, and providing long-term academic support as students pursue an extended task or set of tasks. As implied by this list of aims, it can be short-term (a class period or two) or last an entire term, academic year, or longer. The instructor's role in facilitating good group interaction is largely one of support and feedback, but her role in designing and evaluating the process is crucial. She must specify the goals and objectives for the group, decide who will be in which group, carefully explain the task and goal structure (perhaps more than once) to students, monitor the group progress and effectiveness, intervene when needed, and finally, evaluate students' achievements, including the quality of their cooperation and participation and its contribution to group and individual outcomes (Johnson, Johnson, & Smith, 1991).

Research on collaborative and cooperative learning strategies finds that these approaches typically enhance student learning (Pascarella & Terenzini, 2005). Syntheses of studies of both methods reveal significant advantages in individual achievement, problem solving, and content learning for students in these learning situations when compared with those in individualistic or competitive situations. This advantage is the same whether the cooperative groups are solving well-structured or ill-structured problems. In particular, studies show that college students solving linguistic problems (rather than non-linguistic problems) reaped substantial advantages from cooperative learning strategies (Pascarella & Terenzini, 2005).

Peer Teaching Most instructors have heard the often-quoted statement: To teach is to learn twice (Whitman, 1988). In peer teaching, a variant of collaborative learning, a student learns the material and then teaches it to peers. A wide variety of arrangements are possible. The student acting as teacher may be a tutor, two students may work as a pair, or both may be involved in a workshop group. Whitman (1988) identifies five types of peers: (a) near peers (other undergraduate students), (b) undergraduate teaching assistants, (c) tutors, (d) counselors (with a general focus), and (e) co-peers (partnerships and work groups). Johnson, Johnson, and Smith (1991) offer several ideas for structuring peer teaching using pairs of students: discussion pairs, explanation pairs, note-taking pairs, and feedback pairs.

Psychologists have found that the way students learn material in anticipation of peer teaching is different from the kind of learning that takes place when a student is required to take a test. When students explain to one another, they test their knowledge; when they take notes together, they improve their synthesis skills. Just as articulation in a group learning situation resembles deep processing rather than surface processing of material, peer teaching requires students to elaborate their knowledge rather than simply recalling it. Research evidence suggests that the act of tutoring itself can enhance students' ability to retain what they are learning, thus enhancing content mastery (Pascarella & Terenzini, 2005).

Linking Learning and Life: Experiential Learning

Instruction need not be limited to classroom settings. Many instructional processes, such as undergraduate research opportunities, supervised field work, internships, and academic service learning, are useful tools for initiating students into a field of study by allowing them to experience it first-hand. These activities are particularly well-suited for developing students' problem-solving, interpersonal, and teamwork skills. They also can introduce students to the important role of professional standards and ethics in a field and enhance career development and personal maturity. Career decisions flow from engaging in a broad range of experiences.

Most off-campus learning can be called experiential education. Regardless of the academic field, experiential education helps students understand complex problems in context and helps institutions respond to changes in the nature of work and the new demands of society (Sexton & Ungerer, 1975). Advocates argue that it also helps prepare students for their roles as citizens and provides alternatives for students who are alienated from traditional forms of education.

Cooperative Education Cooperative education allows students to alternate or combine periods of academic study and employment, providing students with opportunities to test career options before graduation while earning wages or salaries in the process. "Co-ops" help students integrate classroom studies and work experience related to their academic or career goals. They are similar to internships, but often provide progressive experiences with the same employer over multiple terms (NCCE, 2002). Students in all fields of study can enroll in cooperative education, but students in professional fields like business and engineering may be most likely to take advantage of these experiences. While students who complete cooperative education reportedly have more job interviews, higher starting salaries, and higher grade point averages than students who do not participate (Yin, 2008), the greatest benefit, from the point of view of educators, may be the opportunity students have to apply what they are learning in the classroom to actual work problems. To make the most of this opportunity to integrate learning, many cooperative education programs require students to report on their experiences with employers. These reports are intended not only to document the work experience, but to prompt students' reflection on the connections between their curricular and co-curricular experiences. Students are often asked to discuss what they learned, as well as what knowledge they used on the job, to think about additional courses that might help them remedy gaps in their educational programs, and to explain how the cooperative education experience is influencing their understanding of potential careers and their vocational interests.

Service Learning During the last two decades, service learning has received national emphasis as an important part of a college education. As this form of experiential learning has developed, some advocates have distinguished community service from academic service learning. Community service can be linked to courses or programs or not, but academic service learning requires an integrated approach in which students apply what is learned in the classroom to address community problems. Service learning is a credit-bearing educational experience requiring participation in organized service activities (Bringle & Hatcher, 1996). Structured reflection on this activity is a mechanism for understanding course content and obtaining a broader appreciation of one's field of study, while enhancing one's sense of civic responsibility.

International Study International study (study abroad) is a well-known form of experiential education that is changing to meet new needs and to take advantage of new technologies. Traditionally, such programs required students to spend a semester or year at a university in another country, taking courses for which their home institution will accept transfer credit. Although subject to criticism that they are superficial, shorter-term international study tours are gaining popularity. These short terms expose students to another culture and provide opportunities to engage in service, research, or design projects with individuals in different countries. Additionally, virtual student exchanges, conducted through teleconferencing and collaborative websites, connect U.S. students with their counterparts in other countries to permit them to learn or work on collaborative projects using communications technology. These practices that change the venue for learning are typically adopted only after lengthy discussions about curricular quality and often require curricular restructuring. The benefit of these out-of-class experiences, however, is that they can increase students' motivation and help them integrate their learning by presenting real-life opportunities in which to apply their knowledge.

Classroom-Based Experiential Learning Some forms of experiential learning can occur in classes and courses. Problem-based learning (sometimes called project-based learning) is a prime example. Students work collaboratively on a structured or unstructured task and persist with the same group for the duration of the task or project while the instructor serves as a learning facilitator. The by-products of problem- and project-based learning are student engagement in the learning process, pride in the group effort, and a sense of personal responsibility for learning. Increasingly used in medical schools to eliminate information overload, problem-based learning represents a major philosophical change in the way instruction is designed. Faculty members change from information dispensers to instructional guides and managers, while students change from listeners to problem-solvers. Research on the method suggests that it works best if the instructor is first a content expert and, second, trained in use of the process (Boud & Feletti, 1991; Davis, Nairn, Paine, Anderson, & Oh, 1992).

Course management systems and new instructional technologies permit the use of experiential learning through face-to-face and online courses. Music and theater performances can be brought into students' living areas via the Internet, as well as through course management systems. Groups working on real-world problems can meet virtually and share work products. As instructors become comfortable with these technologies, more opportunities for interaction can occur outside the classroom, encouraging students to see learning as an ongoing process rather than one that takes place in fifty-minute sessions. For-profit institutions have been leaders in developing materials to simulate experiential learning. The University of Phoenix, for example, has developed a realistic simulated community complete with industries and government that is used by classes in many different disciplines (Wasley, 2008).

Addressing Student Diversity

> • Recognize that students with different beliefs about knowledge have different expectations of their instructors and different attitudes toward learning activities.

Many instructors feel it is impossible to accommodate the needs of the great diversity of learners they encounter in their courses. Research supports the claim that students learn best in settings that accommodate their individual needs and styles. Many learner attributes, such as preferred learning strategies, aptitude, anxiety, previous preparation, and self-efficacy, may all interact with particular instructional processes to influence achievement positively or negatively. Students who enjoy learning with others, for example, may gain from the use of collaborative work groups, whereas others prefer to learn independently rather than working with peers. At a minimum, instructors should consider the prior knowledge and special needs of students in a class when establishing expected types and levels of performance, but other adjustments to a course can provide students with opportunities to pursue their interests.

Giving Students Choices Simply allowing students to choose among supplementary readings or to develop their own term-paper topics accommodates students' interests. In highly structured courses with few options for personalized assignments or readings, it may be possible to include examples from a variety of contexts in order to connect with students in different majors or tap different interests. For example, a biology lecture might include examples from medicine, environmental planning, genetics, and psychiatry.

While most psychologists no longer believe that learning styles are fixed, they acknowledge that individuals do tend to choose certain learning strategies. Since learning strategies can be taught and learned, another way to engage students with different preferences is to vary the types of activities in a course. Students who enjoy hands-on, concrete activities are likely to find observations, simulations, labs, and field work stimulating. Reflective thinkers will be engaged with activities like journaling, discussing, and brainstorming. Instructors, who tend to enjoy abstract thinking, need to be conscious of their own predilections and consider how to motivate students whose experiences, goals, and preferences differ from their own. While every student interest cannot be accommodated in every class, more individualization is possible than most instructors imagine. Importantly, recent thinking about learning and instruction suggests that instructors should not only adapt course activities for diverse learners, but should deliberately help students become competent in various approaches to learning.

Letting Students Vary the Pace In most classes, instructors control the pace of learning by determining the rate at which information is presented to students. Self-paced instructional methods, in contrast, allow the learner to control the pace of learning, and a variety of such methods exist. *Contract learning*, for example, allows students to set and clarify their own objectives for a course, to determine jointly with the professor the activities to achieve those objectives, and sometimes to define the criteria for evaluation (Anderson, Boud, & Sampson, 1996). Although the contract method of teaching may sustain student motivation and increase student-teacher rapport, providing orientation, expertise, guidance, and resources to students requires a greater expenditure of instructor time than more traditional methods.

Mastery learning, another self-paced technique, is based on the assumption that all students can learn the material given sufficient time—a view well-suited to an egalitarian perspective on educational opportunity. In mastery learning, students know the criteria for success, take frequent quizzes or tests to check their performance on each instructional unit of material, and continue to study the material until they have the ability to answer a high percentage of the questions. The technique is best suited for teaching and learning materials that are hierarchically structured and sequential. It works best where there are right and wrong answers and definite criteria for testing.

Competency-based education requires that instructors specify each desired learning outcome in behavioral or performance terms and establish an appropriate criterion level for achievement. Since the system emphasizes achievement instead of "time serving," it challenges the well-established credit-hour system of measuring educational progress. In the 1970s, a few entire colleges (for example, Governor's State University in Illinois, Mars Hill College in North Carolina, and Sterling College in Kansas) developed extensive competency-based programs. Today, Alverno College in Milwaukee is the best-known example of this kind of instructional approach, which relies on the specification of student learning outcomes and continuous and various forms of student assessment to determine an individual's academic progress.

In the 1960s and 1970s, college instructors responded to the emerging recognition that students learned at different rates and saw different aspects of their education as relevant. During this period, a number of colleges and universities experimented with self-paced work. This movement toward individualized learning promoted consciousness of learner needs in designing academic plans and may have improved instruction by requiring faculty discussion to develop objectives and set the competency criteria. These curricular innovations, although no longer common, are precursors to today's emphasis on recognizing individual student variability and specifying criteria to meet demands for assessment of student learning. In fact, individualization has been enhanced by technological advances that allow students to access course materials, readings, simulations, and tests online using web tools developed specifically for that purpose.

Culturally Responsive Teaching   Geneva Gay (2000) argues that most teachers are unaware of how their teaching practices reflect their cultural values or how students from different cultures might perceive those practices. Most instructors, she contends, believe that good teaching "transcends place, people, time, and context . . . and has nothing to do with class, race, gender, ethnicity, or culture of students and teachers" (p. 22). She argues, instead, that ethnicity and culture are filters through which students and instructors apprehend the world.

A culturally responsive approach to instruction strives to create a learning environment that respects the cultures of all students through actions that help students feel respected and connected. Such environments also help students see the personal relevance of what they are learning by including students' perspectives and values at the same time that they develop their sense of competence (Gay, 2000; Ladson-Billings, 1994, 1995; Wlodkowksi & Ginsberg, 1995). Culturally responsive strategies go by different names (such as culturally relevant, congruent, mediated, or centered teaching), but all assume that instructors must understand the cultural orientations of diverse students so that they can create equitable educational experiences and teach "to and through" students' strengths (Gay, 2000, p. 29).

Prior learning and experiences affect how people learn, for example, influencing not only what they notice in their environments but how they organize and interpret this information. This, in turn, influences their abilities "to remember, reason, solve problems, and acquire new knowledge" (Bransford, Brown, & Cocking, 2000, p. 10). Because learners have preconceptions about how the world operates, their initial understandings must be engaged if they are to grasp new ideas and information. Culturally responsive approaches are consistent with these constructivist views of learning, espousing active learning approaches that help students interpret the world around them and make intellectual connections

(Quaye & Lattuca, 2006). Culturally responsive teachers not only call for active learning, they also encourage students to explore the social and political dimensions of their communities and social worlds.

Because proponents of constructivist and culturally responsive instruction view learning as an adaptive activity, they stress the need to engage students in practical activities that enable them to interact effectively in educational environments and the larger community. For cultural minority students, practical activities can be those that help them understand how the values, beliefs, and practices of their families and home communities intersect or even oppose the values, beliefs, and practices they encounter in dominant society. In a diverse society, instructors must become more aware of how cultural norms and mores can interfere with learning unless recognized and addressed (Wertsch, 2002). For minority students, "official" knowledge can be contradictory and exclusionary, creating a disconnect between the knowledge students encounter in school and that of their home communities (Gutierrez & Rogoff, 2003).

Culturally responsive teaching does not suggest that all perspectives are equally valid. Rather, its goal is to encourage students to carefully examine, challenge, and reconstruct knowledge by asking questions about what they believe they know and what they are taught. The end product of this inquiry is an understanding of how and why the views of their instructors, peers, and authors do or do not fit with their personal understandings. Through such inquiry students will learn that some knowledge holds up under scrutiny, while other knowledge does not (Quaye & Lattuca, 2006). Discussing discrepancies between what is learned in school and what is learned at home, Ladson-Billings (1994, 1995) argues that students who are not part of the cultural majority must learn to live in both cultures if they are to succeed in the dominant culture. To ensure all students have the opportunity to learn, culturally responsive teaching asks instructors to create classroom environments in which students feel that they matter. Instructors who create such classrooms acknowledge prior learning of students so that students understand that their experiences and beliefs are an important part of the learning process.

Establishing and Communicating Expectations

One of the most important and possibly most overlooked elements of good instruction is the communication of clear purposes, goals, and standards to students. Wilbert McKeachie, whose book *McKeachie's Teaching Tips* (McKeachie, 2006) has been reprinted many times, writes: "Much of my previous teaching was lacking because I failed to communicate to my students why fieldwork, discussions, essay questions, term papers, team research, lectures, and textbooks were expected to contribute to their learning and to their ability to continue learning.

I believe that all of us could do much more to help our students think about their own learning and become more active, strategic learners" (1987, p. 138).

The extent to which instructors make choices among teaching activities may depend on whether they explicitly state course objectives or leave them implicit. Further, instructors who explicitly identify and discuss course or unit purposes and goals can answer students' questions about the subject matter to be learned, how it relates to other parts of the curriculum, and the instructors' objectives and expectations. These questions can be addressed through a course syllabus and are embodied in other course mechanisms such as tests and grades, but instructors should discuss the syllabus, including how assignments and assessment will assist student learning. Discussions of course goals and structure are more likely to be effective if they are done periodically, not just at the opening of the course (Lowther, Stark, & Martens, 1989), and many faculty members in the course planning studies claimed to reiterate the goals and plan for the course to students at least once a week.

The Syllabus Half of the faculty respondents in the course-planning studies, regardless of field, developed syllabi for their courses to help describe them to students (Stark & others, 1988). In some fields, such as nursing, national norms seem to dictate very complete course syllabi or course manuals with objectives, rationales, and detailed organizing questions for each class session. In other fields, such as mathematics or physics, a syllabus may include only the name of the textbook and the chapters and problems assigned for each week. In addition to acting as a mechanism for improving communication between student and instructor, a complete syllabus also helps students learn effectively by providing a guide to the instructors' thinking. Unfortunately, the course syllabus recently has been increasingly viewed, especially by administrators, as a legal contract that provides grade-based incentives and protects the faculty member from lawsuits. Instead, it should be an important educational tool. An effective syllabus explains to students the rationale and purpose of the course as well as course content and procedures. A carefully designed syllabus is a manifestation of course design and planning.

The checklist in Table 7.2, based on a short guidebook by Lowther, Stark, and Martens (1989), can be used to organize a course and provide students with information about the overall course rationale. New instructors can use the guide as a checklist of what might be included, or it can be used by groups of faculty from different disciplines to stimulate discussion about improving communication with students. Although a number of the items in the guide may seem obvious to the experienced instructor, they are often omitted in syllabi. Each of the items in Table 7.2 need not be included in every syllabus, but a more comprehensive document is preferable to a brief outline. Importantly, instructors should view

TABLE 7.2. RECOMMENDED SYLLABUS COMPONENTS

Basic information
- Name of the instructor, office location and hours, and contact information
- Basic course information such as title, number of credits, class meeting times and places, prerequisites, catalog description, and identification of students for whom the course is intended

Course purpose, goals, and objectives
- A course rationale statement, general course goals, specific objectives, and the relationship of the course to program goals
- Relationship to general education or major requirements

Educational beliefs
- Statement of instructor's beliefs about the purposes of education and teaching role, as well as expectations of students

Course outline
- A topic outline and rationale for this content
- A discussion of the nature of the field, including information about the modes of inquiry, assumptions, and the skills to be applied in the course

Assignments and course calendar
- Readings, papers, required documentation style, if any, tests and quizzes, projects, laboratories, and/or field experiences
- Discussion of the relationship of the course goals to assignments and the objectives of assignments
- Dates for major assignments, exams, quizzes, projects, and special activities

Textbooks
- Title, author, edition, publisher, estimated price, and where textbook(s) can be obtained
- Reason(s) for using a particular text or texts

Supplementary readings
- A list of required and recommended readings or other learning resources (for example, recorded materials, performances, exhibits), keyed to student interests
- The location of supplementary materials and information about the course management system

Methods of instruction
- Description of instructional techniques, the rationale for their use, a description of class form at, and how techniques and the format achieve specified goals

Student feedback and grading procedures
- Information regarding the grading system and expectations for student learning
- Policies on assignments, tests, attendance, incomplete work, and extra credit
- Information on how student learning will be assessed and monitored, such as quizzes and tests, papers, class participation, and/or office visits

From: Lowther, Stark, & Martens, 1989. Reprinted by permission of the University of Michigan.

the syllabus as a flexible tool that can accommodate changes in schedules and be adjusted or supplemented during in a course.

Program Guides Academic programs can establish guides that parallel course syllabi, to communicate program goals to students in their degree programs, just as an instructor provides essential information about a course to students. Although most programs write statements of their general goals, requirements, course listings, and preferred sequence to be published in catalogs and on websites, only a few programs like nursing and teacher education, where professional accreditors have insisted on a total program framework and rationale, generally have complete program guides. The creation of a program guide ensures that the faculty responsible for an academic program have discussed and articulated their plan and supplied the academic advisors with that information. The guide informs students about the intended learning goals of the program and how the program faculty members conceptualize the field and intend to teach it to them, and defines relationships between students and faculty. It also can define how both students and the curriculum plan itself will be evaluated. The academic plan concept provides one possible framework to support the creation of a program guide: faculty members can utilize the elements of the academic plan to frame their discussions and consider each element as they articulate their specific plans.

Teaching for Intentional Learning

- Treat students as apprentices who must be assisted in learning the language, ways of thinking, and inquiry methods of academic fields.
- Promote development of complex views of knowledge and recognize that students are at different stages of epistemological development.

Francis, Mulder, and Stark (1995) portray the optimal college graduate as an "intentional learner" who has an explicit understanding of the learning process. Good instructors, alone and in program groups, carefully orchestrate this process, encouraging students to become self-directed learners who choose to learn, know how to learn, and make decisions about their learning. Five attributes, arranged here in a developmental hierarchy, characterize the intentional learner:

1. *Questioning:* facts, theories, experiences; wanting to learn; asking independent questions about what is to be known.
2. *Organizing:* ideas, meaning, knowledge; developing understanding of what is learned.

3. *Connecting:* new knowledge with old; integrating what is learned into a broader pattern of understanding.

4. *Reflecting:* on what, how, and why one is learning; understanding one's learning needs and strategies.

5. *Adapting:* to new situations and needs; using what is learned in a changing world or profession.

The goals of the intentional learning process in any course or field of study are to enable students to attain content knowledge, develop their intellectual skills, and learn to learn intentionally.

Figure 7.2 depicts the process of becoming an intentional learner as cumulative and cyclical. The specific processes—attaining knowledge, developing intellectual skills, and learning intentionally—parallel the stages of epistemological development discussed in Chapter 6. Research on epistemological development reveals that students operate at different levels of intellectual development. Although instructors do not generally use educational or psychological terms to describe their instructional objectives, excellent instructors try to design experiences that will help students make the transition from dualistic positions that base notions of right and wrong on authority to positions that recognize differences of opinion as legitimate. Some may also lead students toward the development of commitments and values. Particularly at advanced course levels in professional fields, an instructional goal may be to encourage students to move from relativism to positions of moral and ethical commitment that signify professional identity.

Marcia Baxter Magolda (2001) concluded from her longitudinal study of college students' epistemological development that the primary challenge students in their twenties faced, during and after college, is the need to establish a personal set of beliefs and a sense of self that can guide them in their relationships within their worlds. She uses the term "self-authorship" to describe the ability to create this internal compass, which requires young adults to "collect, interpret, and analyze information and reflect on one's own beliefs in order to form judgments" (1998, p. 143). Learning environments that convey the idea that knowledge is complex and socially constructed, acknowledge the centrality of the self in knowledge construction, and demonstrate that knowledge and expertise can be shared and mutually constructed by instructors and peers foster self-authorship. Instructors hoping to encourage this kind of intellectual development will validate students as knowers, situate learning in students' experiences, and engage with students in meaning-making and knowledge-construction. Baxter Magolda's ideas are consistent with constructivist approaches to teaching and the incorporation of multiple perspectives in the classroom. They are

FIGURE 7.2. DEVELOPING INTENTIONAL LEARNERS

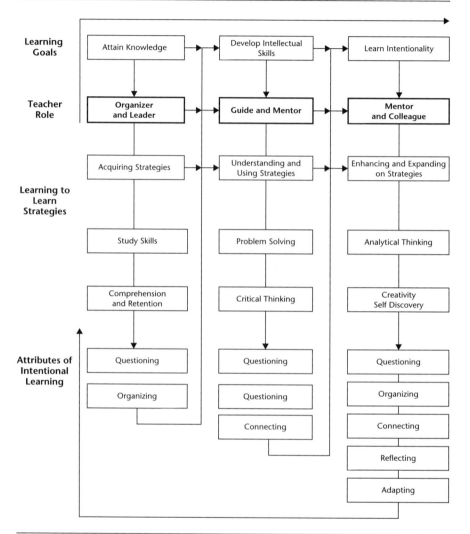

also closely aligned with the principles of culturally responsive teaching discussed earlier.

The teaching goals we associate with intentional learning are also consistent with constructivist approaches to teaching, as well as with research on the role of metacognition in learning. Because students differ in their ability to be intentional learners, and in their status as intentional learners at a given point in time, instructors must select course topics and develop instructional strategies that acknowledge students' current status yet challenge them to move to the next stage.

The skills of questioning, organizing knowledge, connecting ideas, reflecting on knowledge and learning processes, and adapting to new situations result from fundamental educational processes—whether formal or informal. Instructional processes that promote these skills will help students develop into intentional learners who are mature, self-directed, and competent to continue to learn. As the developmental process takes time, an overall view of intentional learning must be addressed by instructional policies at the program level as well as by choice of instructional strategies at the course level.

Questioning: Exploring Inquiry in Academic Fields

Students need to know how an academic field develops knowledge as well as what knowledge it has already developed. Curricular attention to the inquiry processes used in a field is therefore essential. Entering college students often believe that research is a process that occurs primarily in science fields (Shaw, Stark, Lowther, & Ryan, 1990) and thus must be shown that all fields are engaged in the process of developing new knowledge through characteristic research questions and methods of inquiry. The NCRIPTAL course planning interviews revealed that instructors teaching introductory courses devoted little time to increasing students' awareness of research in their fields. Many believed that students must first have a command of vocabulary and basic facts of the field. Discussions of inquiry were postponed to upper-division courses.

Early attention to the processes of inquiry used in a field can help students understand how the field's knowledge is generated and how academic fields are similar to, and different from, one another. It also helps students understand that knowledge is created through social processes that are subject to error. When students learn that researchers can be wrong, that knowledge sometimes grows in unexpected directions, and that scholarly communities often harbor disagreements about concepts, principles, theories, and research findings, they begin to understand that they can be critical consumers of the information they encounter in the world. The development of this kind of critical perspective on knowledge is necessary if students are to become participants in a field of study rather than simply observers on the fringes. To understand the thinking processes of a field, students have to understand the criteria and processes used to validate knowledge in that field.

Different fields of study, of course, stress different thinking skills and different modes of inquiry. Many use the term "critical thinking" to capture the kinds of reasoning or analysis used in their scholarly communities. This term often includes the components of logic, problem solving and abstraction, which are emphasized to different degrees by individual fields (Donald, 2002). In the humanities, scholars focus on developing the skills of interpretation, asking students to construct meaning and defend their understandings of a text or artwork by identifying evidence that text that corroborates their explanations. In contrast, in the physical sciences and engineering, the emphasis is on problem solving. Students learn to define a problem, select and implement procedures for solving it, and verify the logic of that process to validate the answer. Regardless of the field, effective thinking, as defined by the field, is the ultimate goal of instruction in all academic fields.

Enhancing Critical Thinking Most instructors are familiar with the term "critical thinking" and may use it as a synonym for logical thinking, reasoning, or analysis. To be inclusive, we will use these terms as synonyms in the discussion that follows, but we will distinguish problem solving as a specific type of critical or logical thinking.

Ennis (1987) defines critical thinking simply as "reasonable reflective thinking focused on deciding what to believe or do." Not all students enter college with the analytical and evaluative skills needed for this reflective thinking. When instructors assume that they do, they may erroneously create assignments requiring skills that only the most advanced students may have mastered (Arons, 1979). There are, however, specific techniques that appear to successfully cultivate critical thinking in students who lack them.

To motivate the development and use of critical thinking abilities, faculty can act as role models for them, thinking through new problems and articulating their thinking process in front of the class. Through modeling, students can learn that an expert thinker quickly identifies the essentials of a problem, recognizes information that is irrelevant, notes missing information, notices the similarity of a problem to one that has been solved before, and consciously weighs alternative arguments and solutions. Even those who disagree on whether critical thinking is subject-specific or can be taught as a generic skill agree on the importance of modeling such thinking processes (see, for example, McPeck, 1990).

Stephen Brookfield (1988) contends that the instructor's task is to help students examine their beliefs through a variety of approaches, from listening to affirmation to direct confrontation. Although some educators argue that classrooms should be "safe" places for students, bell hooks (1994) argues that learning may sometimes be uncomfortable. Students must learn to discuss difficult and sensitive topics, such as those involving experiences related to race and gender in society, with their classmates, instructors, and others. Instructors bear the responsibility of helping students assess potential risks of critical thinking and the potential repercussions of changes in their thinking and behavior. This, Brookfield argues, is best achieved through personal modeling of appropriate risk-taking behavior, analysis of assumptions, and open discussion of thinking processes.

Transfer of critical thinking skills also can be encouraged by asking students to use their critical thinking skills in diverse situations and by simulating the kinds of decisions that might need to be made in work, family, or community settings. In addition to using diverse examples to build students' skills, instructors can encourage critical thinking by being receptive to students' questions and creative solutions; insisting they clarify, articulate, and defend their thinking about an issue; and encouraging them to challenge—respectfully and constructively—each other's thinking.

Teaching Problem Solving Problem solving is a specific form of critical thinking most often associated with scientific and technical fields. Instruction in problem solving generally includes processes for retrieving information, weighing alternatives, and making decisions. To solve a problem, a student must know what knowledge and skills are applicable to the problem, when to apply them, and why. Although problem solving depends on a knowledge and skill base in the subject, that is usually insufficient to the task. Students must also appropriately apply their knowledge and skills.

To build problem-solving skills, students must do more than find answers to problems that have clear or single answers. These so-called well-structured problems are often found in textbooks and on examinations that test surface-level knowledge. They assess students' ability to recall and apply procedures learned in a course unit. Ill-structured problems, in contrast, do not have a single right solution and cannot be solved through formulaic approaches. They require students to make decisions in the face of limited, incomplete, and ambiguous information to reach a solution and may also require some creativity on the part of the problem-solver. To prepare students for work and for life in their communities, instructors must give them practice in solving ill-structured problems. Thus, they learn to generate alternative solutions to problems and to decide which potential solutions are best given particular contexts and circumstances.

Typically, instructors independently make the choice of whether to introduce principles of critical thinking or problem solving in their courses. Program faculty, however, could work together to identify and formulate appropriate problems for students to solve in various courses and at various points in their academic careers. This kind of exercise is particularly appropriate for programs that are designing or redesigning capstone courses or that require a comprehensive examination for majors. Depending on the field, program faculty might assess students' ability to comprehend, develop, and use concepts and generalizations; recognize and use inductive and deductive reasoning; distinguish between fact and opinion; recognize fallacies in reasoning; synthesize materials from various sources and draw reasonable conclusions from that information; and defend their conclusions or decisions using evidence from texts or experiments.

Enabling Student Inquiry: Undergraduate Research Undergraduate research programs, where students work with a faculty member on specific projects either individually or in small groups, can successfully introduce students to the world of ideas and research. These programs create conditions known to promote student learning: they reveal the nature of intellectual life in the field, encourage students and faculty to interact outside of class, and actively engage students in the learning experience (Pascarella & Terenzini, 1991; 2005). Students doing undergraduate research can apply what they are learning in courses, learn to find information that they have not yet learned, and figure out whether the kind of thinking and research conducted in a field is an appropriate professional choice for them. The programs also increase students' persistence to degree, elevate degree aspirations, and increase the likelihood of students' enrolling in graduate study. The differences in aspirations and graduate study observed between students who engage in undergraduate research and those who do not cannot be attributed to prior preparation, grades, other undergraduate experiences, or peer or family encouragement (Pascarella & Terenzini, 2005).

Hampshire College (Massachusetts), which recognizes the centrality of inquiry in the learning process and the fact that most contemporary problems cannot be solved within the confines of a single discipline, offers many examples of inquiry-based courses in various fields of study. At Hampshire, academic fields are considered tools rather than subjects for study. The curriculum is organized into interdisciplinary "schools of thought" that seek to connect existing fields and bodies of knowledge. In addition, students are encouraged to conduct original research or creative work and to become independent thinkers.

Organizing: Making Sense of What Is Learned

Students must be initiated into the ways of thinking and inquiring in any field of study. Instruction, therefore, should focus in part on helping students understand how a field is structured so that they have a framework for meaningfully connecting the specific ideas and skills they encounter. Students who have such a framework (whether initially provided by the instructor or developed over time as a result of their own experiences) can endure long learning sessions with less fatigue than students who are struggling to connect ideas. Both motivation to learn and learning outcomes can be improved by helping students conceptualize the knowledge structure of a field of study.

College and university faculty members, as experts in their fields of study, have well-developed knowledge bases in their fields and tend to use these to organize their courses. Instructors enhance students' ability to organize their knowledge of a field when they (a) organize and present material in a meaningful way,

(b) require students to actively organize information and ideas, and (c) help students link instructional material to their developing understandings of the field (McKeachie, 2006). To promote accurate and meaningful understandings of course and program content, those designing academic plans can ask, following Posner and Rudnitsky (2006):

1. Is there a set of fundamental concepts that underlie knowledge in this field or topic?
2. How might these concepts and their relationships be represented?
3. How can these fundamental concepts and relationships be taught to the novice?

Besides the traditional well-organized lecture, other instructional techniques can be used to help students organize their burgeoning knowledge. One technique asks students to arrange key concepts and propositions from a text, a lecture, or an experiment into spatial diagrams or hierarchical structures that indicate the relationships among them. Such spatial relationships may be trees and graphs, concept maps, or networks. These diagrams can be used to assess students' existing knowledge structures and identify opportunities for building on prior knowledge and experience. Instructors can then use these assessments to help students make connections, remedy misunderstandings, and begin to map their fields of study. Over the course of a term, students' ways of organizing knowledge become more elaborate and more similar to those of their instructor (Naveh-Benjamin, McKeachie, Lin, & Tucker, 1986). Superior students, at least when judged by grades, organize course concepts much as the instructor does.

The technique of concept mapping can also be used to supply structure in courses. A concept map is simply a diagram representing the conceptual structure of subject matter under study. Instructors might present an explicit concept map for an entire course, revisiting and elaborating on it as the course proceeds to direct students' attention and connect topics to one another. Students also can be asked to construct their own concept maps for a particular learning unit or course. Research consistently shows that the use of concept mapping improves students' textual comprehension and knowledge retention (Pascarella & Terenzini, 2005). Concept maps are also useful diagnostic tools that reveal possible misconceptions about relationships and help instructors assess the extent to which students understand key concepts and relationships in a course.

Concept maps for different fields will take different forms. Instructors teaching in highly structured fields can ask students first to identify the concepts and principles in the course and arrange them in a hierarchical order from the most general to the most detailed. In a field that is not hierarchically structured,

FIGURE 7.3. CONCEPT MAP FOR A PROFESSIONAL PROGRAM

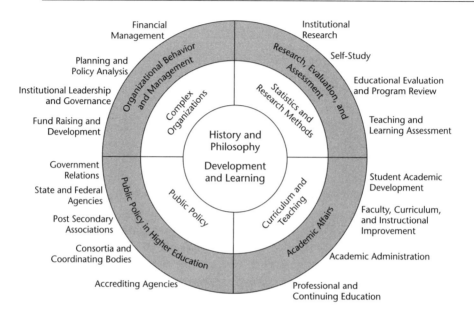

concepts might be arranged as spokes around a central core of general ideas. The academic plan diagram at the beginning of this chapter, and around which this book is organized, is a type of concept map that guides the reader by identifying major ideas and making them easier to remember and relate to one another.

The program faculty is an ideal group to develop a concept map that portrays the curricular connections intended by program requirements and electives. It can be used to assess the coherence of the courses offered and determine course sequences, as well as which courses should be required and which electives, and to help students understand the field and curriculum. In Figure 7.3 we show a concept map that relates requirements and careers for a doctoral program in higher education.

Connecting: Integrating Knowledge

To be successful in college-level learning, students must pay conscious attention to what they are learning, why they are learning it, and how they are doing so. Too often, instructors assume students have relatively sophisticated thinking, reasoning, and linguistic skills, not realizing that development of these intellectual capacities is an ongoing process for students who come to higher education with different capacities and learn at different rates.

Cultivating metacognition takes time; students must be allowed repeated practice in the thinking and reasoning approaches in the fields they study and must be given explicit help and encouragement (Arons, 1979). They should also be urged to "stand back" and examine their reasoning processes and express these in their own words. Although some instructors perceive that this kind of processing comes at the expense of subject-matter coverage, the research literature consistently shows that stressing content coverage while neglecting to encourage awareness of what is being learned, why, and how, encourages surface processing and diminishes learning. Especially in foundational courses that prepare students for intermediate and advanced study, reducing the number of concepts taught by selecting those that are crucial and promoting reflection will improve student comprehension, help them make connections between new prior knowledge, and increase their ability to recall and use what has been learned.

Programs can encourage metacognition by asking students to reflect periodically on their beliefs about knowledge, their approaches to learning, and to understand how these affect their academic achievements. Some students change their conceptions of learning when they realize that the kind of learning they are being asked to do at the university level is different than what they have been asked to do previously (Saljo, 1982). The kinds of metacognitive monitoring of learning that students must do in a field also varies across different academic programs. Because the kinds of monitoring students do in knowledge domains like mathematics and history vary, instructors in all disciplines should build these practices into their courses.

With a modest time investment, program faculty can develop interventions in selected courses that enhance students' awareness of effective strategies for learning and problem solving. In courses for academically underprepared students, metacognitive awareness can begin with basic learning strategies such as rehearsal and elaboration. More often, however, the goal of enhancing college students' metacognitive skills will require instructors to plan courses and programs that help students develop sophisticated learning strategies that connect and integrate new knowledge. For example, explicit attention to the epistemological assumptions that underlie the concepts and principles being studied—and how these align or conflict with personal beliefs—can help students understand that beliefs about knowledge are plural and why individuals in a field may disagree.

One of the great challenges faced by colleges and universities is how to help learners make sense of the many academic fields and the many different thinking processes they encounter. In addition to helping students understand how scholarly inquiry is accomplished in different fields, instruction should develop the ability to connect the different ideas, concepts, and viewpoints. The general education curriculum is an obvious venue for helping students reflect on their knowledge and integrate the concepts, theories, and knowledge they gain into a coherent understanding, but general education courses do not always focus on helping students integrate what they are learning. The National Survey of Student Engagement also reveals considerable differences in the extent to which college seniors report engaging in integrative learning experiences in their major programs. Although students in all fields report engaging in such experiences, seniors in the social sciences and humanities are more likely than those in the sciences, engineering, and business fields to report that they engaged in integrative activities such as writing papers or participating in discussions that required them to incorporate ideas from different sources. Perhaps science and engineering students are more likely to integrate by applying their cumulative knowledge in laboratory work and technical projects. Those in education and professional fields other than business lie in the middle of these groups. All fields, the study concluded, have room for improvement (NSSE, 2005).

Community service, interdisciplinary programs, student work portfolios, and honors programs can provide students with opportunities to connect what they are learning in their courses and apply this knowledge to real-world problems. The Integrative Learning Project, sponsored by the Association of American Colleges and Universities, supported extensive efforts by ten campuses to find other ways to increase students' integrative educational experiences. These included extended core curriculum programs, linked general and professional education courses, cross-disciplinary learning communities, and first- and middle-year initiatives to foster integration. Any instructional form or activity that asks students to consider common problems, issues, or themes, however, can promote integration if it requires students to consider different disciplinary perspectives, connect theory and practice, or wrestle with a variety of viewpoints (Huber, Hutchings, Gale, Miller, & Breen, 2007). The key is to design academic plans, preferably at both the course and program levels, that have integration as a guiding goal.

Learning communities have become a popular curricular response to the need to encourage intellectual connections and coherence. Simply defined, a learning community links two or more courses during an academic term and enrolls a common cohort of students (O'Connor, 2003). It may include a seminar with a unifying theme as a vehicle for bringing students and instructors from different courses together for integrative learning activities. Learning communities often employ collaborative and cooperative learning, discussion-based seminars, and problem-based learning to foster a sense of community among students and instructors and promote deep learning and academic skill development. Learning communities in varied forms have been established in all types of institutions, from community colleges to large research universities (O'Connor, 2003).

Several institutions have had success with interdisciplinary general education programs based on one of the learning community models. They find that student retention rates have increased as the communities create a unique environment based on social and intellectual membership. While extensive studies of student performance have not been done, preliminary data, based on students' self-reported learning gains, suggest that students believe that they benefit from participation. Pascarella and Terenzini (2005) warn that more rigorous studies that control students' abilities and characteristics are needed, but also note that the evidence linking active learning strategies with engagement is consistent with the claim that learning communities enhance students' persistence in college.

Adapting: Using What Has Been Learned

The intentional learner is an individual who can apply what he knows to new situations and problems encountered in the classroom and beyond. The ability to transfer knowledge from one setting to another is affected by the extent to which students have learned with understanding, rather than by simply following procedures or recalling facts (Bransford, Brown, & Cocking, 2000). Unfortunately, while students typically transfer basic skills like reading, writing, and mathematics, research shows that they often do not transfer other kinds of skills (Perkins & Salomon, 1988).

Researchers distinguish between two types of transfer mechanisms—called low-road and high-road transfer—that help explain why students do or do not transfer knowledge or skills and describe how to help them do so. Low-road transfer occurs, and a well-known routine is triggered, when a context or set of circumstances seems similar to one already encountered. For example, a student recognizes that the math skills needed to solve a chemistry problem can also be applied to a physics problem. High-road transfer, in contrast, requires the ability to abstract skills or knowledge for use in new situations. Students must consider, for example, how what they learn in history courses about international cooperation can be applied to current events.

Instructors who want to help students transfer this kind of knowledge highlight patterns (not superficial resemblances) that can link historical and contemporary situations. Helping students reflect, abstract, and make mental connections is the key to encouraging high-road transfer. Instructors can focus on assisting students in abstracting the essential elements of a problem for use in future situations and in identifying key dimensions of a particular problem. Thus, they build students' capacities to recognize and understand which new problems they encounter are like those with which they are already familiar. Helping students organize their knowledge so that it is a coherent set of ideas rather than discrete bits of information further assists transfer and intentional learning. Many of the experiential education strategies we discussed earlier—field work, cooperative education, and simulations—help students adapt their knowledge to new settings and circumstances.

Assessment for Intentional Learning

The term "assessment" includes any strategy that allows instructors to judge students' learning and development, including periodic tests. Although content mastery is one goal of instruction, to move students toward the goal of intentional learning, instructors should also assess students' abilities to apply and integrate what they have learned. Therefore, other assessment options—written assignments such as term papers, short- or long-term projects, portfolios, performances in field experiences and practicum courses, and class participation, for example—can supplement or replace tests. The choice among options depends on what types of knowledge and skills need to be assessed.

The results of any assessment should contribute to students' ability to improve their learning. Effective assessment helps students organize and integrate their learning, and it can also motivate them to question what they learn, moving them toward intentional learning. Information from multiple and diverse assessments tells both instructors and students what students know, understand, and can do as a result of their educational experiences (Huba & Freed, 2000). An increasingly popular assessment tool, the student portfolio, can assess a number of intentional learning skills over the course of a term: the ability to organize knowledge, to integrate knowledge across courses and experiences, to reflect on learning, and to apply knowledge in new situations. As an organized collection of student work, the portfolio aligns with principles of motivation by focusing students' attention on quality standards rather than on grades or test scores, providing informative feedback, and cultivating a more reflective attitude toward academic work. Mary Huba and Jann Freed (2000) contend that assessment should reveal to students what they need to accomplish, what constitutes good performance, and what they must do to improve. The dimensions of "learner-centered assessment" are elaborated in Table 7.3.

Students are attuned to messages about what is important that are conveyed in tests and assignments. Thus, transfer of learning depends both on what is learned and what is assessed (Bransford, Brown, & Cocking, 2000). In developing academic plans, instructors thus need to determine whether the desired types of learning are modeled by the assessment and grading system. When the criteria for good work are made clear and grading systems provide detailed information on levels of performance, assessment can encourage students to become more reflective about their learning. Anecdotally, instructors who use assessment rubrics to communicate evaluation criteria and levels of performance to students report that few students argue about the fairness of the grades they receive.

TABLE 7.3. LEARNER-CENTERED ASSESSMENT

Tell students what they need to accomplish
- Intended learning outcomes
- Nature of the task—what is student asked to "do"
- What students already know that can help them
- What new knowledge is required
- Why the task is important and valuable

Provide information on what constitutes good performance
- Establish and communicate clear evaluation criteria

Inform students about what they must do to improve
- Provide ongoing feedback on the quality of work

From: Huba, Mary E. & Jann E. *Freed Learner-Centered Assessment in College Campuses, 1e* Published by Allyn & Bacon/Merrill Education, Boston, MA. Copyright ©2000 by Pearson Education. Adapted by permission of the publisher.

Effective assessment also benefits instructors by helping them evaluate the extent to which the readings, activities, and assignments are contributing to students' ability to achieve the instructional goals set out in the academic plan. At the program level, comprehensive examinations, theses, portfolios, and field experiences may be used to evaluate program effectiveness. Although these summative exercises can engender student anxiety, faculty can alleviate these concerns by helping students understand the goals of the experience, for example, the opportunity to synthesize and apply what they have learned over the course of a program.

Reflecting on Planning and Teaching

- Learn about learning and discuss with colleagues how knowledge about student learning can be used in courses and programs.

Instructors who construct effective academic plans carefully choose instructional processes that align with course objectives and learners' characteristics and reflect on how these choices are linked to the other elements of their academic plans. They recognize that changes in one element of an academic plan may suggest changes in other elements. For example, changes in learners' preparation for the introductory course in a major may necessitate the development of instructional activities that give students opportunities to learn and practice needed skills. Reciprocally, trying new methods of instruction may prompt reconsiderations of beliefs and assumptions about education and learners and about one's discipline. An instructor who decides to introduce hands-on learning experiences in a course may realize that motivation is situation-specific; students can be motivated by classroom activities that show them the connections between course work and their daily lives or personal goals. While change can be good, evolutionary, rather than revolutionary, changes in academic plans or instructional processes are advisable. Not all elements of an academic plan should be varied simultaneously. As testimony, an accounting professor engaged in curriculum change told his colleagues he had learned that the product of complex topics and complex student thinking is a constant: "You can't move both upward at the same time; you must ratchet up one then the other, seeking a new constant."

One commonly recognized dimension of good teaching is the instructor's preparation and organization. Similarly, we have stressed that good teaching depends on good instructional designs. Such designs can build student interest and motivation, promote learning skills as well as content learning, foster students' academic self-confidence, develop critical thinking and a spirit of inquiry, encourage knowledge retention by making connections, help students integrate knowledge, and increase their proclivity to take responsibility for their own learning. In this sense, good teaching could be recognized as a potential outcome of good planning, although good planning does not ensure good teaching.

Some believe that college teachers need to confront a severe discrepancy, an alternative situation, or a crisis in order to be receptive to new methods of course planning and selection of a wider variety of instructional processes. However, just as instructors should encourage students to reflect on their goals and learning, instructors should be reflective about their teaching—and reflection can produce change. Peer consultations (Katz & Henry, 1988), peer review of instructional materials (Berk, 2006), classroom assessment and research (Conrad, Johnson, & Gupta, 2007; Cross & Angelo, 1988; Cross & Steadman, 1996), the scholarship of teaching and learning (Huber & Hutchings, 2005), course or teaching portfolios (Hutchings, 2000; Seldin, 1997), student ratings of instruction (Theall, Abrami, & Mets, 2001), and other literature on teaching provide opportunities for reflection. Reflection on the specific challenges of teaching a particular course or adjusting the design of a particular program can begin a process of inquiry that helps instructors see the connections among teaching, learning, and assessment (Conrad, Johnson, & Gupta, 2007). The academic plan concept, which encourages instructors to consider these linkages and other linkages among the elements of college curricula, can thus provide a useful tool for instructional development.

A comprehensive set of guidelines, such as the *Seven Principles for Good Practice in Undergraduate Education* (Chickering & Gamson, 1991), can provide a catalyst for reflection and change. Instructors can use the associated Seven Principles Faculty Inventory to help them assess the extent to which their courses encourage:

1. Frequent student-faculty interaction in and outside class which helps to motivate and involve students.
2. Cooperation between students, rather than competitive and isolated study.
3. Active learning through discussion, writing, and application of what is learned.
4. Prompt feedback on student performance to help students assess their existing knowledge and competence.
5. Emphasis on time on task, that is, helping students to learn to use their time effectively.
6. Communication of high expectations to all students, from the poorly prepared to the bright and motivated.
7. Respect for the diverse talents and ways of learning that students bring to college. (Reprinted with permission of John Wiley & Sons, Inc.)

A parallel Seven Principles Institutional Inventory provides quick assessments of program or college-wide educational climates, academic practices, curriculum, faculty, support services, and facilities. The Faculty and Institutional Inventories can be used jointly or separately to spur discussions of existing practices, norms, policies, and expectations, providing a basis for discussions about how to create "educationally powerful environments" (Chickering, Gamson, & Barsi, 1989, p. 3). The National Survey of Student Engagement and the Faculty Survey of Student Engagement also assess these seven principles.

To expand instructors' knowledge of the array of possible instructional processes, professional development opportunities for faculty should parallel the principles we have suggested for student learning: (a) use collaboration to support learning and instructors engaged in learning; (b) start with disciplinary groups that explore and build on existing beliefs and styles; (c) move to groups of instructors from different fields to reveal disciplinary assumptions and encourage reflection on, and discussion of, alternative instructional processes; (d) promote self-confidence through peer support; (e) recognize that emotions and attitudes can hinder instructional innovation and address these obstacles; and (f) improve motivation by basing instructional development on actual teaching challenges, communicating the value of the teaching task widely, and rewarding effective instructors publicly as well as materially.

Which has greater potential to change and improve—the "instructor as planner" (the designer of the curriculum at the course, program, or college level) or "the instructor as actor" (the implementer of the chosen instructional process)? We believe that helping instructors become effective curriculum planners can bring about positive change in classroom instruction. We have also argued that evaluation is a critical element of any academic plan. It is equally important, then, to develop instructors' abilities to assess the success of their instructional plans. We address course, program, and college evaluation processes next.

CHAPTER EIGHT

EVALUATING AND ADJUSTING ACADEMIC PLANS

An emphasis on evaluating and adjusting courses and programs distinguishes our dynamic definition of curriculum as an academic plan from static definitions that merely list or describe courses, groups of courses, or learning experiences. The concept of an academic plan organizes thinking about evaluation because it helps to identify specific aspects of curriculum to change based on new needs and new information. In addition, evaluating the entire plan and its elements may be less threatening to the classroom instructor than evaluating only teaching behaviors; the elements of the academic plan point to essential dimensions of course planning, which are also components of good teaching (although not identical with them).

In Figure 8.1 we illustrate how evaluation and adjustment operate in the academic plan model in three ways. First, evaluations of specific course and program plans provide information that faculty members use to make adjustments (Path A). Second, evaluations of the overall college and university curriculum, often collaborative efforts by faculty and administrators (Paths A and B), provide information regarding needed adjustments in academic plans for an entire college as well as the educational environments in which course and program plans are created. In addition to these evaluation mechanisms that college personnel use directly to improve academic plans, there is another evaluation and adjustment path outside

FIGURE 8.1. ACADEMIC PLANS IN SOCIOCULTURAL CONTEXT: EVALUATING AND ADJUSTING

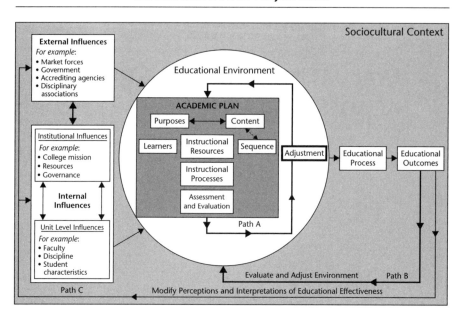

the specific educational environment (Path C). This path suggests a process by which college outcomes are observed, aggregated, and interpreted by the public and policy makers and perceived by these groups to be the "results" of college attendance. Whether well-founded or not, these perceptions are external influences that can affect the nature and strength of other external influences and, in this way, the evaluations captured in Path C operate on the educational environments of colleges and universities, and thus, indirectly, on their academic plans.

In this chapter we focus on evaluation and adjustment processes at the course level (Path A in Figure 8.1) and program level (Paths A and B), and discuss common college-wide evaluation processes such as program monitoring, accreditation, and externally mandated program reviews. Although evaluation processes at the various levels are linked, they differ in where they place primary responsibility and in the degree to which they use formal processes. Paths A and B are often informal faculty activities. However, in the volatile context of increasing accountability, substantial changes following Path B and responses to public perceptions and judgments developed through Path C may merit more systematic attention from both faculty and administrators. Such changes often require effective program or college-wide administrative leadership and more formal processes to enhance and improve curriculum. Consequently, we will examine strategies for making extensive curricular change in more depth in Chapter 10.

Defining Evaluation and Assessment

Many evaluation activities in Paths A and B are aimed directly at improvement and are often referred to as "formative" evaluations. Formative evaluation means that the results of the evaluation are used for decision making, improvement, and planning future courses and programs. Formative evaluations may include measurement of student outcomes (assessment) and satisfaction (student-centered evaluation) as well as estimates of how faculty themselves believe the plan works (professional judgment). The procedures used in formative evaluation may range from informal to formal and from unstructured to structured and often arise from faculty initiatives. In the case of occupational and professional programs, however, forces external to the unit, such as employers or accreditors, may help to define the evaluation of academic plans. Where college-wide review systems dictate standard procedures for the periodic review of academic programs, institutional forces may also affect evaluation plans and adjustments.

When the evaluation processes represented in Paths A and B are intended to inform critical decisions, they are frequently called "summative" evaluations. Summative evaluation can lead to judgments about course and program quality and ultimately to decisions regarding staffing, budget support, and program continuance. These summative reviews, for accountability, program justification, or both, are typically initiated at an institutional level above the program or course being evaluated or by an external agency such as a state agency or an accrediting agency. Evaluations may be conducted at any level of the academic plan.

In our discussion we will use the term "evaluation" in the broadest sense, connoting the process of examining an enterprise and making judgments, either formative or summative, about its effectiveness. Thus evaluation subsumes more specific processes such as assessment of student outcomes, self-study, and external program review.

As commonly used with respect to curriculum, the term "assessment" refers to a subset of evaluation processes focused on student achievement. In the strictest sense, student assessment is conducted to determine whether students are achieving those educational outcomes that the creators of academic plans intended them to achieve. Since educators define both the desired educational outcomes and the measures of success, assessment is sometimes called "goal-focused" evaluation. When defined less strictly, assessment may include examining students' perceptions of their success and self-reports of their attitudes toward or satisfaction with the educational process (student-centered evaluation). Like other types of evaluation, assessment may be formative—that is, initiated by faculty members who wish to understand more about what and how students in their courses or programs are learning. Assessment may also be a summative process required by administrators, accreditors, or a state agency. In the next section we will review some common evaluation strategies, including various assessment techniques, before considering how they are and may be applied at the course, program, and college levels.

Evaluation Strategies

Each element of the academic plan (purpose, content, sequence, learner, resources and materials, instructional processes, evaluation, and adjustment) can be evaluated at the course, program, or college level, although some techniques are clearly more useful at some levels than others. Our discussion begins with evaluation strategies most similar to current practice and moves to those least similar. The four strategies are (a) informal assessment that enhances faculty members' ability to get direct feedback and make adjustments quickly; (b) student-centered evaluation that focuses on students' interpretations of their needs, behavior, and satisfaction; (c) goal-free evaluation in which evaluators look for unintended and undesirable consequences of the curriculum as well as intended ones; and (d) assessment (goal-focused evaluation) that focuses on learning outcomes. The first two strategies focus primarily on the educational process with some attention to outcomes; the third, goal-free evaluation, gives about equal emphasis to process and outcomes; and the fourth, assessment, attends largely to educational outcomes with some attention to process. Most evaluators would assert that these models are rarely used in their "pure" forms and would recommend using combinations based on the evaluation problem at hand.

Informal Evaluation Instructors can select informal evaluation strategies based on their chosen educational purposes, content, sequences, and instructional processes. These informal course-level evaluations require no special skills and can provide prompt feedback in the classroom directly useful to the instructor, who is typically also the course planner. We know a good deal about these strategies from the NCRIPTAL studies of course planning. Some of the new ideas we will suggest later in the chapter supplement traditional processes of instructor-based evaluation rather than substitute for them.

Student-Centered Evaluation Student-centered evaluation examines goal congruence between students and instructors or between students and programs. Surveys, interviews, and focused discussions can provide information on how students with varied goals fared in class or in a program. This type of evaluation attempts to determine whether an academic plan was useful, beneficial, and satisfying to students. It also seeks to illuminate the meanings that students construct in the class or program, which may or may not be the meaning the instructors intend. These assessments may solicit specific information instructors believe is important to evaluate the educational context and process, or they may involve simply listening to students' goals and expectations. Understanding students' goals can better help instructors connect classroom principles and theories to student concerns and interests as well as enhance students' understanding of the field.

Goal-Free Evaluation Goal-free evaluation seeks to illuminate what actually happened to students, but does not focus specifically on what the faculty member(s) intended to happen. Therefore the measures to be taken in a goal-free evaluation cannot be specified in advance. Instead, general questions are posed for both students and professors. These might include: What was achieved? What happened in this course or program? How did you change during this educational experience? What aspects of the course or program were positive for you? Which were negative? Faculty members must be alert to and willing to consider student responses about aspects of the classroom experience that are not specified in course objectives but which occur nevertheless. Some of these outcomes may be positive but unexpected; others may be negative, indicating undesirable outcomes or procedures. Unintended positive outcomes can include: (a) learning to model one's own future teaching behavior after an admired instructor, (b) valuing viewpoints from persons with different experiences and perspectives, (c) consciously developing one's independent learning skills, and (d) acquiring metacognitive skills. Negative outcomes might include: (a) learning to dislike the course material although one is doing satisfactory academic work, (b) unintentional reinforcement of poor learning strategies or use of surface reading strategies that result from overly burdensome workloads, (c) decreases in self-esteem or self-efficacy due to lack of opportunities for course success, and (d) feelings of discomfort during course discussions. Since the questions asked in goal-free evaluations are difficult to ask in a neutral way and may elicit negative responses, obtaining the assistance of a third party is advisable so that students feel free to share their thoughts and experiences. The third party need not be an individual outside the academic program (although it might be).

For example, instructors can team with colleagues, each exploring the course taught by the other.

Assessment (Goal-Focused Evaluation) Assessment is a four-step empirical method of determining the demonstrable intended outcomes of student learning. It includes: (a) establishing clear objectives, (b) developing assessment tools, (c) obtaining the desired information, and (d) interpreting the congruence between achievement and objectives. Most goal-focused evaluation focuses on quantitative assessment of student learning, but alternative forms of assessment, such as judgments of student performances and student portfolios, are becoming more common.

Assessment of student learning outcomes typically takes one of three forms: (a) description of the outcomes achieved, (b) description of change in the outcome from some previous assessment, or (c) attribution of change over time to the course or program being evaluated (Stark, 1990). The simplest of these three possibilities, most often used by faculty, is merely to describe the student outcomes. At the next level of complexity, changes in student outcomes are described by assessing student ability at a stage early in the course or program (for example, a pretest) and at a later point in time (for example, a posttest). At the most complex level, the evaluator adjusts the posttest measures to account for scoring differences on the pretests, and for other student characteristics known or suspected to affect either pretest or posttest (for example, previous knowledge). This method of adjusting gain scores provides evaluators with greater assurance that the change observed can really be "attributed" to the educational program and is a reasonable substitute for procedures that compare randomly assigned experimental and control classes. The first two methods of outcome measurement are familiar to most faculty members; the attribution of gains is more typically left to educational and psychological researchers. (Those considering the use of gain scores or valued-added assessment should consult the literature on student assessment to understand the procedures and their limitations [for example, Banta & Pike, 2007].)

Most faculty members desire to create assessments that tap students' ability to use knowledge, not simply their ability to recall it. This ability to use knowledge often is not easily measured through testing procedures. Authentic assessment is a term for evaluations that directly examine student performance on intellectual or performance tasks. In music, for example, student performances must be judged by faculty (or external experts) to determine student competency. In professional fields such as architecture and engineering, authentic assessment of complex skills, such as design, requires faculty or external judges to evaluate students' ability to complete simulated, job-related tasks. Portfolios—once used only in fields like

TABLE 8.1. REASONS FOR ASSESSING STUDENT OUTCOMES

- To guide student progress
- To improve course planning, program planning, and teaching
- To provide a vehicle for faculty dialogue
- To help students understand the purpose of their educational activities
- To demonstrate accountability
- To enhance public relations
- To reward (or not reward) instructors
- To gain theoretical understanding about how students change and develop

architecture or studio arts—are now increasingly used to demonstrate students' achievement in a variety of fields. Portfolios are collections of students' work products, typically accompanied by reflective essays on the assembled work, that show how an individual student has achieved particular learning goals over time.

Often, portfolios and authentic assessments are utilized at the end of a major program to determine the extent to which students can integrate and apply what they have learned. Capstone courses are thus a source of assessment data on students and on program effectiveness (see Berheide, 2007, for examples in several fields of study). In the context of a goal-focused evaluation, a random-selected sample of portfolios or an evaluation of a set of group projects that requires students to integrate and synthesize what they have learned in a program (such as team-based design project in landscape architecture) can be examined to determine whether a course or program, overall, is achieving its stated learning outcomes.

A broad range of objectives may be evaluated with assessment methods, including not only acquisition of academic concepts and principles, but attitudes such as cultural sensitivity, behaviors such as civic engagement, and longer-range outcomes such as career development. Some reasons for assessing student outcomes are given in Table 8.1.

Evaluating and Adjusting Course Plans

The NCRIPTAL course planning studies provide insights into typical evaluation practices used by college and university faculty at the course level, while the CLUE data inform us about practices at the program level. In the sections that follow, we first report these practices. We then provide models and suggestions for enhancing evaluation at that level.

Interviews with faculty members about course planning reveal that most of them consciously make judgments about the way their academic plans are going (Stark, Lowther, Ryan, Bomotti, Genthon, Martens, & others, 1988). Based on these judgments, most make adjustments frequently, but some deem no changes necessary, and a few neglect to make changes even when the need is clear. Typically, faculty members make several types of observations using four types of indicators: (a) how they feel about the course (using their professional judgment), (b) how students feel about the course (determining satisfaction), (c) how well students achieve course objectives as judged by examination results or similar indicators that describe student achievement, and (d) how peer faculty members judge the course.

Professional Judgment

First and foremost, faculty members rely on their own professional judgment when evaluating their courses, and they have strong confidence in their periodic assessments of student learning. Written assignments, quizzes, monthly examinations, and homework (such as problem sets) can help faculty diagnose problems that must be addressed. Faculty members also learn from informal exchanges with students during class and office hours, the types of questions students ask during help sessions, and the skills demonstrated during practice sessions or internships.

Faculty members in the NCRIPTAL studies described daily monitoring of students' involvement in learning by watching students' faces, observing discussions, and monitoring class attendance. Interviewees also said that they observed how frequently students visited their offices, asked questions after class, and completed assignments (Stark & others, 1988, 1990). Table 8.2 shows the indicators in which faculty had the greatest confidence (Stark & others, 1990).

Student Opinion

Some instructors create mechanisms to solicit and use student feedback regularly during a course. For example, some professors established student committees (or "quality circles") to give them weekly reports about student progress and reaction; others use group interviews to provide end-of-course feedback. There are many variations on this practice; some involve outside consultants, while others are conducted by pairs of faculty working together to improve their respective courses (for examples, see Cross & Angelo, 1988; Heppner & Johnston, 1994; Tiberius, 1995). Most typically in the United States, evidence of student satisfaction with courses

TABLE 8.2. WAYS FACULTY OBSERVE STUDENT INVOLVEMENT IN LEARNING

Indicator	Percent of Faculty with 95 Percent Confidence in Indicator
Examination results	62
Student papers	51
Observing discussions and student participation	50
Completion of assignments	47
Watching student faces	46
Class attendance	40
Observing after-class discussion	21
Student evaluations	21
Number of office visits	15
Student journals	8

From: Stark and others, 1990. Reprinted by permission of the University of Michigan.

is gathered through end-of-term evaluation forms (Berk, 2006; Seldin, 1999). Research has shown that the standard course evaluations used by most colleges are valid sources of information on teaching behavior, consistently revealing common notions of "good teaching" among students (Cashin, 1988; Feldman, 1976; Marsh, 1984, 1987; Marsh & Bailey, 1993; Marsh & Dunkin, 1991). Currently, such forms focus primarily on the instructor's selection of instructional processes and on teacher behavior in the classroom—the two most visible aspects of a course. Extensive research has also documented that a few specific extraneous characteristics (the student's initial interest in the course and possibly class size) influence these evaluations; standard forms therefore usually include questions that allow the effects of such variables to be examined and controlled.

Although use of student rating forms is almost universal, the forms continue to be controversial. Most are geared toward evaluation of lecture- and discussion-oriented courses; thus some faculty members complain that the forms are not well adapted to their particular disciplines and teaching styles or are not helpful for course revision. Despite this controversy, 48 percent of professors in the NCRIPTAL studies said they use the results to make adjustments in their course the next time they plan it.

It is important to distinguish evaluation of academic plans from the evaluation of teaching performance. The selection of instructional processes is only one aspect of the academic plan about which instructors make decisions. Student views on other aspects, such as the choice of content, the usefulness of instructional materials, the appropriateness of sequencing of course content, and the effectiveness of the evaluation and adjustment processes, are also critical to course quality and student learning, and these areas are not always included in course evaluations.

Student Achievement

Instructors who follow systematic course design models often have developed written course objectives and can describe quite clearly the extent to which the students have achieved each one. However, even instructors who do not prepare written objectives for their courses have a strong sense of what they want students to know and are confident that they will recognize the obvious indicators of student intellectual growth. Whether or not they develop written objectives, most college and university instructors tend to cast desired results in terms of content acquisition. When asked how they want students to behave, think, or "be different" at the end of the course, instructors typically answer indirectly by describing the content that they hoped to cover or convey to students. Some have considerable difficulty separating demonstrated student learning from their own intentions to cover material and their proficiency in doing so.

How instructors evaluate courses and examine whether students have achieved the course objectives differs substantially by academic field, paralleling disciplinary variations in educational purposes and objectives. The NCRIPTAL studies revealed that faculty members in structured fields like sciences and mathematics tended to believe that they could quantify student achievement based on demonstrated ability to supply information or solve problems on tests. To them, these methods seemed appropriate in achieving their primary goals of learning the concepts and principles of the field. These professors were more likely than instructors in non-science fields to calculate grades mathematically and to conduct statistical analyses to determine which test items present the most difficulty for students. They tend to emphasize acquisition of content rather than other aspects of student development, such as gaining critical perspective or developing a sense of social responsibility.

Interviews with faculty members in the humanities and many social science fields found them more hesitant to quantify students' learning, and more skeptical of the possibility—and value—of doing so. These instructors tend to use essays, research papers, portfolios of student work, journal writing, and conversation, rather than multiple-choice tests, to judge student development. They may also reward personal insight or a creative flair in students' work because they see student development as a more individualized process than do those in more structured fields. Professors in the social science fields often measured students' achievement by their ability to connect, compare, and contrast ideas and theories in organized essays—and resisted judging students in any way that implied a single "correct" answer to the problem or question posed.

Faculty members in professional and occupational fields tend to have still different views of evaluation. Programs preparing students for entrepreneurial professions often teach (and test for) specific concepts and problem-solving skills, as well as behavioral skills such as accounting techniques or computer programming. Instructors in these fields often evaluate students according to externally established standards—for example, the knowledge of principles tested by exams of the American Institute of Certified Public Accountants. As we noted earlier, the skills taught in the artistic professions such as music, art, and dance are evaluated by professional judgment. In fact, as Schön (1987) pointed out, it may be easier for faculty members in the arts to model and recognize the desired artistic behavior than to verbalize criteria for it. Finally, the fields we have grouped as human services and information services are likely to have both clear-cut criteria for evaluating some student outcomes (such as how to give an injection in nursing or conduct a bibliographic search in library science) and more subjective criteria for others (such as how to help clients deal with anxiety). While all fields emphasize particular thinking skills, the professional fields also emphasize ways of "connecting" with the future occupation.

When NCRIPTAL researchers asked faculty members how they evaluated the success of a course, participants' answers included informal modes of evaluation that were influenced by the instructor's discipline, local context, and professional orientation. No single evaluation strategy is appropriate given the diversity of courses and academic plans in higher education. Academic fields, institutional types, and personal experiences and beliefs all affect how faculty plan courses and how they evaluate achievement of their goals as well.

Peer Opinions

Faculty in the NCRIPTAL studies reported that close colleagues were an important source of help in planning and adjusting their courses. Departmental colleagues and the department chair were considered most helpful, and colleagues in the same field at other institutions were seen as much more helpful than local colleagues in other fields. Part-time faculty were more likely to turn to chairpersons as sources of opinion about course planning and adjustment than full-time faculty were, perhaps because part-timers had less contact with departmental colleagues (Lowther, Stark, Genthon, & Bentley, 1990). When faculty members team up with colleagues to help evaluate and improve each other's courses, they report the experience as satisfying and helpful. Although it was not a common practice, faculty members who used instructional consultants found them helpful in adjusting course design (Diamond, 1998). Based on conversations with faculty, we speculate that, once faculty members have obtained evaluative opinions about their courses from varied sources and found these opinions useful, they tend to seek consultation again.

Making Course Adjustments

Some elements of the course-level academic plans are adjusted far more frequently than others. In the NCRIPTAL interviews, faculty reported that their course purposes and objectives are quite stable; they are more likely to adjust the specific content used to achieve the objectives. The most common adjustments include incorporating advances in knowledge, trying new ways of sequencing material, or using newly available instructional resources such as textbooks and computer programs. These three types of adjustments (content, sequence, and resources) are often combined when refining a course. Instructors make small informal adjustments in their course plans frequently, both as they are teaching and in preparation for the next offering of the course. Modest adjustments may be made in instructional processes but are limited by faculty preference for the lecture/discussion mode of teaching. Only when a major course restructuring occurs, and the academic plan to be created is viewed as unusual or risky, are instructors likely to systematically pilot-test or evaluate their adjustments.

Simple classroom observations can lead to course changes, or even a major overhaul. For example, a literature professor may decide to spend additional class time on a reading after the class discussion falters. Similarly, a biology instructor may make a time adjustment when students' unfamiliarity with laboratory equipment suggests that they will need extra time to finish the lab assignment. While covering the content of the course is always a concern when an adjustment of this sort is made, the time spent thoroughly addressing a difficult topic is time well spent if student learning is enhanced.

Observations, of course, can be deceiving. Katz and Henry (1988) provide a good illustration of the dangers of unexamined assumptions based on classroom observations. They recount the story of one instructor who wondered why some students were not fully engaged in his class. Eventually, he realized that he paced the instructional process based on the eye contact he maintained with students who paid attention consistently. Daydreamers, with whom he never made any eye contact, never influenced his pacing. Once the instructor realized this, he began to select instructional processes and sequence content in ways that would make the class more productive for a larger proportion of the students.

Most changes in courses that instructors make as they teach, or as they plan the next offering of the same course, respond to an internal stimulus such as personal dissatisfaction. While observers might expect an external influence, such as a change in accreditation standards, to be acknowledged as a catalyst to course changes, most engineers reported that the changes they made in their courses were the result of personal initiative (Lattuca, Terenzini, & Volkwein, 2006). Accreditation pressures appear to be more keenly felt by department chairs.

Enhancing Course Evaluation

Faculty members may be required to use end-of-term course evaluations, but they have the opportunity to range far more broadly in their use of evaluative techniques in their courses. Several approaches developed by educational researchers merit trial. Among these are classroom research and assessment strategies.

Classroom Research Classroom assessment and classroom research were first formally outlined in 1985 (Angelo, 1991; Angelo & Cross, 1993; Cross & Angelo, 1988), and new techniques or modifications of existing techniques continue to appear. Some faculty members report that using classroom assessment and research to collect information has fundamentally changed their thinking about their course plans and has significantly improved students' learning.

According to Cross (1998), classroom assessment and classroom research are distinguished by the kinds of questions they ask. Classroom assessment addresses the "what" questions of teaching and learning, such as: What did students learn from today's lesson? What didn't they understand? What additional questions do they have? Classroom research, in contrast, seeks to answer "why" and "how" questions. These can include questions such as: Why did the students respond in that way? Why don't they understand this concept? and How did they approach this task and get "x" results? (Cross, 1998). We focus on classroom assessment techniques, which are more typically employed by faculty who seek to improve their courses. Classroom research, in contrast, is more often conducted by instructors who seek to engage in the scholarship of teaching and disseminate the results of their classroom research efforts to larger audiences.

Classroom assessment techniques can be used to assess (a) course-related knowledge and skills; (b) learner attitudes, values, and self-awareness; and/or (c) learner reactions to instruction. The techniques seek to evaluate, for example, students' prior knowledge, recall, and understanding; analysis and critical thinking skills; problem-solving skills; creative thinking and synthesizing skills; and skills in application and performance. The information sought is that which the instructor believes will be helpful in changing aspects of the academic plan that can be altered.

Classroom assessment techniques are designed to help students learn at the same time that they help the teacher assess what and how well students are learning. By participating in classroom assessment, students reflect on their own learning, reinforce their understanding of course content, strengthen their self-assessment skills, and gain self-confidence from realizing that instructors are interested in their success. Angelo and Cross stress that classroom assessment data should be used only to learn more about how to improve student learning and should not affect student grades. The unit of evaluation is the class rather than the individual student; the class should be viewed as a learning community with whom the results of the assessment are shared.

Classroom assessment techniques are quite adaptable to a variety of classroom situations and academic fields. For example, a calculus professor adapted a classroom assessment technique called "documented problem solutions" to help students become aware of their problem-solving strategies and then to improve them. He asked students to explain, step-by-step and in complete sentences, how they had solved a problem assigned for homework and then to compare their approaches in class. This technique is designed to assess course-related knowledge and skills and is quite different from getting the correct answer by memorized formulas. It helped students recognize that their understanding and problem-solving skills could be improved. Based on the same pool of examination questions used before the classroom assessment techniques, the students earned better grades.

The "one-minute paper," probably the most widely used of the classroom assessment techniques, is used by many faculty members to gather feedback about the success of several aspects of the academic plan, including student preparedness and attention during class. Near the conclusion of a class session, the instructor asks students to write responses on index cards to such questions as: (a) What was the most important thing you learned during this class? or (b) What important question was left unanswered? By examining and summarizing the anonymous student responses, instructors can tell how well students are learning (Angelo & Cross, 1993). Light (1990) concluded from his study of Harvard undergraduates that students appreciate these informal types of course evaluations and believe that they had positive effects on their attitudes toward a course as well as their actual learning.

The *Course-Related Self-Confidence Survey* (Angelo & Cross, 1993) is an example of a technique used to assess learner attitudes and course-related study skills.

It identifies factors that influence student confidence and, therefore, helps instructors develop sequences of material and instructional processes that build confidence. Angelo and Cross offer an example of a nursing instructor who used such a survey to better understand the self-confidence of student nurses in clinical practicum situations. In addition to a list of specific examples to be used in her teaching, she was able to help students create their own checklists of things they could do to monitor their behavior and improve their self-confidence.

Techniques for assessing learner reactions to instruction include the *Group Instructional Feedback Technique (GIFT)* (Angelo & Cross, 1993), a method for gauging students' reactions to teaching and to teachers. It uses student reports about what is helping or hindering their learning and solicits suggestions for improvement. To make the process easier and more comfortable for students, some faculty members ask a colleague to use this feedback technique with their students and then share the aggregated results with them.

Student reactions can also be obtained through reflective essays, focus groups, journals, or surveys that allow students to express themselves without being influenced by the instructor's perspective (as is always true when the instructor creates the items on a survey). Asking students what they want from a course or program may seem like opening Pandora's box, but it can provide useful information for adjusting courses and programs. Students can be quite knowledgeable about their academic needs, and often their comments can suggest simple but responsive changes.

Measuring Student Learning Simply put, the more a student is meaningfully engaged in an academic task, the more he or she will learn (Pace, 1998). In practical terms, the more books a student checks out from the library and reads with interest and comprehension, the more knowledge he will gain about literature. Assessments of student engagement in learning are useful for student-centered evaluation at all levels of the academic plan. Assessment of engagement can focus on evaluating the type, intensity, and frequency of learners' activities. For example, NSSE asks students to report how often they worked with classmates outside of class to prepare class assignments, discussed their grades or assignments with an instructor, or went to class without completing required readings or assignments. Course instructors and program faculty can develop similar kinds of questions based on their academic plans and collect information that helps adjust the plan in ways that encourage learners to pursue more effective strategies.

Describing Outcomes General descriptions of student performance benefit both teachers and students and should be shared more widely than is typical. They clarify objectives for teachers and students and identify areas in which congruence between student and teacher goals exists or is lacking. They make both teacher and student aware of multiple outcomes and objectives for a course or program (some intended, some not intended). They can also provide in-course feedback to a teacher about how the students are progressing toward objectives.

A class of students may be profiled most simply by the instructor's verbal descriptions of how fully the group has achieved specific outcomes. Profiles can also include students' scores on an outcome measure and the average (mean) and dispersion (spread) of those scores. Alternatively, the description could show what students can do or have learned in comparison with a pre-established criterion (criterion-referenced tests). A specific student's performance may be described in terms of the student's deviation from the class average or in terms of achieving the pre-set criteria. When course goals are clear, student-centered descriptions such as portfolios, anecdotal reports, and student journals may also be used.

Of course, the list of possible outcomes instructors consider important and choose to reflect in descriptive profiles of achievement will differ for each college course. Some instructors may stress basic skills, some general learned abilities to be acquired in college, and some learning expected in particular academic fields. The items in Table 8.3 suggest some examples in each of these broad categories within the domain of academic achievement.

TABLE 8.3. EXAMPLES OF COURSE-LEVEL OBJECTIVES

Basic Skills
- Communication skills
- Problem-solving skills
- Numerical skills

Course-Related Learning
- Vocabulary
- Facts
- Principles
- Concepts
- Methods of inquiry
- Methods of application
- Professional and occupational skills

General Abilities and Attributes
- Cognitive characteristics such as conceptual flexibility
- Changes in orientation toward inquiry or toward course or program content
- Evidence of independent thinking
- Evidence of disposition toward continuing learning

Descriptions of student performance on most of the objectives in Table 8.3 have traditionally been based on the results of paper-and-pencil tests, performance tests, or professional judgment by an expert observer. Tests and performance measures may be locally developed, or educators may use norm-referenced tests (so that results can be compared to those of other students similar to those being tested). Many arguments, pro and con, may be made concerning the strengths and weaknesses of locally developed and norm-referenced tests (Courts & McInerney, 1993). A strong point in favor of locally developed tests is that they are likely to assess course and program objectives that instructors planned to achieve. A serious criticism of such tests is that they may not measure achievement of the specified objectives validly and reliably if they are not developed by individuals skilled in test construction. Banta and Schneider (1988) report, for example, that faculty members in eleven fields who attempted to develop examinations for capstone senior seminars had difficulty constructing tests that required high levels of cognitive ability. Additional areas of deficiency in faculty-devised tests may be lack of domain coverage and clarity. Faculty members may find it valuable to work with colleagues who can examine their tests carefully, checking for clarity, for coverage of important domains, and for assurance that the answers require appropriately high levels of effective thinking.

Describing Change Descriptions of learning outcomes at one point in time tell us little about what students gain during a course or program. Analyses of how students change during a course or program provide more useful information and have some other advantages. When appropriate, pretests can help the instructor understand what students know initially and adjust the instructional process accordingly. They may also help the instructor judge whether an academic plan needs adjustments for all students or just for specific subgroups. Pretests must be used cautiously, however, since they can also decrease motivation if the initial tests are so challenging that students feel inadequate to master the material. In contrast, when the results of well-designed pretests and posttests are shared with students, descriptions of change may give students a sense of achievement and enhance motivation.

Change can be described in a number of ways depending on the measure of student achievement used. Researchers can simply (and simplistically) subtract pretest scores from posttest scores and plot distributions of gain scores. They may display pretest and posttest scores as group profiles, as comparisons of percentage of students above a criterion point, or as correlated measures. All of these types of change scores must be interpreted carefully, as students with greater initial proficiency have less opportunity to improve than those who are initially less proficient. Unless adjusted for pretest performance, a distribution of change scores is hard to interpret and may be misleading. Not all assessment requires change scores.

In some cases the source of a change in students is obvious. A complex pretest in an unfamiliar foreign language, for example, will provide an exercise in guessing and frustration but little valuable information that the instructor could not attain by asking which students are familiar with the language from some other source. Pace (1985) provides a useful analogy: it would not be appropriate to push a beginning skier down the slope so you could measure his progress at a later point in time.

Attributing Outcomes The most complete and sophisticated course-level evaluations attempt to attribute student change to the course plan or activities. Assessments of student learning will thus include evidence of change (or "value-added") in a desired direction with respect to skills, attitudes, and behaviors that are the generally expected outcomes of a particular course or program. Attribution of change is not always complex. Suppose American students enrolled in a course in spoken Russian demonstrate considerable ability to speak Russian at the term's end. Although a few students might be sufficiently motivated to enhance their knowledge of Russian from other sources (through language instruction tapes or tutoring from an international student), it would be unusual if the majority of students gained their knowledge of Russian from sources other than the course. In another instance, it might be very difficult to demonstrate that particular learning occurred because the student was enrolled in a specific course. For example, students taking several courses that required essays probably could not attribute improvement in writing to any one of them. Similarly, those taking a course in American political systems during a national presidential election might acquire new knowledge of political systems from TV coverage of the election as well as from the course. A third possibility is that the course had both a direct effect (class material) and an indirect effect (by encouraging them to watch TV coverage of the election). Indirect effects of courses and programs merit more examination.

The first step in attributing learning to a particular educational experience is to clearly specify the expected outcomes. The second step is to be sure the selected pretest reasonably measures students' capabilities before the course begins. A potential third step is to identify and measure other characteristics (mediating variables) related to the subject—for example, speaking Russian at home or on a recent trip to Russia. Finally, the posttest scores are statistically regressed upon the pretest scores and appropriate mediating variables to determine the amount of change beyond that caused by these existing conditions; this result can reasonably be attributed to the course.

These steps represent a more complex procedure than most faculty members will use in evaluating their courses. The statistical techniques in step three substitute for an actual experiment with two classes in which the students are randomly selected. Yet it is important to recognize that, in the absence of randomized or experimental designs, one cannot attribute student change solely to the course. Some evaluation theorists, however, believe that course outcomes can, with careful attention to competing hypotheses, be attributed to educational experiences through this value-added method which substitutes for a true experimental design. (Professors who contemplate using change scores may wish to consult *Assessing for Excellence* by Astin [1991] or the appendix of *How College Affects Students* by Pascarella and Terenzini [1991].)

To account for student effort when attempting to attribute learning to a course, an instructor needs to consider measures of student effort (and perhaps student motivation) as mediating variables that may influence student success in the course. This viewpoint and related strategy are appealing to many instructors who are willing to assess student learning in their courses but who realize that student effort is an important variable that cannot easily be measured or statistically controlled.

Finally, even when student learning outcomes are the primary object of assessment, the basic purpose of evaluation is to adjust elements of the academic plan so that student learning will be improved. Thus, in evaluating a course, the teacher must assess both the plan and the specific student outcomes resulting from the plan. This fact requires documenting the plan, the intended learning outcomes, and the criteria for their successful achievement. It is helpful if each specified outcome is also associated with a measure that will help the professor know if it is achieved.

Using Peer Interaction Colleagues from the same or a related program are a neglected resource for course evaluation. Peer reviews are more effective if they involve consultation in addition to classroom observations. In one successful model (Hutchings, 1995, 1996), two instructors agree to exchange written dialogue focused on discussing: (a) course purposes, content, and rationales; (b) teaching practices; and (c) student learning. They exchange course syllabi, copies of course assignments (complete with the kinds of feedback offered to students), and other materials that make explicit their course decisions, sequence of topics, and reasons for choosing instructional methods. They also identify goals for in-class and out-of-class interaction between instructors and students and ways to determine the success of these activities. These formative written dialogues provide a useful and efficient method of peer evaluation over an entire course. Although existence of the process may provide evidence of interest in teaching improvement for an annual performance review or tenure dossier, the actual dialogue should probably remain privileged between the two colleagues.

Evaluating and Adjusting Program Plans

College and university members tend to use very informal methods to gather data about how their program plans are working. As NCRIPTAL researchers asked faculty about how and why they evaluate and adjust curriculum plans at the program level, they found few systematic processes for collecting information. Rather than set aside time periodically for regular review, faculty members said they dealt with specific problems when they seemed to need attention, as evidenced by major student dissatisfaction or by poor results on examinations. Often faculty members evaluated only a specific component of a program or a selected instructional process, such as an internship, laboratory, or thesis requirement that seems problematic. Faculty members surveyed for the Engineering Change study (Lattuca, Terenzini, & Volkwein, 2006) also were more likely to view curricular decision making as reactive—responding to problems as they arose—rather than periodic and systematic. Furthermore, when asked if curricular decisions in their programs were more often based on opinion than on fact, more than two-thirds of faculty members agreed that decisions tend to be opinion-based rather than evidence-based. In engineering, where assessment of specific student learning outcomes is a requirement for accreditation, reluctance or confusion about how to use assessment data for decision making persists; only about two-thirds of program chairs indicate that more than half of their program members supported the use of assessment information in decision making (Lattuca, Terenzini, & Volkwein, 2006).

When asked what information about learner experiences they use in planning academic programs, faculty members in the NCRIPTAL studies frequently provided anecdotes about a few outstanding or successful students who typically had pursued advanced studies at prestigious institutions. They usually did not offer much information about the larger group of students who had disappeared into society or routine careers. However, in programs selected as exemplars of continuous curriculum planning, such as those in the CLUE studies, faculty members were somewhat more likely to name varied review efforts and measures of program success.

Lack of systematic evaluation of program plans, including failure to assess student learning, is in large part due to a lack of knowledge and experience among program faculty. In the absence of assistance or local expertise, academic programs administer student or graduate satisfaction questionnaires that are roughly parallel to course-rating instruments but not as carefully crafted.

Many program-level adjustments in elements of academic plans arise from faculty initiative. In the absence of external influences, educational purposes typically remain stable while subsidiary objectives and the particular content used to achieve them are gradually adjusted to reflect advances in a field's knowledge base, changing methods of inquiry, and changes in social and professional settings for which students are prepared. Changes in program content are often accompanied by changes in the sequence of courses or topics within courses, while changes in resource materials are especially common when instructors believe students have inadequate foundational knowledge and skills. New textbooks, new scientific equipment or professional tools, new data bases or case studies, and especially the arrival of new faculty with recent training or field experience represent the types of changing resources that stimulate program adjustments. In fields where program faculty monitor the success of student majors on external examinations (for example, chemistry, accounting, nursing), adjustments may be more frequent.

The ethos of respect for faculty autonomy and creativity tends to discourage program chairpersons or faculty from devoting large amounts of time or resources to the systematic adjustment of instructional processes at the program level. Changes in instructional processes are often led by innovative faculty members or strong (and persuasive) academic leaders. One or two professors may develop new instructional processes that other faculty members may adopt of their own volition.

Despite the apparent lack of attention to evaluation at the program level, most colleges and universities expect faculty to evaluate the effectiveness and productivity of their program curricula occasionally through a program review process (Barak & Mets, 1995). Most program evaluations can be placed in one of the following categories: (a) program self-study; (b) program review; or (c) program accreditation. Each of these types of evaluation may include assessment of student outcomes.

Program Self-Study

Many aspects of the program plan can be evaluated, and subsequently adjusted. Faculty may evaluate the content that has been included, determining whether students are well prepared for subsequent courses in the program or successful in careers. They may evaluate the sequence in which the material has been presented or the instructional activities that the program faculty chose to produce learning outcomes. Perhaps most importantly, they may evaluate the evaluation and adjustment plan itself. Assessing student outcomes through performance examinations and assessing student perceptions of their experience are the two most common types of program evaluation. Despite the heavy emphasis on assessment in recent decades by legislators, government officials, and accreditation agencies, relatively few programs have effective plans for performing assessments or using them to evaluate programs as a whole. Professional and occupational programs with external examinations may be in the strongest position to defend the success of their academic plans, while general education programs with broad goals and non-career major programs are in the weakest position.

A program self-study is usually initiated internally and is more likely than course evaluation to involve professional judgment from external experts. Program self-studies often include visits by consultants (usually professors from a similar college and department) who review documents and data and interview students, faculty, and administrators before commenting on program strengths and weaknesses and suggesting possible adjustments. Professional and occupational programs may also seek views on curriculum planning from practitioners in the field. For example, community colleges and occupational programs often survey their local business community about specific training needs. Professional programs may rely on industry advisory councils or boards to advise them on changes in employer needs and to comment on proposed changes in undergraduate curricula. Such advisory boards can be powerful catalysts for program adjustment. Results of external examinations and employment records of program graduates may also be part of self-study for professional programs.

Self-studies may use data already available in institutional research offices, but this information may be limited to characteristics of students, faculty, budget, credit hours, and space allocations. Such input measures, used as proxies for educational quality, may be of little help in determining how well programs have met their educational goals. Institutional research offices can, however, help programs to collect outcome data more useful in self-studies and to do so on a regular basis.

Program Review

In program reviews, a faculty group outside the program may evaluate it to determine whether it should be discontinued, substantially altered, or merged with another unit. Most often, such a review is suggested or mandated at a higher administrative level, either periodically or at a time of crisis. In such evaluations, judgments are made about (a) whether the program is performing well at its task (merit), (b) whether the program is needed (worth), and (c) what actions should be taken to remedy discrepancies from "ideal" merit and worth. A judgment of "worth" concerns whether the college (or society) needs or chooses to have and support such an enterprise (Lincoln & Guba, 1980). Technically, the decisions about merit and worth are independent of whether the evaluation process is formative or summative. Practically, however, a summative process will more often lead to a decision about worth, while a formative process to improve the program's merit will likely assert the worth of the program in advance.

As an example of the distinction between merit and worth, consider a program in social work located at a college that is adjusting its mission to focus primarily on technological fields. The social work program may provide excellent instruction and be judged highly meritorious. Yet because the college is changing its mission, an excellent human service program may be considered of little "worth" to the college. It might be discontinued or transferred to another nearby college focusing on human services, where its merit could continue to be supported.

Institutionally mandated program reviews are sometimes unpopular among faculty because colleagues from other departments can be harsh critics and may be unfamiliar with the norms of the academic field under review. Institutional reviews may also be threatening when triggered by fiscal concerns that threaten closure or reduction of a program. Under such circumstances, programs often must defend their worth in terms of bottom lines—credits generated, instructional costs, or students' time-to-degree. At such times, faculty members may simultaneously dispute data collected by the non-program reviewers and scurry to collect information that might have been collected earlier and used more systematically for self-study. Periodic reviews that are done regularly, rather than during times of crisis, are less threatening and probably more productive.

Community colleges and state-funded colleges typically have more regular evaluative curriculum mechanisms for programs than independent institutions do. Some states require regular program reviews for public colleges. One rationale for these planned reviews is that taxpayers' dollars should be used to support only high-quality programs with an employment market. At some community colleges, for example, deans regularly target occupational programs for review and use information about employment opportunities and student job performance to make summative, as well as formative, decisions. Reviews identify programs that fail to meet established criteria and consequently must be either improved or eliminated.

Professional Program Accreditation

Some academic programs that prepare students for specific professions and occupations voluntarily submit to professional accreditation, although not every occupational or professional program has an accrediting agency, and programs in a given field are not required to seek such approval. Program accreditation requires periodic visits by site teams composed of colleagues in the same field who examine the program and provide feedback. Professional program accreditations are supplemental to and unrelated to regional or national accreditation, which examines the entire institution.

The accrediting agencies endorsed by the Council for Higher Education Accreditation and the U.S. Department of Education include more than sixty agencies—including regional, national, faith-related, and professional (specialized) agencies. (See www.chea.org for a complete listing.) Most of these accreditors require that a program complete a self-study prior to the arrival of the site visit team and make the results of the self-study available to its members. Typically, the accreditor provides a protocol, including the types of questions that should be asked in the self-study and the form in which the answers should be provided. Sometimes the program may designate a particular aspect of its work to be examined to capitalize on a valuable opportunity for peer reaction.

In formal program accreditation or periodic reviews, faculty and administrators tend to follow descriptive models. They might, for example: (a) describe the program and its context, (b) report the description in terms that are understandable to the audience and responsive to their concerns, and (c) suggest some potential program modifications and adjustments based on observed deficiencies and strengths, existing values, and implied standards of merit and worth (often comparisons with other programs). Some professional accreditation agencies require that assessment evidence be included in self-study reports or shared with site-visit teams before or during an accreditation review.

Enhancing Program Evaluation

Systematic use of program-level evaluation strategies requires administrative leadership, substantial coordination, and, sometimes, professional development for faculty. Since program evaluation can determine the extent to which a particular curriculum design is effective and can encourage faculty to adjust those aspects that are least effective, the time and resources spent on coordination and training seem justified. We will discuss varied leadership strategies for broader change and possibilities for professional development for faculty members in Chapters 9 and 10. Here we present some strategies for common program adjustments that parallel those we discussed at the course level.

Program Research A publication of the Association of American Colleges, *Program Review and Educational Quality in the Major* (1992), is useful to a wide range of liberal arts disciplines. The handbook offers guidelines for both informal and formal evaluation strategies. After listing thirteen characteristics of a strong liberal arts major (many of which also apply to majors in professional fields), the handbook provides a framework and series of questions for eight foci of program review: (a) goals, (b) structure of the curriculum, (c) connections (within the major, with student needs, with scholarly inquiry, with other disciplines, with liberal learning), (d) teaching quality, (e) advising, (f) inclusiveness, (g) institutional support, and (h) outcomes assessment. Some of these categories can be evaluated though informal and student-centered strategies. Others lend themselves to more formal evaluation, which may rely on commercially or locally developed tests or instruments.

Using parallels to classroom research, which we have described for courses, program faculty, and academic advisors, might take the "academic pulse" of students in their program through short, written responses to particular questions about program quality. Web-based survey tools, now widely available, can be used to build and administer questionnaires that reach all students enrolled in a particular program. (Survey design, however, is not as simple as it may appear at first glance. Programs that wish to use survey data for program review purposes are urged to seek assistance from knowledgeable sources to ensure good results. Institutional research offices can often provide this type of assistance to faculty seeking to collect data systematically.)

Program faculty members might talk with individuals in charge of their institution's data warehouse to determine what existing data will be helpful. Information on course-taking patterns of particular types of students (for example, those who take remedial math courses), for example, can reveal where students encounter curricular difficulties. Analyses of existing data may also provide provocative findings—for example, that students who enroll in cooperative education internships have higher grade point averages at graduation than those who do not. Such data cannot explain why cooperative education is related to GPA (Is it a cause or a byproduct?), but it can suggest avenues for additional study.

Student-Centered Evaluation Student-centered techniques can be used for programs as well as for courses, but considerable attention must be given to describing for students the scope, goals, and intended linkages of the program being evaluated. Students can be asked to comment on the program in an open-ended reflective essay when they visit their advisor or register for courses, or their opinions can be sought in required courses selected on a rotating basis. As appropriate, program portfolios might include reflective essays in which students consider how and what they have learned as a result of their curricular and co-curricular experiences.

Goal-free evaluation will identify potential negative and positive unintended consequences of a program plan. Elaboration can be obtained through open-ended essay questions and topics for student-led focus groups (Light, 2001). Goal-free evaluation might explore linkages with related academic programs, ascertaining what faculty in related programs think is happening to students, as well as what students believe is happening to them in the other programs.

Students in general education courses might be queried about the connections between the general education courses they take, their major courses, their career plans, and their personal interests and values. In major programs, students may be queried about connections between their courses of study and their future careers. An example of a student-centered essay question to probe the type and nature of such connections is: "Suppose one of your professors in [general education core course] and one of your professors in [your major] were meeting for lunch to discuss important changes in the curriculum to improve your education. What are some topics you believe they should talk about?" Student response will surely be improved if the evaluators are careful to show students that adjustments have been made in the academic plan based on previous student-centered evaluations.

The National Study of Student Engagement (NSSE) can be used in a student-centered evaluation program to provide reliable and valid evidence of the effort students put into their college programs. The NSSE survey instrument taps personal, social, and career matters, as well as knowledge and intellectual skills. This instrument gathers student responses to questions based on five scales: level of academic challenge, active and collaborative learning, student-faculty interaction, enriching educational experiences, and supportive campus environment (NSSE, 2007). Accordingly, NSSE is ideal for getting student reports of the types of activities they have pursued in a program and for understanding what they think they have gained during a specified academic year.

Assessing Outcomes The three levels of assessment we described for courses (description, description of change, and attribution of change) are equally relevant at the program level. For determining attribution of outcomes at the program level, faculty might give serious consideration to Astin's "input, environment, output" (I-E-O) model (1993). This model, which can be adapted to any program, is useful for assessing the experiences of cohorts of students. It clarifies that entering students' characteristics important to program success must be defined and measured (input), the environment (instructional experiences) must be specified (environment), and the outcomes must be measured (output). It calls attention to the "program environment" in which the academic plan is embedded and thus directs attention at the ultimate goal—to discover how to adjust the specific curriculum plan to enhance desired student outcomes. The procedure requires that students' entering characteristics be statistically controlled; thus the design suggests, but cannot determine, causes and effects.

Although we suggest statistically controlling for entering student characteristics to determine whether learning is attributed to a particular program, we also believe student differences are too important to be disregarded as mere "statistical controls." In some cases, programs will want to study students with particular characteristics. For example, in some institutions, large numbers of students have transferred from another two- or four-year college; one cannot ignore the effects of education received at prior institutions. Other kinds of student characteristics may also be important. Students at different stages of knowledge and intellectual development, or those from different cultural backgrounds, may achieve different outcomes from the same courses. Consider, as an example, a course in business ethics enrolling students from many countries with different business cultures and practices. The ethics of U.S. business might be more easily learned by U.S. students who accept U.S. norms of standard-labeled prices than by students from cultures where bargaining is expected and practiced. It is as important to examine these interaction effects between student characteristics and curricular designs as it is to control student characteristics in examining aggregate patterns. This kind of information is needed to inform the development and revision of academic plans.

Assessment requires that an academic program develop clear goals and objectives as part of its academic plan. Different typologies of potential college outcomes may be considered as frameworks within which faculty members can phrase and evaluate important goals that they had not explicitly considered. When existing programs undergo periodic evaluation and revision, the typologies can be useful at each iteration in the cycle of refining academic plans.

The assessment movement of the 1980s encouraged faculty members to pay attention to outcomes that are broader than content acquisition (Ewell, 1991). Students also can be tested for what are typically called "higher order thinking skills" such as ability to synthesize, analyze, and evaluate. The list of "essential learning outcomes" published by the Association of American Colleges and Universities (2007) includes dispositions such as civic engagement, intercultural competence, and lifelong learning. A number of professional accreditors, such as those in nursing and education, consider such attitudes and dispositions to be essential student learning outcomes. Miller (2007) describes the efforts of more than a dozen colleges to develop intentional approaches to meeting such goals and assessing progress toward them.

Astin (1993) offered a general typology with three dimensions: type of outcome (cognitive or affective), type of data to ascertain the outcome (behavioral or psychological), and time (long-term or short-term). Cognitive outcomes include academic ability, subject-matter knowledge, and skills such as critical thinking; affective outcomes include values, attitudes, and beliefs. Examples of behavioral outcomes might be degree attainment, citizenship, or leadership. A general framework such as this one must be refined and made specific by faculty in each program at each institution, a potentially lengthy process. A useful tool in this process is a matrix that arrays the specific types of knowledge and skills expected of students on one dimension, and the various courses and program experiences expected to foster those outcomes on the other. Such a matrix helps to pinpoint where specific types of outcomes are to be learned—and where gaps exist.

Sometimes assessment guides are provided by professional associations. For example, Table 8.4 contains a list of desired outcomes in accounting education. Until the 1980s, accounting educators focused their attention on learning accounting principles and rules. As a result of a nation-wide reform effort in the 1990s, they began to explicitly include attention to how students integrate

TABLE 8.4. DESIRED STUDENT OUTCOMES FOR A PROFESSIONAL PROGRAM

- Working with people to achieve tasks
- Interpersonal skills
- Teamwork
- Leadership skills
- Understanding the work environment
- Communication skills

- Solving problems (general)
- Critical and analytical thinking skills
- Unstructured and structured problem solving and decision making
- Solving problems and making decisions in a business context
- Seeking and gathering information for business decisions
- Understanding the business context
- Understanding the societal/cultural context
- Seeing accounting as a coherent whole
- Using information in business decisions

- Learning to be an independent learner
- Developing motivation
- Developing learning skills
- Developing information-seeking skills

- Developing broad perspectives
- Global perspectives
- Ethical perspectives
- Entrepreneurial perspectives

Stark's observations based on proposals for change in accounting education submitted by more than fifty universities to the Accounting Education Change Commission, 1989 to 1994.

learning into coherent patterns, how students use learning in solving professional problems, and how they adapt learning to a changing society. Furthermore, like educators in dentistry, accounting educators developed a comprehensive assessment handbook for their colleagues (Gainen & Locatelli, 1995).

Establishing goals and objectives and choosing assessment techniques to measure them provide an important opportunity for faculty members to explore the extent of agreement on the basic purposes of education undergirding the selection of specific content. Faculty members in most major fields, as well as those responsible for general education programs, often prefer to construct their own comprehensive examinations to measure students' development. This process of local construction fosters faculty ownership, but also involves considerable effort and sometimes results in poor test validity and reliability. Standard tests that academic program faculty may wish to examine include those published by the Educational Testing Service, such as the Graduate Record Examination for several disciplines and ACT's College Academic Achievement Proficiency tests (CAAP). To avoid a multi-year project in test construction, general education faculty should review the increasing number of examinations that measure general education outcomes. These include the Collegiate Learning Assessment (Council for Aid to Education), COMPASS Test (American College Testing Service), The MAPP Test (Educational Testing Service), and College BASE (University of Missouri-Columbia). A number of handbooks for planning and implementing assessment of major and general education programs are available (for example, Allen, 2006; Palomba & Banta, 1999). Any comprehensive assessment plan should be linked with other types of evaluation we have described, particularly with student-centered evaluation, in order to fully account for student outcomes, adequately describe change, and make appropriate adjustments in the curriculum.

College-Wide Evaluation

College missions, like program goals, tend to be stable and enduring. Yet, over time, U.S. colleges have adapted to changing times and demands. In Chapter 10, we will discuss more fully how higher education may make adaptive responses to external influences. Here we describe some common college-wide evaluation processes that typically lead to changes in elements of academic plans other than purpose.

College-Wide Self-Studies

Many colleges conduct periodic reviews and evaluations of all or most programs, but reviews vary by state and type of control (public or independent). Due to the influence of state governing and budgeting processes, public colleges are more likely than independent schools to regularly review all programs. In some states, a central board coordinates the reviews, and public colleges merely respond. In other states, each public college or university may lead each of its units in a self-study or external review, pruning or even eliminating programs no longer closely linked to mission or worthy of scarce resources.

Self-studies may evaluate the entire academic program by aggregating existing or new data from programs and courses. For example, existing student course evaluations, when used to develop a composite picture of instruction throughout a college, may help to identify needs for change. Information converging from several programs could be used to strengthen or refocus an instructional development center, an instructional technologies center, or a library. Enrollment data viewed over time may reveal patterns that require attention. In an unusually creative study, Stanford University examined student transcripts for several programs and integrated this information with other data to describe patterns of study that students pursued (Boli, Katchadourian, & Mahoney, 1988). Such evaluations seem more likely to lead to adjustments in sequence or instructional processes and resources, however, than to changes in the content and mission elements of the academic plan.

College-wide evaluators frequently use student-centered procedures such as questionnaires to obtain the opinions of graduates or current students about their goal achievement in college. Not surprisingly, colleges with institutional research offices capable of gathering and analyzing the data are more likely to carry out such evaluative studies. In very large universities with a variety of colleges, schools, or programs, it may be necessary to customize surveys for the specific college or program that students or alumni attended. The Association for Institutional Research (AIR) provides member colleges with guidance in survey design and administration, models of the use of survey results, and professional development workshops related to college-wide studies.

Emphasis on assessment of student learning has led to some college-wide reviews of student outcomes. Banta and Associates (1993) and Hutchings (ca. 1989) cite more than ten model programs that have become well known for systematic evaluation and adjustment procedures. In addition to centralized offices of planning or institutional research, campus-wide assessment committees (composed of administrators, faculty, and other constituencies) are sometimes used to guide such reviews, as are existing faculty senate committees. Colleges may also look to professional and discipline associations for leadership and for ideas about various types of planning. In engineering, for example, an annual workshop features best practices in assessment to assist undergraduate programs in meeting accreditation requirements and improving their programs. Similarly, the National Council for the Accreditation of Teacher Education (NCATE) offers a series of web-based conferences that provide guidance about the accreditation process.

Self-Studies for Accreditation

Voluntary accreditation has existed since the early part of the 20th century, when colleges and universities banded together to form regional associations to examine their own activities and recommend needed changes. Today, each college that belongs to one of the six regional associations supports its endeavors with both membership dues and voluntary participation of faculty and administrators in peer evaluation. Several national accrediting agencies have now been formed to serve a similar function for specific types of for-profit and specialized occupational colleges.

During the last sixty years, accreditation has been a very powerful influence for college-wide review because, in 1945 when the G.I. Bill was passed, the U.S. government decided to rely on accrediting agencies to certify quality rather than setting up its own bureaucracy to do so. Thus, regional (or institutional) accreditation is now an eligibility criterion for many federal grant and student aid programs. During the late 1980s, federal officials demanded that accreditors provide assurance that student outcomes are measured, a role the agencies accepted somewhat reluctantly. In keeping with their emphasis on institutional autonomy in determining missions and goals, the regional associations established assessment standards in general terms. Today, some accreditation standards still focus on assessing institutional "capacity" by examining characteristics such as fiscal solvency, library resources and faculty credentials, but recognize that these characteristics alone are not sufficient to guarantee student learning.

The Council for Higher Education Accreditation (CHEA), an organization that coordinates institutional and programmatic accreditation in the United States, views outcomes assessment as an institutional responsibility, asserting that "Quality standards must be set and met by institutions themselves and not by external agencies" (2003, p. 3). Each college and university, therefore, should gather assessment evidence and use it to develop effective strategies for educational improvement. Accrediting organizations, in turn, should evaluate institutions by their performance related to these institutional goals and develop consistent strategies for summarizing and making their findings public.

Institutional accreditation reviews cover the institution's financial status, governance, faculty and staff relations and achievements, student services, and student learning and achievements. The typical components include: (a) a self-study document, which provides a written summary of performance based on the accreditation criteria established by the accreditation agency; (b), a site visit by a non-paid team of peer evaluators (from institutions of similar type and size) who review the institution, using the self-study as a foundation; and (c) a judgment by the accreditor, typically through a "commission" composed of administrators, faculty, and public members who decide to grant accreditation, reaffirm accreditation, grant accreditation "with conditions," or deny it (Volkwein, Lattuca, Caffrey, & Reindl, 2003). Often an institution begins preparing data for the visit a year or two ahead of the scheduled date, but institutions vary in their approach to self-studies for accreditation. Some colleges take self-studies very seriously, creating large committees and producing comprehensive and useful reports that recommend or facilitate change. Others treat the process much more routinely.

For very large universities with many diverse programs, the regional associations sometimes agree on a specific activity or function that will be examined during the accreditation visit. For example, the University of Michigan engaged all its schools and colleges in a focused examination of assessment procedures. The self-study was intended to raise faculty consciousness about the merits of assessment at the same time it documented unit procedures already in place. These focused, or special-emphasis, accreditation reviews are options for accredited, well-functioning institutions, but they must be approved by agency staff. This option is gaining popularity among large institutions that want to address functions such as governance or strategic planning (Alstete, 2004).

Some regional accreditation agencies have developed procedures that embed the accreditation review in ongoing institutional processes (such as strategic planning or program evaluation) to increase the benefits associated with this resource-intensive process (Volkwein, Lattuca, Caffrey, & Reindl, 2003). The North Central Association of Schools and Colleges, for example, offers an alternative assessment program that focuses on ensuring that institutional systems and processes support quality assurance and institutional improvement. The Academic Quality Improvement Project (AQIP), based on the Malcolm Baldrige National Quality Award, requires a comprehensive self-assessment and interest exploration, an annual update (summary of progress), an evaluation of a systems portfolio every four years, and a formal reaccreditation every seven years. Institutions opting for AQIP accreditation identify three to four "action projects" and commit to a timeline for completing those projects. Each fall, the institution provides a report on the progress of current projects, to which AQIP provides written feedback. Improvements in the processes or performance results are incorporated into a published "Systems Portfolio."

External Reviews

External initiatives can increase the stakes for self-studies. In the United States, the majority of states require periodic program reviews for public colleges and universities. While the review process is idiosyncratic, three processes are common (Creamer & Janosik, 1999). In one model, a state agent (the legislature or a state agency) targets programs for review, requiring institutions to conduct self-studies of program effectiveness. Based on these studies, the state agency forms a review committee or other mechanism to determine a program's status. In a second type of review, state agencies delegate authority for the review to the institution without oversight of the process. In a third model, the state allows the institution to conduct the review, but under the supervision of the state agency, which determines the procedures and criteria. State agency staff members may participate in the review process. In this case, the report to the state generally includes descriptive information about the program, assessment information, plans to improve program quality and productivity, and productivity indicators.

Variations on these three general approaches are used in individual states. While some state-mandated reviews are scheduled cyclically, others are triggered by concerns about productivity indicators such as enrollments or credit hours. Some are general in focus, while others have a special focus. The "performance funding" approach established by the state of Tennessee in 1979 illustrates a review process with a special focus. This carrot-and-stick approach to evaluation awarded extra funds to colleges on the basis of program evaluations, including student performance and assessment. As a result, the University of Tennessee and other public Tennessee institutions developed models of student assessment and program evaluation that others built upon.

Enhancing College-Wide Evaluation

Increasingly, government agencies and the media are providing the public with ratings of colleges and universities. Often the criteria used are not directly relevant to the quality of learning. Institutions have many opportunities to collect more appropriate evaluation data that can be used to inform the public as well as stimulate improvements.

Student-Centered Evaluation Direct measurement of educational outcomes for an entire institution is logistically difficult and often meaningless without a program context. In contrast, student-centered evaluation that collects reactions from current and past students is particularly useful as a method of college-wide evaluation. Richard Light (1992; 2001) describes a number of college-wide student-centered assessment projects at Harvard that have focused on particular aspects of students' educational experience, such as the impact of class size or how students improve their writing. The initiative called the Harvard Assessment Seminars involved students as trained collaborators and interviewers in the process. In one of the studies conducted through this initiative, a random sample of students mentioned the need to improve their writing three times more often than any other need. Interviews with graduating seniors helped to determine what efforts students had made personally to improve their writing during college and how they had benefited from course-related writing assignments. Three strong recommendations emerged: (a) emphasize writing in the upper-class years after students have adjusted to college and when writing instruction would be most appreciated; (b) organize writing around a substantive discipline, combining writing instruction with actual assignments; and (c) help instructors avoid inserting their perspectives into a students' work. As a result of these carefully constructed studies, several concrete new strategies emerged for writing instructors as well as for students, and adjustments were made in the college's writing programs.

The National Study of Student Engagement (NSSE) can also provide information on the quality of the educational experience at an institution. NSSE has become popular for college-wide studies because it includes measures directly relevant to the total college experience. For example, students answer questions that assess their engagement in courses (for example, how much they have read and written in a year); report their involvement in out-of-class activities (which research shows are related to learning and academic success); tell how often they have engaged in conversations with faculty outside of class; and indicate how often they have had serious conversations with students of a different race or ethnicity. Survey items also request student perceptions of the extent to which their campus provides the support needed for academic success; the extent to which their collegiate experiences have contributed to their intellectual and personal development; and ratings of services such as advising. A companion instrument, the Faculty Survey of Student Engagement (FSSE), evaluates the extent to which faculty members encourage active student engagement in the learning process both inside and outside the classroom. Benchmark data for different types of institutions make it possible for a college or university to compare the engagement levels of their students, and the extent to which their faculty use engaging practices, with those of peer institutions.

Goal-Free Evaluation Goal-free evaluation techniques can be used at the college level, but qualitative data is expensive to collect and analyze. If goal-free methods are deemed appropriate, random samples of students make the task feasible and computer programs may be used to help evaluators track common themes in the qualitative data. Graduates are excellent sources for goal-free evaluation, as they may recognize positive and negative unintended consequences several years after commencement. Women graduates of the 1950s, for example, became conscious only belatedly that fewer options in sports, music, and careers were open to them than were open to men.

The diversity of students and programs limits evaluative generalizations about a large college or university. Special populations particularly should be sought out for their reflections on the college experience and its unintended consequences. This includes women, underrepresented minority students, transfer, part-time, and physically challenged students, as well as those studying unusual majors. The goals and experiences of such students are sometimes sufficiently different from those of the "average" student and may reveal that educational practices that work for the majority of students do not serve special populations as effectively.

Assessing Outcomes The desire to demonstrate educational quality and the emphasis on accountability in higher education often focus on the need for college-wide assessment. After reviewing thirty years of research on the effects of college on students, Pascarella and Terenzini (2005) concluded, however, that it is necessary to study the educational environment within a department, college, or specific academic program to understand student learning outcomes. Recent research suggests that, even within a given unit, such as a college of engineering, there is substantial variation in curricular and instructional emphases (Lattuca, Lambert, & Terenzini, 2008) and student classroom and out-of-class experiences (Lattuca, Terenzini, Harper, & Yin, 2008). The assumption that all students in a given institution, or even in a given unit in an institution, learn essentially the same thing is flawed. Differences in curricular emphases and student experiences are often related to the nature of the subject matter, which reflect discipline norms or the needs of the practice communities to which students aspire. Understanding when assessment has revealed differences in intellectual goals and when it has uncovered poor educational practices that impede learning may be a complex task.

Strong college-level leadership can help each college and department within the university move forward systematically toward useful assessment data that may later be analyzed or applied on a college-wide basis. Such a comprehensive plan must be flexible and adaptable to differences among academic fields but can focus on college-wide goals by using all of the types of evaluation we have described and more. For example, transcript analysis and other "unobtrusive measures," that is, those that do not involve testing, interviewing, or surveying students directly, may be useful (Terenzini, 1987). Varied methods of transcript analyses have been developed to study the course sequences that students have taken (Zemsky, 1989) and to relate them to learning outcomes (Boli, Katchdourian, & Mahoney, 1988; Ratcliff, 1992). Data on employment, life success, and contributions of graduates to their communities might also be assessed to paint a picture for the entire college.

In a time of challenge for higher education, faculty members and researchers will likely create many more new evaluation methods that, with proper interpretation, may be used at the college level. In some institutions assessment specialists assist with the evaluation of academic programs, and may assist faculty with assessment of agreed-on outcomes that can be reported on a college-wide basis—for example, development of critical thinking abilities and competence in ethical judgment. Specific outcomes to be examined must be carefully chosen, measures must be constructed, random samples of students must be used, and response rates must be maximized as such techniques are refined.

One model of a college-wide assessment program that includes assessment as well as other types of evaluation is described in detail by the State University of New York at Albany (Burke & Volkwein, 1992; B. Szelest, personal communication, April 23, 2008). Albany began assessing programs in the 1960s and launched a long-term assessment program in 1978 with a series of studies of student cohorts. The result is a comprehensive outcomes assessment model (Figure 8.2), an extensive set of data bases about students, and a set of customized department assessment plans. In addition to a total plan for assessing the outcomes of general education, the SUNY Albany plan customizes assessment for departments, offering them a variety of options, ranging from senior essays to

FIGURE 8.2. SUNY ALBANY OUTCOMES ASSESSMENT MODEL

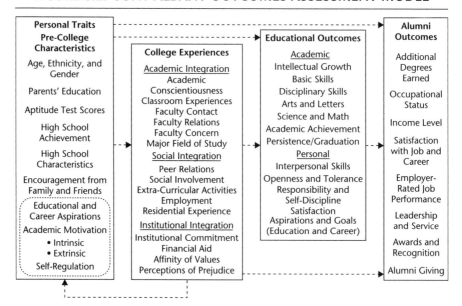

From: The Office for Institutional Research, Planning, and Effectiveness at The University at Albany, The State University of New York, http://www.albany.edu/assessment/ualb_outcomes_model.html

student portfolios and performances. The program has resulted in a wide variety of adjustments and changes to curriculum. The Albany program does not limit itself to the measurement of easily measured academic outcomes; it also assesses personal growth of students and the quality of such support services such as advising. It uses all of the types of evaluation we have discussed in this chapter.

Examining Resources The pressure for greater accountability has also prompted a search for more efficient and effective instructional programs. Evaluation of instructional programs may reveal inefficiencies that can be remedied without sacrificing the primary goal of student learning. The instructional costs benchmarking effort known as the Delaware Study and the course redesign program of the National Center for Academic Transformation suggest two concrete approaches to understanding and controlling instructional costs.

Estimating instructional costs is an imperfect science, but these processes have improved markedly as a result of an ongoing research effort, The University of Delaware's National Study of Instructional Costs and Productivity, which focuses on the development of credible and reliable measures of teaching workloads, instructional costs, and productivity (Middaugh, 2000). Organized class sections taught are reported by type of instructor (tenured or tenure-eligible, supplemental, teaching assistants), division (lower, upper division, and graduate), and type of course (lecture-seminar sections are reported separately from associated labs, discussion, and recitation sections). Thus, calculations may be done to ascertain the proportion of teaching done by full-time faculty, teaching assistants, and adjunct instructors and at what levels (lower, upper, and graduate divisions). Because information on instructional budgets is collected by departments, it is also possible to examine the teaching loads and instructional patterns by academic department. These field-specific instructional costs can be compared against national benchmarks (norms) for a set of peer institutions (derived from the data of the participating institutions).

Instructional costs can also be reduced by redesigning large enrollment courses. A course redesign methodology developed by the non-profit National Center for Academic Transformation (NCAT) allows states and systems to redesign high-enrollment courses that require multiple sections and multiple instructors using information technology to reduce costs while maintaining or improving learning. An evaluation of the implementation of the program at thirty institutions of varying types found that twenty-five institutions showed significant increases in student learning, while five reported outcomes similar to those achieved in courses using a traditional format (Twigg, 2005).

Commitment at all levels of a college or university is needed for a successful course redesign effort, and NCAT's process engages administrators and faculty leaders in early discussions through a team-based approach. This effort involves three sets of partners: (a) state systems or regional groups that provide funding for the transformation effort; (b) NCAT staff who provide expertise and manage the program; and (c) local stakeholders—faculty, administrators, and staff who engage in planning and implementation. The savings from course redesign efforts can be used in a variety of ways, based on institutional needs.

Evaluating Evaluation

We have asserted that every element of the academic plan, including evaluation itself, should be evaluated and the results used to improve the next evaluation. Some evaluation experts refer to the process of examining the evaluation processes as "meta-evaluation," a type of research and reflection on evaluation processes. Key questions to ask about formative evaluations include:

- Was the evaluation of appropriate scope and was it correctly targeted at learning outcomes?
- Did it involve both students and faculty and other relevant parties?
- Was it a reasonable use of student and faculty energy?
- Was there open communication about the results?
- Did it change faculty and student behavior or understanding?
- Did it provide information on how to adjust academic plans?
- Did the adjustments promise improved educational experiences and outcomes?

The credibility and use of evaluation data and assessment results depend heavily on who conducts the assessments, chooses the measures, interprets the results, and is assigned responsibility for improvement. Imposing evaluation requirements and measures of learning violates faculty members' expectations that their subject-matter expertise, professional judgment, and academic responsibility for academic planning of courses and programs will be respected. While not all faculty members will seek active involvement in evaluation and assessment processes, most will have opinions on their quality and usefulness that influence their willingness to act on the results of the evaluation. According to one assessment expert, "Academics are always inventive in finding ways to circumvent external initiatives for which they perceive little value" (Banta, 1994, p. 1). Faculty are more likely to make adjustments to their courses and programs if they contribute to the development of assessment and evaluation procedures voluntarily, if they have opportunities to provide feedback, and if they are engaged in making interpretations and considering plans for improvement. Strong and positive leadership is important, as evaluation alone does not produce curriculum change.

TABLE 8.5. CHARACTERISTICS OF EVALUATION AND ADJUSTMENT AT VARIOUS LEVELS OF ACADEMIC PLANS

Level	Specificity of Outcomes	Formality of Procedures	Ease of Data Collection	Attributes of Learning	Promptness of Adjustment
Course	Specific	Informal	Easy	Somewhat uncertain	Rapid
Program	Both specific and general	Ranges: informal to formal	Range: easy to difficult	Uncertain	Slow
College-wide	General	Formal	Difficult	Very uncertain	Very slow

The level of academic plan being evaluated also strongly affects the interpretation and usefulness of results for improving education. Table 8.5 shows how the characteristics of evaluation and adjustment vary on several dimensions over the three levels of academic plans. As we move from course to college level, the outcomes to be evaluated become less specific; the formality of procedures greater; the difficulty of collecting information about student knowledge, behavior, and opinion greater; the level of attribution less certain; and the promptness of adjustments slower. These observations imply that evaluations and adjustments to improve academic plans should occur at the lowest possible level—with leadership from above to help faculty in planning, implementing, and evaluating the plans. Data responding to educators' needs to improve teaching and advising are more likely to be used (Mentkowski, 1991). Thus, assessment results should be disaggregated to the program level to guide change and adjustment.

Responding to Accountability Demands

As we have noted, the diversity of students, programs, and colleges precludes either standard evaluation procedures or meaningful comparisons of learning outcomes for different institutions, and even for different programs. Yet as college administrators interpret college mission and achievements to the public, policymakers increasingly demand consistent college-wide measures, failing to understand the diversity of missions and the difficulty of confidently attributing learning outcomes to college, or even to a specific college experience. Most colleges and universities can do a better job of demonstrating the quality of their educational experiences and outcome to the public, but rankings based on simple measures fly in the face of good educational evaluation practices. The tension between the public's need for information about educational quality and institutional needs for valid measures is an important issue today.

In the early 2000s, the U.S. Department of Education expanded its attention to student assessment in elementary and secondary schools. In the "No Child Left Behind" program, they required substantial testing of student progress in elementary schools and informed the public of progress through reports showing the percentage of children passing each test in each school district. Thus, assessment of student outcomes and the public comparison of results are well-established in K-12 education but remain uncommon in colleges and universities because college students have multiple complex goals and are not all learning the same content and skills. The introduction of assessment requirements into accountability processes linked to funds for public colleges (by state governments) and discussions of their potential incorporation into accreditation processes are often viewed as intrusive and threatening by those in the higher education sector. Many in higher education, including researchers and evaluation experts, protest that simplistic indicators do not portray what college students are learning very well and are not as helpful for formative purposes as other methods, both traditional and emerging. They cite negative side-effects of standardized testing, such as letting tests determine the content taught; limiting college access to underserved populations by setting rigid, unrealistic standards for admission, progress, or achievement; decreasing students' motivation and increasing their anxiety by over-testing; and "locking in the curriculum" based on the expense of adjusting tests to fit changing academic programs. To forestall uniform measurements and simplistic types of data collection, higher education organizations (such as the National Association of State Universities and Land Grant Colleges and the American Association of State Colleges and Universities), along with higher education institutions, are developing evaluation models that they believe will more accurately assess educational quality (Wheeler, 2007).

Our discussion has focused on two evaluation goals that lead most directly to adjustments in academic plans. These are (a) guiding student progress and (b) improving course and program planning. Indeed, success in achieving these two goals may relieve some of the external pressures on colleges to accept other, less appropriate, types of evaluation goals. Most evaluation experts endorse collection of multiple forms of evidence, as well as encouraging evaluators to seek not only information about how well specific educational objectives were achieved but that they were met without other undesirable consequences. Experimentation with assessment may increase as colleges increasingly state goals in terms of expected student behaviors, develop or adopt measurement instruments, collect data, interpret findings, and develop more systematic recommendations for changes. Academic plans may be improved by attention to an even wider range of evaluation models and potential adjustments. Curriculum leaders in colleges must continue their search for meaningful indicators and evaluation methods that will be acceptable to instructors from various fields as well as useful to the public.

CHAPTER NINE

ADMINISTERING ACADEMIC PLANS

Curriculum administration is the exercise of responsibility and authority to ensure the successful development, coordination, implementation, support, evaluation, and adjustment of academic plans. In most colleges and universities, faculty and administrators share these activities, but responsibilities vary with the type of college, the academic field, and the level of the academic plan. Individual instructors may bear the full responsibility for planning the classes they teach, while faculty and administrators are jointly responsible for program plans and for the curriculum as a whole. Curriculum administration especially includes establishing and maintaining an educational environment in which academic plans can be implemented effectively and improved continuously. Our discussion focuses on three areas of curricular responsibilities. The first focus is the joint responsibility of faculty and administrators as they develop, implement, and foster adjustments of college courses and programs. The second, the responsibility of administrators for the environment in which academic plans are developed, is highlighted in Figure 9.1. The third is the leadership needed for substantial and transformational curriculum change, that is, the path for change often designated in Figure 9.1 by Path C.

Many academics believe that the best curriculum administration is the least possible administration. Instructors, they believe, should be given carte blanche to develop courses and programs consistent with disciplinary tenets and individual interests. The danger in this approach is that uncoordinated programs will serve isolated interests and fail to achieve the goals of colleges, programs, or students.

FIGURE 9.1. ACADEMIC PLANS IN SOCIOCULTURAL CONTEXT: FOCUS ON ADMINISTRATION

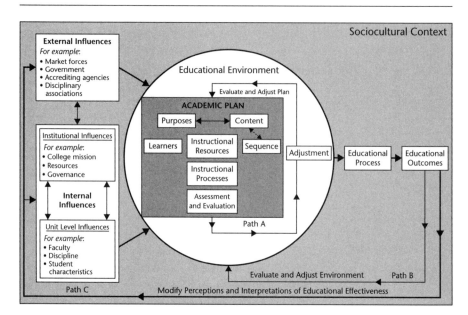

To balance the needs of instructors, students, the college, and society, good curriculum administration does require coordination but of a most deliberate and sensitive sort. Research has shown that college leaders who establish a positive educational environment can provide coordination while fostering strong motivation for program leaders and instructors to take curriculum planning seriously. The effective curriculum administrator must establish dialogue about academic plans and have the perseverance to attend to each element in the plans at all levels. Effective administration also requires an awareness of and concern for the internal, institutional, and external forces that influence curriculum. It is useful as well for administrators to understand and use appropriate change models such as those we will discuss in Chapter 10. When viewed in its entirety, the academic plan framework can serve as a guide and checklist for administrators as well as for faculty who accept curriculum leadership.

In Figure 9.2, we have arrayed the elements of the academic plan in overlapping groups, linking them to five broad administrative functions: development, implementation, coordination, support, and evaluation. All of these functions

FIGURE 9.2. ADMINISTRATIVE ROLES AND ACADEMIC PLANS

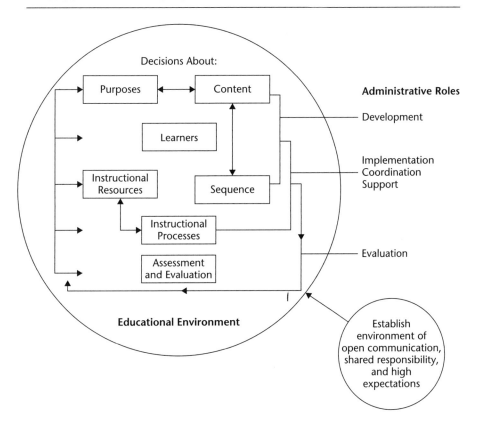

characterize an educational environment where college and program leaders give conscientious attention to curriculum.

Since colleges differ so greatly in mission and organization, our use of the term "administrator" is necessarily general. We will speak of program chairs, deans, and vice presidents as generic categories of administrators, recognizing that this scheme must be adapted for a specific setting. For example, in a small liberal arts college, the academic dean may also serve as the academic vice president. In a large university, associate deans for undergraduate or graduate education may assume a primary curriculum leadership role in the unit. To clarify further the administrative roles that may be appropriate at each of these levels, Table 9.1 provides a matrix of necessary functions if academic programs are to thrive. The functions are grouped into nine categories, depending first on whether they

TABLE 9.1. A MATRIX OF CURRICULUM ADMINISTRATIVE FUNCTIONS

	Development	Implementation	Evaluation
	Purpose, Content, Sequence	*Learners, Resources, Process*	*Evaluation, Adjustment*
Internal Matters (Program Chair)	(A) • Keep abreast of trends in field. • Design program plans and courses. • Describe and communicate plans.	(B) • Staff courses. • Provide incentives for faculty. • Understand learners. • Support and budget. • Select materials. • Select processes.	(C) • Monitor student progress. • Monitor progress of plan. • Determine merit and worth. • Determine costs/benefits. • Adjust plans. • Report to dean.

Organizational Matters (Dean)	(D)
	• Interrelate missions of programs.
	• Relate program missions to college.
	• Coordinate program sequences.
	• Describe academic programs.
	• Create collaborative climate.
		(E)
		• Staff programs.
		• Gather data on learners.
		• Allocate budget.
		• Provide materials, services, instructional resources, and other central services.
			(F)
			• Collect comparative data on:
			  Faculty
			  Students
			  Programs
			  Budgets
			  Planning
			• Encourage adjustment.
			• Report to vice president.

External Matters (Vice President)	(G) • Review college mission. • Relate programs to mission. • Conduct college-wide planning for programs. • Communicate mission. • Establish expectations. • Sense new markets.	(H) • Staff college or departments. • Allocate budget. • Supervise public relations/student recruitment. • Provide central services. • Raise funds.	(I) • Collect comparative data on departments and colleges. • Support new programs. • Adjust existing programs. • Report to president and sponsors.

deal with internal, institutional, or external relations, and second on whether the broad phase of curriculum planning is development, implementation, coordination and resource provision, or evaluation and adjustment. The specific responsibilities appropriate for administrators at the institution (vice president), college (dean and associate deans), or program level (department chair) vary for each type of concern; responsibility is seldom focused at a single level, although it may be more centralized in for-profit institutions.

Curriculum planning is usually specific to a discipline or professional field. Internal leadership is provided by a group of faculty with a program chair who acts as a coordinator. The overall goals are to develop high-quality, coherent academic plans for the designated set of learners; to coordinate the implementation of the plans within the program, including communication with faculty and students; and to evaluate program effectiveness and encourage adjustments. The tasks of this coordinating role in overseeing development, implementation, and evaluation are shown for the program level in Cells A, B, and C. The evaluative tasks in Cell C often are overseen by the individual in the post one administrative level above the responsible program chair, usually a dean.

Institutional leadership for curriculum planning involving several units (Cells D, E, F) is provided by program chairs and deans working together. The primary goals are to develop high-quality academic plans for the designated set of learners; to coordinate implementation of plans and policies, including communication among the various units to ensure linkage and integration among programs; and to work with the next higher level of administrative authority on evaluation and adjustment. A vice president for academic affairs is often the overall coordinator and evaluator.

In external matters (Cells G, H, I), leadership is provided by the deans and vice president for academic affairs working together with coordination by the president. The overall goals are to ensure the development of programs faithful to the college or university mission; to provide resources necessary for implementation; to monitor responsiveness, adaptability, and quality; and to maintain accountability to societal and learner needs as well as to sponsor interests.

In not-for-profit colleges and universities, leadership for curriculum development and day-to-day implementation can and should come from faculty members, while coordination should come from administrators. Evaluation and new vision should involve both groups. The intensity and nature of each group's involvement will vary with the setting and the curriculum task at hand. The faculty should hold some responsibility for curriculum development at all levels from courses to college-wide programs. Similarly, administrators should show their joint ownership and responsibility by remaining informed about even the lowest levels of academic plans. In for-profit institutions with few full-time faculty members, the responsibility for curricular development, coordination, and evaluation tends to rest with administrators. Often the full-time instructors in these institutions serve in administrative roles. Regardless of the formal structure, the primary goal is the design of academic plans that are successful for students and society.

CLUE project researchers interviewed forty-four chairpersons in diverse departments, viewed as effective in curriculum planning, about their curriculum activities and identified seven self-reported leadership roles (Stark & others, 2002). The roles most frequently mentioned (in order of decreasing frequency) were facilitator, sensor, initiator, agenda setter, advocate, coordinator, and standard setter. These roles roughly correspond to the three major functions described in Cells A, B, and C (development, implementation, and evaluation, respectively) of Table 9.1. The results give us a picture of current department chairpersons' activities with respect to curriculum.

Chairpersons playing the roles of facilitator, agenda setter, and initiator are concerned with the process of curriculum planning, especially issues, ideas, and proposals. Thus, these three quite different roles may be viewed as "curriculum development" (Cell A in Table 9.1). Chairpersons most frequently saw themselves as facilitators. They referred to themselves as process leaders, integrators, "first among equals," and prodders. Facilitators try to avoid initiating proposals; rather they use committee appointments and plant ideas to stimulate change. In contrast, initiators provide more direct leadership, sensing what may be needed and bringing proposals to the table for faculty members to consider. Agenda setters bring problems to the discussion table in a neutral way. Their role lies between the facilitator's concern with faculty autonomy and the initiator's development of specific ideas for instructors to consider.

Curriculum implementation (Cell B) encompasses the roles of coordinator and advocate. Coordinators are concerned with smooth internal operation of the program. They provide structure, task orientation, and paperwork support to faculty members who are developing and implementing curriculum decisions. Coordinators may view themselves as supervisors, managers, conflict resolvers, and jugglers of competing interests. This role is frequently associated with multi-field departments or departments that offer large multi-section courses. Although also concerned with implementation, advocates are concerned with institutional relations. Specific activities include procuring resources, setting priorities, obtaining funds, and cultivating positive public relations, especially within the institutional hierarchy.

Two roles emerged that deal with "curriculum evaluation" (Cell C). The standard-setter role focuses on standards, quality, and success. The chairpersons interviewed only infrequently saw themselves as standard setters, but those who did mentioned the roles of monitor, role model, time protector, and "employer of good people." Such chairs attempt to set a model for others by implementing procedures smoothly, facilitating faculty work, and following the institutional rules correctly, especially with respect to monitoring faculty and student progress. The sensor's role is quite different. Sensors concern themselves with both external and internal issues and trends that may suggest the need for curriculum change.

Chairpersons mentioned identifying relevant internal issues, institutional issues, national or regional issues and developing comprehensive visions for the future. Chairpersons who play the sensing role may initiate curriculum proposals based on their external knowledge, but some merely use their knowledge to serve as facilitators. CLUE researchers noted that a role seemed to be missing; they did not find chairpersons who viewed themselves as leading reflective evaluation.

In general, chairpersons in the CLUE interviews were concerned with curriculum renewal, aware of possible need for change, and determined to build consensus and teamwork as well as to find necessary facilities and resources for their academic program. Perhaps because they were selected as exemplars, they were more interested in curriculum development than chairpersons typically represented in the research literature (Hecht, Higgerson, Gmelch, & Tucker, 1999; Leaming, 2007; Lucas, 1994; Tucker, 1992) and more likely to use continuous improvement models of change. Interestingly, however, given the common organizational reporting scheme described in Table 9.1, only a few chairpersons had ever had a discussion with their deans about expectations regarding curricular leadership. Most said that they had no idea what the dean expected!

Curriculum Leadership and Administrative Roles

From the many models available, we selected the "competing values" typology of management model (Quinn, 1988; Quinn, Raerman, Thompson, & McGrath, 1990) as a useful framework in which to examine curriculum leadership and administration. Although managerial in focus, the model's dimensions are congruent with important elements of our academic plan concept. One of its main dimensions—internal-external focus—parallels the internal and external influences on curriculum we have emphasized; the second dimension—flexibility-control—captures the tension between autonomy that instructors need for effective and creative curriculum planning and accountability to sponsors and society. In addition, the model incorporates a wide range of administrative styles that might be used. Thus, consistent with our attempt to present alternatives from which faculty members may choose, it allows curriculum administrators in different settings an opportunity to examine alternative roles relevant to their situations.

Quinn noted that four commonly accepted management models (rational goal, internal process, human relations, and open systems) appear to be based on very different values. For example, the human relations model stresses participation, openness, commitment, and morale. This contrasts with the rational goal model, which is defined by control and an external focus. The open systems model with its view toward environmental adaptation opposes the internal process

FIGURE 9.3. THE COMPETING VALUES MODEL: EIGHT MANAGERIAL ROLES

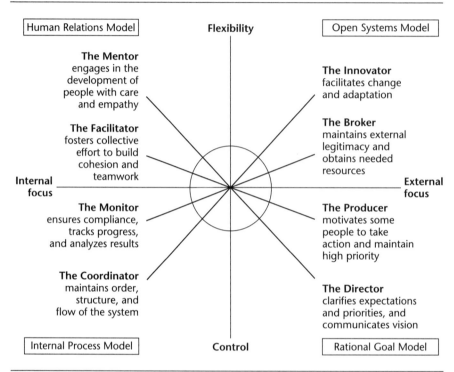

Adapted from: Quinn, 1988; Quinn, Raerman, Thompson, and McGrath, 1990. Reprinted with permission of John Wiley & Sons, Inc.

model, which emphasizes internal coordination and compliance with existing procedures for smooth work flow. Yet each model is similar to another in some respect. For example, the open systems and human relations models share an emphasis on flexibility. The open systems and rational goal models both emphasize external focus; they may be viewed as complementary aspects of the larger construct of managerial leadership, each to be used in appropriate situations. The four models are therefore mapped on two primary dimensions—internal-external and flexibility-control—as shown in Figure 9.3. Taken together, the four models occupy the four quadrants defined by these two axes, and each quadrant includes two roles consistent with that quadrant. Quinn stresses that each managerial role requires a different set of leadership competencies. Thus the total model points to at least eight potentially effective leadership roles that may be used at different times and different organizational levels of responsibility.

As we apply it to higher education, the competing values model supports the prevailing notion in the curriculum administration matrix shown in Table 9.1. This notion is that the most effective and efficient curriculum administration occurs when those with the broadest responsibility provide balanced oversight of the internal, institutional, and external conditions that influence academic plans, but reserve the major role in their development for those closest to implementation of the academic plan.

Project CLUE researchers tested Quinn's competing values model for curriculum administration and leadership in academic departments, surveying 429 department chairs of programs nominated by vice presidents of 137 diverse colleges and universities as especially attentive to continuous curriculum planning. The study aimed to determine (a) the frequency with which the chairpersons carry out activities consistent with each of the eight roles; (b) the curriculum leadership styles that the chairs feel are most effective; and (c) the curriculum leadership styles (groupings of roles) that chairs feel they actually use. (For a detailed discussion of the research methods and results, see Stark, 2002.)

In the next sections, we discuss several aspects of curriculum administration by linking the managerial roles of Quinn's model with the educational environment and the elements of the academic plan. We report data from the CLUE project that indicate whether the relevant roles represent current leadership roles in academic departments, and provide guidelines for administrators who are working toward enhancing curriculum development. These guidelines are necessarily broad and are intended to allow individuals to select those ideas and change strategies appropriate to their own roles and settings.

Establishing the Educational Environment (Roles: Mentor; Facilitator)

To build effective academic plans at the college and program levels, the instructors must have expertise, flexibility to follow their creative talents, opportunities to consider alternatives, and resources to implement the plans. Faculty members tend to feel that curriculum development is worthwhile and challenging but time-consuming and lacking in extrinsic rewards. Thus, they require strong and visible support to maintain vital interest in it. According to one experienced college leader, an environment that motivates instructors is characterized by shared responsibility (a sense of ownership), freedom to experiment (a sense of security), public attention to curriculum (a sense of pride), and keeping pace with knowledge growth (a sense of intellectual vitality and high expectations for quality education) (Guskin, 1981). These conditions are minimal prerequisites for motivating individual faculty, meeting their professional needs, and fostering their sense of obligation to evaluate student learning and adjust academic plans accordingly.

A managerial model promoting these conditions is the one most emphasized in literature written about the department chair role. Of the chairpersons surveyed by CLUE researchers, 48 percent felt that this leadership style was at least somewhat effective. Only 27 percent felt that this style was most like their own.

Shared Responsibility and Freedom to Experiment When curriculum is viewed as an academic plan, every member of a college or university staff holds some responsibility for it. A program coordinator or department chairperson has chief responsibility for leading curriculum development and for coordinating the planned courses and experiences of enrolled students in a program. Program chairpersons (who may or may not have departmental budget authority) usually are accepted as curriculum leaders because they are experts in the subject field of the program. In units in which diverse fields are grouped, the chairperson may be expert in only one of the programs offered. In this case, his or her leadership depends more on formal authority or persuasion than on subject-matter expertise and colleagueship. The more diverse the units under an administrative umbrella, the more distant the leader is likely to be from the actual development of the academic plan.

The pair of inverted triangles shown in Figure 9.4 portrays the typical arrangement in not-for-profit institutions. A top administrator's active role in planning is focused at the college level; his or her role at the course level is less active and may be almost non-existent vis-à-vis such elements of the academic plan as content, sequence, learners, and instructional process. High-level administrative influence is most apparent with respect to resources, evaluation, and adjustment. Instructors, in contrast, are most involved in creating, developing, implementing, and evaluating academic plans at the course level, focusing on

FIGURE 9.4. FACULTY AND ADMINISTRATIVE ROLES IN ACADEMIC PLANNING

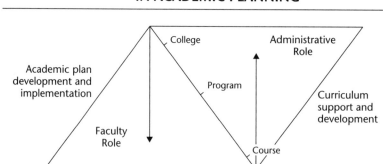

decisions closely linked to the learning process. At the college level, their roles become less active, although in some colleges they may assist both in gathering resources and in defining the college mission.

Considering the wide diversity of colleges and universities, Figure 9.4 represents a theme with many variations. At one end of the spectrum, faculty responsibility for curriculum is well established at many research universities and selective liberal arts colleges. In these settings, administrative decisions about curriculum are actually made by faculty committees, and administrators may be minimally involved at all levels. Faculty may directly recruit students to departments or programs and, in addition to planning the academic program, may engage in fundraising. In colleges and universities with organized faculty unions and collective bargaining, the roles of each group are often defined and distinguished by faculty contracts and "management rights." In such settings, faculty may feel no responsibility for helping the college establish the mission or raise funds; similarly, administrators may have limited participation and authority in decisions about courses and program content or sequence. Depending on local relationships, the codification of responsibilities may either minimize or exacerbate conflict in unionized colleges. In the for-profit sector, there is considerable variation in the reliance on full-time faculty, who have curricular responsibilities similar to those at traditional colleges and universities, and part-time instructors, who teach but may have little input into curriculum planning. Institutions that employ primarily part-time instructors assign most curricular tasks to those in administrative roles.

Even where strongly collegial models operate, the division of responsibility for curriculum can be a source of conflict. Faculty members who chair committees within programs, departments, and colleges become quasi-administrators, leading their colleagues in the details of planning academic programs, but they often lack both authority for budget and accountability to ensure program success. Thus, some carefully formulated committee plans can fail because the necessary resources and staff do not accompany the assignment. While it is philosophically and pedagogically sound for instructors and administrators to share administrative responsibility for curriculum, in most institutions final accountability ultimately rests with the academic administrator.

Even when instructors play the primary role in curriculum development at the course and program level, administrators should not be passive players. They have an obligation to represent the mission strongly. At one institution NCRIPTAL researchers visited, the administration's strong support created an environment in which faculty clearly felt motivated about curriculum change in general, and positive about planning for a new general education program specifically. Faculty members reported: "The president never gives a speech without emphasizing that the university mission is teaching the students of this region.

We feel empowered in our work by the equal attention he gives to the educational program, not just budget and fund-raising." Not only did the chief administrator in this state university regularly remind instructors of institutional mission, he established expectations of careful attention to the curriculum by modeling that behavior himself. He did this by asking important questions that improved and focused the attention instructors gave to the design of academic plans; he encouraged curriculum committees to do the same, abandoning *pro forma* reviews in favor of collegial, but searching, discussions. Curriculum development is often considered hands-off for administrators because they cannot be experts in every field. Yet administrators who accept the shared responsibility for program planning in a supportive, interested way can create a positive climate and use appropriate change strategies to facilitate course and program planning.

Communication about the value of curriculum development is a key factor in fostering the freedom to experiment. Faculty in many colleges feel rewarded for research but believe that they will suffer lack of promotion or lack of salary rewards if they concentrate on curriculum planning and teaching. National studies reveal that a growing proportion of faculty members perceive that research and publications are increasingly important in promotion and tenure decisions, and these perceptions are evident even in four-year colleges outside the university sector (Schuster & Finkelstein, 2006). Yet survey studies show that, even in research universities, both instructors and administrators believe more emphasis should be placed on teaching (Cochran, 1989; Gray, Froh, & Diamond, 1992). In addition, across all institutional types and program areas, faculty members report increased interest in undergraduate education (Schuster & Finkelstein, 2006). Administrators should examine the reward system and the promotions and tenure criteria to be sure that faculty members who devote time to the undergraduate curriculum are likely to be rewarded, not discouraged. Early tenure reviews, as well as final decisions, should make clear that teaching and course planning are important criteria (along with research and service as fits the college mission) for long-term appointments.

The belief that faculty members in research universities do not value teaching in the same way as those in other types of colleges is only one example of misunderstanding that could be helped by open dialogue. The environment necessary to effectively create academic plans requires that such tensions between teaching and research be openly discussed to promote faculty security and vitality. Faculty perceptions of the institutional environment appear to be particularly influential. James Fairweather and Robert Rhoads (1995) concluded, from their analyses of a nationally representative sample of faculty in all types of four-year colleges and universities, that when faculty believe their institution rewards research more than teaching, they are more likely to spend greater time on research. While it may seem obvious, this finding carries important implications for improving the reward system.

Open Communications and High Expectations Academic vice presidents typically think they should give teaching and curriculum development greater attention than they do, yet feel that other demands on their time make such attention impossible (Cochran, 1989). In reviewing research concerning duties of department chairpersons, Stark and Briggs (1998) noted that curriculum matters received little attention compared to personnel, budget, and scheduling issues. On those occasions when academic administrators and faculty discuss curricula, the conversation often focuses on budgets and bureaucratic topics rather than on educational efforts. But it is precisely those missing conversations about educational goals, teaching conditions, student learning, and faculty rewards for teaching and related activities that could lead to effective curriculum development.

Academic leaders can encourage programs to actively discuss their statements of purpose, their program objectives, and their ways of measuring them. To illustrate, the University of Utah David Eccles School of Business developed a matrix of its objectives for students and decided that every course must contribute to one or more objectives. In addition, they asked each faculty member to develop a short "teaching philosophy" for discussion. Administrators and faculty reported that these simple techniques opened many avenues for dialogue about curriculum change and evaluation and generated the feeling of being a learning community (Loebbecke, 1994). Communication about institutional mission and expectations for instructors and students are also critical. Key administrators should spend time engaging faculty in discussions of the college's mission if they expect it to be reflected in course-level and program-level plans.

Administrators might also exhibit a sense of enthusiasm about the importance of good curriculum planning and teaching. They should be sure to publicly acknowledge faculty members who exercise curriculum leadership. During orientation for new instructional staff, they might encourage them to develop peer support groups on curriculum development and teaching and give high importance to curriculum work at program and college levels. Showing special attention to part-time instructors, whose role is primarily teaching, clearly signals the importance of the educational program.

The academic vice president should also comment on the importance of the curriculum at frequent intervals to promote its importance internally. Communication with external audiences like students, sponsors, alumni, and local and state officials is also necessary. For example, the academic vice president's office should ensure that promotional and public relations materials highlight curriculum plans and successes, emphasizing the educational mission and academic

TABLE 9.2. ESTABLISHING A SUPPORTIVE ENVIRONMENT (THE MENTOR AND FACILITATOR ROLE)

- Establish a secure atmosphere. Spell out institutional priorities and the rewards for curricular experimentation. Publicly recognize that the process of curriculum development can be as valuable as the end result. Give ample time to test innovations and allow for revisions and adjustments. Be sure that ownership of the curriculum design and the credit for its success rest with the faculty.

- Foster a system of open communication. Good curriculum plans build on intellectually vital personnel and open processes. Open dialogue helps to establish collaborative relationships among and between faculty and administrators, and helps proponents and opponents to respect one another's views.

- Increase motivation and high expectations through frequent expressions of interest. Provide indications of interest, administrative support, and visibility for curriculum projects as well as high expectations for quality process and product. Praise success. Give public credit both to those who have been successful and to those who were willing to try new ideas.

programs of the institutions as well as its research facilities, athletic programs, and campus amenities. Guidelines for these roles are summarized in Table 9.2.

Developing Academic Plans (Roles: Producer; Director)

After an environment of shared responsibility, freedom to experiment, open dialogue, and high expectations has been established, developing strong academic plans within the college organization requires additional administrative actions. As we have already indicated, these actions are supported by several broad functions. The guidelines we offer are familiar to experienced academic administrators but are important enough to bear repeating with specific emphasis on their relation to developing academic plans. In the CLUE survey, the greatest percentage of the chairpersons (72 percent) believed the producer/director leadership style was most effective, but only 37 percent of them felt they actually played this role. Fully 24 percent reported that the role they did play was not their first choice but instead was influenced by local circumstances, including union contracts, financial stringencies, or organizational expectations.

Choosing Faculty Who Value Teaching A key role for a program administrator (usually assisted by a faculty committee) in colleges and universities is hiring instructors who are competent in their fields. But disciplinary knowledge is insufficient; it is essential that instructors also be competent as curriculum planners and teachers. The importance of interest in curriculum planning and teaching skills should be stated in the advertisements of every faculty position. Candidates can be asked for position papers or statements of philosophy about curriculum development and asked to submit actual course plans or syllabi they have constructed. The hiring process should include discussions of both course planning and teaching; this strategy safeguards against flashy seminar presentations without a solidly developed and clear academic plan.

The Preparing Future Faculty Project (sponsored by the Pew Foundation) has popularized the practice of including information on faculty roles and responsibilities for teaching and curriculum development in graduate education programs. As colleges and universities continue to adopt these ideas, there should be greater numbers of new faculty members with requisite interests and skills. Since other candidates will need to learn on the job by their individual efforts, leaders of curriculum development also need to provide ways for instructors to develop and maintain their competence in both subject matter and curriculum planning. Administrators send clear messages when they sponsor travel to conferences on teaching, learning, and assessment as well as to discipline conferences; encourage exchange visits with other campuses to discuss curriculum development at the program level; or hold workshops on campus. A potent example of a positive change agent in our experience is an academic vice president who not only organized curriculum development workshops but participated fully in every session himself.

Stressing the Centrality of Learners Administrators with responsibility for curriculum should emphasize the centrality of students as learners. Since many administrative problems may deflect attention from student needs, such an emphasis may require conscious effort, particularly in research universities. Alexander Astin urged colleges and universities to incorporate a philosophy of student development into their administrative actions. He contended that college administrators should act on three assumptions: (a) the principal function of educational administration is to enhance student development, (b) the ultimate goal of acquiring resources is to use the resources in educational processes, and (c) institutional quality should be measured in relation to student development goals (Astin, 1979). Astin also believed that this concern for student development should be multidimensional, encompassing intellectual, social, and career development. An administrator who tries to act on these assumptions will support curriculum decisions more effectively than one who sees administrative decisions as ends in themselves.

Although many institutions produce information on student characteristics, goals, and achievement, fewer use it constructively. Administrators who believe learners are central in academic planning will insist that profiles of learner characteristics and achievement are routinely generated and supplied to instructors and programs. They may also request documentation of how this information has been used to improve the academic plan. Engaging the help of instructional development staff is one way to assist in evidence-based decision making. In Astin's words, "The values of an institution are reflected in the kinds of information that it collects about itself and pays attention to" (1991, p. 27).

Administrators can also improve the learning experience of students by working with student affairs and academic affairs offices on initiatives that integrate students' experiences in and out of class. In most institutions, such educational integration is hampered by the organizational practice of dividing responsibility for the college experience between professionals in academic and student affairs. Donald Harward, the former president of Bates College, notes that while the development of the "whole person" has long been a goal of higher education, "on most campuses today, the 'whole person' is fractured into discrete parts. Students themselves are expected to integrate, cumulatively and developmentally, what institutional structures and operations formally divide" (2007, p. 9). Recognizing that both academic and student affairs serve the cause of student learning can foster open and productive dialogues between the two about curriculum development and improvement.

To create a more seamless educational experience, faculty and student affairs professionals can work together to connect course work and co-curricular programs meaningfully and to repair the disconnect that many perceive between students' academic and social lives. Many options for integration exist. Most campuses offer an extensive array of programs featuring guest speakers, films, art installations, musical and theatrical performances, some linked to annual events like Women's and Black History Month, that are potential complements to course offerings. Student affairs professionals can also work with program faculty to address student concerns such as career development. Cooperative education and internship coordinators can also help academic programs identify and disseminate opportunities of particular interest to their students. Many campuses now have a coordinator of service learning who will work with instructors to develop service projects that extend the classroom learning experience to real-world problems. Finally, academic program faculty members should be encouraged to participate in new student orientation programs and first-year seminars that introduce the field and career options to potential majors. On smaller campuses, collaboration between instructors and students affairs professionals may be possible at the institutional level, but on larger campuses, such efforts will likely occur in academic units such as schools and departments.

Promoting Goal Congruence Periodic discussions about goals are valuable even if an institution is not planning extensive curriculum change. One important but often neglected administrative task is to ensure that program-level goals are closely congruent with the college mission. Often, such a consideration is linked with the budgeting process and determines the extent to which the program is eligible for limited resources. Such external forces as accreditation, state examination requirements, and the need to collaborate with practice sites also require administrative attention to program goals in academic planning. College goals need to be discussed regularly too, with special attention to the compatibility of college goals, program goals, and student goals. All are important influences on curriculum planning and must be well understood and consciously addressed. We have summarized guidelines associated with the producer and director roles in curriculum administration in Table 9.3.

TABLE 9.3. ALIGNING TEACHING, LEARNING, AND ACADEMIC GOALS (THE PRODUCER AND DIRECTOR ROLES)

- Ensure that newly hired faculty members demonstrate skills in course planning and teaching. Seek new faculty members with training in curriculum and instruction. Seek experienced faculty members with a record of cooperative team membership in curriculum development. Give attention to enhancing the curriculum planning skills of current instructors.

- Be sure that instructors have the expertise and commitment necessary for the programs planned. If necessary, provide opportunity and incentives for expanding expertise. Resist creating programs based on vague promises of sufficient expertise.

- Provide information about students' characteristics and goals necessary for instructors to develop effective academic plans and ensure its use in planning and decision making.

- Assess curriculum change proposals in light of anticipated student characteristics and interests as well as potential impact of these proposed changes on students.

- Link new and revised academic plans with known student goals and planned student outcomes. At the outset of the new curriculum, create a plan for assessing student learning and goal achievement.

- Be sure that curriculum proposals are consistent with college goals and with the college's public image. Invite participation from a wide spectrum of constituents during the early stages of curriculum development. But be sure it is clear that faculty and administrators are collaborating, rather than making commitments to respond to special-interest groups.

- Determine that academic plans at the program level link with college mission. Help faculty members resist the temptation to offer programs that are beyond the scope of the institutional mission or that have been assigned to other institutional units.

- Be sure that faculty members have an opportunity to associate with curriculum projects most in accord with their values and ideas. However, resist developing programs and sequences of courses that relate to faculty interests but ignore students' interests and demand.

Coordinating Academic Planning (Role: Coordinator)

Several types of academic programs require the coordinator role at the college level because they involve students and faculty from more than one academic planning unit. These include, for example: (a) general education programs, (b) developmental or remedial programs, (c) linkages among programs collaborating to prepare majors, (d) interdisciplinary specializations, and (e) articulation with feeder high schools, community colleges, and graduate programs. These organizational linkages may demand more administrative coordination than academic plans that are contained completely within the bounds of a single field or professional major. In fact, programs spanning organizational boundaries are so frequently neglected that they are sometimes called institutional "orphans." When organizational units compete for limited resources, nurturing such programs may require astute skills for conflict resolution as well as protection and encouragement. In the CLUE survey, chairpersons reported that they performed activities that coordinate curriculum planning far more frequently than activities that initiate it, evaluate it, or link it with external constituencies. Nonetheless, just 30 percent of them reported that a coordinating managerial style was effective, and only 16 percent said that this role was most like their own.

Providing Linkages and Encouraging Articulation Earlier, we emphasized the importance of clearly designated administrative structures for programs that are not under the purview of a single department and suggested some dialogues that might improve the integration of liberal and professional study. We return to these issues of linkage and coordination in both of these cases here.

General and Developmental Education Revisions of general and developmental education programs are often hampered by the lack of administrative responsibility and concern for these areas. Lack of coordination contributes to the gradual attenuation of general education goals and to the proliferation of course options within core and distribution requirements. When colleges that are revising their general education programs recognize these trends, they sometimes establish special associate dean or associate vice president positions for the continued coordination of their general education programs. A next appropriate step would be the assignment of a budget and a stable core faculty.

Developmental education programs can suffer from similar problems. Efficient administrative coordination requires strong leadership to achieve consensus about the philosophy of developmental education, to acquire resources, to implement the program, and to track results. This kind of leadership allowed administrators at Miami Dade Community Colleges to develop a computerized system that guides students to courses of the proper level and tracks their progress.

Program Linkages Many academic programs connect two or more related fields of study. One field may serve the other, as biology and psychology courses serve students in nursing, or they may be related, each reinforcing the other, such as biology courses for chemistry majors and chemistry courses for biology majors. Commonly, instructors designing plans at the program level overlook the need to coordinate these efforts with related departments. We recall a college where a professional field predicated its whole curriculum sequence on the assumed adoption of a new general education program. When the proposed general education program was defeated by the liberal arts faculty, the professional field was in serious trouble. Effective academic planning not only means being alert to these linkages but also developing efforts to promote multidisciplinary approaches involving more than one program. Administrators who have a broad view of several academic programs are in the best position to guide such efforts.

Interdisciplinary programs are increasingly common as students and faculty members seek to address complex problems that cross academic fields. An interdisciplinary program may depend on a fairly permanent link between two or more academic units, as in the case of an American Studies program, or may be created and totally "individualized" for a specific student. Such arrangements challenge faculty members' security and talents by requiring them to develop and sustain new organizational relationships. A fairly common example is the formation of a program such as public policy based on voluntary cooperation from disciplines such as political science, sociology, and history. After a few years of successful existence, public policy may become a department in its own right with less opposition from competing parent departments than at the outset of the collaboration. Because the relationship between faculty members in different programs can be fragile, sensitive coordination is needed.

Articulation Aggressive coordination is needed to develop articulation agreements between two- and four-year colleges, high school and college programs, and undergraduate degree programs. As students increasingly move among colleges and universities and between educational levels, coordination of their progress and advising is required. In institutions that enroll many transfer students from lower-division colleges (such as in the California State University System), administrators, counselors, and instructors must help students choose an academic plan that builds on previous work. In some systems, such as Pennsylvania State University's linked campuses, course and program decisions are centrally approved to ensure equivalent academic programs regardless of campus location. In institutions that lack such mechanisms, administrators may have to insist that agreements about the transferability of courses be worked out, despite faculty concerns about comparable content or quality.

Two- and four-year institutions alike are influenced by the fact that their students increasingly take courses at more than one institution to complete a degree. The receiving institutions, often four-year state colleges and universities, are influenced by the preparation of transfer students coming from other institutions. This influence has grown apace over the last fifty years and is now very strong. For example, in Arizona, the accounting programs at several Mesa Community College campuses teach a course strongly influenced by the receiving programs at Arizona State University. The successful effort to work out articulation agreements between the community colleges and the university was a lengthy process. The growth of the for-profit sector has complicated the transfer credit picture as some two- and four-year institutions have balked at accepting credits from for-profit institutions. The concern on the part of the not-for-profit institutions is the equivalence between courses at the different kinds of institutions; the courses may have similar titles, but vary in terms of content, educational purposes, and instructional methods.

Examining Functions, Structures, Policies, and Processes People create the educational environment in which curriculum development takes place by creating particular administrative functions, policies, structures, and processes. In their role as leaders, administrators have opportunities to examine these to ensure they support effective curriculum development. Although the demarcations are not always clear, administrative functions include tasks that support academic programs either directly or indirectly, including (a) channels of communication, influence, or practice that affect how academic programs operate; (b) policies, that is, deliberate rules of operation that influence the academic program; and (c) processes, namely the ways that positions, structures, and policies actually interact to produce behavior.

Administrative Functions Most institutions would benefit from more dialogue about the roles and responsibilities of administrators and instructors with respect to curriculum. Particularly in large universities where top administration is far removed from the academic program, some instructors are disgruntled about substantial growth in the number of administrators who seem to have no impact on students' education. A healthy habit is to ask whether an administrative position fills the goal of freeing faculty members to use their time and expertise for what they do best. This question should be asked publicly to reinforce the college mission and the high expectations held for quality educational programs.

Structures It is also important to publicly ask substantive questions about how budget, structures, and facilities support the academic plan. In addition, all academically related structures should be examined periodically for their impact on academic plans. Many of these structures—credits, degrees, grades, testing procedures, academic calendars, advising systems, and articulation practices—exist by tradition but affect and constrain the sequence of academic plans. Administrators might temporarily assume that these "curricular structures" do not exist and consider how they might be alternatively conceived.

Policies Academic policies are codified rules and regulations that often are based on the assumption that current structures are appropriate. These include policies regarding comprehensive examinations, laboratories, practica, internships, apprenticeships, cooperative education, credit by examination, and credit for experience. To illustrate, colleges may limit the number of academic credits students may gain through examination, but this policy depends on the existence of a credit structure. If credit as a coin of academic transaction were abolished, the policy would be moot. Like structures, policies should be reexamined regularly for their fit with educational mission and purpose. Course-level and program-level policies regarding course enrollments, the use of library resources faculty workload, course prerequisites, and registration procedures should also be reviewed and adjusted periodically.

Processes The process by which curriculum change takes place is also important. Some procedures may reinforce reluctance to change. For example, one university's written policy on changing course titles, descriptions, or numbers requires that a course change must be originated at the department level (except in a set of approved interdisciplinary programs that allow other origins) and be approved by the (a) department, (b) college, (c) University Council (possibly the Graduate Council as well), (d) University Senate, and (e) University Governing Board, and, for more substantive changes, such as program changes, the State Coordinating Board. Imagine how stagnant business enterprises would become if relatively minor changes in operating procedure followed such a complex route for approval. Many more examples of cumbersome processes could be given, all contributing to the inertia reputedly characteristic of curricular change in colleges and universities. Recently, however, under the umbrella of continuous quality improvement, college administrators have begun to examine structures, policies, and processes in light of the total educational purpose and service to students. Table 9.4 synthesizes the coordination strategies we have discussed.

Implementing Academic Plans (Roles: Broker, Innovator)

When instructors construct academic plans, they make two major choices about the means of implementation: selecting resources and selecting instructional processes.

Often the two choices are linked, just as planning and teaching are linked. The administrative role includes enlarging the set of alternatives from which instructors may choose and reducing the constraints on their choices. In this sense, the administrator may serve not only as coordinator, but also as broker of new knowledge and practices. Of the chairpersons surveyed by CLUE, only 37 percent said the Broker/Innovator managerial style was most or second-most effective. Fifteen percent said that this role was most like their own. Most chairpersons felt ill-prepared to serve as an external sensor to bring new alternatives to faculty members.

Facilitating Instructional Choices Faculty in not-for-profit colleges and universities need considerable autonomy and flexibility to choose appropriate instructional processes, although they increasingly work with other instructors (and instructional development specialists) as partners in curriculum development. Administrators should hold equally high expectations for both individual and team efforts. It is also important to provide instructors with opportunities to try different processes freely and without risk.

Numerous books, newsletters, and checklists are available to help faculty members think about curricular choices. Administrators might assess the overall environment using the Institutional Inventory of Good Practice in Undergraduate

TABLE 9.4. COORDINATING CURRICULUM PLANNING PROCESSES (THE COORDINATOR ROLE)

- Appoint strong leaders to see that the general education and remedial programs are well planned and institutionalized.
- Develop systematic methods to identify duplication and necessary links in existing or proposed curricula among departments. Seek economical solutions to duplication while safeguarding faculty autonomy and disciplinary identity.
- Encourage instructors to experiment with interdisciplinary relationships, recognizing and supporting the risks they take.
- Make articulation a priority; students' needs, not administrative convenience, should take priority.
- Work with faculty members to develop realistic expectations and time lines for discussing curriculum change and implementation. Allow sufficient time for the impact of proposals to be fully discussed but not belabored. Encourage, and if necessary insist, that decisions be made, not avoided. With faculty collaboration, streamline curriculum change processes.
- Require that new proposals have a clear time line for implementation that does not disadvantage enrolled students.
- Be sure counselors and students are informed well in advance of new requirements. Interpret changes and fully explain their rationale to students.

Education, which covers: (a) classroom climate, (b) academic practices, (c) curriculum, (d) faculty, (e) academic support and student services, and (f) facilities. Institutions participating in the Faculty Survey of Student Engagement can utilize program-specific and institutional results to spark conversations in departments and colleges about common instructional practices and the desirability of changes in existing patterns. *FSSE*

Providing Resources Some choices that instructors make as they design academic plans result from constraints on instructional resources; these include staff assistance, schedules, class sizes, rewards and incentives, and working conditions. College instructors are so accustomed to accommodating constraints that they are not fully aware of them until the lack becomes acute or they recognize an exciting opportunity foregone. But observers might attribute great influence to them if they visited some classrooms or departments and observed working conditions that are often far inferior to those in business. Surely, the length of the scheduled class hour and fixed seats in lecture halls propel one toward the lecture; vacations influence the scheduling of tests and the sequencing of content; inadequate staffing contributes to infrequent or hastily done presentations and course websites; and class size often constrains active learning activities. One important role for the administrator, budget concerns notwithstanding, is to create discontent by making new and better alternatives more visible.

Providing Central Services and Facilities Typically a college-wide administrator is responsible for coordinating some central services and units that serve many or all programs in the college. Common service units include learning skills units, libraries, computing centers, media and instructional technology units, instructional development centers, career counseling offices, and bookstores. Supportive services also include test administration, scoring, and analysis; advising; and professional development. The fact that instructors do not use these services extensively argues for a stronger brokering role on the part of administrators who must familiarize instructors with alternatives. In colleges where an unfortunate stigma is attached to the use of instructional development centers, administrators may need to take a strong hand in changing instructors' perspectives. Another challenge is presented by the rapid increase in the use of technology in both planning and implementing academic plans. Administrators need regularly to ascertain that information technology, instructional services, and other support units are prepared to assist in the process of curriculum planning and implementation. See Table 9.5 for a list of guidelines to support instructional development and improvement.

TABLE 9.5. IMPLEMENTING ACADEMIC PLANNING
(THE INNOVATOR AND BROKER ROLES)

- Be sure that financial resources are adequate to carry out academic plans and that the proposals demonstrate a reasonable cost per student. Do not encourage instructors to establish new programs first and plan to use them later to justify the need for additional funds.

- Determine needed facilities for new programs and that they exist or can be acquired. Plan for regular review of facilities for existing programs so that they support educational goals and processes.

- Use the Institutional Inventory of Good Practice in Undergraduate Education to encourage professors to select active instructional processes and create awareness of the importance of teacher-student interaction.

- Develop opportunities for instructors to learn about and select from a wide variety of instructional processes and to experiment with them in their academic plans.

- Identify opportunities for training in both subject matter and pedagogy that faculty will need. Suggest and provide resources for training opportunities.

Encouraging Evaluation (Role: Monitor)

Adjustments based on evaluation paths A and B in our academic plan model help to modify the institution's academic plans directly; changes based on the external cycle (Path C) do so more indirectly by interpreting the views of society to the college and, in turn, the college's processes and outcomes to external constituents. Administrators often must move among the roles of mentor, facilitator, producer, moderator, and coordinator in the internal evaluation path, and the roles of innovator, broker, and monitor in the external evaluation path. Thus, academic administrators who work with curriculum evaluation use all of the roles outlined in the competing values framework. CLUE investigators did not ask chairpersons to react to a leadership style focused solely on monitoring or evaluation activities. However, in a factor analysis of responses to survey items, evaluation activities emerged as a separate group of tasks, seemingly unrelated to other activities and infrequently performed.

Establishing Evaluation Plans and Expectations In public colleges and universities, periodic evaluation cycles may be dictated by state and local governmental agencies as well as by accreditors; independent colleges have more leeway in determining the evaluation activities. Numerous models of cyclical and collaborative evaluation processes are available to guide administrators at each type of college in evaluating curriculum. We mentioned some of these in Chapter 8.

Evaluation professionals agree that evaluating academic plans at any level, especially when many stakeholders are involved, requires a careful four-phase process: (a) planning, (b) information collection, (c) judgment, and (d) use of judgments. Evaluation plans and procedures often must be acceptable to a wide variety of interested groups, including employers, graduate schools, transfer institutions, professional and disciplinary associations, and state and federal officials. The type of evaluation to be used should be deliberately chosen and the purpose clearly stated. Except in goal-free evaluation, criteria must be established to judge merit and worth. The plan should specify the projected use of the information, the decision-makers, the specific object or target of the evaluation, and the clients who will gain. Instructors, especially, must understand the advantages of evaluation and have sufficient opportunity to weigh proposed adjustments before deciding to incorporate them into academic plans.

Developing Faculty Skills For informal methods such as classroom research, instructors must be willing to examine recommended techniques and have the courage to use them. For formal methods such as goal-focused assessment, they need knowledge of testing principles, as well as an understanding of the limitations on test results and their attribution. Statistical skills are needed to identify change through students' test scores and attribute it to classroom events. Statistical consultants may often be found in instructional development units and among social science faculty or institutional researchers.

To help plan an effective evaluation program, instructors need to gather information and use it well. Collaborative work is part of the planning process and instructors therefore also need good interpersonal and teamwork skills, and the willingness and ability to understand others' points of view. Privacy in planning and teaching courses is reduced when a program group engages in a well-planned evaluation program; such collaboration requires new approaches, as well as sensitivity to faculty concerns about professional autonomy.

Finally, if evaluation is to be a positive experience, trained observers and helpers will be needed to collect and process data. If confidentiality is protected by coding records, student workers can assist with these tasks and gain from the experience. Ultimately, of course, administrators have the responsibility for seeing that all of these conditions are possible.

Maintaining Evaluation Standards Evaluation professionals have developed a set of standards—a sort of code of ethics—for the appropriate conduct of evaluation and the use of results for improvement. These standards include statements about:

1. Utility standards: ensuring that the evaluation provides practical information
2. Feasibility standards: ensuring that the evaluation is realistic and prudent

3. Propriety standards: ensuring that the evaluation is conducted legally and ethically

4. Accuracy standards: ensuring that the evaluation reveals and conveys technically adequate information (From: The Joint Committee on Educational Evaluation, 1994, pp. 13–15. Reprinted with permission of Sage Publications, Inc. Books.)

Administrators may delegate the details of the evaluation of academic plans to faculty, but should ensure these standards are available, understood, and used.

 Using Evaluation Results Internally One important administrative role is the interpretation and use of evaluation plans and results within the college. Administrators can encourage instructors to evaluate and make their own interpretations of academic plans at the course level by encouraging the formative use of mid-semester student feedback and classroom research techniques. Internal audiences for these evaluation results include faculty members within a specific program, those in related programs who may learn from the efforts of others, and the students who participated in the activities.

At the program level, the process of self-study is essential if gradual improvement is the intended result, but for administrators there is no escaping the responsibility for program review that moves beyond educational considerations to cost-effectiveness and considerations of worth and merit. Because it includes measures about the program such as enrollment, class size, course cost, workloads, and cost per graduate, program review is often connected with budget allocations and efficiency dimensions, ideas most instructors find alien. Externally, trustees, sponsors, employers, foundations, and state coordinating agencies may be important audiences for these evaluations.

If evaluation or assessment results are summative, that is, to be used for administrative decisions such as program reduction or enhancement, a flow chart and guidelines for the entire evaluation process should be mapped in advance so that questions of fairness or appropriateness to the programs can be raised and dealt with early. The process must be complete enough to be credible but not so cumbersome that an evaluation cycle will never be completed.

To maintain a supportive climate, indicators used for program evaluation should address important educational outcomes, not merely those that are easily measured. These important outcomes call for reliable and valid indicators of learning that are simple enough to be understood by faculty who are not professional evaluators and by the public. Not all evaluation that deserves feedback and discussion involves complex research methods, however. Traditional methods such as peer reviews continue to be important and could be strengthened. Administrators can encourage effective reviews by providing clear charges to review committees, attending key meetings, setting the stage for committee reports, reading and commenting on reports, and publicizing them. But administrators can also cast peer review in a positive light and help faculty use these reviews to build better programs. Finally, administrators can sponsor open dialogue about a program's self-study or review results or add them to data bases maintained by the institutional research office.

Meta-evaluation, the evaluation of an evaluation, not only improves procedures but increases knowledge about how procedures work. Thus, a method must be included for evaluating the evaluation process itself, adjusting it to make it more useful when used again. Administrators can use meta-evaluation to check for unintended negative and positive consequences of evaluation. For example, negative effects of assessing student outcomes may be test anxiety, test fatigue, teaching for the test, and improper use of student assessments for faculty evaluation. Positive effects may include an increased sense of community among instructors, clarification of teaching goals and strategies, and increased sense of student responsibility for personal growth.

Interpreting Evaluation Results Externally States and the federal government have increasingly initiated evaluative activities. Thus, the administrative task of developing cooperative relationships with state and federal officials and accreditors may include providing appropriate data about student outcomes to all three external agencies. Just as essential is the administrator's ability to resist demands for data that may inappropriately represent an institution's educational program. Administrators must weigh the advantages and disadvantages of making evaluation results public and of linking student test results or peer reviews to program budgeting. While some applaud incentive funding, others are convinced that this procedure presents artificial incentives and can lead to both misuse and abuse of evaluation data. Decisions about this depend heavily on the history and context at specific institutions. Monitoring guidelines are listed in Table 9.6.

Adjusting Academic Plans (Roles: Monitor; Facilitator; Innovator)

Most changes in a college's educational environment tend to be gradual and of modest scope. Sometimes a change in the local environment sufficiently supports change or stimulates creative efforts needed to produce substantially new courses or programs. And sometimes creative academic leaders may encourage changes that can be classed as transformational curriculum change based on wide adoption of a new concept, idea, or practice that departs radically from tradition in a specific college or program.

TABLE 9.6. EVALUATING AND INTERPRETING (THE MONITOR ROLE)

- Establish a complete plan for evaluating both existing and new curricula and follow up to see that it is undertaken. Anticipate well in advance the collection of data for future evaluations and accreditations.

- Devote at least as much time in public speeches and discussions to curriculum evaluation as to budget documents, financial planning, and building needs.

- Monitor evaluation processes carefully to be sure that attribution is not made where none is demonstrated.

- Develop careful feedback procedures for the internal use of evaluation information. Create guidelines for the use of evaluation information to influence external constituencies. For example: (a) Don't promise more than the institution can deliver, (b) Get involved in developing state policies rather than reacting to them, (c) Be positive in finding compromises with policy makers, not defensive, (d) Supervise the college image that the public relations office is developing, (e) Anticipate crises and develop contingency responses in advance, and (f) Place personal meetings with important external figures high on the agenda.

- Monitor evaluation processes to ensure that positive student learning outcomes are not attributed to courses or programs without clear evidence.

Although routine changes and new programs meeting specific needs derive mainly from internal influences, transformational changes often stem from external influences acting on the educational environment and are usually guided by instructors and administration leaders who are attuned to these influences. The most common types of change, such as routine adjustment, require administrators to act primarily as monitors and facilitators, roles characterized by internal processes and modest control. Other types of change that are far-reaching or transformational require a much stronger external focus, a high degree of flexibility, and thus a different administrative role, that of innovator. The innovative administrator will want to choose carefully among the change strategies and models that we present in Chapter 10.

Administering Curriculum Adjustments The roles strategists describe for various internal change agents (the rational planner, the collaborator, the facilitator, and the linker or broker [see Lindquist, 1974]), are congruent with some of the roles outlined earlier in Quinn's competing values model. Faculty leaders as well as administrators may play these roles. Much depends on what type of expertise is required in the specific change proposed and how broad participation and credibility can be enhanced. Some studies also suggest that administrators interested in leading change will want to shift roles as the change process progresses (Davis, Strand, Alexander, & Hussain, 1982). In fact, using factor analysis of survey responses, CLUE researchers found four dimensions of chairperson activities related to, but not congruent with, the four quadrants of Quinn's model. They called one important dimension "balanced oversight" since it incorporated some activities that would, at face value, fall into each of the four quadrants. Two additional dimensions were named "coordination" and "evaluation," respectively, both based on activities in the Internal Process quadrant. A fourth (and less practiced) activity dimension was called "external sensing" and fell in the Open Systems quadrant. Currently, chairpersons spend far more time in internally focused management activities than on those with an external sensing or linking focus.

The idea that administrators must use all of the roles in Quinn's model at different times was strongly reinforced by the chairpersons CLUE researchers interviewed. No one leadership style was viewed as best in all circumstances. Rather, many chairpersons commented that all of the styles or some combination of them could be effective, depending on the local culture and the particular talents of the faculty members and chairperson. Although the Quinn model is not an exact map of what curriculum leaders do or should do, it can help them reflect on their own styles and recognize activities that they tend to neglect. As one chairperson said: "The skill is knowing which of the four styles is needed at what point in time" (Stark, 2002, p. 73).

Leading Curricular Change Leadership plays an important role in encouraging substantial change that responds to both external and internal influences as well as in facilitating routine adjustments. Leaders need to be aware of external pressures on their programs, of new developments in their academic fields, and help instructors translate these pressures into change when appropriate. They need to assist instructors in using the results of their own evaluations to initiate improvements and in responding to increasingly rapid changes in the educational context. On any given issue, different perspectives on the proposed change and different power structures exist at each level and setting. Higher education has many change leaders, but not all have the authority, persistence, or expertise to bring about the changes they propose.

Colleges and universities traditionally have placed strong emphasis on achieving consensus and commitment to change at the lowest organizational level where curricular decisions are made. The closer the level of the academic plan to the expertise of faculty members, the more fully they will be involved in and, thus, potentially committed to, a specific curriculum change. Collective decisions are more likely at the program level than at the college-wide level, where change models suggest that the political dimensions of change must be more fully addressed. The collaborative, facilitative, and linking roles are most appropriate when the leader is less expert in the academic field than the followers—surely the case when the leader/change agent is a college-wide administrator. When the leader possesses expertise—as is usually the case at the program chair level—these roles

TABLE 9.7. PROMOTING CURRICULUM ADJUSTMENTS (THE MONITOR, FACILITATOR, AND INNOVATOR ROLES)

- All faculty members should have some involvement in decisions, although the involvement will differ by role.
- Communication should flow in all directions; all organizational members should participate in developing plans for change and in reviewing progress.
- Persons given responsibility for stimulating and implementing change should be knowledgeable, credible, and flexible.
- Goal consensus should be sought, but leaders should be prepared to move forward with less than unanimity.
- All members of the organization should be encouraged to evaluate their own contributions and progress toward goals.
- The need for adjustments in reward systems should be foreseen and adjustments should be made at the beginning of a new program.
- New training needed for organizational members should be assured in advance.
- Administrative leaders should make public statements supporting the change and outlining their expectations for success.

continue to be important, but the leader may also provide stronger leadership for far-reaching curriculum change using multiple change strategies.

Major curriculum changes frequently have been achieved by creating new institutions or departments and by recruiting leaders with commitment to a given idea (Levine, 1978, p. 418). Large research universities are often able to establish entire new departments (for example, nanotechnology, sustainability, center for the study of heart rhythms) using donated funds or research grants. For most smaller institutions, new funds for alternative programs and institutions are severely restricted today so substantial program change may well depend on refining systematic change processes and giving more deliberate attention to opportunities.

Leaders of substantial change efforts especially need to be cosmopolitan, focused on mission, sensitive to opportunities in the external environment, communicative, willing to take risks, and prone to ask difficult questions (Seymour, 1988, pp. 14–17). They must also create the kind of supportive educational environment we have discussed, including: (a) an open decision structure distinguished by free communication patterns, widespread involvement of faculty, effective group processes, and decentralized decision making; (b) consensus about institutional and program goals, coupled with a spirit of self-evaluation; (c) an accepted pattern for achieving change, including an emphasis on continuous improvement; (d) a clear expectation that change will occur when needs are identified; (e) an appropriate reward system; and (f) an expectation that faculty will oversee implementation of the change as well as recommend it. See Table 9.7 for a summary of recommendations for leading curriculum change.

In the slow and indirect process of curriculum change, administrators typically play a small role in planning the content of the curriculum but a large role in establishing purpose, helping to set priorities, obtaining resources, and maintaining a supportive context. They play this role by fostering communication, supporting experimentation, and encouraging full consideration of decision alternatives in an atmosphere of trust. Just as the academic plan gives instructors a guide to follow in developing curricula, it gives administrators a template to maintain a climate consistent with what is known about fostering change.

CHAPTER TEN

MODELS AND STRATEGIES
FOR CURRICULAR CHANGE

Proposals for curricular change arise as faculty and administrators evaluate the effectiveness of academic plans and seek either minor adjustments or major improvements, but they may also result from external influences. Figure 10.1 highlights these two sets of influences. Internal influences typically result in adjustments along Paths A and/or B. External influences often follow Path C. Some adjustments in academic plans are sufficiently broad to be called "curricular change." For example, adjustments in content or sequence made by an instructor in a specific course differ in scope and importance from a decision to alter several elements of an academic plan or modify a significant aspect of the educational environment. Broad changes such as the ones we address in this chapter require leadership, coordination, and, often, professional development for faculty and administrators. Successful leadership for such changes must recognize and build upon the college or university culture, including its institutional traditions, norms, and values; politics and power; individual and collective beliefs and attitudes related to proposed changes; and existing social relations and practices. In this chapter, we focus on factors such as these that can affect the success of a curricular change effort.

Although external influences sometimes create strong currents for change, colleges and universities are not passive recipients of societal pressures. Rather,

FIGURE 10.1. ACADEMIC PLANS IN SOCIOCULTURAL CONTEXT: FOCUS ON CURRICULAR CHANGE

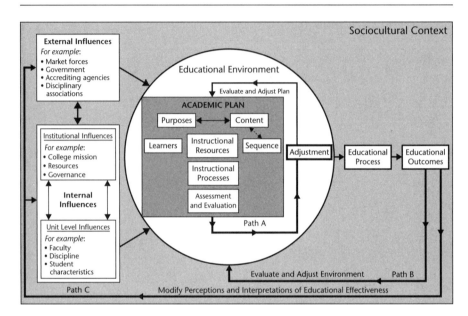

administrators, faculty, and staff are active agents in the curricular change process, sensing, examining, and interpreting external influences and ideas to determine their suitability for local needs, adapting promising ideas, and sharing the responsibility for successful implementation. The models of change we discuss in this chapter offer different perspectives on how and why change occurs (or doesn't). The existence of numerous models suggests that none is complete; as researchers continue to study higher education, additional variables in the change process emerge. Our review of several broad models of change allows us to identify a variety of factors that affect curricular change efforts and offer ideas about how to design and evaluate curricular change processes.

Evolution, Adaptation, and Strategic Change

Throughout this book, we have discussed many environmental factors that have shaped higher education curricula in the United States. Social, cultural, political, and economic shifts have stimulated many changes in higher education generally and in the curriculum specifically. Such contextual factors continue to pressure institutions to change. The responses of colleges and universities to societal influences may be considered part of an evolutionary process. Often, change is an institutional survival response to external conditions. While some view this evolutionary process as largely reactive and uncontrolled by organizational actors (Hrebiniak & Joyce, 1985), others suggest that organizations can anticipate and adapt to change (Cameron, 1984). Examples of effective responses to alterations in the educational environment include: (a) the continuing response of U.S. colleges and universities to changes in student demographics and demands over time; (b) the addition of new programs responding not only to students' calls for career preparation but to changes in the economic base of the nation; (c) the development of flexible delivery options and programs for nontraditional students; and (d) the adoption of college-wide assessment in the face of pressures for accountability from government agencies and accreditors. Some of these changes evolved in a time of budgetary growth in higher education and emphasis on increased access; others occurred during economic recessions. No consistent pattern is apparent; sometimes a confluence of external forces is needed to stimulate change.

These examples also demonstrate how higher education institutions can adapt and change through differentiation and accretion, adding programs (such as computer science and women's studies), responsibilities (such as assessment), and even structures (such as online learning units) that allow them to adapt to changes in their environments without substantially altering existing structures and practices (Clark, 1983; Gumport, 1993). Accretion and differentiation appear to be particularly apt descriptions of much of the history of curricular change.

We have noted that the relative strength of internal and external influences, and thus the emphasis on adoption of different curricular purposes and content, varies over time. To illustrate, government policies always influence the educational environments of colleges and universities, but federal and state governments are more active at some times than others. Moreover, their priorities change periodically. During one period, government funding strongly supports development of occupational programs in community colleges; during a subsequent period, government agencies criticize colleges for excess emphasis on job training and encourage them to place more emphasis on basic communication skills or preparing students for transfer to four-year institutions. Because a curriculum reflects its sociocultural context, external influences act powerfully over time to produce substantial curriculum change. Over the short term, however, the direction of these forces may be inconsistent.

A review of curricular changes over time suggests that college and universities are more reactive than proactive, but such a suggestion may overlook the important role of human agency and the complex interactions among variables that affect change (Kezar, 2001). Especially in higher education institutions, administrators, faculty, and staff assess potential changes by considering them in relation to existing beliefs, identities, structures, and norms. External pressures become crises that must be addressed when they are interpreted as such by individuals within the college or university (Sporn, 1999).

Scope of Curricular Change

One way to understand the scope of curricular change is to consider the extent to which a given change will influence institutional practices. Eckel, Hill, and Green (1998) suggest two measures of this influence: *depth* and *pervasiveness. Depth* describes the extent to which a change affects behavior or alters institutional structures. For example, a course that has been redesigned by incorporating technology profoundly changes the learning experience for students and requires both the instructor and students to think and act differently. Such *deep* changes in any element of an academic plan alter perceptions, values, and assumptions—but they are not necessarily widespread. This kind of course change may affect only a small number of students and faculty in the institution. In contrast, a change is *pervasive* if it affects many units within a college or university. Course management software has made pervasive changes in some colleges and universities because it is used by faculty and students in many different academic programs. Eckel, Hill, and Green (1998) suggest a matrix that combines these two elements of change (see Figure 10.2).

As we noted earlier, most course planning is routine: faculty make adjustments (Quadrant 1) to existing courses by modifying course content, sequence, or instructional processes during and after a course is offered. Although adjustments may represent improvements, they may not substantially change the overall academic plan or the learning experiences of students. "Isolated changes" (Quadrant 2) are high in depth but low on pervasiveness. When online education was new, many colleges and universities limited it to continuing education programs; its adoption was thus an isolated change that affected only one or two units within

FIGURE 10.2. TYPES OF CHANGE

		Depth	
		Low	**High**
Pervasiveness	**Low**	Adjustment (1)	Isolated change (2)
	High	Far-reaching change (3)	Transformational change (4)

the institution. Today, online education has become a far-reaching change (Quadrant 3) in many institutions; online courses enroll hundreds or thousands of students, both residential and non-residential and from undergraduate as well as graduate academic programs. In these institutions, online education can rightfully be viewed as substantive curricular change. Similarly, the adoption of a cohort-based educational program like a learning community can be an isolated change or a transformational one. If a single academic program within a college adopts this instructional process, the change will be deeply felt in that program, but it is not pervasive because students and faculty in only one program are affected. In another college that decides to enroll all first-year students in coordinated courses, all entering students and many faculty members will be affected by the move to a learning communities program. The teaching and learning process will be greatly altered (a deep change), as will the experiences of many students and instructors (pervasive). This change is transformational (Quadrant 4).

Transformational changes in curricula that are both deep and pervasive have occurred throughout U.S. history in response to external influences. An example is the adoption of the land-grant mission. In making this intentional mission adjustment, existing colleges and universities greatly expanded their content and instructional processes; enlarged their enrollments of students interested in agriculture, engineering, and other practical fields of study; internalized a new set of values and institutional purposes; and altered faculty roles. When faculty and administrators consider far-reaching and transformational curricular changes, careful consideration of the impact of the proposed changes on structures, beliefs, and practices can inform decisions about whether and how to change. These deliberations clarify many factors influencing whether curricular changes are accepted and implemented. The literature on organizational change in higher education that we will review can provide guidance to programs and institutions preparing to engage—or already enmeshed—in curricular change efforts. The models of change we discuss add a layer of complexity to the change process, but also permit us to recommend avenues for accomplishing curricular change.

Models of Change

Theories and models of organizational change can be used to analyze three kinds of deep and pervasive curricular changes: (a) those that result from institutional response to external societal pressures; (b) those that result from diffusion of educational ideas developed outside the institution; and (c) those that emerge from planning efforts of faculty and administrators within a program, college, or university. Our review is indebted to scholars who have synthesized the theory and research on change models with respect to higher education, particularly Robert Nordvall (1982) and Adrianna Kezar (2001). As they and other scholars have noted, change models are not mutually exclusive. They may operate—or be intentionally utilized—simultaneously or in sequence (Eckel, Hill, Green, & Mallon, 1999).

Given the emphasis on reason, discussion, and collegial interchange in higher education, most faculty and administrators believe that attempts to reform or revise curricula will be rational and straightforward. They assume that individuals affected by a change will consider the proposed curricular change with an open mind, weigh its advantages and disadvantages for different groups (such as students and faculty in a program, employers, and others), and come to a reasoned conclusion about whether it is needed. Similarly, some models assume that change can be accomplished through planning, implementation, and testing of new ideas. Planned change models, for example, assume this kind of rational process. Political and social cognition models, in contrast, attend to other influences—such as beliefs and attitudes of organizational members—that affect change efforts. Our discussion highlights the array of variables that must be considered in any change effort, focusing on how change models inform the planning and implementation of effective curricular change efforts at the program and institutional level.

Diffusion Theories: Addressing External Influences

Curricular change often occurs by diffusion. Faculty or administrators learn about an emerging content area, a new instructional method that appears to be particularly effective, or consider adding an academic program in order to remain competitive with peer institutions. The decision to try a new teaching method or mount a new program is both an external impetus and an internal decision. The open boundaries between colleges and society foster interactions like these among internal and external influences and allow for transformation of external influences into internal ones.

When an external influence is sufficiently powerful (such as one supported by legal or fiscal authority), convincing (presenting strong ethical or moral obligations for higher education institutions), or economically or politically sound (necessary for the nation's economic and civic welfare or defense), it may gradually come to become viewed as an internal imperative or priority. This interpretive process takes place at different rates, depending on the influence and context and, of course, some external influences are not internalized but fall by the wayside. Some are abandoned due to a lack of persistent emphasis, or changes in local power dynamics. In other cases, authorized funding is not forthcoming or the nation turns its attention to other more immediate matters. The open boundary between colleges and society refutes the common stereotype of the university as an ivory tower, insulated from the society it serves.

Stages of the Diffusion Process The movement of influences across the boundary between institutions and their environments can be viewed as stages in a change process. Three stages common in most diffusion theories are *initiation* (or awareness), *screening* (adaptation), and *adoption* (confirmation) (see Table 10.1). Although early theories presented these stages as linear, recent ones portray a process that is more complex and episodic (Rogers, 1995).

The first phase of response to a period of agitation or ferment in society is *initiation* or *awareness*. At this phase of problem recognition or initial public pressure, external influences are strong but organizations may resist change, either because the source is not perceived as legitimate or credible, because the need for change is not fully recognized, or simply because of organizational inertia. An example may be concern in some sectors of society about environmental sustainability. Not all colleges are addressing this issue in their curricula, but concern is spreading.

TABLE 10.1. STAGES IN CURRICULAR CHANGE INITIATED BY EXTERNAL INFLUENCES

Initiation (Awareness) Stage
- Recognize the need or opportunity (awareness, knowledge, assessment).
- Develop interest, suggest a plan, or formulate a plan.

Screening (Adaptation) Stage
- Develop arguments for and against the change.
- Identify opinion leaders.
- Evaluate the plan or suggested solution.
- Explore similar programs elsewhere.
- Consider a small-scale trial.
- Make tentative decision to adopt.
- Discuss extensively.
- Make second tentative decisions to adopt.

Adoption (Confirmation) Stage
- Adopt the plan.
- Implement the plan.
- Establish future evaluation strategy.

The second phase of response is *screening* or *adaptation*. During this period, the organization evaluates the possibilities for the proposed change and tentatively decides to respond. In the case of curricular change, individuals may actively advocate the need for change or disseminate new models. Institutions may then gradually accept the direction of society, cease active resistance, and begin to incorporate new ideas into academic plans. Although new ideas are being adapted to the local context, at this point, the internalization of the change is still tentative. In our previous example, if society moves on to other issues or is distracted by a crisis, the sustainability issue may disappear. External influences that do not survive the screening or adaptation process either fade away or continue to be external influences.

The process of adaptation often begins by converting the external influence into an institutional influence. For example, exploration of the feasibility and desirability of a curricular change will proceed largely through discussions that involve program interrelationships and financial allocations, governance patterns, and views of the fit of the suggested innovation with institutional or program mission. At this stage, college leaders may well ask about the consequence of *not* adopting the change and how to resolve the organizational tensions that seem to prevent adoption. To illustrate, in many institutions internationalization of the curriculum is at the adaptation stage. Some fields, such as business, have already internalized the need to deal with global problems; other fields have not yet viewed this as relevant. To give another example, as society accords increasingly higher priority to concerns about environmental sustainability, university faculty members in scientific and other fields may persuade their colleagues that leadership from educators is essential and that curriculum change incorporating this issue is imperative.

When the stage of *adoption* or *confirmation* is reached, the degree of acceptance is sufficiently great that the influence may no longer be viewed as external; it is now part of the institution's agenda. The more an influence is perceived as compatible with the college or program mission or values, the more likely it is to become an internal influence (rather than something attributed to an external authority or pressure group). As an illustration of an external influence that was slowly internalized, we again refer to the mission assigned to colleges by the Morrill Act in 1862. For fifty years or more prior to the passage of the legislation, some societal leaders recognized that education in the sciences and agriculture was necessary for the nation's economic growth. Many colleges, however, were not ready to embrace these new educational purposes. At this stage, the desire to include these new subjects in the college curriculum was primarily external to colleges. As awareness rose, professors began to teach these practical studies, or at least acknowledge their value, and the impetus for change became internal as well as external. Eventually, existing colleges designated as land grants, as well as the newly created land-grant colleges, fully integrated new curricula and priorities into their missions. A more recent example is the initiation and growth of diversity course requirements in general education and academic programs in fields such as education. Following *Brown v. Topeka Board of Education*, many colleges and universities began to accept the idea that diversity in the curriculum is an educational necessity. While transformational curricular change is slow, many institutions have incorporated learning outcomes related to diversity into their mission statements, and academic programs have expanded the array of authors and perspectives included in their courses.

Some recent curricular changes appear to have staying power. These include online education, learning communities, and institutional assessment of student learning outcomes. Other curricular changes are fleeting. Examples abound of colleges that in the 1970s began to focus on interdisciplinary study, independent learning, or non-graded study. Many of these have now resumed more traditional practices of offering majors, minors, and grading systems (Cardozier, 1993; Klein, 1990; Levine, 1978; Townsend, Newell, & Wiese, 1992). Cameron Fincher (1988) observed that curriculum decisions take place by "provisional variation" and "selective retention" (p. 282). He described provisional variations as changes that follow prolonged debates and deliberation and, in the end, are made with only tentative faculty commitment. Selective retention is the process of maintaining changes that are subsequently seen as effective while allowing the rest (including many of those that received tentative commitment) to die an uncelebrated death. This process, according to Fincher, makes curricular change slow and indirect, rather than rapid and deliberate. The change models that we review provide keys to understanding why some changes are institutionalized while others fade away.

In his classic study, *Dynamics of Academic Reform* (1969), J.B. Hefferlin suggested that what we think of as change in higher education is often a case of importing a new idea from elsewhere. Hefferlin believed that the major problem in academic change is the difficulty of selecting among external ideas and using them to institute changes that will lead to improvement. He noted, "Academic reform consists far more in the diffusion of educational ideas from one institution to another than in the creation of new ideas" (p. 156). Diffusion theories attempt to describe this process, suggesting that the decision to adopt a particular innovation depends on awareness of the innovation, interest in it, evaluation of its merits, and a small-scale trial.

Everett M. Rogers' model of the diffusion of innovations (1995) delineates a number of factors contributing to an individual's decision to adopt a new idea. According to Rogers, an individual's decision to adopt an innovation depends on four factors: (a) the characteristics of the proposed change; (b) the environment or situation surrounding the potential change; (c) the extent of involvement of those affected in the adoption process; and (d) the leadership strategies used. Once aware of an innovation, the individual considers its features. Does the new practice offer a relative advantage over existing ones? Are there other alternatives? He or she also assesses the compatibility of the innovation with existing norms and expectations. The ease with which an innovation can be understood and communicated is yet another factor influencing adoption, as is the ease of implementation.

If all these assessments are positive, the outcome of this diffusion process is adoption. A few opinion leaders (or linking agents) spread the word about an innovation and a small number of individuals may be "early adopters," while others take a "wait and see" attitude (Lindquist, 1974). In higher education, institutions as well as individuals can serve as early adopters who pave the way for others. Some examples of curricular changes that occurred primarily through diffusion are the elective and general education distribution systems, the academic major, pass-fail grading, and the use of course management software. Some substantive changes have more limited life spans. Competency-based education and the 4-1-4 calendar are examples of changes that were tested briefly in the 1970s by numerous institutions that later abandoned them. Although examples of these curricular changes still exist, they are not common in U.S. higher education.

Planned Change Models

Planned change differs from diffusion. Models of planned change emphasize goal-directed action (rather than reaction to external influences or educational ideas initiated elsewhere). In addition, while the focus in diffusion is on the individual, planned change models focus on the change process. Kezar (2001) identifies four kinds of planned changed models: (a) research and development (R&D), (b) problem solving, (c) organizational development, and (d) continuous improvement.

R&D and Problem Solving The rational side of curricular change is highlighted in the research-and-development and problem-solving models of change. Curriculum change in an R&D model depends on the ability of those advocating change to present convincing arguments, buttressed by research, that identify the need for change and suggest a carefully tested and logical alternative to current practice. For example, writing instructors in a college or university may discuss the wisdom of embedding writing instruction within major programs, rather than offering general writing courses for all students. If these instructors base their decision on research findings (their own and/or those of others) that demonstrate the superiority of the embedded writing approach, they have followed an R&D approach. In engineering one can find examples of curriculum modules and entire courses that were developed through a "design-build-test" approach. Although this deliberate approach may be more common among engineering faculty because systematic design and R&D processes are used in engineering practice and research, examples also exist in other fields. For instance, psychology faculty members at the University of Michigan conducted pilot studies to assess the intellectual and academic growth of undergraduate students who participated with faculty mentors in research projects. These results facilitated decisions about whether to expand the project and its funding (Nagda, Gregerman, Jonides, von Hippel, & Lerner, 1998).

The problem-solving model of change differs slightly from the R&D model because it suggests that change originates in a felt need that is based on either an internal or external diagnosis. In addition to searching deliberately for solutions to a problem (a rational approach), organizational members must be willing to change. According to this model, the need for change can be personally or vicariously experienced, but it must be perceived if individuals are to be persuaded to change. In higher education, the perception that change is needed is often based on knowledge of what colleagues in similar settings are doing (and thus is not entirely separate from the diffusion process). Once convinced of the need for change, faculty members and administrators often will review the work of peer programs and institutions as they evaluate solutions to determine if they are locally appropriate. For example, in the 1950s education faculty members were concerned that some students entered capstone student teaching experiences only to find that they were uncomfortable dealing with children. The far-reaching result, the initiation of a requirement for contact with children very early in the education major, increased graduates' fit with a teaching career. More recently, colleges of education have fostered even closer relationships with local schools. These "professional development schools" provide many more opportunities to engage with teachers and students in elementary and secondary classrooms as part of the undergraduate educational process.

Planned change efforts may combine approaches. The linkage model (Havelock, 1971), for example, contends that planned change starts with (a) a potential user or adopter feels a need for the change (as in the problem-solving model); (b) a diagnosis of the problem leads to a problem statement about what is wrong; (c) a search for potential solutions is conducted; and (d) a solution that meets the needs of the local context is developed and approved (as in the R&D model).

In a study of curriculum change in higher education, Jack Lindquist (1978) tested Havelock's linkage model of change in a multi-institution, longitudinal study.

His findings led to the development of a general theory of planned curricular change, which he called the "adaptive development" model. Lindquist's use of the term "adaptive" signaled his belief that planned change is a local development, but one that is typically stimulated by an external (rather than internal) innovation. None of the campuses he studied started "from scratch." Rather, institutions "took an idea, a few guidelines, some practical tips on what works and what needs avoiding, some evidence to convince local skeptics, and then constructed their own innovation to fit their institutions" (p. 224). Lindquist noted the effects of power and politics, yet the graphic depiction of his model portrays the change process as primarily rational. Critics of rational planning models believe the influence of power and interest groups, informal and behind-the-scenes processes, persuasion, and politics have been neglected (Conrad, 1978; Kezar, 2001).

Organizational Development and Continuous Improvement Like the R&D and problem-solving models of change, the organizational development (OD) and continuous improvement (CI) models focus on diagnosing problems and searching for solutions, but they define these activities as continuing and regular practices rather than occasional efforts. A key to facilitating organizational development is analyzing obstacles to change, so the OD model focuses on understanding the attitudes of organizational members such as staff, administrators, and faculty as well as the role of organizational norms in hindering desired changes. In this way, OD models address a criticism of planned change models—their inattention to the role of personal beliefs, perceptions, and attitudes in change efforts.

The weakness of organizational development models—especially in not-for-profit colleges and universities—is that they place heavy responsibility for successful change efforts on a leader who manages the transition through the phases of an OD process. The norms of collegiality and professional autonomy in most colleges and universities challenge (and may subvert) this top-down approach.

A close cousin to the OD model, continuous improvement, delegates responsibility downward and also stresses collaborative efforts. It thus appears more appropriate to college and university settings than the OD model. Continuous improvement models emerged from the total quality management movement of the 1980s and 1990s, which affected business and industry quite strongly. Not surprisingly, therefore, CI principles have had their greatest impact on the administrative functions of colleges and universities (Harper, 2008). Thus far, CI has received limited trials in assisting academic change except in some academic fields where the CI terminology is familiar and its ideas have been incorporated into the standards of specialized accreditation agencies (such as the Accreditation Board for Engineering and Technology and the Association to Advance Collegiate Schools of Business).

The goal of continuous improvement is proactively planned change. Like OD models, it assumes that diagnosing and solving problems is an ongoing practice. The CI models also emphasize consistent attention to the mission, goals, and outcomes of the organization (or of the unit or program) as a basis for judging the suitability of proposed changes. Moreover, any proposed changes, CI models assert, must be based on evidence of the need for change, and collaborative decision making by those who will be responsible for achieving and sustaining change. In contrast to the central role of the leader in OD models, leaders in a CI model play a supporting role, facilitating organizational efforts and ensuring that ongoing training and individual development are available and valued in the organization.

In the CLUE studies of programs known for regular curriculum planning, the most successful departments exhibited characteristics congruent with those of continuous improvement models, viewing themselves as communities that learn together and share their experiences as they plan (Briggs, 2007). This collaboration was collegial in a positive way, emphasizing voluntary initiative and flexible participation in the group rather than formal roles and timelines for change. The culture of continuous planning reflected this collegiality and shared ownership of the curriculum which, in turn, was exhibited in problem-solving behavior. Group leaders, whether faculty members or department chairs, expressed high expectations for curriculum planning and provided many opportunities for discussion and for staying abreast of trends in their field as faculty members worked together on tangible products such as lab manuals, slide collections, course syllabi, examinations, and web-based tools. In such programs, all instructors and staff, not just a small committee, would be responsible for a self-study for program review or accreditation. The indicators of the CI culture developed through the CLUE study are listed in Table 10.2.

This type of program culture, where academic planning is considered an important responsibility and new faculty are urged to participate in it early, may be less common (and less feasible) in research universities, where the number of instructors is large and emphasis is on discovery of new knowledge rather than teaching. In a study of continuous improvement practices in undergraduate engineering programs, Betty Harper (2008) supported this, finding that programs in baccalaureate institutions were more likely to use continuous improvement practices in their curricular planning than those in research universities. Continuous improvement practices are also less common where the broader institutional culture limits the opportunities for faculty members to exert control over the curriculum, such as when articulation agreements with community colleges or umbrella institutions make academic plans inflexible.

TABLE 10.2. CONTINUOUS CURRICULUM PLANNING CRITERIA AND INDICATORS

Continuous and Frequent Curriculum Planning Processes
- Evidence of ongoing curriculum planning processes
- Committees and leaders facilitate flow of suggestions to agenda
- Dedicated time for discussing curricular issues
- View curriculum planning as ongoing process
- Department has articulated mission, reviews it periodically

Awareness and Responsibilities
- Planning is self-initiated, proactive, and responsive
- Mandates, reviews, accreditation used for genuine self-study
- Internal sensing of faculty and student perceptions
- External sensing of environment
- Develops linkages with other relevant departments and institutions

Participation and Teamwork
- Curriculum considered everyone's job
- Faculty other than chair can discuss curriculum as a whole
- Ideas are welcome; culture of experimentation
- Participatory processes result in decisions
- Faculty collaborate in curriculum planning

Use of Evaluation for Adaptive Change
- Program evaluation procedures are formally organized
- Curriculum decisions are based on relevant information gathered
- Internal data used in decision making is varied
- External data used in decisions making is varied
- Critical examination of trends before adapting, adopting, rejecting

From: Briggs, Stark, and Rowland-Poplawski, 2003. Copyright The Ohio State University Press. Reproduced with permission.

The four planned change models we have discussed—R&D, problem solving, organizational development, and continuous improvement—suggest that several key strategies are needed to facilitate curricular change efforts (see Table 10.3). These models are among the most prominent explanations of change in the literature on higher education, but Kezar (2001) asserts that the evidence supporting their efficacy is mixed. Some strategies associated with these models (for example, organized efforts by leaders to create shared visions of new practices) appear to

TABLE 10.3. PLANNED CHANGE STRATEGIES

- Arguments for change must be persuasive, either supported by evidence of the need for change (R&D model) or by an acknowledged need to change (problem-solving model).
- Those who will be affected by the curricular change must be willing to change.
- The search for solutions to the problem should be deliberate and include those who will be affected by the change.
- The change process should analyze and assess obstacles to change, including those related to the personal beliefs, perceptions, and norms of those affected by the change.
- Alternative solutions must address the needs of the local context. Small-scale trials are useful.
- All those involved must evaluate the merits of alternative solutions proposed.
- All parties must understand each proposed solution.
- Decisions should be evidence-based (and in the case of continuous improvement models, collaborative).
- All parties must have opportunities to learn how to achieve the desired change.
- Leaders must support and facilitate curricular change.

work, but the models downplay or avoid the issues of power and politics. When planned change models have been used successfully in colleges and universities, they have often been paired with the political and social cognition strategies we discuss next (Eckel, Hill, Green, & Mallon, 1999; Nordvall, 1982).

Political Models

Organizations are political entities in which coalitions use their power to preserve their privileges and the conditions that support those privileges (Kezar, 2001). Thus, interest groups often are responsible for creating, supporting, or resisting change. Because interest groups are critical to change efforts, political models consider the interactions among organizational members more important than the activity of rational planning. Continuing informal advocacy for an idea often results in success (Hearn, 1996; Kezar, 2001).

A multi-institution study of curricular change by Clifton Conrad (1990) illustrates the influence of power dynamics in curricular change. Using a grounded theory approach, Conrad explored curricular change processes in four institutions and developed a theory premised on the assumptions that (a) conflict is a natural process in colleges and universities and (b) change involves the exercise of power. Although Conrad acknowledges the usefulness of planned change models in explaining the policy recommendation phase of academic change, he also argues that such models do not adequately explain either the sources of change or the dynamics of the final decision-making process. His research suggests that interest groups, coalitions, brokers, and others are informally active at all phases of change, particularly in the later phases as groups struggle to assert their visions of what the curriculum should be. Some of these visions may be rooted in self-interest, such as the desire to maintain course enrollments in a specific field or unwillingness to accept increased faculty workload. But, with respect to curriculum change, many of the interest groups stem from disciplinary differences or sincere competing beliefs about the efficacy of instructional processes.

Political models like Conrad's expand our understanding of the complex process of curricular change, recognizing that rationality is often compromised by the use of power within organizations. Moreover, research suggests that intentional use of interest groups, power, persuasion, coalition building, and deal making are all effective strategies for promoting change in colleges and universities (Kezar, 2001). Hybrid models that pair planned change strategies with attention to political processes may be particularly effective (Eckel, Hill, Green, & Mallon, 1999).

Social Cognition Models

Social cognition models assume that people acquire knowledge and skills in social contexts that influence what and how they learn. Variations in contexts lead to variations in knowledge and experiences. Social cognition models of organizational change focus on the implications of these variations, recognizing that (a) individuals in the same organization may differently interpret the same event and (b) local contexts (as well as other relevant contexts) influence organizational members' ways of thinking and acting. Any curriculum change proposal will thus be considered in light of individuals' existing knowledge and beliefs and will be compared with familiar ways of doing things. Resistance to change can arise when instructors, administrators, and staff who encounter new ideas view them as contrary to the norms or ways of thinking common among colleagues in their department or college. Although academic and institutional values shape college and university cultures, instructors, administrators, and staff also belong to subgroups whose interests, social contexts, and traditions may differ from one another—and may differently shape responses to curricular change efforts. Social cognition models argue that, for change to succeed, all institutional members must first understand the change and what it means for them and their program, college, or university. In this sense, these models assume that change proceeds from the ground up.

Reflecting on his case studies of curricular change, Lindquist (1978) observed that most committees charged with curricular change worked in isolation. They engaged in a learning process that involved reading, data gathering, discussing, synthesizing, and proposing. Others on campus who were asked to accept a proposed change had not participated in a similar learning process. For that reason, Lindquist argued, none of the committee proposals offered in his case study institutions was approved:

> [Other members of the institution] had not slowly moved through study and interaction to the conclusion that this proposal is the best solution to a real problem. All they experienced was a quick reading of a final proposal and a brief critique of it in committee, senate, or faculty assembly. . . . [F]aculty critics only needed to find one loose brick, and the whole edifice would come crashing down. (p. 235)

Lindquist found that the most successful committees engaged other members of the college in a learning process similar to, although not as extensive as, their own. They presented early drafts of their work, divided their colleagues into small discussion groups to share thoughts about potential curricular changes, and relied on external experts to broaden awareness of options among their faculties. These committees formally solicited early faculty feedback on their ideas and responded to comments by revising their proposals.

Estela Bensimon and Anna Neumann (1994) took an additional step to expand on the role of learning, arguing that teams—such as curricular change committees—must "think together" in addition to acting together to achieve change. In a project based at the University of Southern California, Bensimon relies on strategies consistent with the assumptions of social cognition models to help faculty and administrators in higher education make changes necessary to eliminate racial gaps in student learning outcomes. The vehicles for change are "evidence teams" composed of appointed faculty and administrators who collect and analyze relevant data and engage in a process of learning through inquiry. In doing so, they "confirm or refute untested hypotheses, challenge preconceived ideas, motivate further inquiry, and provide the impetus for change." The goals are to change unproductive ways of thinking and to institutionalize change that leads to student success (Bensimon, 2005, p. 106).

Many different learning activities—reading groups, committees, staff development, town hall meetings, and open forums—provide opportunities for participants to make meanings of new roles, skill requirements, teaching approaches, and educational philosophies potentially associated with curricular change. These kinds of strategies are well aligned with academic culture. They complement the shared governance structure in not-for-profit colleges and universities and build on valued skills such as inquiry, discussion, reflection, and writing (Kezar, 2001). Briggs, Stark, and Rowland-Poplawski (2003) discovered many of these kinds of activities when interviewing faculty and chairs of programs that continuously examine and attempt to improve their curricula.

Jean Lave and Etienne Wenger (1991) view learning as a process of participation in communities of practice with their own structures, rules, norms, artifacts, and discourses. For example, instructors in an academic program come to share norms, practices, and rules that guide their teaching, advising, research, and other activities. Thus the term "community of practice" seems to fit observations of effective curriculum planning in academic programs better than teamwork models that specify rigid tasks and roles (Briggs, 2007). Norms are influenced in part by the field, in part by the institution or unit, and in part by the individuals in the community. Such groups tend to choose new members who will be compatible with these norms.

Changing an academic program requires both knowledge of the group norms and the social skills necessary to work within them. Those who wish to facilitate curricular change should study and understand the history and traditions that shape, in part, the way people in a program, unit, or institution think and act. Values and beliefs are often apparent in local artifacts, such as institutional rituals and ceremonies, reward systems, and teaching practices (Eckel, Hill, & Green, 1998). Such artifacts concretely represent institutional commitments and assumptions. For example, at the program level, artifacts that reveal the depth of commitment to learning-centered practices include the kinds of assignments students complete in capstone courses, the use of assessments that tap essential learning outcomes, and the nature and promptness of feedback to students. In departments that value collegial interchange, final decisions about such issues will be negotiated as individuals learn more about a proposed change, consider its possible repercussions, and weigh the idea of change against personal and community values and priorities. Table 10.4 summarizes key strategies consistent with political and social cognition models of change.

Using Multiple Strategies for Curricular Change

Comprehensive models of change typically acknowledge several key influences on the success of change efforts even as they emphasize a single aspect. R&D and problem-solving models, for example, stress a rational change process while noting the importance of individuals' perceptions of the need for change and their understandings of the change itself. Political and social cognition models acknowledge the role of institutional culture and practices in change, even as they stress political power and learning processes. (These differences and similarities are

TABLE 10.4. POLITICAL AND SOCIAL COGNITION CHANGE STRATEGIES

- Those seeking curricular change must understand and effectively address organizational and disciplinary history, norms, values, and power dynamics. This is especially true when groups with different perspectives are involved.
- Those who seek change must understand local contexts and how they shape organizational members' responses to proposed change.
- Effective change agents recognize and work with interest and power groups both supporting and opposing the proposed change, building coalitions among supporters and engaging opposition groups to increase understanding of both positions.
- Those affected by change must understand the proposed curricular change and what it means for them. This implies a learning process is necessary.
- Those seeking change should address feelings of unfamiliarity, lack of competence, and change in status that may inhibit willingness of members to change.
- Informal, as well as formal, advocacy can facilitate change.
- During consideration of the need for change, proposed changes, and debate about proposals, all parties should be engaged in an inquiry learning process. All findings and viewpoints should be freely shared.
- Leaders should provide professional development for group members and time for involvement in change.

summarized in Table 10.5.) Those who wish to achieve curricular change must use several models simultaneously and consider many factors: institutional and program histories, traditions, and norms; individual and collective understandings of local values and practices; power and interest groups; and the limitations of rational plans.

Change in higher education is a messy, complex, and iterative problem-solving process that includes conflicts over interpretations and solutions, political maneuvering, unspoken assumptions, and agendas that frustrate dialogue (Lueddeke, 1999). The picture may be familiar to those who have attempted to effect transformational or far-reaching curricular changes in colleges and universities. A considerable body of evidence from studies of curricular and organizational change in higher education suggests that change efforts that draw from several models, anticipating and addressing as many factors as possible, stand the best chance of success. Thus, a holistic approach to change is likely to be more successful than a strategy that ignores any of the factors we have discussed. One such holistic approach, Lueddeke's adaptive-generative developmental model, focuses on the role of learning in the change process, while also incorporating political and cultural factors. The outcomes of the change process depend on participants'

TABLE 10.5. TYPES OF CHANGE

Change Model	Stimulus for Change	Change Process
Diffusion • Internal adaptation to external changes	• External change • Survival • Perceived applicability of prospective institutional change	• Scan internal and external environments for ideas • Gather information and consider potential outcomes and benefits • Determine institutional support and compatibility • Filter and choose ideas that sustain institution • Identify opinion leaders • Create tentative plan for implementation
Problem Solving and Research and Development • Methodically identified problems and responses	• Perceived need based on internal/external diagnosis	• Environmental scan, check peer programs • Articulate problem • Collect evidence of need and develop rationale • Set goals • Design, build, and test prototype Analyze and interpret data
Continuous Improvement • Collective and collaborative adjustment cycle	• Regular monitoring of internal and external influences leads to proactive change	• Create collaborative, organizational change structure and process • Analyze opportunities and obstacles to change • Select change(s) to implement • Identify and develop supportive and vested leaders • Communicate expectations • Engage faculty in process and in faculty development programs • Identify funding sources • Monitor peer programs and institutions to ensure comparability • Collect data on internal outcomes and external demands • Regularly and collectively evaluate data based on mission, goals, and established learning outcomes
Political • Acknowledges role of power and consensus building	• Conflict, power, struggle, privilege in current curriculum • Individuals and/or interest groups	• Build coalitions and consensus for change as pertinent to shared values, beliefs, and cultures • Assess available resources and interest group needs • Expect informal advocacy and defense of self-interests

TABLE 10.5. *(continued)*

Social Cognition • Change is viewed as a process of organizational learning	• Aspect of internal and/or external environment identified as potential change opportunity • Environment influences individual response due to need for survival or possible improvement	• Acknowledge how change will be perceived and affect communities of practice that have particular structures, rules, norms, artifacts, and discourses • Develop knowledge of group norms and social skills • Gather feedback and integrate diverse perspectives • Address dissent

prior knowledge and interests, as well as on a group process of defining problems and creating knowledge.

The focus on learning in social cognition and combination models makes good sense. Although faculty members may work in the same program or college, individuals will undoubtedly have different perceptions of the same problem—and thus imagine different solutions. Open discussions are necessary to unearth assumptions that frame individuals' understandings of a curricular change proposal. Once individuals recognize that they are not necessarily starting with the same background and indeed have different understandings of the problem at the root of calls for change, they often recognize the need for a systematic process of redefining what they thought they agreed upon (Engeström, 1987).

Identifying, reflecting on, and even renouncing familiar practices and beliefs, however, may only be a first step toward change. Examining and altering assumptions about current practices can provide the impetus for change, but college and university instructors often need appropriate professional development to devise and implement curricular changes. Even faculty who agree that instructional innovations are necessary to improve student outcomes can balk at the implementation stage if they feel inadequate to the task (Lattuca, 2006b). Acceptance of the idea of change may outdistance their capacity to enact it. Thus, resistance to change may not simply be the result of recalcitrance, but rather reflect unmet needs for confidence- and competence-building. Faculty, administrators, and staff may need both time and practice to learn *how* to change. Although faculty members are independent learners in their own academic fields, they have not necessarily learned to seek out and examine alternative theories and viewpoints with respect to curriculum and teaching.

Learning processes are highly valued in colleges and universities, and change processes that include these kinds of activities are consistent with the cultural values and practices of higher education (Kezar, 2001). Although instructors, administrators, and staff members do not always act rationally, planned change processes emulating the problem-solving processes are a logical—if not sufficient—step toward curricular change. Rather than abandon the idea of planned change, educators need instead to develop a plan that acknowledges existing contexts and provides opportunities to address participants' emotional responses to proposed changes (such as their fear of the new and unfamiliar; the loss of feelings of competence; and the desire to retain the status quo and existing power relations). The challenge posed in Table 10.6 will have a familiar ring to many faculty members and administrators.

Learning to Change in Academic Organizations

Groups spontaneously create problem-solving processes in the course of their work (Engeström, 1987). These processes include periods of data-gathering and discovery, co-construction and testing of possible solutions to existing problems, reflection on what is learned, and public discussion of solutions. A view of learning as problem solving resembles the learning processes that devotees of rational planning imagine are most effective in producing lasting change. Interaction of group members with a shared object—such as a prototype of a new course module, a draft of syllabus for a new course, or an outline for a set of courses for a new minor concentration—capitalizes on these processes by using the practices and products that individuals or groups create to orient their learning (Engeström, 1987). A pilot test of an electronic portfolio system to assess undergraduate engineers' knowledge of design, for example, can direct and shape the interactions and learning of the faculty in a department or program. One study found that these kinds of intentional learning activities allowed engineering faculty to test their ideas about how to incorporate innovative curricular and instructional changes in their undergraduate programs. Data-gathering processes, workshops, task forces, and whitepapers similarly enabled individuals to learn about new content areas or teaching strategies before deciding in favor of implementation (Evensen & Lattuca, 2005).

Evensen and Lattuca found that faculty groups that positioned themselves as "learners" and consciously created learning activities related to their curricular reform tasks moved more effectively toward their curricular reform goals than groups that divided the labor among them. In fact, only those groups with long histories of successful collaborative work were able to divide and sequence the labor associated with curricular change. Groups of faculty that did not recognize the critical role of learning how to change and what to change often short-circuited their own well-intentioned change efforts. Such examples

TABLE 10.6. A CURRICULUM CHALLENGE

- **Setting:** A mid-sized state university offering arts and sciences and several professional programs.

- **Units involved:** All arts and sciences departments and professional schools with undergraduate programs.

- **Problem:** Respond to a challenge from the academic vice president, who cites trustees' demands that the undergraduate basic curriculum include specific attention to global interdependence. The trustees' rationale includes concerns about ethical issues in an increasingly interdependent society as well as the nation's economic welfare and civil defense. The vice president notes that, unlike more routine curriculum planning processes that lead to incremental adjustments in academic plans and the educational environment, this broad issue has potential to be pervasive and to alter basic educational programs. He asks all faculty members and administrators to grapple with this issue over the next year and share some feasible ideas about how to meet the challenge. Although some programs will view their fields as more connected with this issue than others, all are connected in some way and should participate.

A group of program curriculum leaders jotted down the following notes as they considered lessons gleaned from their study of change models (noted in parentheses):

1. Other universities whose programs are examined and possibly emulated should be similar in size, mission, traditions, and discipline organization. (Diffusion)

2. A process is needed in which faculty can learn and share learning about the underlying issue. (Problem solving/Social cognition models)

3. Varied pilot studies should be conducted that involve diverse disciplines or combinations of disciplines. (R&D model)

4. Explicit attention should be given to individuals and work groups most likely to be affected. Negotiations with the vice president's office are needed to ensure budget resources and release time for needed professional development. Care should be taken to encourage the participation of relatively new faculty members who may feel severe time conflicts with their teaching and research. (Organizational development model)

5. Interest groups should be identified and their potential influence (pro or con) assessed. Special meetings for opinion leaders of these groups and engagement in shared learning are essential. Coalitions may be formed and resources provided as incentives. (Political model)

6. Many task forces of varied composition (not just one) should be established to study the problem and learn about potential solutions. A Website should be developed to create an electronic forum where drafts of positions, possible proposals, and possible educational experiences can be shared. Workshops, open forums, and discussions both at unit levels and among units should be planned from the beginning to the end of the deliberation process. Care should be taken not to move to proposals until groups have defined the problem and shared their learning about it. (Social cognition model)

(continued)

TABLE 10.6. *(continued)*

The leaders also jotted down some "Dos and Don'ts":

- Don't conduct decision meetings prematurely or in a way that will harden political positions or leave some fields uninvolved.
- Discourage each academic field from developing solutions independently.
- Seek and show continued interest and involvement from top leadership. Signify commitment in symbolic ways. Keep abreast of opportunities for external funding and initiatives. Provide resources for workshops, speakers, as needed.
- Express high expectations for the university to become a leader and role model on this issue.
- Consider the optimal depth and pervasiveness of change desired.
- Use the academic plan model to ascertain what elements of academic plans potentially could be changed.
- Make provisions for evaluating whatever change(s) are adopted.

of problem solving in action provide empirical support for models of planned change models that purposefully address the learning needs of organizational members.

In another change effort, Stark and Lowther led a large group of faculty members from diverse professional and liberal arts fields in developing rationale and protocols for integrating liberal and professional study. The group members, who initially disagreed vigorously since they differed radically in disciplines and academic traditions, found they were able to understand their colleagues' points of view by engaging briefly as students in unfamiliar fields. Faculty participants engaged, for example, in a project that beginning architecture students might undertake to design a motel room and a simulated nursing project dealing with elderly social service clients. Many of those who participated can still relate twenty years later what they learned about their colleagues' thinking and how they learned it.

Those who seek change in academic settings need to ask also about the social relationships and interactions that influence how colleagues view their workplace and their work, and thus any proposed change. In considering curricular changes, programs must consider how to encourage those involved in a change—faculty members, staff, administrators, and students—to hold their viewpoints and practices up for examination and possible revision. It will be obvious that two faculty members with different instructional viewpoints and who have had a contentious relationship for years will not be successful in collaborating on the details of a new course. But the nature of some relationships will be more subtle and difficult to detect. A group leader can often discover both problem situations and fruitful collaborations by asking group members to do some "free reflections" in writing to express their feelings about the deliberative process.

Varied college programs share many goals and beliefs, but may also place different priorities and values on issues involving students, teaching, research, service, consulting, grants, community engagement, and so on. When a curricular change effort requires input and effort from multiple academic units, these different values add complexity to the change process. In higher education, cultures are of particular interest since academic fields strongly influence instructors' attitudes and behaviors related to research, teaching, and curriculum planning. These contexts influence how individuals view any change effort. Instructors in many institutions can tell about an attempt to provide a generic statistics course to serve many departments that was doomed because of each group's insistence that the course focus on specific statistical examples from its field. In a college-wide curriculum committee, differences in academic values and norms can create tensions that may not lead to participant learning and change unless specifically acknowledged and dealt with. Responses to proposed curricular changes also may vary if faculty groups assess differently the extent to which a given effort is consistent with their scholarly commitments and norms. Proposed curricular changes that involve more than one academic field must, therefore, pay special attention to the traditions and norms of all the fields involved.

Curriculum is an arena in which administrators and faculty leaders can also stimulate desirable change by asking carefully targeted questions that encourage instructors to use rational planning and problem-solving modes while also acknowledging the political and social dimensions of change. Table 10.7 includes questions that faculty members should ask about any curriculum proposal—new or old, adjustment or transformation. The questions establish the expectation that academic planning will be systematic and careful (if not entirely rational) and that, at the same time, it can be appropriately responsive to both external and internal agendas. Table 10.7 also suggests questions for exploring the context in which change will have to occur.

All curricular change efforts are scrutinized, to a greater or lesser extent, by those who will be affected by the change. Mechanical engineering faculty members will ask whether a new master's program in biomedical engineering will "steal" enrollments or the best students from their graduate program. Undergraduate instructors will ask how the introduction or elimination of the undergraduate thesis requirement will influence perceptions of the honors program.

TABLE 10.7. QUESTIONS TO ASK ABOUT CURRICULAR CHANGE PROPOSALS

Is there a need for curricular change?

- What purposes, assessments of student learning, and/or changing social conditions justify the proposed change?
- Is the proposal consistent with research and/or theory on learning?
- Does the planned solution solve an important problem? Are the advantages of the new idea over the status quo clear to those who must adapt, adopt, and implement?

Who and what will be affected by the change?

- How will students be affected by the change? Will the change have differential impacts on particular groups of students (for example, academically underprepared, part-time, those who speak English as a second language)?
- Which elements of current academic plans will the idea affect?
- What will be the likely intended and unintended consequences at course, program, and college levels?

Is the proposed change appropriate for the local context?

- Does the idea link with goals, values, and procedures already accepted in the college or university?
- Does the proposed change require students to adjust to new instructional processes, time schedules, administrative procedures, or individual responsibilities? How will students be aided during the transition?
- Is the current organizational environment supportive of this type of idea? Are knowledgeable, credible, and flexible opinion leaders committed to the idea and willing to work toward its adoption?
- Is the necessary instructional expertise available? Will this expertise need to be developed?
- Will new financial resources or staff be required? If so, what will be their role if the change does not endure?
- Will necessary instructional resources, facilities, and/or equipment be required and available?

What will the change process look like?

- How will those affected by change be included in the curricular change process?
- Is a trial of the proposal feasible? How long a trial period is needed to fully test the concept? What evaluation criteria will guide decision making?
- When will the decision be made? Is it a decision from which an orderly retreat can be made if needed?
- Could a potential implementation proceed in steps?
- How will the curricular change be evaluated? Who will evaluate it and when? What provisions for a continuous evaluation cycle can be built into the change process?

Table 10.8 lists questions intended to identify the sources and types of resistance to curricular change.

Maintaining Change

Despite careful planning and faculty participation, curricular change may not endure. Because of the autonomy of faculty members in not-for-profit institutions, decisions to change academic plans are not always final or binding. They can be (a) optional for members (for example, use classroom research techniques if they fit your style), (b) contingent (that is, rewards and incentives accrue to those who adopt the change), (c) collective (that is, by agreement), or (d) dictated by authority (Rogers, 1968). The extensive differences in educational purposes and instructional approaches among academic fields make it very likely that most college-wide curricular change decisions in large colleges and universities will be optional or contingent, at least at first. Small colleges or single-purpose colleges within a university may be more likely to reach collective agreements. In unionized colleges or occasionally in small denominational colleges, authority may rule. For example, Richard Alfred

TABLE 10.8. ASSESSING THE CONTEXTS FOR CURRICULAR CHANGE

- Which administrators, faculty, students, and staff will be affected by the change?
- What are the various perspectives on the proposed change that must be addressed during the change process?
  - Do individuals understand the nature of the proposed change or must misconceptions be corrected?
  - What is the nature of any concerns about the proposed change and how strong are these concerns?
  - What are the appropriate messages and communication vehicles for each of the affected groups?
- Which groups or individuals within the institution are likely to be advocates of the proposed change?
  - Can respected members of the institution be counted on for active assistance in gaining support for the proposed curricular change?
  - How can alliances with supportive individuals and groups be forged?
- Which groups or individuals are likely to oppose the change, at least at the outset?
  - How can this resistance be effectively countered?
  - What compromises might be required to gain the support of opponents?

and Vincent Linder (1990) reported that strategic decisions in community colleges (which are often unionized) are made 40 percent of the time by the president and board of trustees, with little faculty involvement.

The type of decision for adoption may also vary with the level of the academic plan. The closer the level of the academic plan to the specific expertise of faculty, the more fully faculty will be involved and, thus, potentially committed to, a specific curricular change. Collective decisions are more likely at the program level than at the college-wide level, where conflict models tend to favor optional or contingent decisions. The classic example of a contingent decision is the adoption of general education distribution requirements. The requirements provide flexibility and options for both students and instructors, but, in effect, they allow students the option of avoiding courses they perceive to be difficult. A related contingent decision occurs when faculty members adopt general education core seminars that focus on humanities, treating sciences and mathematics courses as optional because their content is "more structured" and may not lend itself to small-group discussion or problem-centered treatment. In part, a contingent adoption is used because the mathematics and science faculty are unwilling to create courses for nonscientists, and in part because many students will balk at studying this material in the core; in many colleges no one has full authority to force either group to join in a collective decision.

Curricular Change: Past and Future

Curriculum change in American colleges has been extensive and responsive, not moribund or lacking in vigor, as some claim, and has helped higher education adapt to society's perceived needs. True, some changes have failed to endure and some issues are debated repeatedly, but each iteration of each debate has included additional participants, more diverse students, and more complex academic programs and institutions. The variety of actors concerned about curriculum and the set of external pressures have expanded with each major period of change. For example, government agencies that were barely on the scene in the 1940s emerged as active participants in curriculum change in the 1980s, first as promoters of innovation, and then, in the 2000s, as regulators and standard setters.

As colleges attempt to maintain dynamic curriculum equilibrium with their societal environment, they recognize external influences, then attempt to internalize them to achieve stability. Once the influence is internalized, the college deals purposefully with each change influence. The process of internalization and diagnosis of the need for change is likely to promote, not reject, the proposed change. Change serves to modify the effectiveness of academic plans (the process we have called adjustment) and may increase the effectiveness of the planning environment as it also enhances the responsiveness of colleges and universities to society.

The pace of curricular change is increasing today partly because of communication technology and partly because of the increase in the number of interest groups who have a stake in higher education. Diffusion of new ideas and problem-solving activities now takes place rapidly among instructors using web-based technologies. Views of external and internal constituencies about changes that society desires can be conveyed to college and university leaders immediately and forcefully. Increased communication may also increase change based on conflict since it facilitates the organization and political effectiveness of interest groups in society who advocate new concerns.

Curricular change in higher education has seldom been a "transformation" that changes the entire purpose of education (Toombs & Tierney, 1991), but transformations may indeed be imminent, spurred in numerous ways by societal and technological advances that link colleges to specific public concerns not only nationally but globally. Clearly, the role of faculty leaders and academic administrators is key in facilitating faculty involvement in the problem-solving activity necessary for substantive curricular change.

Academic Plans in Context

We have defined curriculum as an academic plan that is developed in a historical, social, and political context. Using this definition, we outlined a model of curriculum that provides an organizing framework for considering curricular issues at the course-, program-, and college-wide levels; serves as a guide for curriculum research; and helps faculty members and administrators design academic plans more effectively. The core of the academic plan theory includes eight elements or decision categories and the relationships among them. The model also acknowledges that all academic plans are constructed in specific educational environments subject to external and internal influences that may modify and thus, directly or indirectly, affect the elements of the plan. The model also links the evaluation of educational outcomes with adjustments in both academic plans and the environments in which they are developed.

Curriculum development is a process by which an instructor or group of instructors solves the complex problem of constructing a learning plan by making a series of decisions. It should be a continuing process of adjustment and renewal, and the participation of faculty groups in problem solving and sharing their learning is crucial to acceptance of new ideas. The academic plan concept and appropriate use of change models can help to convert an unstructured problem into one that is more structured and thus potentially more easily solved. Faculty members and administrators can consciously select strategies that will optimize decisions.

A general model of curriculum development in higher education can have practical value for others by advancing basic knowledge about how academic plans are constructed and implemented. The ideas we have shared in this book will be successful to the extent that they challenge and expand current thinking about curriculum, providing more useful ways of problem solving.

REFERENCES

Ackerman, P. L., & Lohman, D. F. (2006). Individual differences in cognitive functions. In P. A. Alexander & P. H. Winne (Eds.), *Handbook of educational psychology* (2nd ed., pp. 139–161). Mahwah, NJ: Lawrence Erlbaum Associates.

Adelman, C. (1990). *A college course map: Taxonomy and transcript data.* Washington, DC: U.S. Department of Education, Office of Educational Research and Improvement.

Adelman, C. (1992). *Tourists in our own land: Cultural literacies and the college curriculum.* Washington, DC: U.S. Department of Education, Office of Educational Research and Improvement.

Adelman, C. (1999). *Answers in the tool box: Academic intensity, attendance patterns, and bachelor's degree attainment.* Washington, DC: National Association on Postsecondary Education, Libraries, and Lifelong Learning.

Adelman, C. (2000). A parallel universe: Certification in the information technology guild. *Change, 32*(3), 20–29.

Adelman, C. (2004). *The empirical curriculum: Changes in postsecondary course-taking, 1972–2000.* Washington, DC: U.S. Department of Education.

Alexander, P. A. (1997). Mapping the multidimensional nature of domain learning: The interplay of cognitive motivation and strategic forces. In M. L. Maehr & P. R. Pintrich (Eds.), *Advances in motivation and achievement* (Vol. 10, pp. 213–250). Greenwich, CT: JAI Press.

Alexander, P. A. (2003). The development of expertise: The journey from acclimation to proficiency. *Educational Researcher, 32*(8), 10–14.

Alexander, P. A., Jetton, T. L., & Kulikowich, J. M. (1995). Interrelationship of knowledge, interest, and recall: Assessing a model of domain learning. *Journal of Educational Psychology, 87*(4), 559–575.

Alexander, P. A., & Judy, J. E. (1988). The interaction of domain-specific and strategic knowledge in academic performance. *Review of Educational Research, 58*(4), 375–404.

Alexander, P. A., Kulikowich, J. M., & Schulze, S. K. (1994). How subject-matter knowledge affects recall and interest. *American Educational Research Journal, 31*(2), 313–337.

Alexander, P. A., Murphy, P. K., Woods, B. S., Duhon, K. E., & Parker, D. (1997). College instruction and concomitant changes in students' knowledge, interest, and strategy use: A study of domain learning. *Contemporary Educational Psychology, 22*(2), 125–146.

Alexander, P. A., Schallert, D. L., & Hare, V. C. (1991). Coming to terms: How researchers in learning and literacy talk about knowledge. *Review of Educational Research, 61*(3), 315–343.

Alfred, R. L., & Linder, V. P. (1990). *Rhetoric to reality: Effectiveness in community colleges.* Ann Arbor, MI: University of Michigan, Center for the Study of Higher and Postsecondary Education, Community College Consortium.

Allen, I. E., & Seaman, J. (2007). *Online nation: Five years of growth in online learning.* Needham, MA: The Sloan Consortium.

Allen, I. E., Seaman, J., & Garrett, R. (2007). *Blending in: The extent and promise of blended education the United States.* Needham, MA: Sloan Consortium.

Allen, M. J. (2006). *Assessing general education programs.* Bolton, MA: Anker Publishing Company.

Alstete, J. W. (2004). *Accreditation matters: Achieving academic recognition and renewal.* (ASHE-ERIC Higher Education Reports, Volume 30, No. 4). San Francisco: Jossey-Bass.

American Association of State Colleges and Universities. (1986, November). *To secure the blessings of liberty* (Report of the National Commission on the Role and Future of State Colleges and Universities). Washington, DC: Author.

American Association of University Professors (AAUP). (1990). *Joint statement on government of colleges and universities.* Retrieved January 1, 2008, from http://www.aaup.org/AAUP/pubsres/policydocs/contents/governancestatement.htm.

Ames, C. (1992). Classrooms: Goals, structures, and student motivation. *Journal of Educational Psychology, 84*(3), 261–271.

Ames, C., & Archer, J. (1988). Achievement goals in the classroom: Students' learning strategies and motivation processes. *Journal of Educational Psychology, 80*(3), 260–267.

Anderman, E. M., & Wolters, C. A. (2006). Goals, values, and affect: Influences on student motivation. In P. A. Alexander & P. H. Winne (Eds.), *Handbook of educational psychology* (2nd ed., pp. 369–389). Mahwah, NJ: Lawrence Erlbaum Associates.

Anderman, L. H., & Anderman, E. M. (2000). Considering contexts in educational psychology: Introduction to the special issue. *Educational Psychologist, 35*(2), 67–68.

Anderson, G. L. (1974). *Trends in education for the professions* (ERIC/AAHE Research Report No. 7). Washington, DC: American Association for Higher Education.

Anderson, G., Boud, D., & Sampson, J. (1996). *Learning contracts: A practical guide.* London: Kogan Page.

Angelo, T. A. (Ed.). (1991). *Classroom research: Early lessons from success* (New Directions for Teaching and Learning, No. 46). San Francisco: Jossey-Bass.

Angelo, T. A., & Cross, K. P. (1993). *Classroom assessment techniques: A handbook for faculty* (2nd ed.). San Francisco: Jossey-Bass.

Angelo, T. A., & Cross, K. P. (2002). *Classroom assessment toolkit* (Vol. 3). Sarasota, FL: American Accounting Association.

Antony, J., & Boatsman, K. C. (1994, November). *Defining the teaching-learning function in terms of cooperative pedagogy: An empirical taxonomy of faculty practices.* Paper presented at the Annual Meeting of the Association for the Study of Higher Education, Tucson, AZ.

Arons, A. B. (1979). Some thoughts on reasoning capacities implicitly expected of college students. In J. Lockhead & J. Cements (Eds.), *Cognitive process instruction—Research on teaching thinking skills* (pp. 209–215). Philadelphia: The Franklin Institute Press.

Association of American Colleges. (1985). *Integrity in the college curriculum: A report to the academic community*. Washington, DC: Author.

Association of American Colleges. (1994). *Sustaining vitality in general education: Project on strong foundations for general education*. Washington DC: Author.

Association of American Colleges, Project on Liberal Learning, Study-in-Depth, and the Arts and Sciences Major. (1991a). *The challenge of connecting learning* (Vol. 1). Washington, DC: Author.

Association of American Colleges, Project on Liberal Learning, Study-in-Depth, and the Arts and Sciences Major. (1991b). *Reports from the fields* (Vol. 2). Washington, DC: Author.

Association of American Colleges, Project on Liberal Learning, Study-in-Depth, and the Arts and Sciences Major. (1992). *Program review and educational quality in the major: A faculty handbook* (Vol. 3). Washington, DC: Author.

Association of American Colleges, Task Group on General Education. (1988). *A new vitality in general education*. Washington, DC: Author.

Association of American Colleges and Universities (2002). *Greater expectations: A new vision for learning as a nation goes to college*. Washington DC: Author.

Association of American Colleges and Universities. (2004). *Taking responsibility for the quality of the baccalaureate degree*. Washington, DC: Author.

Association of American Colleges and Universities. (2005). *Liberal education outcomes: A preliminary report on student achievement in college*. Washington, DC: Author.

Association of American Colleges and Universities. (2007). *College learning for the new global century*. Washington, DC: Author.

Association of American Colleges and Universities (2008). *High impact educational practices: What they are, who has access to them, and why they matter*. Washington, DC: Author.

Astin, A. W. (1979). Student-oriented management: A proposal for change. In A.W. Astin, H. R. Bowen, & C. M. Chambers (Eds.), *Evaluating educational quality: A conference summary* . Washington, DC: Council on Postsecondary Accreditation.

Astin, A. W. (1991). *Assessment for excellence: The philosophy and practice of assessment and evaluation in higher education*. New York: Macmillan.

Astin, A. W. (1993). *What matters in college? Four critical years revisited*. San Francisco: Jossey-Bass.

Astin, A. W. (2003). *From number crunching to spirituality*. In J. C. Smart & W. G. Tierney (Eds.), *Higher education: Handbook of theory and practice* (Vol. 18, pp. 1–56). New York: Springer.

Attewell, P., & Lavin, D. (2007, July 6). Distorted statistics on graduation rates. *Chronicle of Higher Education, 53*(44), B16.

Ausubel, D. P. (1963). *The psychology of meaningful learning*. New York: Grune & Stratton.

Ausubel, D. P., Novak, J. D., & Hanesian, H. (1978). *Educational psychology: A cognitive view* (2nd ed.). New York: Holt, Rinehart and Winston.

Axelrod, J. (1973). *The university teacher as artist*. San Francisco: Jossey-Bass.

Baldwin, R., & Chronister, J. L. (2001). *Teaching without tenure: Policies and practices for a new era*. Baltimore, MD: The Johns Hopkins University Press.

Bandura, A. (1976). Self-reinforcement: Theoretical and methodological considerations. *Behaviorism, 4*(2), 135–155.

Bandura, A. (1977). Self-efficacy: Toward a unifying theory of behavioral change. *Psychological Review, 84*, 191–215.

Banta, T. W. (1994). Using outcomes assessment to improve educational programs. In M. Weimer & R. Menges (Eds.), *Better teaching and learning in college: Toward more scholarly practice*. San Francisco: Jossey-Bass.

Banta, T. W., & Associates. (1993). *Making a difference: Outcomes of a decade of assessment in higher education*. San Francisco: Jossey-Bass.

Banta, T. W., & Pike, G. R. (2007). Revisiting the blind alley of value-added. *Assessment Update, 19*(1), 1–2, 14–15.

Banta, T. W., & Schneider, J. A. (1988). Using faculty-developed exit examinations to evaluate academic programs. *Journal of Higher Education, 59*(1), 69–83.

Barab, S. A., & Plucker, J. A. (2002). Smart people or smart contexts? Cognition, ability, and talent development in an age of situated approaches to knowing and learning. *Educational Psychologist, 37*(3), 165–182.

Barak, R. J., & Mets, L. A. (Eds.). (1995). *Using academic program review.* (New Directions for Institutional Research, No. 86). San Francisco: Jossey-Bass.

Basken, P. (2007, June 4). Final attempt to reach a consensus on new accreditation rules fails [Today's news]. *The Chronicle of Higher Education*, Retrieved June 4, 2007, from http://chronicle.com/daily/2007/2006/2007060402n.htm

Baxter Magolda, M. B. (1992). *Knowing and reasoning in college: Gender-related patterns in students' intellectual development.* San Francisco: Jossey-Bass.

Baxter Magolda, M. B. (1998). Developing self-authorship in young adults. *Journal of College Student Development, 39*(2), 143–156.

Baxter Magolda, M. B. (2001). *Making their own way: Narratives for transforming higher education to promote student development.* Sterling, VA: Stylus.

Becher, T. (1989). *Academic tribes and territories: Intellectual enquiry and the cultures of disciplines.* Bristol, PA: The Society for Research into Higher Education and the Open University Press.

Belenky, M., Clinchy, B., Goldberger, N., & Tarule, J. (1986). *Women's ways of knowing: The development of self, voice, and mind.* New York: Basic Books.

Bell, D. (1966). *The reforming of general education: The Columbia College experience in its national setting.* Garden City, NY: Anchor, Doubleday.

Bennett, W. (1984). *To reclaim a legacy: A report on the humanities in higher education.* Washington, DC: National Endowment for the Humanities.

Bensimon, E. M. (2005). Closing the achievement gap in higher education: An organizational learning perspective. In A. Kezar (Ed.), *Organizational learning in higher education.* (pp. 99–111). (New Directions for Higher Education, No. 131). San Francisco: Jossey-Bass.

Bensimon, E., & Neumann, A. (1994). *Redesigning collegiate leadership: Teams and teamwork in higher education.* Baltimore: The Johns Hopkins University Press.

Berg, G. A. (2005). *Lessons from the edge: For-profit and nontraditional higher education in America.* New York: Praeger.

Berger, D. (1997). Mandatory assessment and placement: The view from an English department. In J. Ignash (Ed.), *Implementing effective policies for remedial and developmental education* (pp. 33–41). (New Directions for Community Colleges, No. 100). San Francisco: Jossey-Bass.

Bergquist, W. H., Gould, R. H., & Greenberg, E. M. (1981). *Designing undergraduate education: A systematic guide.* San Francisco: Jossey-Bass.

Berheide, C. W. (2007). Doing less work, collecting better data: Using capstone courses to assess learning. *Peer Review, 9*(2), 27–30.

Berk, R. A. (2006). *Thirteen strategies to measure college teaching: A consumer's guide to rating scale construction, assessment, and decision making for faculty, administrators, and clinicians.* Sterling, VA: Stylus.

Bettinger, E., & Long, B. T. (2004). *Shape up or ship out: The effects of remediation on students at four-year colleges.* Cambridge, MA: National Bureau of Economic Research.

Bettinger, E., & Long, B. T. (2005). Remediation at the community college: Student participation and outcomes. In B. L. Bower & K. P. Hardy (Eds.), *From distance education to e-learning: Lessons along the way* (pp. 17–26). (New Directions for Community Colleges, No. 128). San Francisco: Jossey-Bass.

Bezilla, M. (1981). *Engineering education at Penn State: A century in the land-grant tradition.* University Park, PA: The Pennsylvania State University Press.

Bigge, M. L., & Shermis, S. S. (1992). *Learning theories for teachers* (5th ed.). New York: HarperCollins.

Biglan, A. (1973a). Relationships between subject matter characteristics and the structure and output of university departments. *Journal of Applied Psychology, 57,* 204–213.

Biglan, A. (1973b). The characteristics of subject matter in different academic areas. *Journal of Applied Psychology, 57,* 195–203.

Birnbaum, R. (1988). *How colleges work: The cybernetics of academic organization and leadership.* San Francisco: Jossey-Bass.

Blackburn, R. T., Armstrong, E., Conrad, C., Didham, J., & McKune, T. (1976). *Changing practices in undergraduate education: A report prepared for the Carnegie Council on Policy Studies.* Berkeley, CA: Carnegie Foundation for the Advancement of Teaching.

Blackler, F., Crump, N., & McDonald, S. (1999). Managing experts and competing through innovation: An activity theoretical analysis. *Organization, 6*(1), 5–31.

Bloom, B. S. (1956). *Taxonomy of educational objectives: Cognitive domain.* New York: McKay.

Blumenstyk, G. (2005, November 25). Higher education 2015: For-profit outlook. *The Chronicle of Higher Education, 52*(14), A14.

Boehrer, J., & Linsky, M. (1990). Teaching with cases: Learning to question. In M. Svinicki (Ed.), *The changing face of college teaching* (pp. 41–57). (New Directions for Teaching and Learning, No. 42). San Francisco: Jossey-Bass.

Boli, J., Katchadourian, H., & Mahoney, S. (1988). Analyzing academic records for informed administration. *Journal of Higher Education, 59*(1), 54–68.

Bollinger, L. C. (2007, June 1). Why diversity matters [Point of View]. *The Chronicle of Higher Education, 53*(39), B20.

Boud, D., & Feletti, G. (1991). *The challenge of problem-based learning.* London: Kogan Page.

Boyer, E. L. (1987). *College: The undergraduate experience in America.* Princeton, NJ: Carnegie Foundation for the Advancement of Teaching.

Boyer, E. L. (1990). *Scholarship reconsidered: Priorities of the professoriate.* Princeton, NJ: Carnegie Foundation for the Advancement of Teaching.

Bransford, J. D., Brown, A. L., & Cocking, R. R. (Eds.). (2000). *How people learn: Brain, mind, experience, and school.* Washington, DC: National Academy Press.

Braxton, J. M., & Hargens, L. L. (1996). Variation among academic disciplines: Analytical frameworks and research. In. J. C. Smart (Ed.), *Higher education: Handbook of theory and research* (Vol. 11, pp. 1–46). New York: Agathon Press.

Briggs, C. L. (2003, May). *Data for curriculum renewal: What information do continuous planning academic departments collect and use?* Paper presented at the Association for Institutional Research, Tampa, FL.

Briggs, C. L. (2007). Curriculum collaboration: A key to continuous program renewal. *Journal of Higher Education, 78*(6), 676–711.

Briggs, C. L., Stark, J. S., & Rowland-Poplawski, J. (2002). *Instructional resource discussions in continuous planning academic departments: Implications for IR and planning.* Paper presented at the Annual Meeting of the Association for Institutional Research, Toronto, Canada.

Briggs, C. L., Stark, J. S., & Rowland-Poplawski, J. (2003). How do we know a "continuous planning" academic program when we see one? *Journal of Higher Education, 74*(4), 361–385.

Bringle, R. G., & Hatcher, J. A. (1996). Implementing service learning in higher education. *Journal of Higher Education, 67*(2), 221–239.

Brint, S. (2002). Data on higher education in the United States: Are the existing resources adequate? *American Behavioral Scientist, 45*(10), 1493–1522.

Brookfield, S. D. (1988). *Developing critical thinkers: Challenging adults to explore alternative ways of thinking and acting.* San Francisco: Jossey-Bass.

Brown, A. L., & Campione, J. C. (1990). Communities of learning and thinking: Or a context by any other name. *Contributions to Human Development, 21*, 108–126.

Brubacher, J. S., & Rudy, W. (1976). *Higher education in transition: A history of the American colleges and universities, 1636-1976* (3rd ed., rev. and enl. ed.). New York: Harper & Row.

Bruffee, K. A. (1999). Collaboration, conversation, and reacculturation. In *Collaborative learning: Higher education, interdependence, and the authority of knowledge* (pp. 3–20). Baltimore: Johns Hopkins Press.

Burke, J. C. (2002, January/February). Accountability for results—ready or not. *Trusteeship,* 14–18.

Burke, J. C., & Minassians, H. P. (2002). The new accountability: From regulation to results. In J. C. Burke & H. P. Minassians (Eds.), *Reporting higher education results: Missing links in the performance chain* (pp. 5–19). (New Directions for Institutional Research, No. 116). San Francisco: Jossey-Bass.

Burke, J. C., & Serban, A. M. (1997). *Performance funding and budgeting for public higher education: Current status and future prospects* (No. ED41479). Albany, NY: Nelson A. Rockefeller Institute of Government.

Burke, J. C., & Volkwein, J. F. (1992, June). *Outcomes assessment at Albany.* Report to the State University of New York. Albany, NY: State University of New York.

Callan, P. M. (2002). *Coping with recession: Public policy, economic downturns, and higher education.* San Jose, CA: National Center for Public Policy and Higher Education.

Cameron, B. J. (1992, September). What's good and not so good about lectures. *UTS Newsletter,* Winnipeg: University of Manitoba, Centre for Higher Education, Research and Development. 1, 1.

Cameron, K. S. (1984). Organizational adaptation and higher education. *Journal of Higher Education, 55*(2), 122–144.

Cardozier, V. R. (Ed.). (1993). *Important lessons from innovative colleges and universities.* (New Directions for Higher Education, No. 82). San Francisco: Jossey-Bass.

Carey, S. (1985). *Conceptual change in childhood.* Cambridge, MA: MIT Press.

Carini, R. M., Kuh, G. D., & Klein, S. P. (2006). Student engagement and student learning: Testing the linkages. *Research in Higher Education, 47*(1), 1–32.

Carnegie Foundation for the Advancement of Teaching (n.d.). *The Carnegie unit: What is it?* Retrieved on June 3, 2008, from http://www.carnegiefoundation.org/general/sub.asp?key=17&subkey=1874&topkey=17

Carnegie Foundation for the Advancement of Teaching. (1977). *Missions of the college curriculum: A contemporary review with suggestions.* San Francisco: Jossey-Bass.

Carnegie Foundation for the Advancement of Teaching. (2006). *Basic classification tables.* Retrieved June 28, 2007, from http://www.carnegiefoundation.org/classifications/index.asp?key=805

Carnegie Foundation for the Advancement of Teaching. (2007). *Basic classification description.* Retrieved on June 27, 2007, from http://www.carnegiefoundation.org/classifications/index.asp?key=791

Cashin, W. (1988, September). *Student ratings of teaching: A summary of the research* (IDEA Paper No. 20). Manhattan, KS: Kansas State University, Center for Faculty Evaluation and Development.

Cassidy, S. (2004). Learning styles: An overview of theories, model, and measures. *Educational Psychology 24*(4), 419–444.

Cataldi, E. F., Bradburn, E. M., & Fahimi, M. (2005). *2004 national study of postsecondary faculty (NSOPF:04): Background characteristics, work activities, and compensation of instructional faculty and staff: Fall 2003* (NCES 2006-176). Washington, DC: U.S. Department of Education, National Center for Education Statistics.

Chait, R. (1979, July 19). Mission madness strikes our colleges. *The Chronicle of Higher Education, 18*(36), A36.

Chen, C., & Stevenson, H. W. (1995). Motivation and mathematics achievement: A comparative study of Asian-American, Caucasian-American, and East Asian high school students. *Child Development, 66*(4), 1215–1234.

Chen, X. (2007). *Part-time undergraduates in postsecondary education: 2003–2004* (NCES 2007–165). Washington, DC: U.S. Department of Education, National Center for Education Statistics.

Cheney, L. V. (1988). *Humanities in America: A report to the president, the Congress, and the American people.* Washington, DC: National Endowment for the Humanities.

Cheney, L. V. (1989). *50 hours: A core curriculum for college students.* Washington, DC: National Endowment for the Humanities.

Chi, M. T. H., Glaser, R., & Farr, M. J. (Eds.). (1988). *The nature of expertise.* Hillsdale, NJ: Lawrence Erlbaum Associates.

Chickering, A. W., & Gamson, Z. F. (Eds.). (1991). *Applying the seven principles for good practice in undergraduate education* (New Directions for Teaching and Learning, No. 47). San Francisco: Jossey-Bass.

Chickering, A. W., Gamson, Z. F., & Barsi, L. M. (1989). Inventories of good practice in undergraduate education (Faculty Inventory and Institutional Inventory). *The Wingspread Journal, 9*(2), 1–4. Racine, WI: The Johnson Foundation.

Chronicle of Higher Education Almanac. (2008, August 29) Degrees awarded by type of institution, 2005–2006. *The Chronicle of Higher Education Supplement, 55*(1), 20.

Chronicle of Higher Education Almanac. (2007, August 31). College enrollment by age of student. *The Chronicle of Higher Education Supplement, 54*(1), 15.

Clark, B. R. (1983). *The higher education system: Academic organization in cross-national perspective.* Berkeley, CA: University of California Press.

Cochran, L. H. (1989). *Administrative commitment to teaching.* Cape Girardeau, MO: Step-Up Inc.

Cohen, A. M., & Brawer, F. B. (2003). *The American community college* (4th ed.). San Francisco: Jossey-Bass.

College Board. (2007). *2007 College-bound seniors: Total group profile report.* Retrieved November 16, 2007, from http://www.collegeboard.com/prod_downloads/about/ news_info/cbsenior/yr2007/national-report.pdf

Collins, A., Greeno, J. G., & Resnick, L. B. (2001). Educational learning theories. In N. Smelser & P. Baltes (Eds.), *International encyclopedia of the social and behavioral sciences* (pp. 4276–4279). Oxford: Elsevier Sciences.

Common, D. (1989). Master teachers in higher education: A matter of settings. *Review of Higher Education, 12*(4), 375–386.

Conrad, C. F. (1978). A grounded theory of academic change. *Sociology of Education, 41*, 110–112.

Conrad, C. F. (1990). *A grounded theory of academic change.* In D. R. Conrad & J. G. Haworth (Eds.), *Curriculum in transition: Perspectives on the undergraduate experience* (pp. 337–350). Needham Heights, MA: Ginn Press.

Conrad, C. F., Johnson, J., & Gupta, D. M. (2007). Teaching-for-learning (TFL): A model for faculty to advance student learning. *Innovative Higher Education, 32*(3), 153–165.

Conrad, C., & Pratt, A. M. (1983). Making decisions about the curriculum: From metaphor to model. *The Journal of Higher Education, 54*(1), 16–30.

Conrad, C., & Pratt, A. M. (1986). Research on academic programs: An inquiry into an emerging field. In J. C. Smart (Ed.), *Higher education: Handbook of theory and research* (Vol. 2, pp. 235–273). New York: Agathon Press.

Conrad, C. F., & Wyer, J. C. (1980). *Liberal education in transition* (AAHE-ERIC Higher Education Research Report No. 3). Washington, DC: American Association for Higher Education.

Corson, J. J. (1960). *Governance of colleges and universities.* New York: McGraw-Hill.

Council for Higher Education Accreditation. (2003). *Statement of mutual responsibilities for student learning outcomes: Accreditation, institutions, and programs.* Washington, DC: Author.

Courts, P. L., & McInerney, K. H. (1993). *Assessment in higher education: Politics, pedagogy, and politics.* Westport, CT: Praeger.

Creamer, D. G., & Janosik, S. M. (1999). Academic program and review practices in the United States and selected foreign countries [electronic version]. *Education Policy Analysis Archives, 7.* Retrieved April 1, 2008, from http://epaa.asu.edu/epaa/v7n23/

Cross, K. P. (1998, March 24). *What do we know about students' learning and how do we know it?* Paper presented at the American Association of Higher Education's 1998 National Conference on Higher Education, Atlanta, GA.

Cross, K. P. (2005). *On college teaching.* (CSHE.15.05). Berkeley, CA: Center for Studies in Higher Education, University of California Berkeley. (ERIC Document Reproduction Service No. ED492217)

Cross, K. P., & Angelo, T. A. (1988). *Classroom assessment techniques: A handbook for faculty.* Ann Arbor, MI: University of Michigan, National Center for Research to Improve Postsecondary Teaching and Learning.

Cross, K. P., & Steadman, M. H. (1996). *Classroom research: Implementing the scholarship of teaching* (1st ed.). San Francisco: Jossey-Bass.

Cuban, L. (1990). Reforming again, again, and again. *Educational Researcher, 19*(1), 3–13.

Davis, R. H., Strand, R., Alexander, L. T., & Hussain, M. N. (1982). The impact of organizational and innovator variables on instructional innovation in higher education. *Journal of Higher Education, 53*(5), 568–586.

Davis, W. K., Nairn, R., Paine, M. E., Anderson, R. M., & Oh, M. S. (1992). Effects of expert and non-expert facilitators on the small-group process and on student performance. *Academic Medicine, 67*(7), 470–474.

Deci, E. L., & Ryan, R. M. (1991). A motivational approach to self: Integration in personality. In R. Dienstbier (Ed.), *Perspectives on motivation: Nebraska Symposium on Motivation.* Lincoln, NB: University of Nebraska Press.

Delucchi, M. (1997). "Liberal arts" colleges and the myth of uniqueness. *Journal of Higher Education, 68*(4), 414–426.

Dewey, J. (1916). *Democracy and education: An introduction to the philosophy of education.* New York: Macmillan.

Dey, E. L., & Hurtado, S. (1995). College impact, student impact: A reconsideration of the role of students within American higher education. *Higher Education, 30*(2), 207–223.

Diamond, R. M. (2008). *Designing and assessing courses and curricula: A practical guide* (3rd ed.). San Francisco: Jossey-Bass.

Dole, J. A., & Sinatra, G. M. (1998). Reconceptualizing change in the cognitive construction of knowledge. *Educational Psychologist, 33*(2/3), 109–128.

Donald, J. G. (2002). *Learning to think: Disciplinary perspectives.* San Francisco: Jossey-Bass.

Dressel, P. L. (1971). *College and university curriculum* (2nd ed.). Berkeley, CA: McCutchan.

Dressel, P. L. (1976). *Handbook of academic evaluation.* San Francisco: Jossey-Bass.

Dressel, P. L. (1980). *Improving degree programs: A guide to curriculum development, administration and review.* San Francisco: Jossey-Bass.

Dressel, P. L., & DeLisle, F. H. (1970). *Undergraduate curriculum trends.* Washington, DC: American Council on Education.

Dressel, P. L., & Marcus, D. (1982). *On teaching and learning in college.* San Francisco: Jossey-Bass.

Dunkin, M. J., & Barnes, J. (1986). Research on teaching in higher education. In M. Wittrock (Ed.), *Handbook of research on teaching* (3rd ed., pp. 754–777). New York: Macmillan.

Dweck, C. S., & Elliott, E. S. (1983). *Achievement motivation.* In P. Mussen (Ed.), *Handbook of child psychology* (Vol. 4, pp. 643–691). Hoboken, NJ: John Wiley & Sons.

Dweck, C. S., & Leggett, E. L. (1988). A social-cognitive approach to motivation and personality. *Psychological Review, 95*(2), 256–273.

Eckel, P., Hill, B., & Green, M. (1998). *En route to transformation.* (On Change: An Occasional Paper Series of the ACE Project on Leadership and Institutional Transformation). Washington, DC: American Council on Education. (ERIC Document Reproduction Service No. ED435293)

Eckel, P., Hill, B., Green, M., & Mallon, B. (1999). *Taking charge of change: A primer for colleges and universities.* (On Change: Occasional Paper, No. 3). Washington, DC: American Council on Education.

Education Commission of the States. (1986, July). *Transforming the state role in higher education.* Denver, CO: Author.

Einarson, M. K. (2001). *A comparative study of personal, disciplinary, and organization influences on undergraduate faculty use of teaching methods that promote active student involvement in learning.* Unpublished doctoral dissertation. University of Michigan, Ann Arbor.

El-Khawas, E. (1989). *Campus trends, 1989.* Washington, DC: American Council on Education.

El-Khawas, E. (1992). *Campus trends, 1992.* Washington, DC: American Council on Education.

Engeström, Y. (1987). *Learning by expanding: An activity-theoretical approach to developmental research.* Helsinki: Orienta-Konsultit.

Ennis, R. H. (1987). A taxonomy of critical thinking dispositions and abilities. In J. B. Baron & R. J. Sternberg (Eds.), *Teaching for thinking* (pp. 9–26). New York: Freeman.

Entwistle, N. (2008, April 25). *Taking stock: Teaching and learning research in higher education.* Paper presented at the Teaching and Learning Research in Higher Education Symposium in Review prepared for an international symposium on Teaching and Learning Research in Higher Education, Guelph, Ontario, Canada.

Etzioni, A. (1964). *Modern organizations*. Englewood Cliffs, NJ: Prentice-Hall.

Evensen, D. H., & Lattuca, L. R. (2005, July 20). *Educational innovation through interdisciplinary collaboration: Findings from the study of NSF planning grants, 2002-2003 (NSF Grant EEC-0241221)*. Presentation at the National Science Foundation, Engineering Education Directorate, Alexandria, VA.

Ewell, P. T. (1991). Assessment and public accountability: Back to the future. *Change: The Magazine of Higher Learning, 23*(6), 12–17.

Fairweather, J. (1996). *Faculty work and public trust: Restoring the value of teaching and public service in American academic life*. Needham Heights, MA: Allyn & Bacon.

Fairweather, J. (1997). The relative value of teaching and research. In H. Wechsler (Ed.), *The NEA 1997 almanac of higher education* (pp. 43–62). Washington, DC: National Education Association.

Fairweather, J., & Rhoades, R. A. (1995). Teaching and the faculty role: Enhancing the commitment to instruction in American colleges and universities. *Educational Evaluation and Policy Analysis, 17*(2), 179–194.

Farrell, E. F. (2003, February 14). Phoenix's unusual way of crafting courses. *The Chronicle of Higher Education, 49*(23), A10.

Feichtner, S. B., & Davis, E. A. (1984). Why some groups fail: A survey of students' experiences with learning groups. *Journal of Management Education, 9*, 58–73.

Feldman, K. A. (1976). The superior college teacher from the students' view. *Research in Higher Education, 5*(3), 243–288.

Fincher, C. (1988). Provisional variation and selective retention in curricular change. *Research in Higher Education, 28*(3), 281–285.

Fink, L. D. (2003). *Creating significant learning experiences: An integrated approach to designing college courses*. San Francisco: Jossey-Bass.

Fink, L. D. (2007). The power of course design to increase student engagement and learning. *Peer Review, 9*(1), 13–18.

Flavell, J. H. (1979). Metacognition and cognitive monitoring: A new area of cognitive-developmental inquiry. *American Psychologist, 34*, 906–911.

Flavell, J. H. (1985). *Cognitive development:* (2nd ed.). Englewood Cliffs, NJ: Prentice-Hall.

Flavell, J. H. (1987). Speculations about the nature and development of metacognition. In F. E. Weinert & R. H. Kluwe (Eds.), *Metacognition, motivation and understanding* (pp. 21–29). Mahwah, NJ: Lawrence Erlbaum Associates.

Floden, R. E. (1995). Confrontation of teachers' entering beliefs. *ATE Newsletter, 28*(6), 4.

Foucault, M. (1980). *Power/knowledge: Selected interviews and other writings, 1972-1977*. New York: Pantheon Books.

Francis, M. C., Mulder, T., & Stark, J. S. (1995). *Intentional learning: A process of learning to learn in the accounting curriculum*. Sarasota, FL: Accounting Education Change Commission and the American Accounting Association.

Gabelnick, F., MacGregor, J., Matthews, R. S., & Smith, B. L. (1990). Learning community models. In *Creating connections among students, faculty, and disciplines* (pp. 19–37). San Francisco: Jossey-Bass.

Gaff, J. G. (1991). *New life for the college curriculum: Assessing achievements and further progress in the reform of general education*. San Francisco: Jossey-Bass.

Gaff, J. G. (2007). What if the faculty really do assume responsibility for the educational program? *Liberal Education, 93*(4), 6–13.

Gainen, J., & Locatelli, P. (1995). *Assessment for the new curriculum: A guide for professional accounting programs*. Sarasota, FL: Accounting Education Change Commission and the American Accounting Association.

Gansemer-Topf, A., & Schuh, J. H. (2003/2004). Instruction and academic support expenditures: An investment in retention and graduation. *Journal of College Student Retention, 5*(2), 135–145.

Gappa, J. M., Austin, A. E., & Trice, A. G. (2007). *Rethinking faculty work: Higher education's strategic imperative*. San Francisco: Jossey-Bass.

Gardner, H. (1983). *Frames of mind: The theory of multiple intelligences*. New York: Basic Books.

Gardner, H. (1993). *Frames of mind: The theory of multiple intelligences* (10th anniversary ed.). New York: Basic Books.

Gardner, H. (2003). Three distinct meanings of intelligence. In R. Sternberg, J. Lautrey, & T. Lubart (Eds.), *Models of intelligence: International perspectives* (pp. 43–54). Washington, DC: American Psychological Association.

Garland, P. H., & Grace, T. W. (1993). *New perspectives for student affairs professionals: Evolving realities, responsibilities and roles* (ASHE-ERIC Higher Education Reports, No. 7). Washington, DC: The George Washington University.

Garner, R., & Alexander, P. A. (1989). Metacognition: Answered and unanswered questions. *Educational Psychologist, 24*(2), 143–158.

Gay, G. (2000). *Culturally responsive teaching: Theory, research, and practice*. New York: Teachers College Press.

Gay, G. (2002). Preparing for culturally responsive teaching. *Journal of Teacher Education, 53*(2), 106–116.

Geiger, R. L. (2000). *The American college in the nineteenth century* (1st ed.). Nashville, TN: Vanderbilt University Press.

Gerald, D. E., & Hussar, W. J. (1999). *Projections of education statistics to 2009* (NCES 1999038). Washington, DC: National Center for Education Statistics, U.S. Department of Education.

Giroux, H. (1992). *Border crossings: Cultural workers and the politics of education*. New York: Routledge.

Goldin, C. (1992). *The meaning of college in the lives of American women: The past 100 years* (No. 4099). Washington, DC: National Bureau of Economic Research.

Grant, G., & Riesman, D. (1978). *The perpetual dream: Reform and experiment in the American college*. Chicago: University of Chicago Press.

Grasha, A. F. (1994). A matter of style: The teacher as expert, formal authority, personal model, facilitator and delegator. *College Teaching, 42*(4), 142–149.

Gray, P. J., Froh, R. C., & Diamond, R. M. (1992, March). *A national study of research universities: On the balance between research and undergraduate teaching*. Syracuse, NY: Center for Instructional Development.

Green, K. C. (2002). *The 2002 campus computing survey* [electronic version]. Available from http://www.campuscomputing.net.

Greenfield, P. M., Trumbull, E., Keller, H., Rothstein-Fisch, C., Suzuki, L. K., & Quiroz, B. (2006). Cultural conceptions of learning and development. In P. A. Alexander & P. H. Winne (Eds.), *Handbook of educational psychology* (2nd ed., pp. 675–692). Mahwah, NJ: Lawrence Erlbaum Associates.

Greeno, J. G., Collins, A. M., & Resnick, L. B. (1996). Cognition and learning. In D. C. Berliner & R. C. Calfee (Eds.), *Handbook of educational psychology* (pp. 15–46). New York: Macmillan.

Gross, E., & Grambsch, P. V. (1974). *Changes in university organization, 1964-1971*. New York: McGraw-Hill.

Gumport, P. J. (1993). Contested terrain of academic program reduction. *Journal of Higher Education, 64* (3), 283–311.

Guskin, A. E. (Ed.). (1981). *The administrator's role in effective teaching.* (New Directions for Teaching and Learning, No. 5). San Francisco: Jossey-Bass.

Gustafsson, J. E., & Undheim, J. O. (1996). Individual differences in cognitive functions. In D. Berliner & R. Calfee (Eds.), *Handbook of educational psychology* (pp. 186–242). New York: Macmillan.

Gutierrez, K. D., & Rogoff, B. (2003). Cultural ways of learning: Individual traits or repertoires of practice? *Educational Researcher, 32*(5), 19–25.

Halliburton, D. (1977a). Designing curriculum. In A. W. Chickering, D. Halliburton, W. H. Bergquist, & J. Lindquist (Eds.), *Developing the college curriculum* (pp. 51–74). Washington, DC: Council for the Advancement of Small Colleges.

Halliburton, D. (1977b). Perspectives on the curriculum. In A. W. Chickering, D. Halliburton, W. H. Bergquist, & J. Lindquist (Eds.), *Developing the college curriculum* (pp. 37–50). Washington, DC: Council for the Advancement of Small Colleges.

Hammer, D. (2002, April). *Epistemological resources.* Paper presented at the American Educational Research Association, New Orleans, LA.

Hansen, W. L., & Stampen, J. (1993). Higher education: No better access without better quality. *Higher Education Extension Service Review, 4*(2) 1–15.

Harper, B. J. (2008). *Tightening curricular cohesion: The influence of faculty continuous improvement activities on student learning.* Unpublished doctoral dissertation, The Pennsylvania State University.

Harris, K. R., & Graham, S. (1996). *Making the writing process work: Strategies for composition and self-regulation.* Cambridge, MA: Brookline Books.

Hartley, M. (2002). *A call to purpose: Mission-centered change at three liberal arts colleges.* New York: Routledge-Farmer.

Harvard Committee on the Objectives of a General Education in a Free Society. (1945). *General education in a free society: Report of the Harvard Committee.* Cambridge, MA: Harvard University Press.

Harward, D. W. (2007). Engaged learning and the core purposes of liberal education: Bringing theory to practice. *Liberal Education, 93*(1), 6–13.

Hatch Act of 1887, 7 U.S.C. § 361

Hativa, N., Barak, R., & Simhi, E. (2001). Exemplary university teachers: Knowledge and beliefs of law professors. *Instructional Science, 28*, 491–523.

Havelock, R. (1971). *Planning for innovation through the dissemination and utilization of scientific knowledge.* Ann Arbor, MI: University of Michigan, Institute for Social Research.

Hawthorne, E. M. (1996). Institutional contexts. In J. G. Gaff, J. L. Ratcliff, & Associates (Eds.), *Handbook of the undergraduate curriculum: A comprehensive guide to purposes, structures, practices, and change* (pp. 30–52). San Francisco: Jossey Bass.

Hayek, J. C. (2001). *A student-centered approach for identifying high performing colleges and universities.* Bloomington, IN: Indiana University Press.

Hearn, J. C. (1996). Transforming U.S. higher education: An organizational perspective. *Innovative Higher Education, 21*(2), 141–154.

Hebel, S. (2003a, January 3). New York Regents approve CUNY's remediation plan after 3 years of monitoring. *The Chronicle of Higher Education, 49*(17), A30.

Hebel, S. (2003b, February 28). Remedial rolls fall at Cal State. *The Chronicle of Higher Education, 49*(25), A27.

Hecht, I. W. D., Higgerson, M. L., Gmelch, W. H., & Tucker, A. (1999). *The department chair as academic leader*. Phoenix, AZ: Oryx Press.

Hefferlin, J. B. L.(1969). *Dynamics of academic reform*. San Francisco: Jossey-Bass.

Heppner, P. P., & Johnston, J. A. (1994). New horizons in counseling: Faculty development. *Journal of Counseling & Development, 72*(5), 451–453.

Hidi, S. (1990). Interest and its contribution as a mental resource for learning. *Review of Educational Research, 60*(4), 549–571.

Higher Education Act of 1965, 20 U.S.C.A. § 1070 et seq.

Higher Education Amendment of 1968, Pub L. No. 90-575.

Higher Education Amendment of 1972, Pub. L. No. 92-318.

Hofer, B. (2001). Personal epistemology research: Implications for learning and instruction. *Educational Psychology Review, 13*(4), 353–382.

Holland, J. L. (1966). *The psychology of vocational choice: Theory of personality types and model environments*. Waltham, MA: Ginn.

Holland, J. L. (1973). *Making vocational choices: A theory of careers* (1st ed.). Englewood Cliffs, NJ: Prentice-Hall.

Holland, J. L. (1985). *Making vocational choices: A theory of vocational personalities and work environments* (2nd ed.). Englewood Cliffs, NJ: Prentice-Hall.

Holland, J. L. (1997). *Making vocational choices: A theory of vocational personalities and work environments* (3rd ed.). Odessa, FL: Psychological Assessment Resources, Inc.

Hooks, B. (1994). *Teaching to transgress: Education as the practice of freedom*. New York: Routledge.

Horn, L., & Nevill, S. (2006). *Profile of undergraduates in U.S. postsecondary education institutions: 2003–2004. With a special analysis of community college students*. (No. 2006–184). Washington, DC: U.S. Department of Education, National Center for Education Statistics.

Horowitz, H. L. (1993). *Alma mater: Design and experience in the women's colleges from their nineteenth-century beginnings to the 1930s* (2nd ed.). Amherst, MA: University of Massachusetts Press.

Hrebiniak, L. G., & Joyce, W. F. (1985). Organizational adaptation: Strategic choice and environmental determinism. *Administrative Science Quarterly, 30*(3), 336–349.

Huba, M. E., & Freed, J. E. (2000). *Learner-centered assessment on college campuses: Shifting the focus from teaching to learning*. Boston: Allyn & Bacon.

Huber, M. T., & Hutchings, P. (2005). *The advancement of learning: Building the teaching commons*. San Francisco: Jossey-Bass.

Huber, M. T., Hutchings, P., Gale, R., Miller, R., & Breen, M. (2007). Leading initiatives for integrative learning. *Liberal Education, 93*(2), 57–60.

Hutcheson, P. A. (1997). *Structures and practices*. In J. G. Gaff, J. L. Ratcliff, & Associates (Eds.), *Handbook of the undergraduate curriculum: A comprehensive guide to purposes, structures, practices, and change* (pp. 100–117). San Francisco: Jossey-Bass.

Hutchings, P. (ca. 1989). *Six stories: Implementing successful assessment*. Washington, DC: American Association for Higher Education.

Hutchings, P. (1995). *From idea to prototype: The peer review of teaching: A project workbook* Washington, DC: AAHE Teaching Initiative, American Association for Higher Education.

Hutchings, P. (1996). *Making teaching community property: A menu for peer collaboration and peer review*. Washington, DC: American Association for Higher Education.

Hutchings, P. (2000). *Opening lines: Approaches to the scholarship of teaching and learning*. Princeton, NJ: Carnegie Foundation for the Advancement of Teaching.

Ignash, J. (1997). Who should provide postsecondary remedial/developmental education? In J. Ignash (Ed.), *Implementing effective policies for remedial and developmental education.* (pp. 5–20). (New Directions for Community Colleges, No. 100). San Francisco: Jossey-Bass.

Ingels, S. J., Curtin, T. R., Kaufman, P., Alt, M. N., & Chen, X. (2002). *Coming of age in the 1990s: The eighth-grade class of 1988 12 years later.* (NCES 2002–321). Washington, DC: U.S. Department of Education, National Center for Education Statistics.

Institute of International Education. (2007). *Open doors 2007: Report on international educational exchange.* New York: Institute of International Education.

Jarvis, P. (1985). Thinking critically in an information society: A sociological analysis. *Life-long Learning, 8*(6), 11–14.

Jenkins, D., & Boswell, K. (2002, September). *State policies on community college remedial education: Findings from a national survey.* Denver, CO: Education Commission of the States.

Johnson, D. W., Johnson, R. T., & Smith, K. A. (1991). *Cooperative learning: Increasing college faculty instructional productivity* (ASHE-ERIC Higher Education Reports, No. 4). Washington, DC: The George Washington University.

Johnson, G. R., Eubanks, I. D., Fink, L. D., Lewis, K. G., & Whitcomb, D. B. (1987). The higher education curriculum crisis. *Community/Junior College Quarterly, 11,* 253–265.

Johnston, J. S. Jr., Shaman, S., & Zemesky, R. (1988). *Unfinished design: The humanities and social sciences in undergraduate engineering education.* Washington, DC: Association of American Colleges.

The Joint Committee on Standards for Educational Evaluation. (1994). *The program evaluation standards: How to assess evaluations of educational programs* (2nd ed.). Thousand Oaks, CA: Sage.

Kagan, J., & Kogan, N. (1970). Individual variation in cognitive process. In P. Mussen (Ed.), *Carmichael's manual of child psychology* (Vol. 1, pp. 1273–1365). Hoboken, NJ: John Wiley & Sons.

Kane, R., Sandretto, S., & Heath, C. (2002). Telling half the story: A critical review of research on the teaching beliefs and practices of university academics. *Review of Educational Research, 72*(2), 177–228.

Katz, J., & Henry, M. (1988). *Turning professors into teachers: A new approach to faculty development and student learning.* New York: Macmillan.

Keller, F. S. (1968). Goodbye teacher… *Journal of Applied Behavior Analysis, 1,* 76–89.

Keller, G. (1983). *Academic strategy.* Baltimore, MD: The Johns Hopkins University Press.

Kember, D., & Gow, L. (1994). Orientations to teaching and their effect on the quality of student learning. *Journal of Higher Education, 65*(1), 58–74.

Kezar, A. J. (2001). *Understanding and facilitating organizational change in the 21st century: Recent research and conceptualizations* (ASHE-ERIC Higher Education Reports, Vol. 28, No. 4). San Francisco: Jossey-Bass.

Kezar, A., Lester, J., Carducci, R., Gallant, T. B., & McGavin, M. C. (2007). Where are the faculty leaders? *Liberal Education, 93*(4), 14–21.

King, A. R. Jr. & Brownell, J. A. (1966). *The curriculum and the disciplines of knowledge: A theory of curriculum practice.* Hoboken, NJ: John Wiley & Sons.

King, P. M., & Kitchener, K. S. (2004). Reflective judgment: Theory and research on the development of epistemic assumptions through adulthood. *Educational Psychologist, 39*(1), 5–18.

Kinser, K. (2007, March 30). For-profit institutions need to be classified, too [The Chronicle Review]. *The Chronicle of Higher Education, 53*(30), B9.

Kinzie, J., Schuh, J., & Kuh, G. D. (2004, November). *A deeper look at student engagement: An examination of institutional effectiveness.* Paper presented at the Annual Meeting of the Association for the Study of Higher Education, Kansas City, MO.

Kirst, M. W. (1998, September 9). Bridging the remediation gap [Electronic Version]. *Education Week, 18.* Retrieved July 2, 2007, from http://www.stanford.edu/group/bridgeproject/gap/remedgap.pdf.

Kitayama, S., & Markus, H. R. (Eds.). (1994). *Emotion and culture: Empirical studies of mutual influence.* Washington, DC: American Psychological Association.

Klein, J. T. (1990). *Interdisciplinarity: History, theory, and practice.* Detroit, MI: Wayne State University Press.

Krapp, A., Hidi, S., & Renninger, K. A. (1992). Interest, learning and development. In K. A. Renninger, S. Hidi, & A. Krapp (Eds.), *The role of interest in learning and development* (pp. 3–25). Mahwah, NJ: Lawrence Erlbaum Associates.

Kuh, G. D. (2007). *Piecing together the student success puzzle: Research, propositions, and recommendations.* (ASHE-ERIC Higher Education Report, Vol. 32, No. 5). San Francisco: Jossey-Bass.

Kuh, G. D., Kinzie, J., Schuh, J. H., Whitt, E. J., & Associates. (2005). *Student success in college: Creating conditions that matter.* San Francisco: Jossey-Bass.

Kuh, G. D., Nelson Laird, T. F., & Umbach, P. D. (2004). Aligning faculty and student behavior: Realizing the promise of greater expectations. *Liberal Education, 90*(4), 24–31.

Kuhn, D., Amsel, E., & O'Loughlin, M. (1988). *The development of scientific thinking skills.* San Diego, CA: Academic Press.

Ladson-Billings, G. (1994). *The dreamkeepers: Successful teachers of African American children.* San Francisco: Jossey-Bass.

Ladson-Billings, G. (1995). Toward a theory of culturally relevant pedagogy. *American Educational Research Journal, 32*(3), 465–491.

Lattuca, L. R. (2001). *Creating interdisciplinarity: Interdisciplinary research and teaching among college and university faculty.* Nashville, TN: Vanderbilt University Press.

Lattuca, L. R. (2002). Learning interdisciplinarity: Sociocultural perspectives on academic work. *Journal of Higher Education, 73*(6), 711–739.

Lattuca, L. R. (2006a). Curricula in international perspective. In J. J. F. Forest & P. G. Altbach (Eds.), *International handbook of higher education, part one: Global themes and contemporary challenges* (pp. 39–64). The Netherlands: Kluwer/Springer.

Lattuca, L. R. (2006b, April). *Learning to change: A study of NSF planning grants.* Paper presented at the Annual Meeting of the American Educational Research Association, San Francisco, CA.

Lattuca, L. R., Lambert, A. D., & Terenzini, P. T. (2008, March). *Academic environments and student learning: A finer-grained examination.* Paper presented at the Annual Conference of the American Educational Research Association, New York, NY.

Lattuca, L. R., Terenzini, P. T., & Volkwein, J. F. (2006). *Engineering change: Findings from a study of the impact of EC2000, final report.* Baltimore, MD: Accreditation Board for Engineering and Technology.

Lattuca, L. R., Terenzini, P. T., Harper, B. J., & Yin, A. C. (2008, March). *Academic environments in detail: Holland's theory at the subdiscipline level.* Paper presented at the Annual Conference of the American Educational Research Association, New York, NY.

Lave, J. (1977). Cognitive consequences of traditional apprenticeship training in West Africa. *Anthropology and Education Quarterly, 8*(3), 177–180.

Lave, J. (1997). The culture of acquisition and the practice of understanding. In D. Kirshner & J. A. Whitson, (Eds.), *Situated cognition: Social, semiotic, and psychological perspectives* (pp. 17–35). Mahwah, NJ: Lawrence Erlbaum Associates.

Lave, J., & Wenger, E. (1991). *Situated learning: Legitimate peripheral participation.* New York: Cambridge University Press.

Leaming, D. R. (2007). *Academic leadership: A practical guide to chairing the department* (2nd ed.). Boston: Anker Publishing.

Lechuga, V. M. (2006). *The changing landscape of the academic profession: The culture of faculty at for-profit colleges and universities.* New York: Routledge.

Lemann, N. (2000). *The big test: The secret history of the American meritocracy* New York: Farrar, Straus and Giroux.

Levine, A. (1978). *Handbook on the undergraduate curriculum.* San Francisco: Jossey-Bass.

Li, X. (2007). *Characteristics of minority-serving institutions and minority undergraduates enrolled in these institutions* (No. 2008-156). Washington, DC: National Center for Education Statistics, U.S. Department of Higher Education.

Light, R. J. (1990). *The Harvard assessment seminars: Explorations with students and faculty about teaching, learning, and student life* (First Report). Cambridge, MA: Harvard University Press.

Light, R. J. (1992). *The Harvard assessment seminars: Explorations with students and faculty about teaching, learning, and student life* (Second Report). Cambridge, MA: Harvard University Press.

Light, R. J. (2001). *Making the most of college: Students speak their minds.* Cambridge, MA: Harvard University Press.

Lincoln, Y. S., & Guba, E. G. (1980). The distinction between merit and worth in evaluation. *Educational Evaluation and Policy Analysis, 2*(4), 61–71.

Lindblom-Ylanne, S., Trigwell, K., Nevgi, A., & Ashwin, P. (2006). How approaches to teaching are affected by discipline and teaching context. *Studies in Higher Education, 31*(3), 285–298.

Lindholm, J. A., Szelényi, K., Hurtado, S., & Korn, W. S. (2005). *The American college teacher: National norms for the 2004–2005 HERI faculty survey.* Los Angeles: Higher Education Research Institute, UCLA.

Lindquist, J. (1974). Political linkage: The academic innovation process. *Journal of Higher Education, 45*(5), 323–343.

Lindquist, J. (1978). *Strategies for change.* Berkeley, CA: Pacific Sounding Press.

Locke, L. (1989, July/August). General education: In search of facts. *Change, 21*(4), 20–23.

Loebbecke, J. (1994). Presentation to the Accounting Education Change Commission. Paper presented at the Accounting Education Change Commission, Salt Lake City, UT. (Photocopy in our possession).

Long, W. F. (2003). Dissonance detected by cluster analysis of responses to the Approaches and Study Skills Inventory for Students. *Studies in Higher Education, 28*(1), 21–36.

Lowther, M. A., Stark, J. S., Genthon, M. L., & Bentley, R. J. (1990). Comparing introductory course planning among full-time and part-time faculty. *Research in Higher Education, 31*(6), 495–517.

Lowther, M. A., Stark, J. S., & Martens, G. G. (1989). *Preparing course syllabi for improved communication.* Ann Arbor, MI: The University of Michigan, National Center for Research to Improve Postsecondary Teaching and Learning. (ERIC Document Reproduction Service No. ED314997)

Lucas, A. F. (1994). *Strengthening departmental leadership.* San Francisco: Jossey-Bass.

Lucas, C. J. (2006). *American higher education: A history* (2nd ed.). New York: Palgrave Macmillan.

Lueddeke, G. R. (1999). Toward a constructivist framework for guiding change and innovation in higher education. *Journal of Higher Education, 70*(3), 235–260.

Lueddeke, G. R. (2003). Professionalising teaching practice in higher education: A study of disciplinary variation and "teaching-scholarship." *Studies in Higher Education, 28*(2), 213–228.

Marsh, H. W. (1984). Students' evaluation of university teaching: Dimensionality, reliability, validity, potential biases, and utility. *Journal of Educational Psychology, 76*(5), 707–754.

Marsh, H. W. (1987). *Students' evaluation of university teaching: Research findings, methodological issues, and directions for future research.* Elmsford, NY: Pergamon Press.

Marsh, P. T. (Ed.). (1988). *Contesting the boundaries of liberal and professional education: The Syracuse experiment.* Syracuse, NY: Syracuse University Press.

Marsh, H. W., & Bailey, M. (1993). Multidimensional students' evaluations of teaching effectiveness: A profile analysis. *Journal of Higher Education, 64*(1), 1–18.

Marsh, H. W., & Dunkin, M. J. (1991). Students' evaluations of university teaching: A multi-dimensional perspective. In J. Smart (Ed.), *Higher education: Handbook of theory and research* (Vol. 8, pp. 143–233). New York: Agathon Press.

Martin, E., Prosser, M., Trigwell, K., Ramsden, P., & Benjamin, J. (2000). What university teachers teach and how they teach it. *Instructional Science, 28*(5), 387–412.

Maruyama, G., & Moreno, J. F. (2000). University faculty views about the value of diversity on campus and in the classroom. In *Does diversity make a difference? Three research studies on diversity in college classrooms.* Washington, DC: American Council on Education and American Association of University Professors.

McCormick, A., & Zhao, C. (2005). Rethinking and reframing the Carnegie Classification. *Change, 37*(5), 50–57.

McGaghie, W. C. (1993). Evaluating competence for professional practice. In L. Curry, J. Wergin, & Associates (Eds.), *Educating professionals: Responding to new expectations for competence and accountability* (pp. 229–261). San Francisco: Jossey-Bass.

McGlothlin, W. J. (1964). *The professional schools.* New York: Center for Applied Research in Education.

McKeachie, W. J. (1987). Teaching, teaching, teaching, and research on teaching. *Teaching of Psychology, 14*(3), 135–138.

McKeachie, W. J. (2006). *McKeachie's teaching tips: Strategies, research, and theory for college and university teachers.* Boston: Houghton Mifflin.

McKeachie, W. J., Pintrich, P. R., Lin, Y., & Smith, D. A. F. (1986). *Teaching and learning in the college classroom: A review of the research literature.* Ann Arbor, MI: University of Michigan, National Center for Research to Improve Postsecondary Teaching and Learning.

McKeachie, W. J., Pintrich, P. R., Lin, Y., Smith, D. A. F., & Sharma, R. (1990). *Teaching and learning in the college classroom: A review of the research literature* (2nd ed.). Ann Arbor, MI: University of Michigan, National Center for Research to Improve Postsecondary Teaching and Learning.

McPeck, J. E. (1990). *Teaching critical thinking.* New York: Routledge, Chapman & Hall, Inc.

Mentkowski, M. (1991). Creating a context where institutional assessment yields educational improvement. *The Journal of General Education, 40,* 225–283.

Mentkowski, M., & Associates. (2000). *Learning that lasts: Integrating learning, development, and performance in college and beyond.* San Francisco: Jossey-Bass.

Merisotis, J., & Phipps, R. (2000). Remedial education in colleges and universities: What's really going on? *The Review of Higher Education, 24*(1), 67–85.

Middaugh, M. F. (1998). How much do faculty really teach? *Planning for Higher Education, 24*(2), 1–11.

Middaugh, M. F. (2000). Using comparative data costs. In M. F. Middaugh (Ed.), *Analyzing costs in higher education: What institutional researchers need to know* (pp. 55–74). (New Directions for Institutional Research, No. 106). San Francisco: Jossey-Bass.

Middaugh, M. F. (2001). *Understanding faculty productivity: Standards and benchmarks for colleges and universities.* San Francisco: Jossey-Bass.

Miller, N. E., & Dollard, J. (1941). *Social learning and imitation.* New Haven, CT: Institute of Human Relations & Yale University Press.

Miller, R. (2007). *Assessment in cycles of improvement: Faculty designs for essential learning outcomes.* Washington, DC: Association of American Colleges and Universities.

Minnich, E. (1990). *Transforming knowledge.* Philadelphia: Temple University Press.

Mitchell, M. (1993). Situational interest: Its multifaceted structure in the secondary school mathematics classroom. *Journal of Educational Psychology, 85*(3), 424–436.

Morphew, C. C., & Hartley, M. (2006). Mission statements: A thematic analysis of rhetoric across institutional type. *Journal of Higher Education, 77*(3), 456–471.

Morrill Land Grant Act of 1862, Pub. L. No. 37-108, 7 U.S.C. § 301.

Morrill Land Grant Act of 1890 § 841, 7 U.S.C. 322 (1890).

Murphy, P. K. (1998). *Toward a multifaceted model of persuasion: The interaction of textual and learner variables.* Unpublished doctoral dissertation, University of Maryland.

Murphy, P. K., & Mason, L. (2006). Changing knowledge and beliefs. In P. A. Alexander & P. H. Winne (Eds.), *Handbook of educational psychology* (pp. 305–324). Mahwah, NJ: Lawrence Erlbaum Associates.

Murrell, P. C. (2002). *African-centered pedagogy: Developing schools of achievement for African-American children.* Albany, NY: State University of New York Press.

Nagda, B. A., Gregerman, Jonides, J., von Hippel, W., & Lerner, J. S. (1998). Undergraduate student-faculty research partnerships affect students' retention. *Review of Higher Education, 22*(1), 55–72.

National Association of State Universities and Land-Grant Colleges. (1995). Development of the land-grant system: 1862–1994. Retrieved July 2, 2007, from http://www.nasulgc.org/publications/Land_Grant/Development.htm

National Center for Academic Transformation. (2005). *Welcome to the National Center for Academic Transformation.* Retrieved January 10, 2008, from http://www.center.rpi.edu/

National Commission for Cooperative Education (NCCE). (2002). *The cooperative education model.* Retrieved December 8, 2008, from http://www.co-op.edu/aboutcoop.htm

National Center for the Study of Collective Bargaining in Higher Education and the Professions. (2006). *Directory of faculty contracts and bargaining agents in institutions of higher education.* New York: Author.

National Commission on the Role and Future of State Colleges and Universities. (1986). *To secure the blessings of liberty: Report of the National Commission on the Role and Future of State Colleges and Universities.* Washington, DC: American Association of State Colleges and Universities.

National Defense Education Act of 1958. P.L. No. 85–86.

National Governors' Association, Center for Policy Research and Analysis. (1986). Time for results: The governors' 1991 report on education. Washington, DC: Author.

National Institute of Education. (1984). *Involvement in learning: Realizing the potential of American higher education* (Report of the NIE Study Group on the Condition of Excellence in American Higher Education). Washington, DC: U.S. Government Printing Office.

National Survey of Student Engagement (NSSE). (2005). *Annual report 2005.* Bloomington, IN: Center for Postsecondary Research, School of Education, Indiana University Bloomington. Retrieved on September 6, 2008, from http://nsse.iub.edu/pdf/NSSE2005_annual_report.pdf

National Survey of Student Engagement (NSSE). (2007). *Annual report 2007.* Bloomington, IN: Center for Postsecondary Research, School of Education, Indiana University Bloomington. Retrieved on September 6, 2008, from http://nsse.iub.edu/NSSE%5F2007%5FAnnual%5FReport/docs/withhold/NSSE_2007_Annual_Report.pdf

Naveh-Benjamin, M., McKeachie, W. J., Lin, Y., & Tucker, D. (1986). Inferring students' cognitive structure and their development using the "ordered-tree" technique. *Journal of Educational Psychology, 78*(2), 130–140.

Newman, F. (1985). *Higher education and the American resurgence: A Carnegie Foundation special report.* Lawrenceville, NJ: Princeton University Press. (ERIC Document Reproduction Service No. ED265759)

Nicholls, J. G. (1984). Achievement motivation: Conceptions of ability, subjective experience, task choice and performance. *Psychological Review, 91*, 328–346.

NLRB v. Yeshiva University, 444 U.S. 672 (1980).

Nordvall, R. C. (1982). *The process of change in higher education institutions* (ASHE-ERIC Higher Education Research Reports, No. 7). Washington, DC: American Association for Higher Education.

Nussbaum, M. C. (1997). *Cultivating humanity: A classical defense of reform in liberal education.* Cambridge, MA: Harvard University Press.

Nyre, G. F., & Reilly, K. C. (1979). *Professional education in the eighties: Challenges and responses.* Washington, DC: American Association for Higher Education.

O'Connor, J. (2003). *Learning communities in research universities* [National Learning Communities Project Monograph Series]. Olympia, WA: The Evergreen State College, Washington Center for Improving the Quality of Undergraduate Education, in cooperation with the American Association for Higher Education.

Ory, J. C., & Parker, S. A. (1989). Assessment activities at large research universities. *Research in Higher Education, 30*(4), 375–385.

Pace, C. R. (1980). *Measuring outcomes of college: Fifty years of findings and recommendations for the future.* San Francisco: Jossey-Bass.

Pace, C. R. (1985). Perspectives and problems in student outcomes research. In P. T. Ewell (Ed.), *Assessing educational outcomes* (pp. 7–18). (New Directions for Institutional Research No. 47). San Francisco: Jossey-Bass.

Pace, C. R. (1998). Recollections and reflections. In J. C. Smart (Ed.), *Higher education: Handbook of theory and research,* (*13*, pp. 1–34). New York: Agathon Press.

Pajares, F. (1992). Teachers' beliefs and educational research: Cleaning up a messy construct. *Review of Educational Research, 62*(3), 307–332.

Palomba, C. A., & Banta, T. W. (1999). *Assessment essentials: Planning, implementing, and improving assessment in higher education.* San Francisco: Jossey-Bass.

Parsad, B., & Lewis, L. (2003). *Remedial education at degree-granting postsecondary institutions in fall 2000.* (No. NCES-010). Washington, DC: U.S. Department of Education, National Center for Education Statistics.

Pascarella, E. T., & Terenzini, P. T. (1991). *How college affects students: Findings and insights from twenty years of research* (Vol. *1*). San Francisco: Jossey-Bass.

Pascarella, E. T., & Terenzini, P. T. (2005). *How college affects students: A third decade of research* (Vol. 2). San Francisco: Jossey-Bass.

Perkins, D. N. & Salomon, G. (1988). Teaching for transfer. *Educational Leadership, 46*(1): 22–32.

Perry, W. G., Jr. (1970). *Forms of intellectual and ethical development in the college years: A scheme.* New York: Holt, Rinehart and Winston.

Phenix, P. H. (1986). *Realms of meaning: A philosophy of the curriculum for general education.* New York: McGraw-Hill. (Original work published in 1964).

Phillips, D. C., & Soltis, J. F. (2004). *Perspectives on learning* (4th ed.). New York: Teachers College Press.

Pike, G. R. (1999). The effects of residential learning communities and traditional residential living arrangements on educational gains during the first year of college. *Journal of College Student Development, 40*(3), 269–284.

Pike, G. R., Schroeder, C. C., & Berry, T. R. (1997). Enhancing the educational impact of residence halls, the relationship between residential learning communities and first-year college experiences and persistence. *Journal of College Student Development, 38*(6), 609–621.

Pike, G. R., Smart, J. C., Kuh, G. D., & Hayek, J. C. (2006). Educational expenditures and student engagement: When does money matter? *Research in Higher Education, 47*(7), 847–872.

Pintrich, P. R. (1988a). A process-oriented view of student motivation and cognition. In J. S. Stark & L. A. Mets (Eds.), *Improving teaching and learning through research* (pp. 65–79). (New Directions for Institutional Research, No. 57). San Francisco: Jossey-Bass.

Pintrich, P. R. (1988b). Student learning and college teaching. In R. E. Young & K. E. Eble (Eds.), *College teaching and learning: Preparing for new commitments* (pp. 71–86). (New Directions for Teaching and Learning, No. 33). San Francisco: Jossey-Bass.

Pintrich, P. R., Marx, R. W., & Boyle, R. A. (1993). Beyond cold conceptual change: The role of motivational beliefs and classroom contextual factors in the process of conceptual change. *Review of Educational Research, 63*(2), 167–199.

Pintrich, P. R., McKeachie, W. J., & Lin, Y. (1987). Teaching a course in learning to learn. *Teaching of Psychology, 14*(2), 81–86.

Pintrich, P. R., & Schrauben, B. (1992). Students' motivational beliefs and their cognitive engagement in classroom academic tasks. In D. H. Schunk & J. L. Meece (Eds.), *Student perceptions in the classroom* (pp. 149–184). Mahwah, NJ: Lawrence Erlbaum Associates.

Pintrich, P. R., & Schunk, D. H. (2002). *Motivation in education: Theory, research, and applications* (2nd ed.). Upper Saddle River, NJ: Merrill.

Posner, G. J. (1974). Tools for curriculum research and development: Potential contributions from cognitive science. *Curriculum Inquiry, 8*(4), 311–340.

Posner, G. J., & Rudnitsky, A. N. (2006). *Course design: A guide to curriculum development for teachers* (7th ed.). Boston, MA: Pearson.

Posner, G. J., & Strike, K. A. (1976). A categorization scheme for principles of sequencing content. *Review of Educational Research, 46*(4), 665–689.

Posner, G. J., Strike, K. A., Hewson, P. W., Gertzog, W. A. (1982). Accommodation of a scientific conception: Toward a theory of conceptual change. *Science Education, 66*(2), 211–227.

Powell, J. P., & Shanker, V. S. (1982). The course planning and monitoring activities of a university teacher. *Higher Education, 11*(3), 289–301.

Powers, D., & Enright, M. (1987). Analytical reasoning skills in graduate study. *Journal of Higher Education, 58*(6), 658–682.

Prados, J., Peterson, G., & Lattuca, L. R. (2005). Quality assurance of engineering education through accreditation: The impact of engineering criteria 2000 and its global influence. *Journal of Engineering Education, 94*(1), 165–184.

Prosser, M., & Trigwell, K. (1999). *Understanding learning and teaching: The experience in higher education*. Buckingham: Open University Press.

Pryor, J. H., Hurtado, S., Saenz, V. B., Korn, J. S., Santos, J. L., & Korn, W. S. (2006). *The American freshman: National norms for fall 2006*. Los Angeles: Higher Education Research Institute, University of California Los Angeles.

Quaye, S. J., & Lattuca, L. R. (2006, November). *More than meets the eye: Critical race theory, culturally relevant pedagogy, and learning*. Paper presented at the Annual Meeting of the Association of Higher Education, Anaheim, CA.

Quinn, R. E. (1988). *Beyond rational management: Mastering the paradoxes and competing demands of high performance*. San Francisco: Jossey-Bass.

Quinn, R. E., Raerman, S. R., Thompson, M. P., & McGrath, M. R. (1990). *Becoming a master manager: A competency framework*. Hoboken, NJ: John Wiley & Sons.

Ramsden, P., & Entwistle, N. J. (1981). Effects of academic department on students' approaches to studying. *British Journal of Educational Psychology, 51*(3), 363–383.

Ratcliff, J. L. (1992). What we can learn from coursework patterns about improving the undergraduate curriculum. In J. L. Ratcliff (Ed.), *Assessment and curriculum reform* (pp. 5–22). (New Directions for Higher Education, No. 80). San Francisco: Jossey-Bass.

Ratcliff, J. L. (1997). What is a curriculum and what should it be? In J. G. Gaff & J. L. Ratcliff (Eds.), *Handbook of the undergraduate curriculum: A comprehensive guide to purposes, structures, practices, and change* (pp. 5–29). San Francisco: Jossey-Bass.

Ratcliff, J. L., Johnson, D. K., La Nasa, S. M., & Gaff, J. G. (2001). *The status of general education in the year 2000: Summary of a national survey*. Washington, DC: Association of American Colleges & Universities.

Redden, E. (2007, May 16). "College prep" without "college" or "prep" [News]. *Inside Higher Ed*. Retrieved May 16, 2007, from http://www.insidehighered.com/news/2007/2005/2016/act

Reed, H. J., & Lave, J. (1979). Arithmetic as a tool for investigating relations between culture and cognition. *American Ethnologist, 6*(3), 568–582.

Renniger, K. A. (2000). Individual interest and its implication for understanding intrinsic motivation. In J. M. Harackiewicz & C. Sansone (Eds.), *Intrinsic and extrinsic motivation: The search for optimal motivation and performance* (pp. 373–404). San Diego, CA: Academic Press.

Rhoades, G. (1993). Retrenchment clauses in faculty union contracts: Faculty rights and administrative discretion. *Journal of Higher Education, 64*(3), 312–347.

Richardson, K. (2000). *The making of intelligence*. New York: Columbia University Press.

Rogers, E. M. (1968). The communication of innovations in a complex institution. *Educational Record, 49*(1), 67–77.

Rogers, E. M. (1995). *Diffusion of innovations* (4th ed.). New York: Free Press.

Rogoff, B. (2003). *The cultural nature of human development*. New York: Oxford University Press.

Rogoff, B., & Chavajay, P. (1995). What's become of research on the cultural basis of cognitive development? *American Psychologist, 50*(10), 859–877.

Rudolph, F. (1977). *Curriculum: A history of the American undergraduate course of study since 1636.* San Francisco: Jossey-Bass.

Ryan, J. F. (2004). *Institutional expenditures and student engagement: A role for financial resources in enhancing student learning and development.* Paper presented at the Annual Forum of the Association of Institutional Research, Boston, MA.

Saljo, R. (1982). *Learning and understanding.* Gothenberg, Sweden: Acta Universitatis Gothoburgenesis.

Schneider, C. G. (1997). The arts and sciences major. In J. G. Gaff & J. L. Ratcliff (Eds.), *Handbook of the undergraduate curriculum: A comprehensive guide to purpose, structures, practices, and change* (pp. 235–261). San Francisco: Jossey-Bass.

Schommer, M. (1990). Effects of beliefs about the nature of knowledge in comprehension. *Journal of Educational Psychology, 82*(3), 498–504.

Schommer-Aikins, M. (2002). An evolving theoretical framework for an epistemological belief system. In B. Hofer & P. Pintrich (Ed.), *Personal epistemology: The psychology of belief about knowledge and knowing* (pp. 103–118). Mahwah, NJ: Lawrence Erlbaum Associates.

Schommer-Aikins, M., Mau, W., Brookhart, S., & Hutter, R. (2000). Understanding middle students' beliefs about knowledge and learning using a multidimensional paradigm. *The Journal of Educational Research, 94* (2), 120–127.

Schön, D. A. (1987). *Educating the reflective practitioner: Toward a new design for teaching and learning in the professions.* San Francisco: Jossey-Bass.

Schubert, W. H. (1986). *Curriculum: Perspective, paradigm, and possibility.* New York: Macmillan.

Schunk, D. H. (2004). *Learning theories: An educational perspective* (4th ed.). Upper Saddle River, NJ: Pearson/Merrill/Prentice Hall.

Schunk, D. H., & Zimmerman, B. J., (2006). Competence and control beliefs: Distinguishing the means and ends. In P. A. Alexander & P. H. Winne (Eds.), *Handbook of educational psychology* (2nd ed., pp. 349–367). Mahwah, NJ: Lawrence Erlbaum Associates.

Schuster, J. H., & Finkelstein, M. J. (2006). *The American faculty: The restructuring of academic work and careers.* Baltimore, MD: The Johns Hopkins University Press.

Schwartz, R. A. (2002). The rise and demise of deans of men. *The Review of Higher Education, 26*(2), 217–239.

Seely Brown, J., Collins, A., & Duguid, P. (1989). Situated cognition and the culture of learning. *Educational Researcher, 18*(1), 32–42.

Seldin, P. (1997). *The teaching portfolio: A practical guide to improved performance and promotion/tenure decisions* (2nd ed.). Boston, MA: Anker.

Seldin, P. (1999). *Changing practices in evaluating teaching: A practical guide to improved faculty performance and promotion/tenure decisions.* Boston, MA: Anker.

Servicemen's Readjustment Act of 1944, Pub. L. No. 85-857, 38 U.S.C. § 1 et seq.

Sexton, R. F., & Ungerer, R. A. (1975). *Rationales for experiential education* (ERIC-AAHE Research Reports, No. 3). Washington, DC: American Association for Higher Education.

Seymour, D. T. (1988). *Developing academic programs: The climate for innovation* (ASHE-ERIC Higher Education Reports, No. 3). Washington, DC: Association for the Study of Higher Education.

Shavelson, R. J. (1974). Methods for examining representations of a subject matter structure in students' memory. *Journal of Research in Science Teaching, 11*, 231–250.

Shaw, K. M., Stark, J. S., Lowther, M. A., & Ryan, M. P. (1990, April). *Students' goal changes as an indicator of academic socialization in college subjects.* Paper presented at the American Educational Research Association, Boston, MA.

Shuell, T. J. (1986). Cognitive conceptions of learning. *Review of Educational Research, 56*(4), 411–436.

Slavin, R. E. (2000). *Educational psychology: Theory and practice* (6th ed.). Boston: Allyn & Bacon.

Slaughter, S., & Rhoades, G. (2004). *Academic capitalism.* Baltimore, MD: The Johns Hopkins University Press.

Smart, J. C., & Ethington, C. A. (1995). Disciplinary and institutional differences in undergraduate education goals. In N. Hativah (Ed.), *Disciplinary differences in teaching and learning: Implications for practice* (pp. 49–57). (New Directions for Teaching and Learning, No. 64). San Francisco: Jossey-Bass.

Smart, J. C., Ethington, C. A., Riggs, R. O., & Thompson, M. D. (2002). Influences of institutional expenditure patterns on the development of students' leadership competencies. *Research in Higher Education, 43*(1), 115–132.

Smart, J. C., Feldman, K. A., & Ethington, C. A. (2000). *Academic disciplines: Holland's theory and the study of college students and faculty.* Nashville, TN: Vanderbilt University Press.

Smith, B. L., & MacGregor, J. T. (1992). What is collaborative learning? In A. S. Goodsell, M. R. Maher, V. Tinto, B. L. Smith, & J. T. MacGregor (Eds.), *Collaborative learning: A sourcebook for higher education* (pp. 10–30). University Park, PA: National Center in Postsecondary Teaching, Learning, and Assessment. (ERIC Document Reproduction Service No. ED357705)

Smith, B. L., & McCann, J. (Eds.). (2001). *Reinventing ourselves: Interdisciplinary education, collaborative learning, and experimentation in higher education.* Boston, MA: Anker Publishing Co.

Snyder, T. (Ed.). (1993). *120 years of American education: A statistical portrait.* Washington, DC: Department of Education, National Center for Education Statistics.

Snyder, T. D., Tan, A. G., & Hoffman, C. M. (2006). *Digest of education statistics, 2005* (No. NCES 2006-030). Washington, DC: U.S. Department of Education, National Center for Education Statistics.

Soares, J. A. (2007). *The power of privilege: Yale and America's elite colleges.* Stanford, CA: Stanford University Press.

Southern Regional Education Board. (1979). The search for general education: The pendulum swings back. *Issues in Higher Education No. 15.* Newsletter of the Southern Regional Education Board, Atlanta, GA.

Sporn, B. (1999). *Adaptive university structures: An analysis of adaptation to socioeconomic environments of U.S. and European universities.* London: Jessica Kingsley.

Stark, J. S. (1990). Approaches to assessing educational outcomes. *Journal of Health Administration Education, 8*(2), 210–226.

Stark, J. S. (1998). Classifying professional preparation programs. *Journal of Higher Education, 69*(4), 353–383.

Stark, J. S. (2002). Testing a model of program curriculum leadership. *Research in Higher Education, 43*(1), 59–82.

Stark, J. S., & Associates. (1977). *The many faces of educational consumerism.* Lexington, MA: D. C. Heath.

Stark, J. S., & Briggs, C. L. (1998, November). *Program leadership for college curriculum development: A background paper and guide to future research.* Paper presented at the annual meeting of the Association for the Study of Higher Education, Miami, FL.

Stark, J. S., Briggs, C. L., & Rowland-Poplawski, J. (2002). Curriculum leadership roles of chairpersons in continuously planning departments. *Research in Higher Education, 43*(3), 329–356.

Stark, J. S., & Lattuca, L. R. (1997). *Shaping the college curriculum: Academic plans in action.* Boston: Allyn & Bacon.

Stark, J. S., & Lowther, M. A. (1986). *Designing the learning plan: A review of research and theory related to college curricula.* Ann Arbor, MI: University of Michigan, National Center for Research to Improve Postsecondary Teaching and Learning. (ERIC Document Reproduction Service No. ED287439)

Stark, J. S., & Lowther, M. A. (1988a). Perspectives on course and program planning. In J. S. Stark & L. Mets (Eds.), *Improving teaching and learning through research* (pp. 39–52). (New Directions for Institutional Research, No. 57). San Francisco: Jossey-Bass.

Stark, J. S., & Lowther, M. A. (1988b). *Strengthening the ties that bind: Integrating undergraduate liberal and professional study.* Ann Arbor, MI: University of Michigan, Professional Preparation Network. (ERIC Document Reproduction Service No. ED304951)

Stark, J. S., Lowther, M. A., Bentley, R. J., Ryan, M. P., Martens, G. G., Genthon, M. L., & others. (1990). *Planning introductory college courses: Influences on faculty.* Ann Arbor, MI: University of Michigan, National Center for Research to Improve Postsecondary Teaching and Learning. (ERIC Document Reproduction Service No.ED330277)

Stark, J. S., Lowther, M. A., Hagerty, B. M. K., & Orczyk, C. (1986). A conceptual framework for the study of preservice professional programs in colleges and universities. *Journal of Higher Education, 57*(3), 231–258.

Stark, J. S., Lowther, M. A., Ryan, M. P., Bomotti, S. S., Genthon, M. L., Martens, G., & others. (1988). *Reflections on course planning: Faculty and students consider influences and goals.* Ann Arbor, MI: University of Michigan, National Center for Research to Improve Postsecondary Teaching and Learning. (ERIC Document Reproduction Service No. ED316067)

Stark, J. S., Lowther, M. A., Shaw, K. M., & Sossen, P. L. (1991). *Student goals exploration: User's manual* (Institutional Research Guide: Classroom Research Guide). Ann Arbor, MI: University of Michigan, National Center for Research to Improve Postsecondary Teaching and Learning. (ERIC Document Reproduction Service No.ED338127)

Stark, J. S., Shaw, K. M., & Lowther, M. A. (1989). *Student goals in college and courses: A missing link in assessing student achievement* (ASHE-ERIC Higher Education Reports, No. 6). Washington, DC: The George Washington University.

Stark, J. S., & Thomas, A. M. (1994). *Assessment and program evaluation* (ASHE Reader Series). Needham Heights, MA: Simon and Schuster.

Sternberg, R. J. (1985). *Beyond IQ: A triarchic theory of human intelligence.* Cambridge, MA: Cambridge University Press.

Sternberg, R. J. (1986). *Intelligence applied.* New York: Harcourt Brace Jovanovich.

Svinicki, M. (circa 1989). If learning involves risk-taking, teaching involves trust-building. *Teaching excellence: Toward the best in the academy* (newsletter of the Professional and Organizational Development Network, sample issue).

Svinicki, M.D. (1991, December). So much content, so little time. *UC Ideas: A Forum for the Exchange of Information, 6*(1), 1–2.

Terenzini, P. T. (1987). The case for unobtrusive measures. In *Assessing the outcomes of higher education* (pp. 47–61). Proceedings of the 1986 ETS Invitational Conference. Princeton, NJ: Educational Testing Service.

Terenzini, P. T., & Reason, R. (2005, November). *Parsing the first year of college: A conceptual framework for studying college impacts.* Paper presented at the Association for the Study of Higher Education, Philadelphia, PA.

Theall, M., Abrami, P. C., & Mets, L. A. (Eds.). (2001). *The student ratings debate: Are they valid? How can we best use them?* (New Directions for Institutional Research, No. 109). San Francisco: Jossey-Bass.

Thelin, J. R. (2004). *A history of American higher education* Baltimore, MD: Johns Hopkins University Press.

Thielens, W. (1987, April). *The disciplines and undergraduate lecturing.* Paper presented at the American Educational Research Association, Washington, DC.

Tiberius, R. G. (1995). From shaping performances to dynamic interaction: The quiet revolution in teaching improvement programs. In W. A. Wright and Associates (Eds.), *Teaching improvement practices: Successful strategies for higher education.* Boston, MA: Anker.

Tierney, W. G., & Hentschke, G. C. (2007). *New players, different game: Understanding the rise of for-profit colleges and universities.* Baltimore, MD: The Johns Hopkins University Press.

Toombs, W. (1977–1978). The application of design-based curriculum analysis to general education. *Review of Higher Education, 1,* 18–29.

Toombs, W., Amey, M., & Fairweather, J. (1989, January 7). *Open to view: A catalog analysis of general education.* Paper presented at the Association of American Colleges, Washington, DC.

Toombs, W., & Tierney, W. G. (1991). *Meeting the mandate: Renewing the college and departmental curriculum* (ASHE-ERIC Higher Education Reports, No. 6). Washington, DC: The George Washington University.

Toombs, W., & Tierney, W. G. (1993). Curriculum definitions and reference points. *Journal of Curriculum and Supervision, 8*(3), 175–195.

Toulmin, S. E. (1962). *The philosophy of science: An introduction.* London: Hutchinson.

Toutkoushian, R., & Smart, J. C. (2001). Do institutional characteristics affect student gains from college? *The Review of Higher Education, 25*(1), 39–61.

Townsend, B. K., Newell, L. J., & Wiese, M. D. (1992). *Creating distinctiveness: Lessons from uncommon colleges and universities* (ASHE-ERIC Higher Education Reports, No. 6). Washington, DC: The George Washington University.

Trigwell, K. (2002). Approaches to teaching design subjects: A quantitative analysis. *Art, Design & Communication in Higher Education, 1*(2), 69–80.

Trigwell, K., & Prosser, M. (2004). Development and use of the approaches to teaching inventory. *Educational Psychology Review, 16,* 409–426.

Trigwell, K., Prosser, M., & Waterhouse, F. (1999). Relations between teachers' approaches to teaching and students' approaches to learning. *Higher Education, 37*(1), 57–70.

Tucker, A. (1992). *Chairing the academic department: Leadership among peers* (4th ed.). Phoenix, AZ: Oryx.

Twigg, C. A. (2005). Improving quality and reducing costs: The case for redesign. In *Course corrections: Experts offer solutions to the college cost crisis* (pp. 32–48). Indianapolis, IN: Lumina Foundation for Education.

Umbach, P. D. (2007). How effective are they? Exploring the impact of contingent faculty on undergraduate education. *Review of Higher Education, 30*(2), 91–117.

U.S. Bureau of the Census. (1975). *Historical statistics of the United States, Colonial times to 1970* (bicentennial ed.). Washington DC: Author.

U.S. Census Bureau. (2008). *Educational attainment of the population 18 years and over, by age, sex, race, and Hispanic origin: 2007.* Retrieved on July 1, 2008, from http://www.census.gov/population/www/socdemo/education/cps2007.html.

U.S. Department of Education, National Center for Education Statistics. (2004). *The condition of education 2004* (No. NCES 2004-077). Washington, DC: U.S. Government Printing Office.

U.S. Department of Education; National Center for Education Statistics. (2005). *The condition of education 2005* (No. 2005-094). Washington, DC: U.S. Government Printing Office.

U.S. Department of Education. (2006). *A test of leadership: Charting the future of U.S. higher education.* Retrieved November 16, 2007, from http://www.ed.gov/about/bdscomm/list/hiedfuture/reports/final-report.pdf

U.S. Department of Education; National Center for Education Statistics. (2007). *The condition of education 2007* (No. NCES 2007-064). Washington, DC: U.S. Government Printing Office.

Volkwein, J. F., Lattuca, L. R., Caffrey, H. S., & Reindl, T. (2003). What works to ensure quality in higher education institutions. *AASCU/CSHE Policy Seminar on Student Success, Accreditation, and Quality Assurance.* Washington, DC: AASC&U and The Pennsylvania State University.

Wallenstein, P. (2008). *Higher education and the civil rights movement: White supremacy, black southerners, and college campuses.* Gainesville, FL: University Press of Florida.

Walters, E. (2001/2002). Institutional commitment to diversity and multiculturalism through institutional transformation: A case study of Olivet College. *Journal of College Student Retention, 3*(4), 333–350.

Wasley, P. (2008, August 8). U. of Phoenix lets students find answers virtually. *Chronicle of Higher Education, 54*(48), A1, A10.

Wechsler, H. S. (1977). *The qualifying student: A history of selective college admissions in America.* Hoboken, NJ: John Wiley & Sons.

Weimer, M. G. (Ed.). (1987). *Teaching large classes well.* (New Directions for Teaching and Learning, No. 32). San Francisco: Jossey-Bass.

Weiner, B. (1986). *An attributional theory of motivation and motion.* New York: Springer-Varlag.

Weinstein, C. E., & Mayer, R. E. (1986). The teaching of learning strategies. In M. Wittrock (Ed.), *Handbook of research on teaching* (pp. 315–327). New York: Macmillan.

Weinstein, C. E., & Palmer, D. R. (2002). *LASSI user's manual for those administering the Learning and Study Strategies Inventory* (2nd ed.). Clearwater, FL: H&H Publishing Company, Inc.

Wertsch, J. V. (1985). *Vygotsky and the social formation of mind.* Cambridge, MA: Harvard University Press.

Wertsch, J. V. (2002). *Voices of collective remembering.* Cambridge, MA: Cambridge University Press.

Wertsch, J. V., Del Rio, P., & Alvarez, A. (1995). Sociocultural studies: History, action, and mediation. In J. V. Wertsch, P. Del Rio, & A. Alvarez (Eds.), *Sociocultural studies of mind* (pp. 1–34). New York: Cambridge University Press.

Weston, C., & Cranton, P. A. (1986). Selecting instructional strategies. *Journal of Higher Education, 57*(3), 259–288.

Wheeler, D. L. (2007, November 23). State universities adopt accountability measures. *The Chronicle of Higher Education, 54*(13), A19.

Whitley, R. (1976). Umbrella and polytheistic scientific disciplines and their elites. *Social Studies of Science, 6*(3/4), 471–497.

Whitman, N. A. (1988). *Peer teaching: To teach is to learn twice* (ASHE-ERIC Higher Education Reports, No. 4). Washington, DC: The George Washington University.

Whitman, N. A., Spendlove, D. C., & Clark, C. H. (1984). *Student stress: Effects and solutions* (ASHE-ERIC Higher Education Reports, No. 2). Washington, DC: Association for the Study of Higher Education.

Wiggins, G. T., & McTighe, J. (2005). *Understanding by design.* Alexandria, VA: Association for Supervision and Curriculum Development.

Wingspread Group on Higher Education. (1993, December). *An American imperative: Higher expectations for higher education.* Racine, WI: The Johnson Foundation and others.

Wittrock, B. (1993). The modern university: The three transformations. In S. Rothblatt & B. Wittrock (Eds.), *The European and American university since 1800: Historical and sociological essays* (pp. 303–362). New York: Cambridge University Press.

Wlodkowski, R. J., & Ginsberg, M. E. (1995). *Diversity and motivation: Culturally responsive teaching.* San Francisco: Jossey-Bass.

Woolfolk Hoy, A., Davis, H., & Pape, S. J. (2006). Teacher knowledge and beliefs. In P. A. Alexander & P. H. Winne (Eds.), *Handbook of educational psychology* (2nd ed.) (pp. 715–737). Mahwah, NJ: Lawrence Erlbaum Associates.

Yin, A. C. (2008, March). *Developing design and problem-solving skills through cooperative education: Findings from a national study of engineering education.* Paper presented at the Annual Meeting of the American Educational Research Association. New York, NY.

Yinger, R. J. (1979). Routine in teacher planning. *Theory into Practice, 18,* 163–169.

Zemsky, R. (1989). *Structure and coherence: Measuring the undergraduate curriculum.* Washington, DC: Association of American Colleges.

NAMES INDEX

SUBJECT INDEX

Page references followed by *fig* indicate an illustrated figure; followed by *t* indicates a table.

A

Academic communities: examining differences in academic field, 101–102; Holland personality types of different, 102–105; promoting linkages among, 105–111. *See also* Institutions

Academic fields: academic communities of different, 101–111; characterizing, 91–93; Collaboration/ Integration Matrix, 109–110*fig*, 111; components of professional fields and, 94*t*; differences in course planning among, 93–101; eight cells framework classification of, 92–93; learning process in, 174–179; liberal education outcomes of, 112*t*; outcomes important to liberal arts/undergraduate professional programs, 108*t*–109*t*; substantive structures and service roles of, 95; typical groupings of, 91*t*

Academic organizations. *See* Institutions

Academic plan administration: academic beliefs regarding, 269–273; CLUE project research on, 274–275, 277; curriculum leadership and administrative roles of, 275–299; illustrated diagram on roles in, 271*fig*; issues and research on, 269–275; matrix of curriculum functions of, 272*t*–275; sociocultural context focus on, 270*fig*; three areas of responsibilities for, 269. *See also* Administration

Academic plan administration roles: academic planning, 278*fig*; adjusting academic plans (monitor/ facilitator/innovator), 295–299; competing values model on, 276*fig*, 296–297; coordinating academic planning (coordinator), 286–289; developing academic plans (producer/director), 282–285*t*; encouraging evaluation (monitor), 292–295; establishing educational environment (mentor/ facilitator), 277–282*t*; implementing academic plans (broker/innovator), 289–292*t*

Academic plan elements: content, 9; evaluation and adjustment, 11; instructional process/learning activities, 10; instructional resources, 10–11, 76–77; learner characteristics and needs, 10; listed, 6–7*fig*; purposes of, 7–9, 25; sequence of instructional process, 9. *See also specific element*

Academic plan model (sociocultural context): administration focus of, 270*fig*; curricular change focus of, 302*fig*; evaluation and adjustment focus of, 230*fig*; external influences focus of, 24*fig*; instructional processes focus of, 183–228; internal influences focus of, 67*fig*; learner focus of, 146*fig*, 184*fig*; overview of issues and elements of, 5*fig*–22; purposes, content, and sequence focus of, 90*fig*

Academic plans: administration of, 269–299; contextual influences on, 11–15; defining curriculum as, 4–11, 329–330; evolution of concept, 16–20; sharing